Stanley McNeil
Stacy

Angela Jefferson

Patterns for College Writing

A Rhetorical Reader and Guide

Patterns for College Writing

A Rhetorical Reader and Guide

LAURIE G. KIRSZNER
Philadelphia College of Pharmacy and Science
STEPHEN R. MANDELL
Drexel University

St. Martin's Press   New York

For information, write St. Martin's Press, Inc.,
175 Fifth Avenue, New York, N.Y. 10010

cover design: Frederick Charles
typography: James M. Wall

ISBN: 0-312-59813-0

ACKNOWLEDGMENTS

NARRATION

John M. Bresnahan, "Monday, March 5, 1770: Who Was to Blame?" Reprinted with permission from the March 1967 issue of *Yankee Magazine*, published by Yankee, Inc., Dublin, N.H.

Bonnie Smith-Yackel, "My Mother Never Worked." Copyright © 1975 by *Women: A Journal of Liberation*, 3028 Greenmount Avenue, Baltimore, Md. 21218.

Martin Gansberg, "38 Who Saw Murder Didn't Call the Police." © 1964 by The New York Times Company. Reprinted by permission.

"A Letter from Mississippi." From *Letters from Mississippi*, edited by Elizabeth Sutherland. Copyright © 1965 by McGraw-Hill Book Company. Used with permission of McGraw-Hill Book Company.

George Orwell, "Shooting an Elephant." From *Shooting an Elephant and Other Essays* by George Orwell, copyright 1950 by Sonia Brownell Orwell; renewed 1978 by Sonia Pitt-Rivers. Reprinted by permission of Harcourt Brace Jovanovich, Inc. and Martin Secker & Warburg Ltd.

Acknowledgments and copyrights continue at the back of the book on pages 375–377, which constitute an extension of the copyright page.

Preface

More than anything else, we want students to find this book useful, and one of the many things our students have taught us is that their needs as college writers extend far beyond the English classroom. They write also for sociology and education and biology and business and all of their other courses. In *Patterns for College Writing* we have sought to address the diverse requirements of college students both in the variety of the essays we have chosen and in the practical focus of our introductions, questions, and writing assignments.

Throughout the book we repeatedly stress the importance of a clear purpose and concept of audience, and in preparing the book we kept our own purpose and audience always in mind. We wanted to explain and illustrate the writing process and the rhetorical options available to student writers. We felt that students need fuller explanations than most other rhetorically organized anthologies provide. And we hoped to present the principles in such a way that students would find them immediately applicable to college writing tasks of all sorts.

The book begins with a comprehensive introductory chapter devoted to the writing process. Here we explain how students can learn to move confidently through the process of invention by understanding their assignment, establishing general boundaries, narrowing a subject to a workable topic, brainstorming to generate ideas, and formulating a thesis. The chapter goes on to discuss arrangement, analyzing the part of the essay in some detail. Finally, the chapter deals with writing and revising and examines two successive versions of a sample student essay.

After explaining and illustrating the writing process, we consider, in nine separate chapters, the rhetorical patterns available to students as they write to fulfill their college assignments: narration, description, exemplification, process, cause and effect, comparison and contrast, classification and division, definition, and argumentation. Each chapter begins with a comprehensive introduction that first defines and illustrates the rhetorical pattern and then provides a thorough analysis of an annotated student example to show how the chapter's concepts can be applied to a particular college writing situation. Each chapter then goes on to illustrate the pattern with a number of selections, diverse in subject and style, by professional writers. Like the student examples in the introductions, these essays are not intended to be imitated (though they may indeed serve as stimuli for student writing). Rather, in the possibilities they offer for arranging material and developing ideas, they are meant to be analyzed and understood.

Each reading selection is followed by three types of questions designed to help students measure their comprehension of the essay's content, their understanding of the author's purpose and audience, and their recognition of the stylistic and structural techniques used to shape the essay. Finally, with every selection we include a Writing Workshop. These suggestions for student writing, many of which ask students to respond to a given situation and to consider a specific audience and purpose, are designed to reinforce the students' understanding of the essay's subject matter as well as its form.

We hope that by offering interesting and accessible reading selections, by fully analyzing student writing that represents many academic disciplines, by stressing the importance of purpose and audience in our questions and assignments, and by presenting writing as a flexible, individualized process, we may encourage students to approach college writing not as a chore but as a challenge. Moreover, we believe that our pragmatic approach to writing as a skill that can be learned and applied will motivate our readers to work to master it.

Friends, colleagues, students, and family all helped this project along. We are grateful to Tom Broadbent and Nancy Perry of St. Martin's Press for their able editorial assistance, to Peter Phelps for his timely encouragement and enthusiasm, and to Marcia Muth for her meticulous and imaginative copy editing. For reading the manuscript and suggesting countless improvements, we thank Carol H. Adams, Elizabeth L. Barnes, Peter B. DeBlois, Richard Elias, Stephen H. Goldman, William Heim, Carolyn Matalene, Leo Rockas, and James M. Williams. We also wish to thank Helen Falls, our extraordinary typist, for making sure we met our deadlines; Caroline Ferree and Dot Elmendorf, who typed the Instructor's

Manual; and our very special department chairmen, Beauveau
Borie of the Philadelphia College of Pharmacy and Science and
Martha Montgomery of Drexel University, for their friendship and
support. And on the home front we thank Mark, Adam, and Rebecca
Kirszner and Demi and David Mandell—our links to the "real
world."

LAURIE G. KIRSZNER
STEPHEN R. MANDELL

Contents

"But was the Massacre a case of cold-blooded murder, or a case of self-defense on the part of the British soldiers? The full account of the event and the following trial of the British soldiers leave room for speculation."

"From her wheelchair she canned pickles, baked bread, ironed

4. Exemplification   103

meningococci. These cells are far less numerous than the red variety; the proportion of white to red under normal conditions is 1 to 400 or 500."

"Begun by the Beatles a decade ago, the rock revolution succeeded beyond everyone's wildest dreams. Rock defined an emerging segment of America, financed a counterculture, and spawned a $2 billion industry." `

"What is sorely lacking in textbooks and thus desperately needed in the classroom is a new image of adult women and a wide range of adult role models for young girls. Girls—and boys too—should learn about the history of women in this country, about suffrage and the current women's liberation movement, and about female heroines of our country and the world."

"The best of friends, I still believe, totally love and support and trust each other, and bare to each other the secrets of their souls, and run—no questions asked—to help each other, and tell harsh truths to each other when they must be told."

"Scientific verifiability rests upon the external observation of facts, not upon the heaping up of judgments. If one person says, 'Peter is a deadbeat,' and another says, 'I think so too,' the statement has not been verified."

"The Talmud was for centuries known to the Christian world only in random and garbled extracts. It was damned and outlawed and torn to shreds or cast into flames—in Paris, Rome, Toledo, Constantinople—by churchmen and emperors, from Justinian down to the Nazis and other fanatics in our midst."

government becomes destructive of these ends, it is the right of the people to alter or to abolish it. . . ."

"As public spirit and public services decline, so does the quality of life. So I ask myself why cannot we put it all together and ask our young people to volunteer in peacetime to serve America?"

"The present rate of increase of Earth's swarming human population qualifies Homo sapiens as an ecological cancer, which will destroy the ecology just as surely as any ordinary cancer would destroy an organism. The cure? Just what it is for any cancer. The cancerous growth must somehow be stopped."

"For years now I have heard the word 'Wait!' It rings in the ear of every Negro with piercing familiarity. This 'Wait' has almost always meant 'Never.' We must come to see, with one of our distinguished jurists, that 'justice too long delayed is justice denied.' "

"The atmosphere of the liberal-arts college is being poisoned by premedical students. It is not the fault of the students, who do not start out as a necessarily bad lot. They behave as they do in the firm belief that if they behave any otherwise they won't get into medical school."

Alternate Table of Contents
Arranged by Subject

SCIENCE AND TECHNOLOGY

LANGUAGE AND LITERATURE

Patterns for College Writing

A Rhetorical Reader and Guide

1

The Writing Process

Every essay in this book is the result of a struggle—one that went on between a writer and his or her material. Every writer starts with an idea or an assignment and then must work to translate his or her thoughts about the subject into a clear and easily read essay. If the writer's struggle is successful, the finished essay is welded together without a seam, and the reader has no sense of the writer's frustration while hunting for the right word or rearranging the ideas. Writing is no easy business, and even professional writers can have a very difficult time. Still, although there is no simple formula for good writing, some ways of writing are easier and more productive than others.

At this point, you may be asking yourself, "So what? What has this got to do with me? I'm not a professional writer." True enough, but during the next few years you will be doing a good deal of writing. Throughout your college career, you may need to write midterms, final exams, quizzes, lab reports, short essays, summaries, progress reports, proposals, personal letters, business correspondence, memos, or resumés. As diverse as these assignments seem to be, they all have one thing in common: they can be made easier if you know something about the writing process—the way in which successful writers begin with a subject, come up with a thesis or unifying idea, and eventually put together an essay.

In general, the writing process has three stages. During *invention*, sometimes called *prewriting*, you progress from subject to topic to thesis. As you develop your thesis, you also generate ideas that might be used to support it. During the next stage, *arrangement*, you decide how you are going to organize your ideas. And finally, during *writing and revision,* you write your essay, progressing through several drafts as you refine style, structure, and mechanics.

When you write, you do not move mechanically from one stage to another because the three stages overlap. Most writers engage in some aspects of invention, arrangement, and writing and revision simultaneously—finding ideas, thinking of possible methods of organization, and looking for the right words all at the same time. Even as writers compose or revise their essays, they may discover ideas that had not occurred to them during the prewriting stage. In addition, no two writers approach the writing process in exactly the same way. Some people outline, and others do not. Some take elaborate notes during the invention stage while others keep track of everything in their heads. But regardless of the differences in their particular systems, almost all successful writers work in some orderly way. If you, too, can approach your writing in college as an orderly process, it will be easier for you to carry out your assignments and to become a more efficient, competent, and relaxed writer. The rest of this chapter will look at the writing process more closely in order to suggest techniques that may work for you.

STAGE ONE: INVENTION

Prewriting, or invention, is probably the most important part of the writing process. Oddly enough, many people totally ignore this stage because they do not know how to plan to write or because they underestimate the importance of preparation. Since many writing assignments begin as general subjects provided by your instructor, you might be tempted to start writing immediately. Before you even attempt to draft your essay, however, you should probe your subject and decide what you are going to say about it. This entails narrowing your general subject to a manageable topic and arriving at a thesis. To accomplish this, your first step during invention should be to make sure you understand the assignment your instructor has given you. Next, you should establish the boundaries of your subject by considering your essay's purpose and audience. Then, you can move from your broad subject to a narrow topic by using questions to probe your subject. When you have discovered a limited topic, brainstorming will help you generate ideas until, finally, you are prepared to formulate a thesis—the main idea of your essay.

Assignments

Almost everything you write in college will begin as an assignment. Some will be direct and easy to understand:

> Write about an experience that changed your life.

> Discuss the procedure you used in this experiment.

But others will be difficult and complex:

> According to Wayne Booth, point of view is central to the understanding of modern fiction. In a short essay discuss how Henry James uses point of view in his *Turn of the Screw*.

Therefore, before you begin to write, it is important that you understand what you are being asked to do. If the assignment is a written question, read it carefully several times. You might even want to underline its most important parts. If the assignment is dictated to you by your instructor, be sure to copy it accurately since a missed word can make quite a difference. Whatever the case, don't be afraid to ask your instructor for clarification if you are confused. Remember that an essay, no matter how well written, will be unacceptable if it doesn't fulfill the assignment.

Establishing Boundaries

Once you are certain you understand your assignment, you are ready to establish the boundaries of your essay by considering its length, purpose, audience, and occasion, and your own knowledge of the subject.

Length.   Since the length of your paper sets an important limitation on your treatment of a subject, this consideration is an obvious way to begin the narrowing process. Often, your instructor will specify an approximate length or your writing situation will determine how much you can write. For example, you would need a narrower topic for a two- or three-page essay than you would for a ten-page paper. Similarly, during an hour exam you could not discuss a question as thoroughly as you might in a paper prepared over several days. If your instructor sets no length, consider how other aspects of the assignment might indirectly determine length. A summary of a chapter or an article, for instance, should be much shorter than the original, whereas an explication of a poem might have to be longer than the original. If your instructor says that the length of your paper should suit your topic and you are uncertain what this means, discuss your ideas for the paper with your instructor rather than asking for a page limit.

Purpose.   The purpose of your writing establishes a second boundary which may affect your subject matter as well as your approach. For example, if you were to write to a prospective employer about a summer job, you would emphasize different aspects of your college life than you would in a letter to a friend. In the first case, you would want to convince your reader to hire you. In the second, you would want to inform, and perhaps entertain, your reader. When you are assigned a college paper, your instructor may give you some guidelines about purpose. Often, an assignment may seem to require only an informational paper (such as a discussion of three economic causes of the Spanish-American War). But, in fact, the successful paper will do more than provide information. It will convince your reader that your position is valid and that you know what you are talking about.

Audience.   To be effective, your essay should be written with a particular audience in mind. Audiences, however, can be extremely varied. An audience can be an *individual,* such as your instructor, or it can be a *group,* like your classmates or co-workers. Your essay could address a *specialized* audience, like a group of medical doctors or engineers, or a *general* or *universal* audience that has no particular expertise, like a radio or television audience.

When you write in college, your audience considerations are usually fairly obvious, especially if the occasion of your writing is a midterm or final examination. Your audience is your instructor, and your purpose is to convince him or her that your facts are valid and your conclusions are reasonable and intelligent. But other audiences can be harder to define. It is just as difficult (and misleading) to categorize groups as it is individuals, and audiences on the job or in the community can be very complex. Considering the age of your audience, its income level, its political and religious leanings, and its educational level may help you define it. Similarly, thinking about your purpose in relation to the values and interests of your audience may also help. For example, if you were selling life insurance, you might prepare different sales letters for people with young children and for single people. Likewise, you might promote a local park differently for retired people and for working couples.

Many times, even after considering the characteristics of your audience as a group, you may find that your audience is simply too diverse to be categorized. In cases like this, many writers simply aim at a universal audience, trying to make points that will appeal to many different readers. Sometimes, writers try to think of one typical or fictional individual in the audience so that they can imagine writing to someone specific. Other times, writers solve this problem by finding a common denominator, a role that could interest or involve all those in the audience. For example, when a report on toy safety asserts, "Now is the time for concerned consumers to demand that dangerous toys be removed from the market," it automatically casts its audience in the role of "concerned consumers."

Occasion. In academic writing, the occasion is most often a classroom writing exercise or a take-home assignment. Although these may not seem to be real life situations, they serve as valuable practice for writing you do outside the classroom—writing a memo or a report for your job, writing a letter to your representative in Congress, or preparing a flyer for an organization. Each of these occasions, in college or out, requires a different approach to your writing. A memo to your co-workers, for instance, might be more informal than a report to your company's president. A notice about a meeting, sent to your fellow beer can collectors, might be strictly informational, whereas a letter to your senator about preserving a local historical landmark would be persuasive as well as informational. Similarly, when you are writing a classroom exercise, remember that there are different kinds of classes, each with different occasions for writing. A response suitable for a psychology class or a history class might not be acceptable for an English class, just as a good answer on a quiz might be insufficient on a midterm.

Knowledge. Your knowledge about a subject also will help you to limit it since what you know determines what you are able to write about. In addition, different assignments or writing situations require different kinds of knowledge. One essay may draw on your personal experiences or your observations; another may call for reading or research. Although your experience riding city buses might be sufficient for an English composition essay, you might need to do research about rapid transit for a paper for your urban sociology class. Sometimes, you will be readily able to increase your knowledge about a particular topic because you have a strong background in its general subject area. Other times, when a subject is new to you, you will need to select a topic particularly carefully so that you are not too ambitious. Often, the time allowed to do the assignment and its page limit will guide you as you consider what you already know and what you need to learn before you can plan a paper.

EXERCISES

1. Decide if the following topics are appropriate for the boundaries noted next to them. Write a few sentences for each topic to justify your conclusions.
   a. *A five-hundred word paper:* A history of the Louisiana American Civil Liberties Union
   b. *A final exam:* The role of France and Germany in the American Revolutionary War
   c. *A one-hour in-class essay:* An interpretation of Andy Warhol's Campbell Soup cans
   d. *A letter to your college paper:* A discussion of your school's investment practices

2. Make a list of different audiences you have to speak to or write to in your daily life. (Consider all the different types of people you see regularly, such as your family, your roommate, your instructors, your boss, your friends, and so on.)
   a. How do you speak or write to each? How do your approaches to these people differ?
   b. Which subjects would interest some of these people but not others? How do you account for these differences?
   c. Describe how you would treat a subject differently if you spoke or wrote to each audience about it. (For example, how would you describe your English class or the last party you attended to these different people?)

From Subject to Topic: Questions for Probing

Once you have considered the boundaries of your assignment, you need to narrow your subject to a topic you can work with. Many writing assignments begin as general fields of interest or concern. These *general subjects* are always too broad and need to be narrowed or limited until they are *topics* that can be reasonably discussed. For example, a subject like DNA recombinant research is certainly interesting and offers a number of exciting writing possibilities. But writing about it would be a mistake because the vastness of your subject would overwhelm you. What you need to do is narrow such subjects down into manageable topics.

Subject	*Topic*
DNA recombinant research	Some benefits of DNA recombinant research
Herman Melville's *Billy Budd*	Billy Budd as a Christ figure
Constitutional law	One result of the Bakke case
Stereo engineering	A comparison of air suspension and electrostatic speakers

In order to limit a general subject, you need to explore the subject so that you discover what topics are available within the boundaries you have established and what you have to say about each of them. Do not make the mistake of skipping this stage of the writing process, hoping that ideas will suddenly come to you. Not only will you waste time with this haphazard approach, but you also may fail to realize the potential of your subject. Instead, you can continue to systematically approach invention using two of the most productive techniques, questions for probing and brainstorming, to help you generate and organize ideas. Like most other writers, you will probably combine several methods of invention and discover by trial and error what works best for you.

The first technique involves asking a series of questions about your subject. These questions are useful because they reflect ways in which the human mind operates: finding similarities and differences, for instance, or dividing a whole into its parts. By running through these questions for probing in a systematic way, you can view your subject from a number of different angles. Although each question can provoke many different responses, not all questions will work for every subject. Still, each question represents a potential topic for your paper, and each answer you provide might be expanded into an essay.

What happened?
When did it happen?
Where did it happen?
What does it look like?
What are its characteristics?
What are some typical cases or examples of it?
How did it happen?
What makes it work?
How is it made?

Why did it happen?
What caused it?
What does it cause?
What are its effects?
How is it related to something else?
How is it like other things?
How is it different from other things?
What are its parts or types?
How can its parts or types be separated or grouped?
Do its parts or types fit into a logical order?
Into what categories can its parts or types be arranged?
On what basis can it be categorized?
What is it?
How does it resemble other members of its class?
How does it differ from other members of its class?
What are its limits?

To probe your subject, ask as many of these questions as you can. Even a few of them can yield many workable topics—some you might never have considered had you not asked the questions. By applying this approach to a general subject, such as "the Brooklyn Bridge," you can generate more ideas and topics than you need:

A short history of the Brooklyn Bridge (What happened?)
The construction of the Brooklyn Bridge (How is it made?)
The effect of the Brooklyn Bridge on American writers (What are its effects?)
A present-day description of the Brooklyn Bridge (What does it look like?)
Innovations in the design of the Brooklyn Bridge (How is it different from other things?)

At this point in the writing process, you are primarily concerned with exploring possible topics, and the more ideas you have, the wider your range of choice. You can even repeat the process of probing several times as you develop more limited topics. For instance, you might begin probing the subject of television programs and then repeat the process after you have narrowed the subject to game shows or even to a particular program. Of course, as you probe, some questions will yield results when applied to a subject, and others will not. Once you have generated many ideas, you should not hesitate to eliminate those that don't interest you or seem difficult to develop or are too complex or too simple. After all, when you have discarded your weaker ideas, you will still have choices left. Then, from these possible topics you can select the one that best suits your paper's length, purpose, audience, and occasion, as well as your knowledge of the subject.

EXERCISES

1. Indicate whether the following are general subjects or limited topics. Be prepared to explain your choices.
   a. Skiing
   b. A comparison of metal and fiberglass skis
   c. The Book of Genesis
   d. Two creation myths in the Book of Genesis
   e. Water fowl and fresh water plants
   f. The Haber Process for the fixation of atmospheric nitrogen
   g. Michelangelo's Sistine Chapel paintings
   h. The advantages of term over whole life insurance
   i. An argument for gun control
   j. An analysis of McDonald's television marketing strategy

2. Choose two of the following subjects and generate topics by using as many of the questions for probing as you can. (Assume that the essay you are preparing is due in three days for your English class and that it should be about five hundred words.)
   a. Television programs
   b. Pocket calculators
   c. Pinball machines
   d. Computers
   e. Teachers
   f. Video games
   g. CB radios
   h. Doctors
   i. Motorcycles
   j. Radio stations
   k. Diets
   l. Fatherhood or motherhood
   m. Grading
   n. Abortion
   o. Inflation

Finding Something to Say: Brainstorming

After you have used the questions for probing to discover a topic, you still have to find something to say about it. Brainstorming is a method of invention that can help you do this. When you brainstorm, you quickly write down everything you can think of that relates to your topic. Your list might include words or phrases or full sentences (statements or questions). Jot them down in whatever order you think of them, allowing your thoughts to wander freely. Some of the items may be inspired by notes you remember taking in class; others may be ideas you got from talking with friends or things you heard in class but didn't write down. Still others may be things you have begun to wonder about, points you thought of while generating your topic, or ideas that spontaneously occur to you as you brainstorm.

An engineering student, assigned to choose one of five topics for an English composition essay, might settle on "advantages and disadvantages of alternate energy sources" as the one most closely related to his interests. His brainstorming list might look like this:

Alternate Energy Sources
Solar
Fusion
Wind
Tidal
Nuclear
Nuclear technology already exists
Nuclear plants can leak radioactivity
Synthetic fuels
Steam power plants
Free fuel for solar
Inefficiency of solar collectors
High temperature of fusion reaction
Difficulty of containing fusion reaction
Solar collectors safe
Disposal of nuclear wastes—dangerous
Proliferation of plutonium
Breeder reactors
Sophisticated technology needs to be developed for fusion
Fusion relatively clean—little radioactive waste
Unlimited fuel source for fusion—H_2O
Limited uranium resources
Solar—no waste—no pollution
Oil will run out by 2020
Limited energy resources
Long lines at gas stations
Congress and president worried
Development money

Certain alternate sources still too expensive
Coal gasification
Shale oil
Decontrol
Raising prices
Rationing

Looking at this brainstorming list, we can see that the student who made it was at no loss for ideas. He immediately focused on the topic and jotted down a number of valuable points. Although this student is an engineering major and could easily discuss many of these items, because the assignment was due in two days and was to be only two or three pages long, he realized he would have to cut down his list. After reading his list over several times, he decided that he would concentrate on the advantages and disadvantages of the three alternate energy sources about which he knew the most: solar, fusion, and nuclear. They would require no research, would fit the limitations of time and space, and could easily be adapted to suit his nontechnical audience in English composition. His next step was to organize the ideas by grouping the items from his brainstorming list under the appropriate headings:

Solar
    Inefficiency of solar collectors
    Solar collectors safe
    Free fuel source
    No waste—no pollution
Fusion
    Sophisticated technology needs to be developed
    Difficulty of containing fusion reaction
    Unlimited fuel source—H_2O
    Relatively clean—little radioactive waste
Nuclear
    Nuclear technology already exists
    Nuclear plants can leak radioactivity
    Limited uranium resources
    Disposal of nuclear wastes—dangerous

Now that the student has decided what he is going to discuss, he is ready to sum up in one sentence the main idea or thesis of his essay: "Although solar, fusion, and nuclear power are promising energy sources with many advantages, each also has a number of serious disadvantages."

EXERCISES

Imagine that your English composition instructor has given you the following list of subjects and told you to select one for a five-hundred word essay, due in two days. Prepare at least three of these subjects following the procedures for invention just discussed. First, use the questions for probing. Next, pick the best topic developed from each subject, and then brainstorm about it. Finally, select and arrange the ideas about each topic that you would use if you were actually writing the paper.

a. Grandparents
b. Science-fiction movies
c. Gay rights
d. Divorce
e. The draft
f. Fast-food restaurants
g. Grading
h. Music
i. Religion
j. The death penalty
k. Cats
l. Television comedy
m. Textbooks
n. Local politics
o. The space program

Formulating a Thesis

Once you have decided what your essay is going to discuss, your next job is to formulate a thesis. Your topic determines what your essay is about; your thesis states your essay's main idea, your specific point about the topic. A thesis is usually a single sentence and most often appears at the beginning of an essay. Three things characterize a good thesis. First, a thesis should be so *clear* that it leaves no doubt in your mind, or in your reader's, about what you are going to discuss in your essay. It is the proposition that enables your readers to make sense of your ideas and to follow their progression throughout your essay.

Subject: Coeducational dormitories
Topic: An examination of the pros and cons of coeducational dormitories
Thesis: Despite predictions to the contrary from parents and church groups, coeducational college dormitories have not proved to be hotbeds of promiscuity.

Here, the general subject, "coeducational dormitories," has been limited to a narrower topic that gives a general idea of what the essay will be about. This topic, however, still gives no indication of the writer's stand on this issue. The thesis statement, on the other hand, explicitly reveals the writer's attitude toward the subject of coeducational dormitories.

This is the second characteristic of a good thesis—it *takes a stand*. It is an idea that your readers can agree or disagree with. In either case, your thesis should generate serious discussion in your essay and prompt serious consideration by your reader. A thesis, therefore, is much more than a title of an essay or an announcement of a subject.

Announcement: In this paper I will discuss Ezra Pound's editing of T. S. Eliot's poem *The Wasteland*.
Title: The English Country House

Neither of these examples is a thesis statement. Although both do tell what these writers are going to discuss, neither indicates what the writer's stand will be. With some revision, these examples can be turned into thesis statements.

Thesis: Far from being superficial, Ezra Pound's editorial changes shaped T. S. Eliot's *The Wasteland* into the great poem it is today.
Thesis: Despite its grandeur, the English country house did not provide a comfortable life for those who lived in it.

The third requirement for a thesis statement is that it be *specific* enough to give your essay direction and purpose. For example, the statement "The president has failed to control inflation" indicates the writer's topic and general stand, but it includes no specific information and establishes no center around which to construct the essay. A revised version, including specific information about the writer's topic and position, is more effective.

Thesis: Even though the president had promised to control inflation, his efforts to date have been tentative and ineffective.

Now, a reader could anticipate the exact direction of the essay, and the writer could build the essay around this thesis, explaining ways in which the president's efforts have been tentative and ineffective.

A clear, specific thesis that takes a stand unifies an essay and establishes its direction and purpose. Every piece of writing should have this clear sense of purpose, this unifying idea that draws the different details presented into a logical whole. Not every kind of writing, however, requires an explicitly stated thesis like the ones above. Sometimes, a thesis may be only implied. Like an explicit thesis, an implied thesis is clear and specific and takes a stand, but it is not directly stated in a single sentence. Instead, it is suggested by the selection and arrangement of the essay's details. Although an implied thesis requires a writer to plan and organize especially carefully, many of the professional writers whose essays are included in this book prefer to use this technique because it is more subtle.

Furthermore, in some types of writing, thesis statements (whether explicit or implied) are neither necessary nor appropriate. A lab report describing the method of typing blood, for instance, merely provides factual information and presents no arguments with which readers might agree or disagree. Trying to force an argumentative thesis on such an assignment (for example, "Typing blood can be fun") may distort your purpose and distract your readers from the solid information you are presenting. Nevertheless, whether a piece of writing has an explicitly stated thesis, an implied thesis, or no thesis at all, it should have a unifying idea—that is, an idea to which everything in the essay relates. (In most college writing situations, since you want to avoid any risk of being misunderstood, you will probably want to include an explicit thesis.)

No fixed rules determine when you formulate your thesis; it depends on the type of assignment, your knowledge of the subject, and your own particular method of writing. Some people prefer to formulate a tentative thesis statement before they start brainstorming or even probing their subject. Others wait until after this process—slowly reviewing all their material and then drawing it together into a single statement. Occasionally, your assignment may specify a thesis statement by telling you to take this or that position about a given subject. Whatever the case, you should arrive at your thesis before you begin actually writing your essay. Keep in mind that the thesis you develop at this point is not final. It is a tentative statement of the direction your essay will take and may be revised as you write. Nonetheless, it gives you guidance and purpose and is thus necessary at this stage of the writing process.

EXERCISES

1. Which of the following are effective thesis statements? Be able to point out the defects of those statements you reject as well as the strengths of those you select.
   a. Myths and society.
   b. Myths serve an important function in society.
   c. Contrary to popular assumptions, myths are more than fairy stories; they are tales that express the underlying attitudes a society has toward important issues.
   d. Today, almost two marriages in four will end in divorce.
   e. Skiing, a popular sport for millions, is a major cause of winter injuries.
   f. If certain reforms are not instituted immediately, our company will be bankrupt within two years.
   g. Early childhood is an important period.
   h. By using the proper techniques, parents can significantly improve the learning capabilities of their preschool children.
   i. Science fiction can be used to criticize society.
   j. Science fiction, in the hands of an able writer, can be a powerful tool for social reform.

2. For three of the following general subjects and topics, go through as many steps as you need to formulate workable thesis statements.
   a. The importance of your family
   b. Writing
   c. Space exploration
   d. The difficulty of adjusting to college
   e. One thing you would change about your life
   f. Air pollution
   g. Gasoline prices
   h. Humor in television commercials
   i. The objectivity of newspaper reporting
   j. Atheism

STAGE TWO: ARRANGEMENT

Let's pause to sum up what we have already considered. So far, we have progressed through the following steps:

- Understanding your assignment
- Establishing the boundaries of your subject
- Moving from subject to topic by using questions for probing
- Brainstorming to generate ideas
- Formulating a thesis

Each of these steps represents a series of choices you have to make about your material. Now, before you actually begin writing, you have another choice to make—how to arrange your material into an essay. This extremely important choice determines how clear your essay will be and how your audience will react to it. Sometimes the decision about how to arrange your ideas is easy because your assignment specifies a particular pattern of development. This may often be the case in your freshman English class where your instructor may assign, say, a descriptive or a narrative essay. In addition, certain assignments or examination questions imply how your material should be structured. Probably no one except an English composition instructor will say to you, "Write a narrative," but you will have assignments in other courses that begin, "Give an account of . . . " Likewise, many teachers will never directly assign a process essay or a classification essay, but they will do so indirectly when they ask you to explain how something works or to discuss the different types of something. An examination question might ask you to trace the events leading up to an event. If you are perceptive, you will realize that this question calls for a narrative or cause and effect answer. The important thing is to recognize the clues that such assignments give and to structure your essay accordingly.

Besides the phrasing of your assignment, your brainstorming list and even your thesis itself can indicate a pattern of development. For instance, the thesis statement on page 12 ("Despite predictions to the contrary from parents and church groups, coeducational college dormitories have not proved to be hotbeds of promiscuity") suggests an *example* structure—a series of examples illustrating that coed dorms encourage loyal friendships and brother-sister relationships—or a *description* of what the dorms are really like. In addition, the questions you used for probing your subject may suggest how to arrange your material:

What happened?
When did it happen?   } Narration
Where did it happen?

What does it look like?   } Description
What are its characteristics?

What are some typical cases or examples   } Exemplification
   of it?

How did it happen?
What makes it work?   } Process
How is it made?

Why did it happen? What caused it? What does it cause? What are its effects? How is it related to something else?	Cause and Effect
How is it like other things? How is it different from other things?	Comparison and Contrast

What are its parts or types?
How can its parts or types be separated or
    grouped?
Do its parts or types fit into a logical order?
Into what categories can its parts or types
    be arranged?
On what basis can it be categorized?
	Division and
	Classification

What is it?
How does it resemble other members of its
    class?
How does it differ from other members of
    its class?
What are its limits?
	Definition

These questions correspond to the general categories of narration, description, exemplification, process, cause and effect, comparison and contrast, division and classification, and definition. And the categories, in turn, correspond to patterns of development that help you order your ideas. As you will see, the rest of this book explains and illustrates each of these patterns. If, when you probed your subject, you found questions under narration most helpful, your essay should be organized as a narrative. This is true of process, cause and effect, and all the other question categories in this list.

Parts of the Essay

As Aristotle, the ancient Greek philosopher, pointed out in *The Poetics,* a piece of writing has a beginning, a middle, and an end. No matter which pattern of development you use, this is true. Every essay has an introduction, a body, and a conclusion.

The Introduction.   This part of your essay, usually one paragraph and rarely more than two, introduces your subject, engages your reader's interest, and states (or at least implies) your thesis or unifying idea. Although it presents your subject and your thesis, the introduction should not include an in-depth discussion or a summary of your topic.

You can introduce an essay and engage your reader's interest in a number of ways. Here are several methods you can employ.

1. You can begin your essay with a direct movement to your thesis. This approach works well in any writing situation where you want immediate clarity and straightforwardness. It is especially useful for midterms and finals where subtlety is undesirable.

> With double-digit inflation taking its toll, it is understandable that many companies have been forced to raise prices, and the oil industry should be no exception. But well-intentioned individuals begin wondering whether high rates are justified when increases occur every week. It is at this point that we should start examining the pricing policies of the major American oil companies.
>
> (economics take-home exam)

2. You can introduce an essay with a definition of a relevant term or concept. This technique is especially useful for research papers or examinations where the meaning of a specific term is crucial.

> Democracy is a form of government in which the ultimate authority is vested in and exercised by the people. This may be so in theory, but recent elections in our city have caused much concern for the future of democracy here. Extensive voting machine irregularities and ghost voting have seriously jeopardized the people's faith in the democratic process.
>
> (political science paper)

3. You can begin with a question.

> What was it like to live through the holocaust? Elie Wiesel, in *One Generation After,* answers this question. As he does so, he challenges many of the assumptions we hold in our somewhat smug and highly materialistic society.
>
> (sociology book report)

4. You can begin an essay with a quotation. If it is well chosen, it can interest your audience in reading further.

> "The rich are different," said F. Scott Fitzgerald fifty years ago. Apparently, they remain so today. As any examination of the tax laws

shows, the wealthy receive many more benefits than do the middle class or the poor.

(business law essay)

5. Finally, you can begin your essay with an anecdote or story.

Upon meeting the famous author James Joyce, a young student stammered, "May I kiss the hand that wrote *Ulysses*?" "No!" said Joyce. "It did a lot of other things, too." As this conversation shows, Joyce was an individual who valued humor. This tendency is also present in his final work, *Finnegans Wake*, where comedy is used to comment upon the human condition.

(English literature paper)

No matter which method you select, an introduction should be consistent in tone and approach with the rest of your essay. If it is not, it can misrepresent your intentions to your readers and, in many cases, destroy your credibility. A final examination or technical report, for instance, should have an introduction that reflects the formality and seriousness of the occasion. An autobiographical essay or a personal letter, on the other hand, should be informal and relaxed.

The Body Paragraphs.   The middle section of your essay supports and expands your essay's thesis. The body paragraphs form the longest section of your essay and present the detailed arguments and evidence (such as examples, descriptions, and facts) that will convince your audience that your thesis is reasonable and valid. Generally, a body paragraph contains a *topic sentence,* a statement that tells your audience the specific point you are discussing in that paragraph. Like the thesis, the topic sentence acts as a guidepost and makes it easier for your audience to follow the flow of your essay.

The body paragraphs develop the thesis or unifying idea that you stated or implied in your introduction. Their contents—supporting ideas and information related to your topic—usually grow from your brainstorming list. This list often provides enough material to develop your thesis fully. If it does not, you can brainstorm again, review your notes, ask questions of your friends and instructors, read about your topic, or go to the library and do some research. Of course, your assignment and your topic will determine the kind and quantity of information you need.

Once you have gathered enough material, you need to review it to decide exactly what to present in your essay. Sometimes you will need to drop one point, even a good one, because it does not fit with your other ideas or support your thesis. Other times, particularly if you have collected much new material, you will need to reconsider your thesis so it continues to reflect the actual content of your essay. In either case, once you have selected your material, you need to arrange it according to the pattern of development that suits it best. For instance, an essay in which you discuss the causes of Hitler's defeat in Russia could be organized following a cause and effect pattern:

Introduction: Thesis
Cause 1:   The Russian winter
Cause 2:   The opening of a second front
Cause 3:   The problem of logistics
Cause 4:   Hitler's refusal to take advice
Conclusion

A lab report on the synthesis of aspirin could be organized like this, following a process pattern of development:

Introduction: Unifying idea
Step 1:   Mix 5 g. of salicylic acid, 10 ml. of acetic anhy-
              dride, and 1–2 ml. of sulphuric acid.
Step 2:   Wait for the mixture to cool. Then add 50 ml. of
              water and collect on a Büchner filter.
Step 3:   Dry the residue.
Step 4:   Recrystallize the aspirin from benzene.
Conclusion

These patterns, and others, will be outlined and analyzed in detail throughout the rest of this book.

The Conclusion.   This part of your essay provides closure and at the same time reinforces your thesis or unifying idea. Because readers remember best what they read last, the final section is extremely important. Like your introduction, your conclusion should be brief. In a five-hundred-word essay, it can be as short as one line and most often is no longer than a paragraph. Regardless of its length, however, your conclusion should accurately reflect or review the content of your essay. Thus, it should not introduce new points or material that you have not discussed earlier. Frequently, a conclusion will end an essay by restating the thesis.

Conclusions can be as challenging to construct as introductions. Here are several ways to conclude an essay.

1. You can conclude by simply reviewing your main points and restating your thesis.

> Rotation of crops provided several benefits. It enriched soil by giving it a rest; it enabled farmers to vary their production; and it ended the cycle of "boom or bust" that had characterized the prewar South's economy when cotton was the primary crop. Of course, this innovation did not solve all the economic problems of the postwar South, but it did lay the groundwork for the healthy economy this region enjoys today.
>
> (history exam)

2. You can end an essay by recommending a course of action.

> While there is still time, American engineering has to reassess its priorities. We no longer have the luxury of exotic and wasteful experiments such as automobile airbags. Instead, we need technology grounded in common sense and economic feasibility. That Volkswagen, rather than an American company, developed an outstanding and inexpensive passive restraint system illustrates how far we have strayed from old-fashioned Yankee ingenuity.
>
> (engineering ethics report)

3. You can also conclude by making a prediction based on the points you have made in the essay. Be careful, however, that your prediction logically extends the implications of your ideas and does not introduce new points.

> It is too late to save parts of the Everglades in northern Florida, but it is not too late to preserve this natural resource in the southern part of the state. With intelligent planning and an end of the dam building program by the Army Corps of Engineers, we can halt the destruction of what the Indians called the "Timeless Swamp."
>
> (environmental science essay)

4. Finally, you can use a quotation in your conclusion. If selected carefully, it can add authority to an already strong essay.

> In *Walden* Henry David Thoreau said, "The mass of men lead lives of quiet desperation." This sentiment is reinforced when you drive through the Hill District of our city. Perhaps the work of the men and women who run the health clinic on Jefferson Street cannot totally change this situation, but it can give us hope to know that some people, at least, are working for the betterment of us all.
>
> (public health essay)

STAGE THREE: WRITING AND REVISION

When you finally begin writing your essay, your major concern should be getting your ideas down on paper. Since an essay usually goes through a number of preliminary drafts before it is ready to be handed in, your final draft probably will be very different from your first draft. The major function of your rough draft is simply to get you going. At this point, you should not let worries about sentence proportion or word choice interfere with your flow of ideas. All you want to do is to build momentum and finish the first draft of your essay. When you write the second or third draft, you can polish your essay, making sure as you revise that each part does what it should do.

Remember that revision is not something you do after your paper is finished. It is a continuing process during which you consider the logic and clarity of your ideas as well as the effective and correct expression of them. Thus, revision is more than proofreading or editing, crossing out one word and substituting another; it may involve extensive addition, deletion, and reordering of whole sentences or paragraphs as you reconsider what you want to communicate to your audience.

After you have written your first draft, you should put it aside for several hours or even a day or two, if you have the time. This "cooling off" period enables you to distance yourself from your essay so that you can go back to it and read it more objectively. Then, when you read it again, check your thesis statement to see if it is still accurate. If you departed from your original goal while you were writing, you will need either to revise the thesis so that it accurately sums up the ideas and information contained in your essay or to revise any unrelated sections so that they logically follow from your thesis. Next, look at your body paragraphs to see if they need strengthening. You might have to add more facts or examples to one to make it as strong as the others. Read your conclusion to see if it accurately reflects the content of your essay. Rework it if it does not sufficiently reinforce your thesis or unifying idea. Finally, get a sense of your whole essay. Is your thesis clear and specific? Does it take a stand? Do the points you make support your thesis? Are they convincing? Would other points be better? Only now, after doing all your revision, should you go back and edit your essay. Polish your sentence structure, check your spelling, and make sure your punctuation and grammar are correct. Revision can take a lot of time, so don't be discouraged if you have to go through three or four drafts of your essay before you feel it is ready to hand in.

The following two drafts of an essay were written by a student, Michael Ginsberg, for his class in business management. His assignment was to choose a local corporation and, in about five hundred words, discuss two or three of its management problems. He was able to do this easily because he had already analyzed the management structure of Acme Power and Light Company for his work-study project. Ginsberg realized that the assignment itself suggested a thesis (company X has management problems) and a pattern of development (example). As part of his process of invention, Michael Ginsberg prepared this outline before he began writing his essay:

Introduction:	Thesis—Acme Power and Light has management problems.
Example 1:	Too many managers
Example 2:	Long record of bad management decisions
Example 3:	Poor customer relations
Conclusion:	Restatement of thesis

Here is the rough draft of his essay:

ACME POWER AND LIGHT

Introduction:
Quotation

When the city said, "Let there be light," Acme was ready. Acme Power and Light Corporation has supplied the city's power since 1962, when it was formed as a city owned and subsidized company. During the years since its inception, Acme has consistently lost money despite a yearly subsidy by the taxpayer. This

Thesis

financial trouble is no doubt due to Acme's management practices, which are downright shocking.

Examples 1
and 2

Acme has too many managers and has made bad decisions that have cost consumers tens of millions of dollars. During the last ten years, the company has increased its middle and upper level management by two and one half times and built a costly atomic power plant to meet a projected increase in demand for electricity. This proliferation of management has added almost five million dollars in salaries and benefits to the company's expenses, and the

power plant cost another seventy-five million
dollars.

Example 3   Perhaps the most blatant management problem Acme
has is its seemingly callous attitude toward
consumers. On any given day, Acme is flooded by
hundreds of calls about errors in billing.

Conclusion   It is clear that Acme's financial problems are
costing the consumer too much.

Points for Special Attention

The Introduction.   The day after he wrote his draft, Michael Ginsberg analyzed it and determined what he wanted to revise. First,
he reconsidered his catchy opening. Although he thought his
opening would have been excellent for another situation, he
decided it was inappropriate for his practical, business-minded
audience and the no-nonsense purpose of his assignment. Next, he
realized that, since all his points about Acme were negative, his
neutral audience might think he was being a little too hard on the
company. Instead of blaming everything on management, he decided to introduce the company's financial problems more fairly so
that his thesis would seem more reasonable. He also reconsidered
his title because he decided that it did not describe his essay as
precisely as it might.

The Body Paragraphs.   Although Ginsberg knew he had outlined
three fairly good examples of the company's poor management
practices, he discovered he had jumbled together the first two
examples—too many managers and bad decisions—while he was
writing. As a result, he suspected that his second paragraph blurred
his ideas, and he decided to revise it so that each example was
developed in its own separate paragraph. Finally, he reviewed his
third example—the company's attitude toward customers—and
concluded that it was insufficiently developed. Just mentioning the
phone calls did not support his assertion that Acme was "callous
toward customers," so he decided to add more information here.

The Conclusion.   Rather than giving his readers a feeling of closure
or providing them with something to think about, Ginsberg knew
that he had simply quit writing. He felt that his single concluding

sentence was too brief and abrupt. Most importantly, he realized that it did not restate his thesis about Acme's management practices. Instead, it left his readers thinking solely about Acme's financial difficulties. Since Ginsberg knew that his audience would remain unconvinced if he let them forget the thrust of his argument, he decided to completely rewrite his last paragraph.

After his careful analysis, Michael Ginsberg reordered and expanded his original paper to look like this final draft:

THE MANAGEMENT PRACTICES OF

ACME POWER AND LIGHT

Introduction:
Direct approach
Acme Power and Light Corporation has supplied the city's power since 1962 when it was formed as a city owned and subsidized company. During the years since its inception, Acme has consistently lost money despite a sizable yearly subsidy from the taxpayers. It would be unfair to single Acme out for criticism because it suffers the ills that all public utilities face—antiquated equipment and increased operating costs. But there is one area where Acme can be faulted, and this is in the quality of its

Thesis
management. Even a cursory examination of this company reveals management practices that are downright shocking.

Example 1
One management problem Acme has is obvious—too many managers. During the last ten years, the company has increased its middle and upper level management by two and one half times. This was done even though Acme's area of service has actually decreased. This proliferation of management has added almost five million dollars in salaries and benefits to the company's expenses which, of course, the electric consumers are required to absorb.

Example 2
Another management problem Acme has is its long record of bad decisions that have cost consumers

tens of millions of dollars. An example was the
decision ten years ago to construct an atomic power
plant to meet a projected increase in demand for
electricity. Despite subsequent projections of
decreasing energy demands, Acme proceeded with
their project. As a result, seventy-five million
dollars later they have an atomic power plant that
operates at 25 percent capacity because the demand
for electricity has gone down instead of up.

Example 3   Perhaps the most blatant management problem Acme
has is its inability to handle customer complaints.
On any day, Acme is flooded by hundreds of calls
about errors in billing, equipment malfunction, or
any number of other complaints. As a recent
newspaper article asserts, the majority of these
problems result from negligence or from Acme's
inability to supervise its employees adequately. If
this were not enough, statistics provided by the
Better Business Bureau show that it takes between
two and three service calls for Acme fully to correct
most problems. The cost of this poor management
represents about 20 percent of Acme's operating
budget.

Conclusion   These are just a few examples of the problems that
Acme Power and Light has. In any private
corporation, such inefficiency would lead to
stockholder charges of mismanagement or to

Restatement   bankruptcy. But because Acme is owned by the city, it
of thesis   is kept afloat by taxpayer money and regular rate
increases. Price increases caused by inflation and
rising fuel costs affect all of us, including
corporations, and must be accepted, but increases
caused by mismanagement should be unacceptable to
everyone.

Points for Special Attention

The Introduction. Michael Ginsberg's introduction follows the direct approach discussed earlier. Because he felt that a paper for a management course should sound businesslike, Ginsberg wisely chose to eliminate the rough draft's opening. His introduction is straightforward and simple. He begins by briefly outlining the history of Acme Power and Light Company and moves right into his thesis statement that the company's "management practices are downright shocking." In the process, Ginsberg demonstrates to his audience that he is reasonable by granting that Acme has some of the problems every public corporation has. Still, he maintains that poor management, the subject of his paper, is something different.

The Body Paragraphs. Ginsberg supports his thesis by presenting examples of Acme Power and Light Company's inefficient management. He now presents each example in a separate paragraph and introduces each paragraph with a clearly stated topic sentence. Following each topic sentence are facts to support it. Perhaps the major weakness of Ginsberg's paper is that he could still have used more supporting data in his first and second body paragraphs. Although his third body paragraph has been adequately expanded, he presents only one example in each of the preceding paragraphs to support his assertions that Acme has too many managers and that it has a long record of bad decisions. Although they are good examples, they are not enough in themselves to convince his audience that what he asserts is reasonable.

The Conclusion. In his conclusion, Ginsberg now not only restates his thesis but also restates his essay's main points. Because his essay is actually a report on the management status of Acme Power and Light, he wants to be sure that his audience does not forget his thesis or the implications of the material he has presented. To make sure, he ends his conclusion with a statement designed to stay with his readers. Fuel costs, price increases, and inflation we have to put up with, he says, but increased costs caused by mismanagement are unacceptable to everyone.

SUMMARY

The following list can be used as a checklist when you write. Keep in mind that, as you become a more confident writer, you will develop your own approaches to the writing process.

- Make sure you understand your assignment.
- Establish the boundaries of your subject.
- Move from subject to topic by using questions for probing.
- Brainstorm to generate ideas.
- Formulate a thesis.
- Arrange your material.
- Write and revise your essay.

Each of the essays in the chapters that follow is organized around one dominant pattern. It is not at all unusual, however, to find more than one pattern used in a single essay. For example, a narrative essay might contain an introduction that is descriptive. As you can see, these patterns are not to be followed blindly but should be adapted to your subject, your audience, and your writing occasion.

2

Narration

WHAT IS NARRATION?

A narrative tells a story by presenting a sequence of events in chronological order. Narration can be the dominant pattern in many types of writing—formal, such as history, biography, autobiography, and journalism, as well as less formal, such as personal letters and entries in diaries and journals. Narration is also an essential part of casual conversation, and it may dominate tall tales, speeches, and shaggy-dog stories, as well as news and feature stories presented on television. In short, any time you "tell what happened," you are using narration.

Although a narrative may be written for its own sake—that is, simply to recount events—in most college writing situations narration is used for a purpose, and a sequence of events is presented to prove a point. For instance, in a narrative essay about your first date, your purpose may be to show your readers that dating is a bizarre and often unpleasant ritual. Accordingly, you do not simply "tell the story" of your date. Rather, you select and arrange details of the evening that show your readers why dating is bizarre and unpleasant.

Often, too, narrative writing may be part of an essay that is not primarily a narrative one. In an argumentative essay in support of stricter gun control legislation, for example, you may devote one or two paragraphs to a story of a child killed with a handgun. These narrative paragraphs, though only a small portion of the essay, will still have a definite purpose. They will support your point that stricter gun control laws are needed.

In this chapter, however, we are concerned with narration when it is the dominant pattern in a piece of writing. During your college career, you will have many assignments that call for such writing.

In an English composition class, for instance, you may be asked to write about an experience that was important to your development as an adult; in American history, you may need to relate the events preceding the attack on Fort Sumter; in a technical writing class, you may be asked to write a letter of complaint reviewing in detail a company's negligent actions. In each of these situations (as well as in case studies for business management classes, reports for criminal justice classes, and many additional assignments), the piece of writing has a structure that is primarily narrative, and the narrative is presented not for its own sake but for a specified purpose.

The skills you develop in narrative writing will also be helpful to you in other kinds of writing. A process essay, such as an account of a laboratory experiment, is like narration in that it outlines a series of steps in chronological order; a cause and effect essay, such as your answer on a history midterm that directs you to "analyze the events that led to World War I," also resembles narrative in that it traces a sequence of events. A process essay, however, presents events to explain how to do something, and a cause and effect essay presents them to explain how they are related. (Process essays and cause and effect essays will be dealt with in chapters 4 and 5, respectively.) Writing both process and cause and effect essays will be easier if you master narration, telling what events took place.

Narrative Detail

Narratives, like other types of writing, need rich, specific detail to be convincing. Each detail should help form a picture for the reader; even exact times, dates, and geographical locations can be helpful. Look, for example, at the following excerpt from the essay "My Mother Never Worked," which appears in its complete form later in this chapter:

> In the winter she sewed night after night, endlessly, begging cast-off clothing from relatives, ripping apart coats, dresses, blouses, and trousers to remake them to fit her four daughters and son. Every morning and every evening she milked cows, fed pigs and calves, cared for chickens, picked eggs, cooked meals, washed dishes, scrubbed floors, and tended and loved her children. In the spring she planted a garden once more, dragging pails of water to nourish and sustain the vegetables for the family. In 1936 she lost a baby in her sixth month.

In this excerpt, the list of details makes the narrative genuine and convincing. The central figure in the narrative is a busy, productive woman, and the readers know this because they are presented with a specific list of her actions.

Narrative Variety

Because narratives are often told from one person's perspective and because they present a series of events in chronological order, a constant danger is that all the sentences will begin to sound alike: "She sewed dresses . . . She milked cows . . . She fed pigs . . . She fed calves . . . She cared for chickens . . ." A narrative without sentence variety may affect your readers like a ride down a monotonous stretch of highway. You can avoid this monotony by varying your sentence structure: "In the winter she sewed night after night, endlessly . . . Every morning and every evening she milked cows, fed pigs and calves, cared for chickens . . ."

Narrative Order

Most narratives present events in exactly the order in which they occurred, moving from beginning to end, from first event to last. Whether or not you follow a strict chronological order, though, depends on the purpose of your narrative. If you are writing a straightforward account of a historical event or presenting a series of poor management practices, you will probably want to move efficiently from beginning to end. Often, however, in writing personal experience essays, you may choose to engage your reader's interest by beginning with a key event from the middle of your story, or even from the end, and then presenting the events that led up to it. In fictional narratives or in personal experience essays, you may also begin in the present and then use a series of flashbacks to tell your story. Whatever ordering scheme you use, it should shape and direct your narrative. Without some plan for clear and orderly progression, your readers will be unable to follow your story.

Because verb tense is an extremely important clue in writing that recounts events in a fixed order, when you write narrative you must be especially careful to keep verb tense accurate and consistent. Naturally, there are times when you must shift tense to reflect an actual time shift in your narrative. For instance, a flashback may require a shift from present to past tense. But it is important to avoid unnecessary shifts in verb tense because such unwarranted shifts will make your narrative confusing.

Transitions—connecting words or phrases—are essential in narrative writing because they signal movement from one time period to another. Transitions can indicate the order in which events in a narrative occurred (*first, second, after that, next, then, later*) or their simultaneous occurrence (*at the same time, meanwhile*). Transitional words and phrases can also show how much time has passed between events (*just then* or *three years later*). Without these guides, your essay would lack coherence, and your readers would be unsure of the correct sequence of events. Other transitions commonly used to signal shifts in time include *immediately, soon, before, earlier, after, afterward, now,* and *finally*.

STRUCTURING A NARRATIVE ESSAY

Like other essays, narratives usually have an introduction, a body, and a conclusion. As we have observed, a pure narrative may tell a story for its own sake or in order to create a particular mood or effect, without trying to prove a point. On the other hand, most of the full-length narratives you will be assigned will use narrative for a particular purpose—for instance, to support an argument. Thus, each of your narrative essays will probably have an arguable thesis which, if it is explicitly stated, will appear in the *introduction*. Once the thesis or significance of your narrative is established in the introduction, the *body* of your essay will recount the series of events that makes up your narrative, following a clear and orderly plan. Finally, the *conclusion* will give your reader the sense that your story is complete, perhaps by restating your thesis if it is explicit. Thus, to plan a five-paragraph narrative essay, you would follow this outline:

¶1   Introduction—including thesis
¶2   First event or events in sequence
¶3   Next event or events in sequence
¶4   Last event or events in sequence
¶5   Conclusion—including restatement of thesis

Let's suppose that you are assigned a short history paper about the Battle of Waterloo. You plan to support the thesis that if Napoleon had kept more troops in reserve, he might have defeated the British troops under Wellington. Based on this thesis, you decide that the best way to organize your paper is to present the five major phases of the battle in strict chronological sequence. An outline of your essay might look like this:

¶1   Introduction—thesis: Had Napoleon kept more troops in reserve, he might have broken Wellington's line with another infantry attack and thus reversed the outcome of the Battle of Waterloo.

¶2   Phase one of the battle: Napoleon attacks the Château of Hougoumont.

¶3   Phase two of the battle: The French infantry attacks the British lines.

¶4   Phase three of the battle: The French cavalry stages a series of charges against the British lines that had not been attacked before.

¶5   Phase four of the battle: The French capture La Haye Sainte, their first success of the day but an advantage which Napoleon, having committed troops elsewhere, could not maintain without reserves.

¶6   Phase five of the battle: The French infantry is decisively defeated by the combined thrust of the British infantry and the remaining British cavalry.

¶7   Conclusion—restatement of thesis: Had Napoleon had reinforcements ready to capitalize on his capture of La Haye Sainte, he could have broken through the British lines with another infantry attack.

By discussing the five phases of the battle in chronological order, you clearly demonstrate the validity of your thesis. In turning your outline into a historical narrative, you realize that exact details, dates, times, and geographical locations will be extremely important. Without them, your mere assertions will be open to question. In addition, you plan to select appropriate transitional words and phrases carefully and pay special attention to verb tenses to keep your readers aware of the order in which the events of the battle took place.

The following essay is typical of the informal narrative writing many freshmen are asked to do in English composition classes. It was written by a student, Derek Wilson, in response to the assignment "Write an essay about an event which had a significant effect upon you."

DO I BELIEVE IN MIRACLES?

**Introduction
(implied thesis)**

Do miracles still happen? Do supernatural healings still take place? Kathryn Kuhlman was known as the "love healer," and her famous words were "I believe in miracles." But these strange occurrences were reserved for famous people; everyone knows that. At least this is what I thought until I was sixteen years old—when I saw the impossible happen.

Narrative begins

It was on a Friday, just after dinner. I was reading when my mother came into the living room.

"Derek," she said, "will you take your aunt Elitia to the gospel meeting? I promised I would take her, but I'm just too busy."

"But, Mama, why would I want to go there?"

"Derek," she snapped, "I don't want any more arguments. You know your aunt is sick, and she can't go on her own. You go on, get dressed, and take her."

Flashback

Aunt Elitia had been sick for years, but during the last few months she had gotten worse. The doctor finally convinced her to go into the hospital for tests, and when they were completed he told her she had a tumor. My aunt had always been religious, but when she heard the doctor's diagnosis she stopped going to the Baptist Church and began attending a faith-healing service. I thought the whole thing was ridiculous, but I did feel sorry for the old woman, so I agreed to take her that Friday night.

**Narrative
continues**

The Faith Gospel Healing Church was an old store that had been gutted, painted, and filled with chairs. We arrived late, and the service was in full swing. The preacher was singing a hymn, and the congregation was swaying and clapping in time to the music. As we sat down, the music ended, and the healing part of the service began. The preacher read

a verse from the Bible about praying and healing and
then began talking about Jesus and faith. After what
seemed like an hour, he asked those in the audience
who wanted to be healed to stand up. My aunt
struggled to her feet and leaned on me for support.

Ten women were standing. The preacher began at
the front of the room. He moved from person to
person. He took each one by the arm. He placed his
hand on each one's head and prayed. As he touched
them, they would close their eyes, begin to moan or
pray, and finally declare loudly that they were
healed.

As I watched the preacher slowly come closer, I
began to wonder why I had ever let my mother talk me
into this. Suddenly, the preacher was standing in
front of us, and every person in the church was
looking. I felt very hot, and sweat ran down my face.
I didn't hear a word the preacher said until he was
almost finished. ". . . Father heal this woman's
tumor. In Jesus's name, Amen."

One minute I was holding my aunt and thinking I
was the biggest fool in the world, and the next I was
struggling to keep her tremendous bulk from
collapsing onto the seats. She had fainted. The
preacher and several men from the congregation
carried her prostrate body to the open door of the
church.

"I'm healed," she mumbled. "Praise the Lord. I'm
healed," she said over and over.

"Sure you are, Aunt Elitia," I said. "Just relax.
You'll be all right."

Three weeks later my aunt went back into the
hospital for more tests. And to everyone's surprise,
except Aunt Elitia's, the doctors found that the
tumor had receded and that there was no need for an

operation. She was positive that a miracle had taken
place and that God, because of her faith, had healed
her.

Conclusion
(return to
implied thesis)

In spite of my experience, I remain unconvinced.
I still would rather go to a doctor than the corner
store—front church. But I do not dismiss what I saw
three years ago with my own eyes. Whenever I see a
faith healer on television on Sunday morning, I no
longer laugh. I watch and listen and remember when I
saw the impossible happen.

Points for Special Attention

Thesis.   Because the assignment does not call for pure narrative
but rather for narrative that will illustrate a point, Derek Wilson's
introduction includes an implied thesis: miracles do happen. The
narrative itself begins with the second paragraph.

Detail.   Personal narratives, like Wilson's, are especially dependent upon detail because the authors ask the audience to see and
hear and feel what they did. In order to present a picture of the
scene, Wilson supplies all the significant details he can remember:
the description of the church, the swaying of the congregation, the
physical bulk of his aunt. He could have presented even more (a
description of his aunt's face, her clothes, or the preacher's appearance), but he chose not to because he wanted to keep his
account focused on the events that related to his thesis.

Dialogue.   Wilson characterizes himself, his mother, the preacher,
and Aunt Elitia through bits of dialogue. As a result, his narrative
is more interesting and immediate than it would be if he simply
described events. (In order to avoid confusion, Derek begins a new
paragraph each time a character speaks.) Using convincing dialogue
is one way to give your audience a sense of reality. Of course,
dialogue is rarely used on exams or in academic papers, but when
it is appropriate (as it is in this personal experience essay), it gives
the narrative an added dimension.

Sentence Variety.   In most of his essay, Wilson's sentences are
sufficiently varied to sustain reader interest. In one section, how-

ever, he could have revised to vary his sentence structure by combining some of his sentences. For instance,

> Ten women were standing. The preacher began at the front of the room. He moved from person to person. He took each one by the arm. He placed his hand on each one's head and prayed.

could have become

> Ten women were standing, and the preacher, beginning at the front of the room, moved from person to person, taking each one by the arm, placing his hand on her head, and praying.

This version eliminates the monotonous string of choppy sentences. In addition, it moves right along with the preacher and ends only when he does, to pray. Its vitality and movement thus help to sustain and direct a reader's attention.

Verb Tense. Derek Wilson knows that chronological order is very important in narrative and that it is essential that he avoid unwarranted shifts in verb tense that could confuse his readers. (Wouldn't you have been puzzled if he had said, "I *thought* the whole thing was ridiculous, but I *do* feel sorry for the old woman so I *agreed* to take her"?) Wilson also realizes that a shift in tense is necessary to indicate a time shift in his narrative. For instance, at the beginning of the sixth paragraph he changes from the past tense of paragraph five (*snapped*) to the past perfect (*had been*). He does this in a brief flashback to introduce some background events that had occurred before the Friday evening he is writing about. The flashback and the corresponding shift in tense make clear that Aunt Elitia was sick *before* she heard the news about the tumor (Aunt Elitia *had been* sick) and also that she was religious *before* the doctor's diagnosis (My aunt *had* always *been* religious).

Transitions. In "Do I Believe in Miracles?" Wilson effectively uses transitional words like *after, then, as, when,* and *suddenly,* as well as transitional expressions like *three weeks later.* For the most part, however, he relies on chronological order to clarify the sequence of events for his reader. Still, there are places where the addition of a transitional word or phrase could have helped. For instance, compare Wilson's "We arrived late, and the service was in full swing" with a possible revision, "When we arrived, the service was in full swing." On the other hand, see how effectively his "One minute I was holding my aunt . . . and the next I was struggling . . ." carries the reader along with the action of the story.

The following selections illustrate the many possibilities open to writers of narrative. They range from a personal letter to an analytical glance back at history, yet all are characterized by a strong narrative thread. Most of these selections have a thesis, but in several cases the thesis is implied rather than explicitly stated.

Monday, March 5, 1770: Who Was to Blame?

JOHN M. BRESNAHAN, JR.

Tensions between citizens of Boston and British government troops erupted on March 5, 1770, in what has come to be called the Boston Massacre. The American colonists, angered by the presence of the British regiments, provoked an argument with the soldiers. In the scuffle that followed, five colonists were killed. Although only two of the soldiers were convicted of manslaughter and the rest were found not guilty, many historians today remain convinced that a deliberate "massacre" took place. In this narrative essay, which originally appeared in Yankee *magazine, John M. Bresnahan, Jr., tries to resolve this controversy by reconstructing the events.*

Everyone who has studied American History in school has read of   1
the Boston Massacre. The account given in most textbooks tells the
story of how the murdering British opened fire on a group of boys
"playfully" throwing snowballs.

But was the Massacre a case of cold-blooded murder, or a case   2
of self-defense on the part of the British soldiers? The full account
of the event and the following trial of the British soldiers leave
room for speculation.

On Monday, March 5, 1770, Boston was still feeling the effects   3
of a bad winter. Ice coated the ground and streets. During the day
a light snow fell. By early evening the sky had cleared and the
moon rose over Boston Bay, brightly reflecting off the white snow
to give the town a ghostly look.

The evening started calmly. A lone British sentry was on duty   4
at the front of the Custom House on King Street. As the evening
wore on, waterfront toughs got involved in brawls with British
patrols. News of the brawls spread among the citizenry of Boston,
and men began to roam the streets with sticks and cudgels, looking
for trouble wherever it might be.

In Dock Square near Fanueil Hall a crowd of about 200 gathered.   5
A tall man in a red cloak and a white wig harangued the crowd.
Who he was is still a mystery.

After the speech, the listeners left Dock Square and headed for   6
King Street. As they moved toward King Street, the bell in an old
brick church in the North End of town was rung, giving the signal

for fire. Men turned out with buckets but were told there was no fire.

The crowd from Dock Square then merged with the men who had been called out by the fire bell. By the time the moving mob reached King Street there were far more than 200 in the group. The lone British sentry, Hugh Montgomery, held his ground in front of the Custom House. From the throng came shouts and threats, "Kill the soldier, Kill the damned coward, Kill the bloody lobster." 7

Missiles began to fly at the soldier. Not just snowballs, but ice, rocks, and frozen clumps of mud were thrown. The sentry yelled for help from the guard house nearby. Captain John Preston of the 29th Worcestershires heard the cry and sent seven men over to help. The church bells began to peal the signal for fire again, and Preston ran to join his men. By now it was 9:20 P.M. 8

The crowd slowly pushed forward—200 strong against nine lone soldiers. Shouts, curses, and threats split the air, "Lobsters, Bloody-backs, Kill them all." The crowd was now throwing sticks and clubs as well as rocks, ice, and sharp-edged seashells. 9

Captain Preston shouted to his men not to fire and even pushed down the muzzles of some raised muskets. But one of the Colonials, armed with a highland broad sword, took a swipe at Hugh Montgomery. Montgomery quickly moved, and the sword hit the butt of the gun only inches from Montgomery's wrist. The impact knocked Montgomery over and to the side, his gun clattering to the ground. He quickly retrieved it and, believing the sword might swing his way again, fired blindly into the crowd. 10

Crispus Attucks, a Negro from Framingham, Massachusetts, was hit by the shot and instantly killed, although he was not the person with the sword. The panicky soldiers then fired, one by one; but apparently there was no order to fire given by Captain Preston. 11

Quickly Samuel Gray fell, hit by a musket ball which tore off a large portion of his skull. He was followed by James Caldwell, who was killed by two musket balls in the back. Two others, James Maverick, a youth of 17, and Patrick Carr, an Irishman, were mortally wounded and would die in the next few days. 12

As the smoke cleared, the gathering was totally silent, frozen motionless by the sight of the five bodies bleeding in the snow. The quiet was broken by the British as they reloaded. Quickly reinforcements of British troops came to the aid of Preston and his men, followed by hundreds of townspeople. 13

The situation showed signs of turning into a major battle. But luckily Governor Thomas Hutchinson had heard the commotion and rushed to the scene. There he was jostled and pushed about. 14

Finally he made it into the State House and out onto the balcony facing King Street.

A hush fell as he began to speak. He was not the best liked man 15 in Boston, but he was respected. He promised that the law would take its course and justice be done. At the suggestion of Colonel Dalrymple, the Commander in Chief of the British soldiers in Boston, Preston and his men were taken directly to the town jail. Dalrymple felt they would be safer there than in the barracks.

As the soldiers marched off with Preston and his men under 16 arrest, the crowd dispersed. The crisis was over.

Preparations were made for a trial, but no one would defend 17 Preston or the soldiers. A friend of Captain Preston, Mr. Forester, nicknamed the "Irish Infant," had tried to persuade every lawyer in Boston, including the crown lawyers, to defend Preston and his men. In desperation, Forester went to John Adams, an avowed Patriot, and pleaded with him to take the case.

John Adams was shocked and angered that no lawyer would 18 defend the accused men. He felt that every person had the right to a fair trial and that a defense lawyer was essential to fair trial. Adams took the case and convinced two other Boston lawyers, Robert Auchmuty and Josiah Quincy, Jr., to help him.

Their first step was to get a postponement of the trial. The town 19 of Boston was in too emotional a state to be able to hold a trial which was fair. To this, Governor Hutchinson readily agreed, and he put the trial off until October.

Actually there were to be two trials: first the trial of Captain 20 Preston, then the trial for the eight soldiers.

Captain Preston's trial began on October 23, 1770. The defense 21 contention was that a soldier had the right to kill when he felt his life was in danger from a physical attack—the same right as any citizen. By the last day of October, the jury had returned a verdict of not guilty.

The second trial had nearly the same outcome. Six of the eight 22 soldiers were found not guilty. The other two, Matthew Kilroy, who had shot Samuel Gray, and Hugh Montgomery, who had shot Crispus Attucks, were found not guilty of murder, but guilty of manslaughter.

John Adams asked benefit of clergy, which was granted. The two 23 men were then branded on the thumb and released.

Thus only eight months after the Boston Massacre, the British 24 soldiers involved in the event were found innocent of murder.

Yet in our history books these men are made out to be cold- 25 blooded murderers. Why? Because Samuel Adams, the master propagandist of the American Revolution, used every means available to make people remember the dead killed by the British soldiers, and to forget the trial which exonerated the soldiers of murder. To this day Samuel Adams's spell has not been broken.

COMPREHENSION

1. Why did some colonists "roam the streets . . . looking for trouble"?

2. Who fired the first shot? Why?

3. What kept the situation from "turning into a major battle"?

4. What part does Bresnahan say Samuel Adams played after this encounter between the British and the colonists?

PURPOSE AND AUDIENCE

1. What does Bresnahan assume his audience knows about the Boston Massacre? What did you know about the incident before you read this essay?

2. The essay has an explicitly stated thesis. Where does it appear? State it in your own words.

3. Why do you think the author refers to so many minor characters by name?

4. Why doesn't Bresnahan use the word *massacre* in the title?

5. Find a brief discussion of the Boston Massacre in an American history textbook or an encyclopedia. How does this treatment differ from Bresnahan's? How can you account for these differences?

STYLE AND STRUCTURE

1. Adjectives in this essay are, for the most part, limited to those that give objective, photographic details such as *white, lone, frozen,* and *seven.* Why does the author use such adjectives? Can you find exceptions, adjectives that convey strong emotion and opinion?

2. Most of this essay presents a sequence of events. The first two paragraphs and the last paragraph, however, have another function. What is this function?

3. In what way is the style of this essay similar to newspaper reporting? In what way is it different?

4. Identify the transitional words and phrases in this essay. How well would the action itself move the reader along if these linking words had been omitted?

5. The author uses dialogue sparingly. Why do you think he doesn't include more? Would more dialogue make the piece more real or more convincing?

WRITING WORKSHOP

1. Find a newspaper story about the incidents at Kent State University or Jackson State University in the spring of 1970. Write a narrative of one of these two incidents titled "Who Was to Blame?" Be sure to use your own words in your account.

2. Imagine yourself one of the British soldiers. Prepare a factual, first-person account of your actions for your superior officer.

3. Reconstruct an incident from your childhood indicating how your original impression of what happened has changed.

My Mother Never Worked
BONNIE SMITH-YACKEL

Although this essay draws on personal experience, it makes a general point about what society thinks of "women's work." According to federal law, a woman who is a homemaker is entitled to social security benefits only through the earnings of her husband. Thus, a homemaker who becomes disabled receives no disability benefits, and her husband and children are allowed no survivors' benefits if she should die. Although this law is being challenged in the courts, a woman who does not work for wages outside the home is still not entitled to social security benefits in her own right. Without explicitly stating her thesis, Bonnie Smith-Yackel comments on this situation in her narrative.

"Social Security Office." (The voice answering the telephone sounds very self-assured.) 1

"I'm calling about . . . I . . . my mother just died . . . I was told to call you and see about a . . . death-benefit check, I think they call it. . . ." 2

"I see. Was your mother on Social Security? How old was she?" 3

"Yes . . . she was seventy-eight. . . ." 4

"Do you know her number?" 5

"No . . . I, ah . . . don't you have a record?" 6

"Certainly. I'll look it up. Her name?" 7

"Smith. Martha Smith. Or maybe she used Martha Ruth Smith. . . . Sometimes she used her maiden name . . . Martha Jerabek Smith." 8

"If you'd care to hold on, I'll check our records—it'll be a few minutes." 9

"Yes. . . ." 10

Her love letters—to and from Daddy—were in an old box, tied with ribbons and stiff, rigid-with-age leather thongs: 1918 through 1920; hers written on stationery from the general store she had worked in full-time and managed, single-handed, after her graduation from high school in 1913; and his, at first, on YMCA or Soldiers and Sailors Club stationery dispensed to the fighting men of World War I. He wooed her thoroughly and persistently by mail, and though she reciprocated all his feeling for her, she dreaded marriage. . . . 11

"It's so hard for me to decide when to have my wedding day— that's all I've thought about these last two days. I have told you 12 dozens of times that I won't be afraid of married life, but when it comes down to setting the date and then picturing myself a married woman with half a dozen or more kids to look after, it just makes me sick. . . . I am weeping right now—I hope that some day I can look back and say how foolish I was to dread it all."

They married in February, 1921, and began farming. Their first baby, a daughter, was born in January, 1922, when my mother was 26 years old. The second baby, a son, was born in March, 1923. They were renting farms; my father, besides working his own fields, also was a hired man for two other farmers. They had no capital initially, and had to gain it slowly, working from dawn until midnight every day. My town-bred mother learned to set hens and raise chickens, feed pigs, milk cows, plant and harvest a garden, and can every fruit and vegetable she could scrounge. She carried water nearly a quarter of a mile from the well to fill her wash boilers in order to do her laundry on a scrub board. She learned to shuck grain, feed threshers, shock and husk corn, feed corn pickers. In September, 1925, the third baby came, and in June, 1927, the fourth child—both daughters. In 1930, my parents had enough money to buy their own farm, and that March they moved all their livestock and belongings themselves, 55 miles over rutted, muddy roads.   13

In the summer of 1930 my mother and her two eldest children reclaimed a 40-acre field from Canadian thistles, by chopping them all out with a hoe. In the other fields, when the oats and flax began to head out, the green and blue of the crops were hidden by the bright yellow of wild mustard. My mother walked the fields day after day, pulling each mustard plant. She raised a new flock of baby chicks—500—and she spaded up, planted, hoed, and harvested a half-acre garden.   14

During the next spring their hogs caught cholera and died. No cash that fall.   15

And in the next year the drought hit. My mother and father trudged from the well to the chickens, the well to the calf pasture, the well to the barn, and from the well to the garden. The sun came out hot and bright, endlessly, day after day. The crops shriveled and died. They harvested half the corn, and ground the other half, stalks and all, and fed it to the cattle as fodder. With the price at four cents a bushel for the harvested crop, they couldn't afford to haul it into town. They burned it in the furnace for fuel that winter.   16

In 1934, in February, when the dust was still so thick in the Minnesota air that my parents couldn't always see from the house to the barn, their fifth child—a fourth daughter—was born. My father hunted rabbits daily, and my mother stewed them, fried   17 them, canned them, and wished out loud that she could taste hamburger once more. In the fall the shotgun brought prairie chickens, ducks, pheasant, and grouse. My mother plucked each bird, carefully reserving the breast feathers for pillows.

In the winter she sewed night after night, endlessly, begging   18
cast-off clothing from relatives, ripping apart coats, dresses, blouses, and trousers to remake them to fit her four daughters and son. Every morning and every evening she milked cows, fed pigs and calves, cared for chickens, picked eggs, cooked meals, washed dishes, scrubbed floors, and tended and loved her children. In the spring she planted a garden once more, dragging pails of water to nourish and sustain the vegetables for the family. In 1936 she lost a baby in her sixth month.

In 1937 her fifth daughter was born. She was 42 years old. In   19
1939 a second son, and in 1941 her eighth child—and third son.

But the war had come, and prosperity of a sort. The herd of   20
cattle had grown to 30 head; she still milked morning and evening. Her garden was more than a half acre—the rains had come, and by now the Rural Electricity Administration and indoor plumbing. Still she sewed—dresses and jackets for the children, housedresses and aprons for herself, weekly patching of jeans, overalls, and denim shirts. She still made pillows, using the feathers she had plucked, and quilts every year—intricate patterns as well as patch-work, stitched as well as tied—all necessary bedding for her family. Every scrap of cloth too small to be used in quilts was carefully saved and painstakingly sewed together in strips to make rugs. She still went out in the fields to help with the haying whenever there was a threat of rain.

In 1959 my mother's last child graduated from high school. A   21
year later the cows were sold. She still raised chickens and ducks, plucked feathers, made pillows, baked her own bread, and every year made a new quilt—now for a married child or for a grandchild. And her garden, that huge, undying symbol of sustenance, was as large and cared for as in all the years before. The canning, and now freezing, continued.

In 1969, on a June afternoon, mother and father started out for   22
town so that she could buy sugar to make rhubarb jam for a daughter who lived in Texas. The car crashed into a ditch. She was paralyzed from the waist down.

In 1970 her husband, my father, died. My mother struggled to   23
regain some competence and dignity and order in her life. At the rehabilitation institute, where they gave her physical therapy and trained her to live usefully in a wheelchair, the therapist told me:

"She did fifteen pushups today—fifteen! She's almost seventy-five years old! I've never known a woman so strong!"

From her wheelchair she canned pickles, baked bread, ironed   24
clothes, wrote dozens of letters weekly to her friends and her "half dozen or more kids," and made three patchwork housecoats and one quilt. She made balls and balls of carpet rags—enough for five rugs. And kept all her love letters.

"I think I've found your mother's records—Martha Ruth Smith;   25
married to Ben F. Smith?"

"Yes, that's right."   26

"Well, I see that she was getting a widow's pension. . . . "   27

"Yes, that's right."   28

"Well, your mother isn't entitled to our $255 death benefit."   29

"Not entitled! But why?"   30

The voice on the telephone explains patiently: 31

"Well, you see—your mother never worked."   32

COMPREHENSION

1. Why wasn't Martha Smith eligible for a death benefit?

2. What kind of work did Martha Smith do while her children were growing up? How does the government define work?

PURPOSE AND AUDIENCE

1. What is the essay's thesis? Why is it never explicitly stated?

2. This essay appeared in *Ms.* magazine and other journals whose audiences are sympathetic to feminism. Could it just as easily have appeared in a magazine whose audience was not? Why or why not?

3. How can you tell that this essay's purpose is to persuade and not simply to entertain or to inform?

STYLE AND STRUCTURE

1. Is the title effective? Why or why not?

2. The author could have outlined her mother's life without framing it with the telephone conversation. Why does she include this frame?

3. This narrative piles details one on top of another almost like a list. For instance, paragraph 13 says, "My town-bred mother learned to set hens and raise chickens, feed pigs, milk cows, plant and harvest a garden, and can every fruit and vegetable she could scrounge." Why does the author list so many details?

WRITING WORKSHOP

1. If you can, interview your mother or grandmother (or another woman you know who might remind you of Bonnie Smith-Yackel's mother) about her work, and write a chronological narrative based on what she tells you. Try to give your narrative a strong thesis.

2. Should homemakers be entitled to social security coverage? Why or why not? Write a narrative essay to answer this question. Or, use a narrative to structure an essay that takes a stand on another issue you feel strongly about. For instance, should alimony be outlawed? Should nuclear power plants be closed? Should medicaid funds be used to pay for abortions? Should plagiarism be grounds for a student's expulsion from college?

3. Write Martha Smith's obituary as it might have appeared in her hometown newspaper. If you are not familiar with the form of an obituary, read a few in your local paper.

4. Write a narrative account of the worst job you ever had. Include a strong thesis.

38 Who Saw Murder Didn't Call the Police

MARTIN GANSBERG

In March 1964 a number of observers stood by as Kitty Genovese was murdered after being repeatedly attacked by an assailant. The entire country was shocked by this incident, which was seen as a comment on the apathy of the time. The story of Kitty Genovese has been told in countless articles and editorials, as well as a television movie, and it is cited even today when public indifference is discussed. Martin Gansberg wrote this article for the New York Times *two weeks after the murder; his thesis, although a powerful one, is not explicitly stated.*

For more than half an hour 38 respectable, law-abiding citizens in   1
Queens watched a killer stalk and stab a woman in three separate
attacks in Kew Gardens.

Twice their chatter and the sudden glow of their bedroom lights   2
interrupted him and frightened him off. Each time he returned,
sought her out, and stabbed her again. Not one person telephoned
the police during the assault; one witness called after the woman
was dead.

That was two weeks ago today.   3

Still shocked is Assistant Chief Inspector Frederick M. Lussen,   4
in charge of the borough's detectives and a veteran of 25 years of
homicide investigations. He can give a matter-of-fact recitation on
many murders. But the Kew Gardens slaying baffles him—not
because it is a murder, but because the "good people" failed to call
the police.

"As we have reconstructed the crime," he said, "the assailant   5
had three chances to kill this woman during a 35-minute period.
He returned twice to complete the job. If we had been called when
he first attacked, the woman might not be dead now."

This is what the police say happened beginning at 3:20 A.M. in   6
the staid, middle-class, tree-lined Austin Street area:

Twenty-eight-year-old Catherine Genovese, who was called   7
Kitty by almost everyone in the neighborhood, was returning home
from her job as manager of a bar in Hollis. She parked her red Fiat
in a lot adjacent to the Kew Gardens Long Island Rail Road Station,
facing Mowbray Place. Like many residents of the neighborhood,

she had parked there day after day since her arrival from Connecticut a year ago, although the railroad frowns on the practice.

She turned off the lights of her car, locked the door, and started   8
to walk the 100 feet to the entrance of her apartment at 82–70 Austin Street, which is in a Tudor building, with stores in the first floor and apartments on the second.

The entrance to the apartment is in the rear of the building   9
because the front is rented to retail stores. At night the quiet neighborhood is shrouded in the slumbering darkness that marks most residential areas.

Miss Genovese noticed a man at the far end of the lot, near a   10
seven-story apartment house at 82–40 Austin Street. She halted. Then, nervously, she headed up Austin Street toward Lefferts Boulevard, where there is a call box to the 102nd Police Precinct in nearby Richmond Hill.

She got as far as a street light in front of a bookstore before the   11
man grabbed her. She screamed. Lights went on in the 10-story apartment house at 82–67 Austin Street, which faces the bookstore. Windows slid open and voices punctuated the early-morning stillness.

Miss Genovese screamed: "Oh, my God, he stabbed me! Please   12
help me! Please help me!"

From one of the upper windows in the apartment house, a man   13
called down: "Let that girl alone!"

The assailant looked up at him, shrugged, and walked down   14
Austin Street toward a white sedan parked a short distance away. Miss Genovese struggled to her feet.

Lights went out. The killer returned to Miss Genovese, now   15
trying to make her way around the side of the building by the parking lot to get to her apartment. The assailant stabbed her again.

"I'm dying!" she shrieked. "I'm dying!"   16

Windows were opened again, and lights went on in many   17
apartments. The assailant got into his car and drove away. Miss Genovese staggered to her feet. A city bus, O–10, the Lefferts Boulevard line to Kennedy International Airport, passed. It was 3:35 A.M.

The assailant returned. By then, Miss Genovese had crawled to   18
the back of the building, where the freshly painted brown doors to the apartment house held out hope for safety. The killer tried the first door; she wasn't there. At the second door, 82–62 Austin Street, he saw her slumped on the floor at the foot of the stairs. He stabbed her a third time—fatally.

It was 3:50 by the time the police received their first call, from   19 a man who was a neighbor of Miss Genovese. In two minutes they were at the scene. The neighbor, a 70-year-old woman, and another woman were the only persons on the street. Nobody else came forward.

The man explained that he had called the police after much [20] deliberation. He had phoned a friend in Nassau County for advice and then he had crossed the roof of the building to the apartment of the elderly woman to get her to make the call.

"I didn't want to get involved," he sheepishly told the police. [21]

Six days later, the police arrested Winston Moseley, a 29-year- [22] old business-machine operator, and charged him with homicide. Moseley had no previous record. He is married, has two children and owns a home at 133–19 Sutter Avenue, South Ozone Park, Queens. On Wednesday, a court committed him to Kings County Hospital for psychiatric observation.

When questioned by the police, Moseley also said that he had [23] slain Mrs. Annie May Johnson, 24, of 146–12 133d Avenue, Jamaica, on Feb. 29 and Barbara Kralik, 15, of 174–17 140th Avenue, Springfield Gardens, last July. In the Kralik case, the police are holding Alvin L. Mitchell, who is said to have confessed that slaying.

The police stressed how simple it would have been to have [24] gotten in touch with them. "A phone call," said one of the detectives, "would have done it." The police may be reached by dialing "O" for operator or SPring 7–3100.

Today witnesses from the neighborhood, which is made up of [25] one-family homes in the $35,000 to $60,000 range with the exception of the two apartment houses near the railroad station, find it difficult to explain why they didn't call the police.

A housewife, knowingly if quite casually, said, "We thought it [26] was a lovers' quarrel." A husband and wife both said, "Frankly, we were afraid." They seemed aware of the fact that events might have been different. A distraught woman, wiping her hands in her apron, said, "I didn't want my husband to get involved."

One couple, now willing to talk about that night, said they heard [27] the first screams. The husband looked thoughtfully at the bookstore where the killer first grabbed Miss Genovese.

"We went to the window to see what was happening," he said, [28] "but the light from our bedroom made it difficult to see the street." The wife, still apprehensive, added: "I put out the light and we were able to see better."

Asked why they hadn't called the police, she shrugged and [29] replied: "I don't know."

A man peeked out from a slight opening in the doorway to his 30
apartment and rattled off an account of the killer's second attack.
Why hadn't he called the police at the time? "I was tired," he said
without emotion. "I went back to bed."

It was 4:25 A.M. when the ambulance arrived to take the body 31
of Miss Genovese. It drove off. "Then," a solemn police detective
said, "the people came out."

COMPREHENSION

1. How much time elapsed between when Kitty Genovese was first stabbed and when the people finally came out?

2. What excuses did the neighbors make for not having come to Kitty Genovese's aid?

PURPOSE AND AUDIENCE

1. This article appeared in 1964. What effect was it intended to have on its audience? Do you think it has the same impact today, or has its impact diminished?

2. The author of this article tells his readers very little about Kitty Genovese. Why, for instance, doesn't he tell us what she looked like? Would additional details have increased the impact of the essay?

3. What is the article's main idea? State it in one sentence as a thesis.

4. What is Gansberg's purpose in describing the Austin Street area as "staid, middle-class, tree-lined"?

5. Why does Gansberg provide the police department phone number in his article?

STYLE AND STRUCTURE

1. The author is very precise in this article, especially in his references to time, addresses, and ages. Why?

2. The objective newspaper style is dominant in this article, and yet the author's anger shows through. Point to words and phrases that reveal his attitude toward his material.

3. Identify the transitions in the article. Characterize the kinds of expressions that are used.

4. Because this article was originally set in the narrow columns of a newspaper, there are many short paragraphs. Would it be more effective

if some of these brief paragraphs were combined? If so, why? If not, why not? Give examples to support your answer.

5. Examine the dialogue. Does it strengthen the author's presentation? Would the article be more compelling without dialogue? Why or why not?

6. This article does not have a formal conclusion; nevertheless, the last paragraph sums up the author's attitude. How?

WRITING WORKSHOP

1. In your own words, write a ten-sentence summary of the article. Try to reflect the author's order and emphasis as well as his ideas.

2. Rewrite the article as if it were a diary entry of one of the thirty-eight people who watched the murder. Outline what you saw, and explain why you didn't call for help.

3. If you have ever been involved in or witnessed a situation where someone was in trouble, write a narrative essay about the incident. If people failed to help the person in trouble, note why you think no one acted. Or, if people did act, tell how.

A Letter from Mississippi

In the summer of 1964, a group of 650 young Northern men and women, largely white college students, traveled to Mississippi to help with education and voter registration of blacks. The volunteers were greeted by most white Southerners with suspicion, hostility, and even outright violence; three young people were savagely murdered in Philadelphia, Mississippi, during that summer. In a personal letter, a volunteer describes his own encounter with violence. Although this letter has no explicitly stated thesis, the writer's attitude and purpose are clear.

Laurel, August 24

Dear family,

Saturday afternoon, several of us were invited out to a farm 6 miles from town for a day of picnicking, swimming, relaxation and V.R.[1] work out in the country.... Bill Haden, a white COFO[2] worker from Oregon, a local Negro and myself were sitting along the edge of the lake about 400 yards from the farmhouse singing some songs and playing the guitar. Just after finishing the last verse of Dylan's "Who Killed Davy Moore," we saw two whites coming towards us down the path from the farmhouse. Since we were expecting other people from the COFO office to be joining us, we didn't think anything strange about this. When they got somewhat closer and I didn't recognize them, I asked Bill if he knew who they were. He didn't know. A few seconds later, the younger man (about 5 feet 10, 200 lbs.) came up to me and asked me if I knew "Dixie." I told him, I wasn't sure, to which he responded, "Well, you'd better be sure, and quick." I told him, "Well, sit down. Maybe we could work it out together." He told me just to play it. I've never learned a song quite so fast in all my life.

Apparently, he didn't appreciate my efforts, because the next thing I know, the guitar was out of my hands, kicked, and thrown out into the lake. Almost simultaneously, about 15 other rednecks, about 25–55 yrs. in age, emerged from the trees and brush surrounding the lake. The other man, who had first come up, began beating me with the big wooden club. I saw that it would be impossible for me to run around the edge of the lake back to the

1

2

---

[1]Voter registration.—EDs.
[2]Council of Federated Organizations, a Mississippi-based association of the Student Non-Violent Coordinating Committee (SNCC), the Congress on Racial Equality (CORE), and other groups.—EDs.

house without being further attacked and beaten. So, since I was
born for the water, home I went. After I was 15 or 25 feet out, he
pulled a pistol from beneath his shirt and began firing in my
direction. Ten or twelve of the other men began shooting in the
direction of the house and the fleeing COFO worker with pistols,
rifles, and shotguns.

When the bullets began hitting the water, not five feet from my   3
head, I thought it was time to make a submarine exit. Coming up
about a hundred and fifty feet further out, the bullets were splat-
tering even beyond me, perhaps 30–40 feet. Since I didn't see any
men at the other end of the lake, I was hoping to swim there, get
out, and try and make it to the house. About ten minutes later, as
I got out of the lake, two men came towards me out of the brush.
The man in front had a forked tire iron and the man behind him
had a steel chain.

Since old freedom fighters never give up, I again tried to   4
humanize with the cat, asking him "Wouldn't you like to sit down
so we can talk this thing over? Although we might have our
differences. . . ." While I was saying this, I was gradually taking a
few steps back toward the lake, just in case he did not respond
positively. Well, he didn't. Menacing the tire iron, he ordered me
to get over to where the rest of the men were and not get wise. For
a few more seconds, I tried to reason with him. . . . Just about at that
moment, one of them comes from the brush around the lake with
his club. He swings it at me across the back and the man with the
tire iron hits me across the knee while I think the man with the
chain hit me across the ribs and back. Deciding that it was better
to be a live chicken than a dead duck, I got the hell out of there.
By some miracle, I was able to make it through the brush, barbed
wire and all the shooting (by now from both sides) up to the
farmhouse.

When I arrived, the COFO office had already been notified and   5
I got on the phone immediately to the FBI in Laurel. After about
five minutes, an FBI agent called back and wanted to know what
was going on. I told him that the Civil War was reoccurring and
would he *please* come on out—with the rest of the Federal Gov't.
He wanted to know if we had notified the local police and sheriff's
office. I told him we had, but they refused to be of any assistance.
I then asked him if he could not protect us, would he be so kind
as to come out and take pictures down by the lake of the man who
had been firing on us? We exchanged a few more words, and I
went to lie down on the floor. I vaguely remember the sheriff
arriving maybe a half hour or 40 minutes later and taking the names

of everybody in the house. We asked him if he would give us protection back to Laurel or at least ride with us. He replied, "I didn't carry you trouble-makers out here and I'm sure not going to take you back." With this, he left us. About 15–20 minutes later, the ambulance arrived and we were taken to Jones County Community Hospital. . . .

That's all for now, take care, don't worry.   6

Love,
Dave

COMPREHENSION

1. Because Dave believes in principles of nonviolence, he makes no attempt to fight violence with violence. What tactics does he try instead? How do his attackers react in each case?

2. How does Dave finally escape danger?

3. What is the attitude of the local sheriff toward Dave?

PURPOSE AND AUDIENCE

1. Although this letter does not have a thesis, it does have a strong unifying idea. What is that idea?

2. Could the fact that Dave was writing to his family have made him change any of the details of what happened? What might he have changed? Do you think he did? Why or why not?

3. Dave was singing "Who Killed Davy Moore," a song about a black boxer who died in the ring; the man who kicked Dave's guitar told him to play "Dixie". How does the contrast between these two songs advance the writer's purpose?

STYLE AND STRUCTURE

1. Although Dave must surely have been frightened, he uses both humor and understatement in recounting the events. Give examples of places where each is used in the letter. Are these devices effective in lessening the tension, or do they heighten it?

2. How do you think Dave's closing, "don't worry," affected his family? What does this line tell you about Dave?

3. Toward the end of paragraph 4, Dave suddenly switches from the past tense in which he is telling the story to the present tense and then back to the past tense again. Why do you think he does this? Does it make the narrative hard to follow? Why or why not?

4. A number of characters figure in Dave's narrative, and he characterizes several of them with dialogue; in other cases, he paraphrases their words. How do these techniques strengthen his narrative?

5. What transitional words and phrases does Dave use to indicate the passing of time?

6. Dave clearly is writing a personal letter and not a formal report for the F.B.I. What stylistic clues tell you that the letter is casual and informal? Why, in such an informal account, does Dave make a point of including details like his attackers' ages, heights, and weights?

WRITING WORKSHOP

1. Some people have said that the volunteers in Mississippi were just "asking for trouble." Could any of your actions have been misunderstood in the same way? Write a narrative essay in which you support the thesis "Although many people thought I was just asking for trouble, I know that what I was doing was right."

2. Imagine you are Dave today, remembering that day in Mississippi. Write a narrative about what happened.

3. Imagine you are a member of Dave's family, and answer his letter. Use a narrative to structure your letter, perhaps telling about an event in Dave's childhood or incidents up North affecting the family while he is away.

Shooting an Elephant
GEORGE ORWELL

George Orwell, author of the widely read novels Animal Farm *and* 1984, *is also well known for his essays. A socialist through much of his life, Orwell wrote this essay about British colonialism, a system he despised. Set in Burma, "Shooting an Elephant" relates an incident that clarified for Orwell the nature of British rule. Notice that Orwell uses an extended narrative to support his thesis and includes much specific detail to increase its impact.*

In Moulmein, in Lower Burma, I was hated by large numbers of people—the only time in my life that I have been important enough for this to happen to me. I was sub-divisional police officer of the town, and in an aimless, petty kind of way anti-European feeling was very bitter. No one had the guts to raise a riot, but if a European woman went through the bazaars alone somebody would probably spit betel juice over her dress. As a police officer I was an obvious target and was baited whenever it seemed safe to do so. When a nimble Burman tripped me up on the football field and the referee (another Burman) looked the other way, the crowd yelled with hideous laughter. This happened more than once. In the end the sneering yellow faces of young men that met me everywhere, the insults hooted after me when I was at a safe distance, got badly on my nerves. The young Buddhist priests were the worst of all. There were several thousands of them in the town and none of them seemed to have anything to do except stand on street corners and jeer at Europeans.

All this was perplexing and upsetting. For at that time I had already made up my mind that imperialism was an evil thing and the sooner I chucked up my job and got out of it the better. Theoretically—and secretly, of course—I was all for the Burmese and all against their oppressors, the British. As for the job I was doing, I hated it more bitterly than I can perhaps make clear. In a job like that you see the dirty work of Empire at close quarters. The wretched prisoners huddling in the stinking cages of the lock-ups, the grey, cowed faces of the long-term convicts, the scarred buttocks of the men who had been flogged with bamboos—all these oppressed me with an intolerable sense of guilt. But I could get nothing into perspective. I was young and ill-educated and I had had to think out my problems in the utter silence that is imposed on every Englishman in the East. I did not even know that the British Empire is dying, still less did I know that it is a great deal better than the younger empires that are going to supplant it. All I knew was that I was stuck between my hatred of the empire I served and my rage against the evil-spirited little beasts who tried to make my job impossible. With one part of my mind I thought of the British Raj as an unbreakable tyranny, as something clamped down, in *saecula saeculorum*, upon the will of prostrate peoples; with another part I thought that the greatest joy in the world would be to drive a bayonet into a Buddhist priest's guts. Feelings like these are the normal byproducts of imperialism; ask any Anglo-Indian official, if you can catch him off duty.

One day something happened which in a roundabout way was enlightening. It was a tiny incident in itself, but it gave me a better glimpse than I had had before of the real nature of imperialism—the real motives for which despotic governments act. Early one morning the sub-inspector at a police station the other end of the town rang me up on the phone and said that an elephant was ravaging the bazaar. Would I please come and do something about it? I did not know what I could do, but I wanted to see what was happening and I got on to a pony and started out. I took my rifle, an old .44 Winchester and much too small to kill an elephant, but I thought the noise might be useful *in terrorem*. Various Burmans stopped me on the way and told me about the elephant's doings. It was not, of course, a wild elephant, but a tame one which had gone "must." It had been chained up, as tame elephants always are when their attack of "must" is due, but on the previous night it had broken its chain and escaped. Its mahout, the only person who could manage it when it was in that state, had set out in pursuit, but had taken the wrong direction and was now twelve hours' journey away, and in the morning the elephant had suddenly reappeared in the town. The Burmese population had no weapons and were quite helpless against it. It had already destroyed some-body's bamboo hut, killed a cow and raided some fruit-stalls and devoured the stock; also it had met the municipal rubbish van and, when the driver jumped out and took to his heels, had turned the van over and inflicted violences upon it.

The Burmese sub-inspector and some Indian constables were waiting for me in the quarter where the elephant had been seen. It was a very poor quarter, a labyrinth of squalid bamboo huts, thatched with palm-leaf, winding all over a steep hillside. I remember that it was a cloudy, stuffy morning at the beginning of the rains. We began questioning the people as to where the elephant had gone, and, as usual, failed to get any definite information. That is invariably the case in the East; a story always sounds clear enough at a distance, but the nearer you get to the scene of events the vaguer it becomes. Some of the people said that the elephant had gone in one direction, some said that he had gone in another, some professed not even to have heard of an elephant. I had almost made up my mind that the whole story was a pack of lies, when we heard yells a little distance away. There was a loud, scandalized cry of "Go away, child! Go away this instant!" and an old woman with a switch in her hand came round the corner of a hut, violently shooing away a crowd of naked children. Some more women followed, clicking their tongues and exclaiming; evidently there was something that the children ought not to have seen. I rounded the hut and saw a man's dead body sprawling in the mud. He was an Indian, a black Dravidian coolie, almost naked, and he could not have been dead many minutes. The people said that the elephant had come suddenly upon him round the corner of the hut, caught him with its trunk, put its foot on his back and ground him into the earth. This was the rainy season and the ground was soft, and his face had scored a trench a foot deep and a couple of yards long. He was lying on his belly with arms crucified and head sharply twisted to one side. His face was coated with mud, the eyes wide open, the teeth bared and grinning with an expression of unendurable agony. (Never tell me, by the way, that the dead look peaceful. Most of the corpses I have seen looked devilish.) The friction of the great beast's foot had stripped the skin from his back as neatly as one skins a rabbit. As soon as I saw the dead man I sent an orderly to a friend's house nearby to borrow an elephant rifle. I had already sent back the pony, not wanting it to go mad with fright and throw me if it smelled the elephant.

The orderly came back in a few minutes with a rifle and five cartridges, and meanwhile some Burmans had arrived and told us that the elephant was in the paddy fields below, only a few hundred yards away. As I started forward practically the whole population of the quarter flocked out of the houses and followed me. They had seen the rifle and were all shouting excitedly that I was going to shoot the elephant. They had not shown much interest in the elephant when he was merely ravaging their homes, but it was different now that he was going to be shot. It was a bit of fun to them, as it would be to an English crowd; besides they wanted the meat. It made me vaguely uneasy. I had no intention of shooting the elephant—I had merely sent for the rifle to defend myself if necessary—and it is always unnerving to have a crowd following you. I marched down the hill, looking and feeling a fool, with the rifle over my shoulder and an ever-growing army of people jostling at my heels. At the bottom, when you got away from the huts, there was a metalled road and beyond that a miry waste of paddy fields a thousand yards across, not yet ploughed but soggy from the first rains and dotted with coarse grass. The elephant was standing eight yards from the road, his left side towards us. He took not the slightest notice of the crowd's approach. He was tearing up bunches of grass, beating them against his knees to clean them and stuffing them into his mouth.

I had halted on the road. As soon as I saw the elephant I knew   6
with perfect certainty that I ought not to shoot him. It is a serious matter to shoot a working elephant—it is comparable to destroying a huge and costly piece of machinery—and obviously one ought not to do it if it can possibly be avoided. And at that distance, peacefully eating, the elephant looked no more dangerous than a cow. I thought then and I think now that his attack of "must" was already passing off; in which case he would merely wander harmlessly about until the mahout came back and caught him. Moreover, I did not in the least want to shoot him. I decided that I would watch him for a little while to make sure that he did not turn savage again, and then go home.

But at that moment I glanced round at the crowd that had   7
followed me. It was an immense crowd, two thousand at the least and growing every minute. It blocked the road for a long distance on either side. I looked at the sea of yellow faces above the garish clothes—faces all happy and excited over this bit of fun, all certain that the elephant was going to be shot. They were watching me as they would watch a conjurer about to perform a trick. They did not like me, but with the magical rifle in my hands I was momentarily worth watching. And suddenly I realized that I should have to shoot the elephant after all. The people expected it of me and I had got to do it; I could feel their two thousand wills pressing me forward, irresistibly. And it was at this moment, as I stood there with the rifle in my hands, that I first grasped the hollowness, the futility of the white man's dominion in the East. Here was I, the white man with his gun, standing in front of the unarmed native crowd—seemingly the leading actor of the piece; but in reality I was only an absurd puppet pushed to and fro by the will of those yellow faces behind. I perceived in this moment that when the white man turns tyrant it is his own freedom that he destroys. He becomes a sort of hollow, posing dummy, the conventionalized figure of a sahib. For it is the condition of his rule that he shall

spend his life in trying to impress the "natives," and so in every crisis he has got to do what the "natives" expect of him. He wears a mask, and his face grows to fit it. I had got to shoot the elephant. I had committed myself to doing it when I sent for the rifle. A sahib has got to act like a sahib; he has got to appear resolute, to know his own mind and do definite things. To come all that way, rifle in hand, with two thousand people marching at my heels, and then to trail feebly away, having done nothing—no, that was impossible. The crowd would laugh at me. And my whole life, every white man's life in the East, was one long struggle not to be laughed at.

But I did not want to shoot the elephant. I watched him beating   8 his bunch of grass against his knees, with that preoccupied grand-motherly air that elephants have. It seemed to me that it would be murder to shoot him. At that age I was not squeamish about killing animals, but I had never shot an elephant and never wanted to. (Somehow it always seems worse to kill a *large* animal.) Besides, there was the beast's owner to be considered. Alive, the elephant was worth at least a hundred pounds; dead, he would only be worth the value of his tusks, five pounds, possibly. But I had got to act quickly. I turned to some experienced-looking Burmans who had been there when we arrived, and asked them how the elephant had been behaving. They all said the same thing: he took no notice of you if you left him alone, but he might charge if you went too close to him.

It was perfectly clear to me what I ought to do. I ought to walk   9 up to within, say, twenty-five yards of the elephant and test his behavior. If he charged I could shoot, if he took no notice of me it would be safe to leave him until the mahout came back. But also I knew that I was going to do no such thing. I was a poor shot with a rifle and the ground was soft mud into which one would sink at every step. If the elephant charged and I missed him, I should have about as much chance as a toad under a steam-roller. But even then I was not thinking particularly of my own skin, only of the watchful yellow faces behind. For at that moment, with the crowd watching me, I was not afraid in the ordinary sense, as I would have been if I had been alone. A white man mustn't be frightened in front of "natives"; and so, in general, he isn't frightened. The sole thought in my mind was that if anything went wrong those two thousand Burmans would see me pursued, caught, trampled on and reduced to a grinning corpse like that Indian up the hill. And if that happened it was quite probable that some of them would laugh. That would never do. There was only one alternative. I shoved the cartridges into the magazine and lay down on the road to get a better aim.

The crowd grew very still, and a deep, low, happy sigh, as of 10 people who see the theatre curtain go up at last, breathed from innumerable throats. They were going to have their bit of fun after all. The rifle was a beautiful German thing with cross-hair sights. I did not then know that in shooting an elephant one would shoot to cut an imaginary bar running from ear-hole to ear-hole. I ought, therefore, as the elephant was sideways on, to have aimed straight at his ear-hole; actually I aimed several inches in front of this, thinking the brain would be further forward.

When I pulled the trigger I did not hear the bang or feel the 11 kick—one never does when a shot goes home—but I heard the devilish roar of glee that went up from the crowd. In that instant, in too short a time, one would have thought, even for the bullet to get there, a mysterious, terrible change had come over the elephant. He neither stirred nor fell, but every line on his body had altered. He looked suddenly stricken, shrunken, immensely old, as though the frightful impact of the bullet had paralyzed him without knocking him down. At last, after what seemed a long time—it might have been five seconds, I dare say—he sagged flabbily to his knees. His mouth slobbered. An enormous senility seemed to have settled upon him. One could have imagined him thousands of years old. I fired again into the same spot. At the second shot he did not collapse but climbed with desperate slowness to his feet and stood weakly upright, with legs sagging and head drooping. I fired a third time. That was the shot that did for him. You could see the agony of it jolt his whole body and knock the last remnant of strength from his legs. But in falling he seemed for a moment to rise, for as his hind legs collapsed beneath him he seemed to tower upwards like a huge rock toppling, his trunk reaching skywards like a tree. He trumpeted, for the first and only time. And then down he came, his belly towards me, with a crash that seemed to shake the ground even where I lay.

I got up. The Burmans were already racing past me across the 12 mud. It was obvious that the elephant would never rise again, but he was not dead. He was breathing very rhythmically with long rattling gasps, his great mound of a side painfully rising and falling. His mouth was wide open—I could see far down into the caverns of pale pink throat. I waited a long time for him to die, but his breathing did not weaken. Finally I fired my two remaining shots into the spot where I thought his heart must be. The thick blood welled out of him like red velvet, but still he did not die. His body did not even jerk when the shots hit him, the tortured breathing continued without a pause. He was dying, very slowly and in great agony, but in some world remote from me where not even a bullet could damage him further. I felt that I had got to put an end to that dreadful noise. It seemed dreadful to see the great beast lying there, powerless to move and yet powerless to die, and not even to be able to finish him. I sent back for my small rifle and poured shot after shot into his heart and down his throat. They seemed to make no impression. The tortured gasps continued as steadily as the ticking of a clock.

In the end I could not stand it any longer and went away. I heard later that it took him half an hour to die. Burmans were bringing dahs and baskets even before I left, and I was told they had stripped his body almost to the bones by the afternoon. 13

Afterwards, of course, there were endless discussions about the shooting of the elephant. The owner was furious, but he was only an Indian and could do nothing. Besides, legally I had done the right thing, for a mad elephant has to be killed, like a mad dog, if its owner fails to control it. Among the Europeans opinion was divided. The older men said I was right, the younger men said it was a damn shame to shoot an elephant for killing a coolie, because an elephant was worth more than any damn Coringhee coolie. And afterwards I was very glad that the coolie had been killed; it put me legally in the right and it gave me a sufficient pretext for shooting the elephant. I often wondered whether any of the others grasped that I had done it solely to avoid looking a fool. 14

COMPREHENSION

1. Why was Orwell "hated by large numbers of people" in Burma?

2. Orwell had mixed feelings toward the Burmese people. Explain why.

3. Why did the local officials want something done about the elephant?

4. Why did the crowd want Orwell to shoot the elephant?

5. Why did Orwell finally decide to kill the elephant? What made him hesitate at first?

6. Why does Orwell say at the end that he was glad the coolie had been killed?

PURPOSE AND AUDIENCE

1. One of Orwell's purposes in telling his story is to show how it gave him a glimpse of "the real nature of imperialism." How does the story illustrate this?

2. Do you think Orwell wrote this essay to inform or to persuade his audience? How did Orwell expect his audience to react to his ideas? How can you tell?

3. What is the essay's thesis?

STYLE AND STRUCTURE

1. What is the function of Orwell's first paragraph? Where does the introduction end and the narrative itself begin?

2. Orwell uses a good deal of detail in this essay to describe the narrative's setting and characters. Locate some examples of this detail. Why is detail so important?

3. Point out some of the transitional words and phrases Orwell uses to indicate the passing of time. Why are they so important in this essay?

4. The essay includes almost no dialogue. Why do you think Orwell's voice as narrator is the only one the reader hears? Is this a strength or a weakness? Explain why.

5. Why does Orwell devote so much attention to the elephant's misery (paragraphs 11 and 12)? How does this compare with his treatment of the coolie's death (paragraph 4)?

6. Orwell's essay includes a number of editorial comments inserted into his text between parentheses or pairs of dashes. What kind of comments are these? Why are they set off from the text?

WRITING WORKSHOP

1. Orwell says that even though he hated British imperialism and sympathized with the Burmese people, he found himself a puppet of the system. Write a narrative essay about a time you had to do something with which you disagreed.

2. Orwell's experience taught him something not only about himself but also about something beyond himself—the way imperialism worked. Write a narrative essay that reveals how an incident in your life taught you something about yourself and about some larger social or political force.

3

Description

WHAT IS DESCRIPTION?

Almost every essay includes some descriptive passages, for description is one of the basic ways we interpret the world. We are surrounded by persons, places, and objects—all of which have their own qualities and all of which affect us in different ways. We begin to understand our world by observing these things that make it up. Usually we describe what we observe before we make judgments about the world, before we compare or contrast or classify our experiences. Scientists observe and describe whenever they conduct experiments, and you do the same thing whenever you write a paper. In a comparison and contrast essay, for example, you may describe the performance of two cars to show that one is superior to another. In an argumentative essay, you may describe a fish kill in a local river to show that factory pollution is a problem. Through description, you introduce your view of the world to your readers. If your readers come to understand or share your view, they are more likely to accept your conclusions and judgments as well. Thus, for almost every essay you write, knowing how to describe effectively is important. In this chapter, we go even further; we examine descriptive writing as a strategy for a whole essay.

A narrative essay presents a series of events; it tells a story. A descriptive essay, on the other hand, tells what something looks like and perhaps what it feels like, smells like, sounds like, or tastes like. When you write description, you use these sensory observations to create a vivid impression for your reader. As we mentioned in chapter 2, a good narrative may depend heavily on descriptive details. It is important, however, not to confuse these two types of writing. A narrative always presents events in time, in some sort of chronological order, whereas a description tells about things in spatial rather than temporal order.

Like a narrative essay, a descriptive essay may or may not have a thesis. You can describe a person, place, or thing for its own sake, simply to share your sensory observations with your reader. You can also use description to support an implied or explicit thesis. Whether or not your description has a thesis, its details should be tailored to create a particular dominant impression. In college writing situations, you are most likely to use description to support an idea or assertion, as this thesis for an architectural design paper suggests: "The sculptures that adorn Philadelphia's City Hall form a catalogue of nineteenth-century artistic styles."

Objective and Subjective Descriptions

There are two basic approaches to description: objective and subjective. In an *objective* description, you focus on the object you are portraying rather than on your personal reactions to it. Many writing situations require precise descriptions of apparatus or conditions, and in these cases your goal is to supply information— to construct as accurate a picture as you can for your audience. A biologist describing what he sees through a microscope and a historian describing a Civil War battlefield would both write objectively. The biologist would not, for instance, say how exciting his observations were, nor would the historian say how surprising she thought the outcome of the battle was. Newspaper reporters also try to achieve this cameralike objectivity, and so do writers of technical reports, scientific papers, and certain types of business correspondence. Of course, objectivity is an ideal that writers aim for but never achieve. Any time writers select some details and eliminate others, they cannot be completely objective.

In the following descriptive passage, Thomas Marc Parrott tries to achieve objectivity by giving his readers all the factual information they need to visualize Shakespeare's theater.

> When James Burbage built the Theatre in 1576 he naturally designed it along the lines of inn-yards in which he had been accustomed to play. The building had two entrances—one in front for the audience; one in the rear for actors, musicians, and the personnel of the theatre. Inside the building a rectangular platform projected far out into what was called "the yard"—we know the stage of the Fortune ran halfway across the "yard," some twenty-seven and a half feet.

Note that Parrott is not interested in responding to or evaluating the environment he describes. Instead, he uses impersonal words that are calculated to convey sizes, shapes, and distances. His choice of adjectives such as *two* and *rectangular* reflects this intent. Only one word in the paragraph—*naturally*—suggests that the author is expressing a personal opinion.

In contrast to objective description is *subjective* or *impressionistic* description, which discloses your responses to what you see. These responses are not expressed directly, through a straightforward statement of your opinion or perspective. Rather, they are revealed indirectly, through your choice of words and phrasing. For instance, if an assignment in freshman English asked you to describe a place that had special meaning for you, you would write about your topic by selecting and emphasizing details that showed your feelings about the place. Similarly, editorial writers on newspapers are expected to use their personal feelings and opinions to shape their descriptions; their function is to interpret, to give their impressions of the events they describe.

Thus, a subjective or impressionistic description should convey not just a factual record of sights and sounds but also their meaning or significance. For example, if you objectively described a fire, you might include its temperature, its duration, and its dimensions. In addition to these quantifiable details, you might describe, as accurately as possible, its color, its movement, and its intensity. If you subjectively described the fire, however, you would include more than these unbiased observations about it. Through your choice of language and your phrasing, you would try to re-create for your audience a sense of how the fire made you feel: your reactions to the crackling noise, to the dense smoke, to the sudden destruction.

In the following passage, Mark Twain subjectively describes the Mississippi River.

> I still kept in mind a certain wonderful sunset which I witnessed when steamboating was new to me. A broad expanse of the river was turned to blood; in the middle distance the red hue brightened into gold, through which a solitary log came floating, black and conspicuous; in one place a long, slanting mark lay sparkling upon the water; in another the surface was broken by boiling, tumbling rings, that were as many-tinted as an opal.

In this passage, Twain's colorful language and unusual imagery express how he felt about what he was describing. By emphasizing the blood red color, the solitary log "black and conspicuous," and the "boiling, tumbling rings," he shares with his readers his vivid perception of the river's beauty.

Neither of the two approaches to description exists independently. Objective description is always the product of a subjective selection of details; subjective description captures reactions to an objective reality. The skillful writer, however, adjusts the balance between objectivity and subjectivity to suit the topic, thesis, audience, purpose, and occasion of an essay.

Objective and Subjective Language

As the passages by Parrott and Twain illustrate, objective and subjective descriptions are characterized by different uses of language. Both depend on specific and concrete words to convey, as precisely as possible, a picture of the person, place, or thing that the observer is describing. Objective descriptions rely on language that is as unbiased and impersonal as possible. They describe things with words and phrases so unambiguous that many observers could agree that the descriptions were appropriate and exact. Ideally, their language conveys identical meanings to all readers. Subjective descriptions, however, generally rely on richer and more suggestive language than objective descriptions. Subjective descriptions are more likely to play on the ambiguities of language, on the multiple meanings of words. They may deliberately provoke the individual reader's imagination with striking phrases or vivid comparisons. For example, a subjective description might liken the behavior of an exotic peacock spreading its feathers to that of a pet Siamese cat posturing and posing, thus evoking a lively image in the reader's mind.

When you write such descriptions, you can use several kinds of comparisons. You can compare two similar things, using the familiar parakeet to describe the unfamiliar peacock. Or, instead of comparing two things that are alike, you can find similarities between things that are unlike, such as the peacock and the cat, and provide a fresh view of both. Such special comparisons are known as *figures of speech*. Three of the most common are simile, metaphor, and personification.

A *simile* compares two things that are unlike using *like* or *as*. These comparisons occur constantly in everyday speech when, for example, someone claims to be "happy as a clam," "slow as molasses," or "hungry as a bear." Effective writers, however, strive to use more original similes than these. For instance, in his short story "A & P," John Updike likens people going through the check-out aisle of a store to balls dropping down a slot in a pinball machine.

A *metaphor* identifies two unlike things without using *like* or *as*.

Instead of saying that something is like something else, a metaphor says that it *is* something else. Twain uses a metaphor when he says that "a broad expanse of the river was turned to blood."

Personification endows animals or objects with the qualities of human beings. If you say that the wind whispered or that the engine died, you are personifying them.

Your purpose and audience determine whether you should use predominately objective or subjective description. Legal, medical, technical, business, and scientific writing assignments frequently require objective descriptions, but even in these areas you may be encouraged to tailor your descriptions so that they develop your own interpretations and arguments. Still, in all these instances, your primary purpose is to give your audience factual information about your subject. On the other hand, an assignment that specifically asks for your reactions demands a subjective or impressionistic description.

Selection of Detail

All good descriptive writing, whether objective or subjective, relies heavily on specific details which enable readers to visualize what you are describing. Your aim is not simply to *tell* your readers what something looks like but to *show* them. Every person, place, or thing has its special characteristics, and you must use your powers of observation to detect them. Then, you must select the concrete words that will enable your readers to see, feel, hear, taste, touch, or smell what you are describing as you do. Don't be satisfied with "he looked angry" when, with a bit more work and some careful observation, you can say, "His face flushed, and one corner of his mouth twitched as he tried to control his anger." What's the difference? In the first case, you simply name the abstract, emotional condition of a man. In the second case, you provide enough detail that a reader can actually picture the man's behavior, the concrete, physical signs of his emotional state. Of course, you could have provided even *more* detail by noting the man's beard or his wrinkles or any number of other features. In a given description, however, not all details are equally useful or desirable. Only those that add to the *dominant impression* you wish to create should be included. If you were to describe a man's face to show how angry he was, you would not necessarily have to describe the shape of his nose or the color of his hair. The number of details you use is less important than their quality. In order to avoid an indiscriminate list, you must select and use only those specific details that are relevant to your purpose.

STRUCTURING A DESCRIPTIVE ESSAY

When you write a descriptive essay, you will probably begin with a brainstorming list of details that need to be organized. You don't want to present them randomly, of course, but rather to arrange them in a way that advances your thesis or unifying idea. For example, you can move from a specific description of an object to a general description of other things around it. Or you can reverse this order, beginning with the general and proceeding to the specific. You can progress from the least important feature to a more important feature until you finally focus on the most important one. You can also move from the smallest to the largest item or from the least unusual to the most unusual detail. Finally, you can present the details of your description in a straightforward spatial order, moving from left to right or right to left, from top to bottom or bottom to top. The particular *organizing scheme* you choose depends upon the dominant impression you want to convey to your readers, your thesis or unifying idea, and your purpose and audience.

Let's suppose that your English composition instructor has assigned a short essay describing a person, place, or thing. After thinking about the subject for a day or two, you decide to write an objective description of the Air and Space Museum in Washington, D.C., since you have just visited it and many details are fresh in your mind. Because the museum is so large and has so many different exhibits, you realize at once that you will not be able to describe them all. Therefore, you decide to concentrate on one, the heavier-than-air flight exhibit, and you choose as the topic for your essay the particular display that you remember most vividly: Charles Lindbergh's airplane, *The Spirit of St. Louis*. You brainstorm to recollect all the details you can, and when you read over your list, you immediately see that the order of presentation in your essay could be based on your actual experience in the museum. You decide to present the details of the airplane in the order in which the eye takes them in, from front to rear. The dominant impression you wish to create is how fragile *The Spirit of St. Louis* appears. The outline for your essay might look like this:

¶1   Introduction—thesis: It is startling that a plane as small as *The Spirit of St. Louis* was able to fly across the Atlantic.

¶2   Front of plane: engine, cockpit

¶3   Middle of plane: wings, extra gas tanks

¶4   Rear of plane: more gas tanks, landing gear

¶5   Conclusion—restatement of thesis

The following student essays both illustrate the principles of effective description. The first one, by Richard Ross, is an objective description of a building, the Parthenon. The second, by Mary Lim, is a subjective description of an area in Burma.

THE TECHNOLOGY OF THE PARTHENON

Introduction

Many great buildings of ancient Greece still stand today. These are monumental buildings that combine beauty, technology, and mystery. As a careful examination of these structures shows, the Greeks' use of mathematics and their understanding of optics were extremely advanced. But there were

Thesis

some definite limitations to this technology, as an examination of the Parthenon, the most impressive Greek structure still standing today, will demonstrate.

Description (general)

Built on the Acropolis overlooking the city of Athens in the fifth century B.C., the Parthenon is the ideal expression of Greek architecture. It was a temple of the gods and was very important to the people. Although at first glance its structure seems to be perfect, on closer examination it becomes clear that it is a static, two-dimensional object. As long as you stand in the center of any of its four sides to look at it, its form will appear to be perfect. The strong Doric columns seem to be equally spaced, one next to another, along all four of its sides. But if you take a step to the right or left, the Parthenon's symmetry is destroyed.

Description (specific) and first point

You can understand this phenomenon if you look at a number of cylinders equally spaced along a line. As you look down the line, the cylinders seem to get larger, and the voids between them seem to get smaller due to your optical angle. The Greeks compensated for this distortion by increasing the

spaces between the Parthenon's columns the farther
they were from the middle, thus making it appear as
if there were equal solid and void portions.
Unfortunately, the resulting symmetry holds only
when a viewer is standing at the geometrical center
of any one of the four sides.

Description (specific) and second point

The Greeks also corrected for another optical
peculiarity. Because the lens of the eye bends
light, images to the far left or right are slightly
distorted. Thus, as you stand at one end of a
colonnade, columns at the other end seem to bend away
from you. To allow for this deflection by the eye,
the Greeks tilted each column slightly inward—
again creating a structure that was symmetrical only
when viewed from certain points along each side.
Although the goal of the architect was to achieve
perfection, he actually succeeded in creating a
distorted structure which appears perfect only from
certain angles. In this, the Parthenon is very much
like a painting made to be viewed from a fixed point
at a fixed angle.

Conclusion (restatement of thesis)

For a culture that existed so many years ago, the
Greeks had an impressive understanding of
mathematics and light. The Parthenon, perhaps the
greatest example of Greek technology, shows us the
strengths and limitations of that technology.
Dedicated over two thousand years ago, it stands as a
challenge and a lesson to those students of
architecture who are willing to examine the
subtleties and complexities of its construction.

Points for Special Attention

Objective Description.   Richard Ross, an architecture major, has
written this paper for a class in design. Because of the nature of his
class and his assignment (to describe briefly the architecture of an

ancient structure), Ross wisely chose to write an objective description of the Parthenon. As he does so, he avoids the temptation of reacting subjectively to the building itself—of stressing its grandeur, its beauty, and its power. Instead, his description emphasizes two structural subtleties that support his thesis that there were limitations to Greek architectural technology.

Objective Language. Because his essay is written for a class in architectural design, Richard Ross keeps his description objective and technical. He uses factual language that concentrates on what the phenomenon he is describing looks like, not how it affects him. For this reason he does not use unusual imagery or elaborate figures of speech.

Selection of Detail. Ross is writing for a specialized audience which he can assume is familiar with the general structure of the Parthenon. A detailed description of the building itself is therefore unnecessary. Ross limits his description to the aspects of the Parthenon that will serve his purpose and presents a thorough, precise picture of the spacing and inward tilt of the columns.

Structure. In organizing his essay, Ross moves his audience from a general view of the Parthenon to a more specific view of two of its architectural peculiarities. In his second paragraph, Ross introduces the idea that the Parthenon is a two-dimensional structure; in his third and fourth paragraphs, he explains why the building appears symmetrical only if viewed from the center of a side.

Unlike "The Technology of the Parthenon," Mary Lim's essay uses subjective description so that the reader can share, as well as understand, her experience.

THE VALLEY OF WINDMILLS

Introduction   In my native country of Burma, strange occurrences and strange scenery are not unusual. For it is a strange land that in some areas seems to have been ignored by time. Mountains stand jutting their rocky peaks into the clouds as they have for thousands of years. Jungles are so dense with exotic vegetation that human beings or large animals cannot

Description
(moving toward
the valley)
even enter. But one of the strangest areas in Burma
is The Valley of Windmills, nesting between the tall
mountains near the fertile and beautiful city of
Taungaleik. In this valley there is beautiful and
breathtaking scenery, but there are also old,
massive, and gloomy structures that can disturb a
person deeply. The road to Taungaleik twists out of
the coastal flatlands into those heaps of slag,
shale, and limestone that are the Tennesserim
Mountains in the southern part of Burma. The air
grows rarer and cooler, the stones become grayer,
the highway a little more precarious at its edges
until ahead, standing in ghostly sentinel across the

Description
(immediate view)
lip of a pass, is a line of squat forms. They straddle
the road and stand at intervals up the hillsides on
either side. Are they boulders? Are they
fortifications? Are they broken wooden crosses on
graves in an unused cemetery?

These dark figures are windmills standing in the
misty atmosphere. They are immensely old and
distinctly evil, some merely turrets, some with
remnants of arms hanging derelict from their snouts,
and most of them covered with dark green moss. Their
decayed but still massive forms seem to turn and

Description
(more distant
view)
sneer at visitors. Down the pass on the other side is
a circular green plateau that lies like an arena
below, where there are still more windmills. Massed
in the plain behind them, as far as the eye can see,
in every field, above every hut, stand ten thousand
iron windmills, silent and sailless. They seem to
await only a call from a watchman to clank, whirr,
flap, and groan into action. Visitors suddenly feel
cold. Perhaps it is a sense of loneliness, the cool
air, the desolation, or the weirdness of the arcane
windmills—but something chills them.

| Description (immediate view contrasted with city) | As you stand at the lip of the valley, contrasts rush as if to overwhelm you. Beyond, glittering on the mountainside like a solitary jewel, is Taungaleik in the territory once occupied by the Portugese. Below, on rolling hillsides, are the dark windmills, still enveloped in morning mist. These |
| Conclusion | ancient windmills can remind you of the impermanence of life and the mystery that still surrounds these hills. In an odd way, the scene in the valley can disturb you, but it also can give you an insight into the darkness that seems to define our lives here in Burma. |

Points for Special Attention

Subjective Description.   One of the first things you notice when you read Mary Lim's essay is her use of vivid details. The road to Taungaleik is described in specific terms: it twists "out of the coastal flatlands" into the mountains which are "heaps of slag, shale, and limestone." The iron windmills are decayed and stand "silent and sailless" on a green plateau that "lies like an arena." Using language in this way, Lim creates her dominant impression of The Valley of Windmills as dark, mysterious, and disquieting.

Subjective Language and Figures of Speech.   Lim conveys the sense of foreboding she felt by describing the windmills in several different ways. Upon first introducing them to us, she questions whether these "squat forms" are "boulders," "fortifications," or "broken wooden crosses." After telling the reader what they are, she personifies the windmills by describing them as dark, evil, sneering figures with "arms hanging derelict"; she sees them as ghostly sentinels awaiting a call from a watchman to spring into action. Through this imagery, Mary Lim masterfully recreates the unearthly scene she witnessed in Burma.

Structure.   Lim's purpose in writing this paper is to create the sensation of actually being in The Valley of Windmills in Burma. Her description takes the reader along the road to Taungaleik, into the Tennesserim Mountains to the pass where the windmills are. From the perspective of the lip of the valley, she describes the details closest to her and then moves farther away. She ends by bringing her reader back to the lip of the valley and contrasts Taungaleik "glittering on the mountainside" with the windmills "enveloped in morning mist." Through her description, she helps the reader learn something about the point of her essay, the nature of life in Burma. She withholds the explicit statement of this point until her last paragraph, when the reader has been fully prepared for it.

The following essays illustrate different types and uses of description. "Water Striders" by Lorus and Margery Milne and "Shakespeare's Theatre" by Thomas Marc Parrott are both objective descriptions; Mark Twain's "Reading the River," Nathan Irvin Huggins's "Uptown in Harlem," and Studs Terkel's "Brett Hauser: Supermarket Box Boy" are subjective descriptions.

Water Striders
LORUS J. MILNE AND MARGERY J. MILNE

"Water Striders" is from the book A Multitude of Living Things. *In the essay, as its title indicates, Lorus J. Milne and Margery J. Milne describe the life of a small aquatic insect, the water strider. Essentially scientific in their approach, the authors aim for objectivity and focus on the subject being described rather than on their own impressions.*

When you sit by a pond or a slowly winding stream, the city's 1 impatient tempo drains away, and from the corners of the mind thoughts come out and sun themselves. Before you on the water surface, bugs and beetles skip about. They stay afloat because the liquid's surface tension acts as a skin, elastic and smooth, preventing them from falling in. Yet this animal activity on the water seems to contradict all human experience. That "water is wet" is one of the first facts learned by every child. In more mature years this wetness is so taken for granted that any exceptions to the rule arouse great interest. Thus the sewing needle that can be lowered gently onto the surface of a tumblerful of water, there to float completely dry, is a startling paradox. But to a large number of animals and plants, this problem of wetness and dryness is a matter of life or death. Many of them find the "dry" surface of water a place on which to live, albeit precariously. Suspended between the air above and the depths below, they inhabit the surface film of ponds, streams, lakes, and even oceans. Theirs is an almost two-dimensional realm—a special niche in nature for use of which certain requirements must be met.

When a substance attracts water molecules more strongly than 2 water molecules attract each other, the water wets the surface. The liquid creeps along, invading every crevice, clinging tightly to each irregularity. But some materials, such as waxes and oils, attract water molecules so little that the water draws away, pulling back into itself and leaving the surfaces dry. Aquatic birds take advantage of these differences by regularly adding oil to their outer plumage, thereby keeping their feathers from becoming watersoaked. The many creatures that walk on water do so by means of well-waxed, hair-booted feet that the water cannot wet.

Best known of all the animals that walk dry-shod on ponds and 3 streams are the water striders—insects with four long legs stretching out to the sides and a shorter pair held under the head. Texans call them "Jesus bugs," whereas in Canada they are "skaters." Their slender feet are covered with a short pile of greasy hairs that the water fails to invade. Each foot presses the water surface and makes a dimple there, but the water does not let the foot fall through the surface film as it would if the fine waxy bristles were absent. Instead, the insect's weight is supported, partly by the buoyant force of the water displaced from the dimples, partly by the surface tension that tends to erase the depressions and bring all the water film to the same level. The strider stands chiefly on its hind and foremost legs, while with the middle pair as oars it sculls along, its body well above the smooth and slippery surface of the pond. Mirrored in the water film below the bug is its image—a reflected "double" seldom seen except by small creatures close to the water surface. Below the strider, on the bottom of a shallow stream, are dark shadows cast not only by the insect, but also by the dimples in the surface film where its feet press downward. Sometimes, on sunny days, these shadows on a sandy bottom are more conspicuous than the insect making them. They drift along and follow every movement of the rowing strider on the film above.

A considerable *length* of surface must be called upon to support an insect as heavy as a full-grown water strider. If its hair-booted feet pressed on the film at only six small points, the bug would penetrate into the water and sink at once. But the strider's legs are spread so widely as to be almost parallel to the surface, and its feet make elongated dimples which are really furrows in the water film. So secure is the insect on a quiet pond or stream that it can shift its weight freely among its feet. Most spectacular are the demonstrations of this when a strider cleans itself. Drawing its rowing legs far back, it stands with its head almost in the water, while its hind legs are raised well above the surface and rubbed one on the other much in the manner of a housefly. Then the insect rests on forefeet and one hind foot, with the rowing leg on that side as an outrigger, while the middle and rear feet of the opposite side are elevated into the air and rubbed free of clinging particles by a similar fiddling movement. To accomplish this contortion the bug practically lies down on its side. The water film stands the strain, but the shadows cast on the bottom shift and spread as the pressures on the fewer surface furrows are increased. Finally the strider stands on rowing feet and rear pontoons while its body and forelegs are raised high above the water. The insect washes itself much as a kitten does, transferring dust particles from feelers, beak, and body to the forefeet. Then it rubs these together until they are satisfactorily clean. If uninterrupted, such a complete toilet operation may take ten minutes, and the bug seems to give great care to every detail. At last, with antennae brushed, the insect rows forth alertly to seek its fortune.

Water striders dive upon occasion, but only under threat of serious danger. They have difficulty breaking through the film, but once below they sink to the bottom. Afterwards they crawl out, wet and obviously miserable, to dry and comb themselves into respectability. All active stages in a water strider's life are spent on the water surface, but for winter they fly or crawl (some are wingless even as adults) under leaves on the shore.

Other animals that spread their weight on outstretched feet may rest with safety on the water film. Small gnats and midges flit from place to place on ponds, alighting with equal equanimity on film or foliage. Even large craneflies settle with surprising grace upon the water's skin, and rise again with their long legs trailing after. Each foot combines the advantages of waxed hair covering and slender length that can distribute the insect's weight along the surface film. But Jesus bugs are not averse to live meat when they can catch it. Many of their dashes over the pond surface are rewarded with small flies that fail to take to flight in time. Occasionally, too, a cranefly dies of unknown causes while resting on the water surface. Without muscular effort to hold its body well above the water, the insect sags into the pond, sinking in or barely floating. Water striders gather around it to salvage such nourishing juices as remain. It is but one of the many types of food they seek as they push their way along the transparent but rubbery surface film. Some of their sustenance floats up to them from below; each dead fish attracts a crowd of striders. But most of the food of these insects falls into the water from the air above. Ants tumble from leaves overhanging the water. Beetles close their wings and drop or blunder into ponds and streams where the water wets them and renders them helpless prey for the predacious bugs. Striders investigate every particle, often making great leaps over the water to reach some newly fallen object. A green leaf floating down a small stream draws the attention of the these bugs, one after the other, as it passes through each quiet stretch. Small articles such as drowning ants are picked out of the surface film and held on a slender black beak while the liquid contents are drained away. Often a strider is seen carrying with it a gnat or other carcass as it glides along the water surface. Occasionally other striders chase the food-bearing relative across the pond, just as chickens do a hen fortunate enough to find a large grub. But when not in the act of feeding, each strider defends some section of shoreline or creek surface, driving away invaders that trespass on the unmarked watery hunting ground.

Only on quiet days do striders venture far from shore. If a breeze springs up they hurry to reach calm water near the bank before the surface becomes ruffled. Rain and winter drive the striders from the water, to crawl out upon the bank. In spite of these precautions, the insects do get wet at times. Although they show great ability in navigating streams and can spring ahead to make progress against the current, an occasional bug is swept through a riffle and fails to stay afloat. Air clinging to its body usually keeps the creature just below the surface film, where it rows to shore to crawl out, dry, and clean itself.

COMPREHENSION

1. Paragraph 1 identifies a sewing needle floating on water as a paradox, an apparent contradiction that is somehow true. Why is this a paradox? How is this paradox related to the water strider's situation?

2. How is the water strider able to walk on water?

3. What other animals rest with safety on the water?

4. Why does the water strider occasionally get wet?

5. What are other names for the water strider? Why is each appropriate?

PURPOSE AND AUDIENCE

1. Is this essay written for a general or a scientific audience? How can you tell?

2. What is the authors' thesis? What evidence do they provide to support it?

STYLE AND STRUCTURE

1. "Water Striders" is an objective description. Does it also convey its authors' attitudes toward their material? If so, where?

2. What is the function of the essay's first sentence?

3. What is the organizing scheme which determines how the details are presented in this essay? Is it the best scheme for this topic? Explain.

4. In paragraph 4, why do the authors compare the water strider to a kitten? What other similes do they use?

5. This predominately descriptive essay also contains one major section that explains a process. Locate this section. What process does it explain?

WRITING WORKSHOP

1. Describe the activity of an animal or insect. Make sure that the essay you write is objective and that it has an organizing scheme.

2. Imagine you are a water strider observing human beings, and write an objective description of their behavior. You might want to focus on one activity, such as swimming or walking.

Shakespeare's Theatre
THOMAS MARC PARROTT

Thomas Marc Parrott was a professor of English at Princeton University and an expert on William Shakespeare. In this essay, from a handbook designed to introduce college students to Shakespeare, he objectively describes the structure of an Elizabethan theater. Because Shakespeare's theater was so different from theaters today and because this difference can give us insight into Shakespeare's plays, Parrott wants to make certain that his audience understands his description. To accomplish this end, he provides pertinent specific details and accompanies his description with two illustrations.

... Of greater importance [than props and costumes] to the art of the dramatist is the physical structure of the stage itself. On this point there is now a practical agreement among scholars; differences remain only on a few minor details.

The Elizabethan theatre may be regarded as evolving from the inn courtyards which were, long before the first playhouse was built, favorite places for dramatic performances by the old companies of actors. . . .

When James Burbage built the Theatre in 1576 he naturally designed it along the lines of the inn-yards in which he had been accustomed to play. The building had two entrances—one in front for the audience; one in the rear for the actors, musicians, and the personnel of the theatre. Inside the building a rectangular platform projected far out into what was called "the yard"—we know that the stage of the Fortune ran halfway across the "yard," some twenty-seven and a half feet. Here the common herd of spectators, the "groundlings," stood—there were no seats on the ground floor in the old public theatres—in front and on both sides of the stage. Around and above the yard ran three galleries approached by interior stairs and divided into "rooms" or boxes where the better class of spectators who paid an additional price for the accommodation sat more or less comfortably on stools. There was no front curtain and the performance was viewed not from the front alone but from three sides by the spectators in the yard and in the galleries. On this projecting platform the greater part of the action took place. As a rule the playwright made no attempt to localize such action; the platform was, so to speak, neutral ground. It might

be any place, outdoors or in, and if the poet wished to designate
a locality he wove an allusion to it into the dialogue. "This is the
forest of Arden" says Rosalind when the scene has shifted from the
Court to the greenwood.

Over a large part of this platform there extended a wooden roof,   4
called "the heavens" or "the shadow," which served partly to
protect the actors from bad weather, but primarily to contain the
machinery needed to let down on the stage certain properties—
"the creaking throne" at which Jonson laughed—or actors imper-
sonating fairies or gods. In the sketch of the Swan we see this
"shadow" supported by strong pillars resting on the platform.
These, one would suppose, must have interfered with the action,
but they could no doubt be used by an actor to conceal himself
from others on the stage. We hear once of a pick-purse caught
plying his trade in the yard who was hoisted up on the stage and
tied to a post for the rest of the performance.

Across the back of the platform ran a wall partly concealed by   5
arras, woven or painted cloth set on frames standing out three feet
or so from the wall. This cloth was sometimes painted in perspective,
but rarely, if ever, presented a realistic background and certainly
was not shifted to denote a change of scene. It served a decorative
rather than an illusion-producing purpose. In the narrow space
between the arras and the back wall an actor might hide himself,
as Polonius does in *Hamlet,* and it was here that Falstaff was found
"fast asleep and snorting like a horse" by the Prince and Peto.

Directly behind the back wall, in the centre under the balcony,   6
was a recess, variously known as the "rear-stage" or the "alcove."
It was cut off from the front by a "traverse," i.e. a curtain hanging
before it. This was drawn back to disclose an action taking place
in the rear-stage and pulled over it again at the close of such a
scene. This "alcove" was an essential feature of the Elizabethan
stage. Since it was concealed from the front by a curtain it could
be set beforehand with properties to suggest a definite locality, a
scholar's study (*Dr. Faustus*), a lady's bed-chamber (*Cymbeline*),
a magician's cell (*Tempest*), or a tomb (*Romeo and Juliet*). An action
beginning in this alcove, like the last scene of *Othello,* might be
transferred to the front stage—the alcove being too small for the
numbers of actors involved—which then became for the time the
same locality as that indicated by the setting of the alcove. At the
close of such a scene the curtain was drawn and the front stage
became again "neutral ground," ready for whatever action the
playwright needed. It may be noted here that the sketch of the

Swan shows no trace of this alcove, only a flat back wall of the front stage pierced by two doors. But the existence of such a recess on the Elizabethan stage is quite certain; either the Swan differed from the other theatres of the day in this respect or, which is perhaps more likely, De Witt failed to represent it.

To right and left of the alcove were doors, set flat in the back wall, as in the Swan sketch, or possibly set on the bias, so that actors emerging from them would meet each other in the centre of the stage. These doors connected the stage with the "tiring-room," the modern "green room," from which another entrance was possible through the alcove to the front stage.

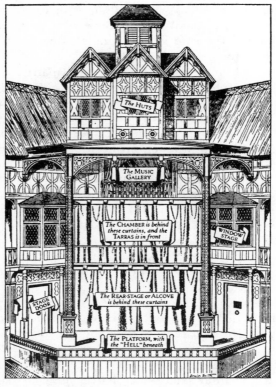

THE MULTIPLE STAGE OF THE GLOBE PLAYHOUSE

As reconstructed by John Cranford Adams

Above this rear-stage was the upper-stage, a gallery, slightly projecting over the platform and provided with a curtain by which it could at need be cut off from the view of the audience and like the alcove could be set with properties. This space seems at first to have been occupied by specially favored spectators and was known as "the lord's room"; occasionally the musicians needed for a performance were placed here. Its peculiar value in the presentation of plays, however, was soon realized and it became a positive asset to the playwright. It was used especially to designate a locality above the plane of the main action on the lower stage: the wall of a city from which the defenders could converse with an opponent below, the window or the balcony of a private house, a high rock, or Cleopatra's monument up to which she and her women draw the dying Antony. This upper-stage was entered as a rule by back stairs from the tiring-room, but it was also possible to reach it from the front by temporary stairs, by a practicable tree set on the main-stage, or by a rope-ladder. It is by such a ladder that Romeo is seen to descend from Juliet's balcony after their wedding-night. In some of the later theatres there seem also to have been boxes over the back doors which could be used at need for the windows of an upper room.

Such was in general the structure of the Elizabethan stage in one of the large public theatres; the Swan seated, De Witt reckons, about three thousand people. There was no essential difference in the so-called "private" theatres. These consisted simply in the adaptation of a hall in a private house for theatrical purposes. The private theatre like the public had its uncurtained front stage, its curtained alcove and balcony. The whole space—stage, pit, and gallery—was under cover, whereas in the public theatre the "yard" was open to the sky and only the galleries and the shadow were roofed with thatch or tile. An upper room or attic served the purpose of the shadow in providing space for the necessary machinery. Performances took place by artificial light and there is reason to believe that the alcove was larger and better lighted. The same plays were produced at public and private theatres, as when Shakespeare's company played both at the Globe and the private Blackfriars; and there is no evidence that any reconstruction of these plays was necessary. The main part of the audience sat on benches on the floor or in the one gallery which sufficed the private theatre. The custom of sitting on a stool upon the stage itself which seems to have originated in public theatres became especially fashionable, and objectionable, in the private houses where a more select audience was ready to pay as much as a shilling extra for such a seat.

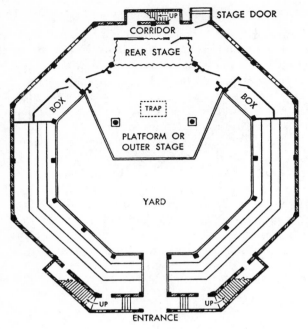

FLOOR-PLAN OF THE GLOBE PLAYHOUSE

As reconstructed by John Cranford Adams

COMPREHENSION

1. From what did the Elizabethan theater evolve?

2. Who were the groundlings?

3. What was the alcove? Why does Parrott say it was an essential feature of the Elizabethan stage?

4. How does the stage of the Elizabethan theater differ from the stage of the modern theater? Explain.

PURPOSE AND AUDIENCE

1. How does Parrott's definition of his audience affect his presentation?

2. What is the essay's thesis?

STYLE AND STRUCTURE

1. Are the illustrations necessary for readers to understand Parrott's description? Explain.

2. Why does Parrott include so many references to plays that Shakespeare wrote?

3. What is the organizing scheme of this essay? Why do you think this particular arrangement was chosen?

4. Are there any passages in this predominantly objective description that seem to you to express opinions or impressions? If so, which ones? Why?

5. Parrott's description at times seems to be mathematically precise, presenting exact measurements and distances and specifying the physical relationships among objects. Are there any sections of the essay where the description is not precise enough? If so, how can you account for this?

WRITING WORKSHOP

1. Objectively describe a building that you are familiar with. Before you write your description, visit the building if you can, and jot down its outstanding characteristics, making note of as many significant details as possible.

2. Write an objective description of the house or apartment building in which you grew up.

Reading the River
MARK TWAIN

In this brief selection from Life on the Mississippi, *Mark Twain (the pseudonym of Samuel L. Clemens) tries to convey to his readers the conflict he felt as he became an experienced steamboat pilot instead of just a passenger. To do so, he personalizes his subjective description of the river by frequently using the first person and intensifies his description with vivid adjectives and figures of speech.*

... The face of the water, in time, became a wonderful book—a book that was a dead language to the uneducated passenger but which told its mind to me without reserve, delivering its most cherished secrets as clearly as if it uttered them with a voice. And it was not a book to be read once and thrown aside, for it had a new story to tell every day. Throughout the long twelve hundred miles there was never a page that was void of interest, never one that you could leave unread without loss, never one that you would want to skip, thinking you could find higher enjoyment in some other thing. There never was so wonderful a book written by man, never one whose interest was so absorbing, so unflagging, so sparklingly renewed with every reperusal. The passenger who could not read it was charmed with a peculiar sort of faint dimple on its surface (on the rare occasions when he did not overlook it altogether) but to the pilot that was an *italicized* passage; indeed it was more than that, it was a legend of the largest capitals with a string of shouting exclamation-points at the end of it, for it meant that a wreck or a rock was buried there that could tear the life out of the strongest vessel that ever floated. It is the faintest and simplest expression the water ever makes, and the most hideous to a pilot's eye. In truth, the passenger who could not read this book saw nothing but all manner of pretty pictures in it, painted by the sun and shaded by the clouds, whereas to the trained eye these were not pictures at all, but the grimmest and most dead-earnest of reading matter.

Now when I had mastered the language of this water, and had come to know every trifling feature that bordered the great river as familiarly as I knew the letters of the alphabet, I had made a valuable acquisition. But I had lost something, too. I had lost something which could never be restored to me while I lived. All the grace, the beauty, the poetry, had gone out of the majestic river! I still kept in mind a certain wonderful sunset which I witnessed when steamboating was new to me. A broad expanse of the river was turned to blood; in the middle distance the red hue brightened into gold, through which a solitary log came floating, black and conspicuous; in one place a long, slanting mark lay sparkling upon the water; in another the surface was broken by boiling, tumbling rings, that were as many-tinted as an opal; where the ruddy flush was faintest, was a smooth spot that was covered with graceful circles and radiating lines, ever so delicately traced; the shore on our left was densely wooded, and the somber shadow that fell from this forest was broken in one place by a long, ruffled trail that shone like silver; and high above the forest wall a clean-stemmed dead tree waved a single leafy bough that glowed like a flame in the unobstructed splendor that was flowing from the sun. There were graceful curves, reflected images, woody heights, soft distances; and over the whole scene, far and near, the dissolving lights drifted steadily, enriching it every passing moment with new marvels of coloring.

I stood like one bewitched. I drank it in, in a speechless rapture. [3] The world was new to me, and I had never seen anything like this at home. But as I have said, a day came when I began to cease from noting the glories and the charms which the moon and the sun and the twilight wrought upon the river's face; another day came when I ceased altogether to note them. Then, if that sunset scene had been repeated, I should have looked upon it without rapture, and should have commented upon it, inwardly, after this fashion: "This sun means that we are going to have wind to-morrow; that floating log means that the river is rising, small thanks to it; that slanting mark on the water refers to a bluff reef which is going to kill somebody's steamboat one of these nights, if it keeps on stretching out like that; those tumbling 'boils' show a dissolving bar and a changing channel there; the lines and circles in the slick water over yonder are a warning that that troublesome place is shoaling up dangerously; that silver streak in the shadow of the forest is the 'break' from a new snag, and he has located himself in the very best place he could have found to fish for steamboats; that tall dead tree, with a single living branch, is not going to last long, and then how is a body ever going to get through this blind place at night without the friendly old landmark?"

No, the romance and beauty were all gone from the river. All the [4] value any feature of it had for me now was the amount of usefulness it could furnish toward compassing the safe piloting of a steamboat. Since those days, I have pitied doctors from my heart. What does the lovely flush in a beauty's cheek mean to a doctor but a "break" that ripples above some deadly disease? Are not all her visible charms sown thick with what are to him the signs and symbols of hidden decay? Does he ever see her beauty at all, or doesn't he simply view her professionally and comment upon her unwholesome condition all to himself? And doesn't he sometimes wonder whether he has gained most or lost most by learning his trade?

COMPREHENSION

1. How is the Mississippi River like a book?

2. When the passenger sees a dimple in the water's surface, what does the pilot see?

3. What did Twain gain as he became a skilled pilot? What did he lose?

4. Why does Twain say, in his conclusion, that he feels sorry for doctors? What do doctors and pilots have in common?

PURPOSE AND AUDIENCE

1. Is Twain's purpose in describing the Mississippi to inform, to entertain, or to persuade? Explain.

2. State Twain's thesis in your own words.

3. Is Twain writing primarily for an audience of pilots or passengers? Explain.

STYLE AND STRUCTURE

1. In the first lines of this selection, Twain compares the Mississippi River to a book. Trace this metaphor and variations of it (that is, other references to language, punctuation, or reading) throughout the selection. Is the comparison between river and book an effective one? Explain.

2. This description, unlike many others, does not really use spatial order for its organizing scheme. Why not?

3. What things are paired and contrasted in Twain's description? Why does he use this technique?

4. What is the function of the description of the sunset in paragraph 2? Would this description have had the same effect if it had been briefer? Explain.

5. Where does Twain restate his thesis? Is this restatement necessary? Why or why not?

WRITING WORKSHOP

1. Write a subjective description of a scene you remember from your childhood. In your thesis statement and in your conclusion, explain how your adult impressions of the scene differ from your childhood impressions.

2. Write a descriptive essay in which you show how increased knowledge of an academic subject has either increased or spoiled your enthusiasm for it.

Uptown in Harlem
NATHAN IRVIN HUGGINS

Nathan Irvin Huggins is a professor of history at Columbia University. In this section from his book Harlem Renaissance, *he describes what Harlem meant to white Americans in the 1920s. To accomplish his ends, Huggins uses specific details to paint an impressionistic picture of an area of New York City—a picture that existed more in fantasy than in fact.*

Postwar America was prepared to view the Negro from a different angle. Afro-Americans and Harlem could serve a new kind of white psychological need. Even if Harlem blacks had wanted it, there was little chance that they would have been left alone to shape and define their own identity. White Americans had identities of their own to find, and black men were too essential to them to be ignored. Men who sensed that they were slaves to moral codes, that they were cramped and confined by guilt-producing norms which threatened to make them emotional cripples, found Harlem a tonic and a release. Harlem Negroes' lives appeared immediate and honest. Everything they did—their music, their art, their dance— uncoiled deep inner tensions. Harlem seemed a cultural enclave that had magically survived the psychic fetters of Puritanism. 1

How convenient! It was merely a taxi trip to the exotic for most white New Yorkers. In cabarets decorated with tropical and jungle motifs—some of them replicas of southern plantations—they heard jazz, that almost forbidden music. It was not merely that jazz was exotic, but that it was instinctive and abandoned, yet laughingly light and immediate—melody skipping atop inexorable driving rhythm. The downtown spectator tried to encompass the looseness and freedom of dance. Coffee, chocolate, and caramel-brown girls whose lithe long legs kicked high, bodies and hips rolling and tossing with insinuation; feline black men—dandies—whose intuitive grace teased and flirted at the very edge of chaos, yet never lost aplomb. In the darkness and closeness, the music, infectious and unrelenting, drove on. Into its vortex white ladies and gentlemen were pulled, to dance the jungle dance. Heads swaying, rolling, jerking; hair flying free and wild; arms and legs pumping, kicking, thrusting—going wherever they, themselves, would go— chasing the bass or drum or cornet; clenched eyes and teeth, 2 staccato breath, sweat, sweat—bodies writhing and rolling with a drum and a beat as they might never with a woman or a man.

It was a cheap trip. No safari! Daylight and a taxi ride rediscovered   3 New York City, no tropic jungle. There had been thrill without danger. For these black savages were civilized—not head-hunters or cannibals—they would not run amok. At worst, if a man strayed from the known paths in search of the more forbidden exotic, he might get fleeced, but in a most "civilized" way. So, as if by magic, convention returned with little evidence that it had gone, except, perhaps, for the deeply insinuated music, the body-remembered rhythm, and the subliminal tease; the self had been transported to a region of its own honesty which it could know again.

How much was illusion? The white hunter in New York's heart   4 of darkness would not see (doubtless, would not recognize) his "savage-primitive" drummer and dancer, on sore, bunioned feet, picking their way on morning's concrete to cold-water flats, to lose their rhythm-weary bodies in sexless sleep. Nor could he know the deep desolation of "savage" life that found only slight escape in alcohol, exotic fantasies in cocaine. Primitive, romantic Harlem was too simple a conception to survive the cold light of day. So, too, was the romantic view of Africa. Illusion though it was, it served the deep needs of those who nurtured it, provided some black men a positive image of themselves, and, most important, it brought downtown money uptown. What was looked for was found.

COMPREHENSION

1. Why did whites find Harlem "a tonic and a release"?

2. What does Huggins mean when he says, "Even if Harlem blacks had wanted it, there was little chance that they would have been left alone to shape their own identity"?

3. What was the downtown white's view of Harlem? How did this view correspond to the real Harlem?

4. Why does Huggins call the white's romantic view of Harlem "a simple conception"?

PURPOSE AND AUDIENCE

1. This selection is from a history book, yet Huggins chooses to present a subjective description instead of just facts. Why?

2. Although this is a section of a chapter and not an independent essay, it does have a thesis. What is it?

STYLE AND STRUCTURE

1. What makes this description subjective? List some of the impressionistic details the author uses in this selection.

2. In paragraphs 2 and 3, Huggins introduces an extended comparison. What points of comparison does Huggins use in both paragraphs? What function does this section serve in the whole essay?

3. What is the organizing scheme of this essay? What elements of Harlem does Huggins choose to emphasize?

4. Identify the restatement of the thesis in the conclusion.

WRITING WORKSHOP

1. Describe the misconceptions a group of tourists might have as they visited your neighborhood. Use as much specific detail as you can.

2. Take a walk or ride through an area you are not familiar with, and describe your impressions of it.

Brett Hauser: Supermarket Box Boy
STUDS TERKEL

*In this essay, Studs Terkel presents his edited version of an interview
with Brett Hauser, a supermarket box boy, who talks about his job.
Hauser's account, like the others in Terkel's book* Working, *is a subjective description which reveals his attitude toward the work he does. By
editing the interview to emphasize certain details and by focusing on
selected incidents, Terkel enables his readers to grasp Brett Hauser's
contradictory feelings about his work.*

He is seventeen. He had worked as a box boy at a supermarket in 1
*a middle-class suburb on the outskirts of Los Angeles. "People
come to the counter and you put things in their bags for them. And
carry things to their cars. It was a grind."*

You have to be terribly subservient to people: "Ma'am, can I 2
take your bag?" "Can I do this?" It was at a time when the grape
strikers were passing out leaflets. They were very respectful people.
People'd come into the check stand, they'd say, "I just bought
grapes for the first time because of those idiots outside." I had to
put their grapes in the bag and thank them for coming and take
them outside to the car. Being subservient made me very resentful.

It's one of a chain of supermarkets. They're huge complexes with 3
bakeries in them and canned music over those loudspeakers
—Muzak. So people would relax while they shopped. They played
selections from *Hair*. They'd play "Guantanamera," the Cuban
Revolution song. They had *Soul on Ice*, the Cleaver book, on sale.
They had everything dressed up and very nice. People wouldn't
pay any attention to the music. They'd go shopping and hit their
kids and talk about those idiots passing out anti-grape petitions.

Everything looks fresh and nice. You're not aware that in the 4
back room it stinks and there's crates all over the place and the
walls are messed up. There's graffiti and people are swearing and
yelling at each other. You walk through the door, the music starts
playing, and everything is pretty. You talk in hushed tones and are
very respectful.

You wear a badge with your name on it. I once met someone I 5
knew years ago. I remembered his name and said, "Mr. Castle,
how are you?" We talked about this and that. As he left, he said,
"It was nice talking to you, Brett." I felt great, he remembered me.
Then I looked down at my name plate. Oh shit. He didn't remember

me at all, he just read the name plate. I wish I put "Irving" down on my name plate. If he'd have said, "Oh yes, Irving, how could I forget you . . . ?" I'd have been ready for him. There's nothing personal here.

You have to be very respectful to everyone—the customers, to   6
the manager, to the checkers. There's a sign on the cash register that says: Smile at the customer. Say hello to the customer. It's assumed if you're a box boy, you're really there 'cause you want to be a manager some day. So you learn all the little things you have absolutely no interest in learning.

The big thing there is to be an assistant manager and eventually   7
manager. The male checkers had dreams of being manager, too. It was like an internship. They enjoyed watching how the milk was packed. Each manager had his own domain. There was the ice cream manager, the grocery manager, the dairy case manager . . . They had a sign in the back: Be good to your job and your job will be good to you. So you take an overriding concern on how the ice cream is packed. You just die if something falls off a shelf. I saw so much crap there I just couldn't take. There was a black boy, an Oriental box boy, and a kid who had a Texas drawl. They needed the job to subsist. I guess I had the luxury to hate it and quit.

When I first started there, the manager said, "Cut your hair.   8
Come in a white shirt, black shoes, a tie. Be here on time." You get there, but he isn't there. I just didn't know what to do. The checker turns around and says, "You new? What's your name?" "Brett." "I'm Peggy." And that's all they say and they keep throwing this down to you. They'll say, "Don't put it in that, put it in there." But they wouldn't help you.

You had to keep your apron clean. You couldn't lean back on the   9
railings. You couldn't talk to the checkers. You couldn't accept tips. Okay, I'm outside and I put it in the car. For a lot of people, the natural reaction is to take out a quarter and give it to me. I'd say, "I'm sorry, I can't." They'd get offended. When you give someone a tip, you're sort of suave. You take a quarter and you put it in their palm and you expect them to say, "Oh, thanks a lot." When you say, "I'm sorry, I can't," they feel a little put down. They say, "No one will know." And they put it in your pocket. You say, "I really can't." It gets to a point where you have to do physical violence to a person to avoid being tipped. It was not consistent with the store's philosophy of being cordial. Accepting tips was a cordial thing and made the customer feel good. I just couldn't understand the incongruity. One lady actually put it in my pocket, got in the car, and drove away. I would have had to throw the quarter at her or eaten it or something.

When it got slow, the checkers would talk about funny things   10
that happened. About Us and Them. Us being the people who
worked there, Them being the stupid fools who didn't know where
anything was—just came through and messed everything up and
shopped. We serve them but we don't like them. We know where
everything is. We know what time the market closes and they don't.
We know what you do with coupons and they don't. There was a
camaraderie of sorts. It wasn't healthy, though. It was a put-down
of the others.

There was this one checker who was absolutely vicious. He took   11
great delight in making every little problem into a major crisis from
which he had to emerge victorious. A customer would give him a
coupon. He'd say, "You were supposed to give me that at the
beginning." She'd say, "Oh, I'm sorry." He'd say, "Now I gotta
open the cash register and go through the whole thing. Madam, I
don't watch out for every customer. I can't manage your life." A
put-down.

It never bothered me when I would put something in the bag   12
wrong. In the general scheme of things, in the large questions of
the universe, putting a can of dog food in the bag wrong is not of
great consequence. For them it was.

There were a few checkers who were nice. There was one that   13
was incredibly sad. She could be unpleasant at times, but she
talked to everybody. She was one of the few people who genuinely
wanted to talk to people. She was saying how she wanted to go to
school and take courses so she could get teaching credit. Someone
asked her, "Why don't you?" She said, "I have to work here. My
hours are wrong. I'd have to get my hours changed." They said,
"Why don't you?" She's worked there for years. She had seniority.
She said, "Jim won't let me." Jim was the manager. He didn't give
a damn. She wanted to go to school, to teach, but she can't because
every day she's got to go back to the supermarket and load groceries.
Yet she wasn't bitter. If she died a checker and never enriched her
life, that was okay, because those were her hours.

She was extreme in her unpleasantness and her consideration.   14
Once I dropped some grape juice and she was squawking like a
bird. I came back and mopped it up. She kept saying to me, "Don't
worry about it. It happens to all of us." She'd say to the customers,
"If I had a dime for all the grape juice I dropped . . ."

Jim's the boss. A fish-type handshake. He was balding and in his   15
forties. A lot of managers are these young, clean-shaven, neatly
cropped people in their twenties. So Jim would say things like
"groovy." You were supposed to get a ten-minutes break every two
hours. I lived for that break. You'd go outside, take your shoes off,

and be human again. You had to request it. And when you took it, they'd make you feel guilty.

You'd go up and say, "Jim, can I have a break?" He'd say, "A break? You want a break? Make it a quick one, nine and a half minutes." Ha ha ha. One time I asked the assistant manager, Henry. He was even older than Jim. "Do you think I can have a break?" He'd say, "You got a break when you were hired." Ha ha ha. Even when they joked it was a put-down. 16

The guys who load the shelves are a step above the box boys. It's like upperclassmen at an officer candidate's school. They would make sure that you conformed to all the prescribed rules, because they were once box boys. They know what you're going through, your anxieties. But instead of making it easier for you, they'd make it harder. It's like a military institution. 17

I kept getting box boys who came up to me, "Has Jim talked to you about your hair? He's going to because it's getting too long. You better get it cut or grease it back or something." They took delight in it. They'd come to me before Jim had told me. Everybody was out putting everybody down . . . 18

COMPREHENSION

1. What does Brett Hauser think of the customers of the supermarket? What is his opinion of the supermarket itself? What statements lead you to your conclusions?

2. What does Brett Hauser think of himself?

3. What does Brett Hauser mean when he says that the camaraderie that existed among the workers in the store "wasn't healthy"?

4. Describe Brett Hauser's physical appearance on the job.

5. Give some examples of the "put-downs" Hauser describes.

PURPOSE AND AUDIENCE

1. Hauser's audience during this interview was Studs Terkel, but Terkel expected his collection of interviews to be read widely. (In fact, it was a best seller.) What do you think Hauser's purpose was in talking to Terkel? What do you think Terkel's purpose was in collecting interviews about how people feel about their jobs?

2. Formulate a thesis statement for this interview.

3. Hauser states that he had the luxury to hate his job and even to quit. How does this affect your reaction to his complaints?

STYLE AND STRUCTURE

1. Studs Terkel prefaces Brett's remarks with an introduction. Is this introductory paragraph necessary? Is it complete enough? If so, why? If not, what else do you think Terkel should tell the reader?

2. Originally this was not a formal written essay; Hauser told his story to Terkel. Can you tell by the style or organization that this was spoken rather than written? If so, how? Be specific.

3. Terkel has Hauser tell his own story instead of telling Hauser's story for him. Why do you think Terkel chooses this option here (and throughout the book *Working*)?

4. Does this selection have an organizing scheme? If so, what is it? If not, why not?

5. This selection contains several narrative sections. Identify them. What is their purpose?

WRITING WORKSHOP

1. Write a descriptive essay about the physical environment of the worst job you ever had. Select and order the details you use so they convey to the reader your feelings about the work you had to do.

2. Visit a supermarket to observe the employees. Describe the physical appearance or behavior of several of the people you see working there.

4

Exemplification

WHAT IS EXEMPLIFICATION?

You have probably noticed when watching television talk shows or listening to classroom discussions that the most lively and interesting exchanges take place when those involved support and illustrate their general assertions with specific examples. It is one thing to say, "The mayor is corrupt and should not be reelected," and another to exemplify his corruption by saying, "The mayor should not be reelected because he has fired two city employees who refused to contribute to his campaign fund, put his family and friends on the city payroll, and used public funds to pay for improvements on his home." The same principle applies to writing, and many of the best essays extensively use examples. Exemplification is used in every kind of academic and nonacademic writing situation, either as a basic essay pattern or in combination with every other pattern of development, to explain, to add interest, and to persuade.

Examples Explain and Clarify

On a film midterm, you may present the thesis "Even though horror movies seem modern, they really aren't." You may think your statement is perfectly clear, but don't be surprised when your exam comes back with a question mark in the margin next to this sentence. After all, your statement goes no further than making a general assertion or claim about horror movies. It is not specific, nor does it anticipate a reader's questions about the ways in which horror movies are not modern. Furthermore, it includes no examples, your best means of ensuring clarity and avoiding ambiguity. To make sure your audience knows exactly what you mean, you should state your point precisely: "Despite the fact that horror movies seem modern, the most memorable ones are adaptations of nineteenth-century Gothic novels."

More important, you must illustrate your point thoroughly by analyzing specific films like *Frankenstein,* directed by James Whale, and *Dracula,* directed by Todd Browning, and by linking them with the novels on which they are based. With the benefit of these specific examples, a reader knows that you mean that the literary roots of such movies are in the past, not that their cinematic techniques or production methods are dated. Moreover, a reader understands which literary sources you mean. With these additions, your point is clear.

Examples Add Interest

The more relevant detail you provide for your readers, the more intriguing and engaging your essay will be. Well-chosen examples provide such detail and add life to relatively bland or straightforward statements. Lawrence J. Peter and Raymond Hull skillfully use this technique in their essay "The Peter Principle," which appears later in this chapter. In itself, their assertion that each employee in a system rises to his or her level of incompetence is not particularly engrossing. It becomes intriguing, however, when supported by specific examples, such as the cases of the affable foreman who becomes the indecisive supervisor, the exacting mechanic who becomes the disorganized foreman, and the charismatic battlefield general who becomes the impotent and self-destructive field marshal.

When you choose examples to support your assertions, don't be afraid to use imagination. Test the vigor of your examples by putting yourself in your reader's place. If you wouldn't find your own essay lively and interesting, you need to rewrite it with more spirited examples. After all, your goal is to communicate your ideas to your readers, and energetic, imaginative examples can make the difference between an engrossing essay and one that is a chore to read.

Examples Persuade

Although you may use examples simply to help explain an idea or to interest or entertain your readers, examples are also an effective way of convincing others that what you are saying is reasonable or valid. A few well-chosen examples can eliminate pages of general, and many times unconvincing, explanations. The old cliché that a picture is worth a thousand words is equally true for an example. For instance, a statement on an economics quiz that "rising costs and high unemployment have changed life for many Americans" needs such support to be convincing. Noting appropriate examples—that in a typical working-class neighborhood one out of every six primary wage earners is now jobless and that many white collar workers can no longer afford to go to movies or to eat any beef except hamburger—can persuade a reader that the statement is valid. Similarly, a statement in a biology paper that "despite recent moves to reverse its status, DDT should not be released to commercial users and should continue to be banned" is unconvincing without persuasive examples like these to back it up:

- Even though DDT has been banned for more than a decade, traces are still being found in the eggs of various fish and water fowl.
- Certain lakes and streams cannot be used for sport and recreation because DDT levels are dangerously high, presumably because of farmland runoff.
- DDT has been found in the milk of a significant number of nursing mothers.
- DDT residues, apparently carried by global air currents, have even been found in meltwater samples from Antarctica.
- Because of its stability as a compound, DDT does not degrade quickly, and, therefore, existent residues will threaten the environment well into the twenty-first century.

Examples are often necessary to convince, so choosing effective examples to support your ideas is important. When deciding which ones to include in an essay, you should consider both the quality and the quantity of your examples.

Using Effective Examples

The best examples succeed in clarifying, interesting, and convincing because they are specific, lively, and appropriate. For instance, let's suppose you plan to write a paper for your mathematics education class about the drop in math scores of high school students nationwide. In your essay, you introduce the issue by citing the statistics reported in the *New York Times* on September 25, 1979. You note not just that scores are lower but, more specifically, that the National Institute of Education has reported that the scores for seventeen-year-old students have fallen 4 percent over the last five years.

Your thesis is that competent math teachers could solve the problem, and you plan to discuss a teacher you observed during your internship at Lincoln High School. You know that your argument, to be effective, must illustrate the techniques of this teacher. You maintain that Ms. Harrison is a fine teacher, but you don't simply mention examples of her strengths—her attentive class, her organized lessons, and her prompt return of papers—as examples of her successful teaching. You develop these illustrations in a lively way, remembering her students leaning forward in their seats to listen and crowding around her desk after class, her outline on the board to accompany her straightforward explanation of the lesson, and her careful review and prompt return of a test.

Finally, you conclude with one last example. You note that the test results for Ms. Harrison's classes are 15 percent above the district norm. You know this example is convincing because it is specific; as a result, it cements together your introduction, your thesis, and your classroom observations. With this example, you're confident that a reader will accept your concluding argument that, regardless of other factors, more teachers like Ms. Harrison could reverse the national trend on high school math exams.

Of course, your essay is a success not simply because you use examples effectively but because you keep your essay focused on your point. A constant danger when using examples is that you may get so involved with one that you lose sight of what your paper is really about. Then the result is that you wander off into a digression. You could, for instance, have given in to the temptation to present a lengthy description of one particularly attentive student who always sat in the second row and wore a brown sweater. Disregarding your paper's topic in this way not only could confuse your readers but also could render much of your essay irrelevant. Thus, no matter how carefully they are developed, no matter how specific, lively, and appropriate they are, to be effective all of your examples must address the main idea of your essay.

Using Enough Examples

Unfortunately, there is no general rule to tell you whether to use one example or many to support your ideas. In some cases, one example will be sufficient, and in others, more will be needed. Simply stated, the number of examples you should use depends upon your thesis. If, for instance, your thesis is that an educational institution, like a business, needs careful financial management, a detailed consideration of your school or university could work well.

This one *extended example* could provide all the detail necessary for you to make your point. In this case, you would not need to include examples from a number of schools. In fact, too many examples could prove tedious to your readers and undercut your points.

On the other hand, if your thesis were that conflict between sons and fathers is a recurrent theme throughout the works of Franz Kafka, several examples would be necessary. One example would show only that the theme of conflict was present in *one* of Kafka's works. In this case, the more examples you include, the more effectively you prove your point. Of course, for some theses even a great number of examples would not be enough. You would, for instance, have a very difficult time finding enough examples to demonstrate convincingly that children from small families have more successful careers than children from large families. This thesis would require nothing less than a statistical study to prove its validity, certainly an impractical, if not impossible, procedure for most of us.

Selecting a sufficient range of examples is just as important as choosing an appropriate number of examples to support your ideas. If you wanted to convince a reader that Douglas MacArthur was an able general, you would choose examples from more than just the early part of his career. Likewise, if you wanted to argue that outdoor advertising was ruining the scenic view from local highways, you would discuss an area larger than your immediate neighborhood. Your object in every case is to select a cross section of examples appropriate for the boundaries of your topic.

Just as professional pollsters take great pains to assure that their samples actually do reflect the makeup of the general public, so your examples should fairly represent the total group about which your thesis makes an assertion. If you wanted to support a ban on smoking in all public buildings, you could not base your supporting points solely on the benefits of such a ban for restaurants. To be convincing, you would have to widen your scope to include other public places such as city buildings, hospital lobbies, and movie theaters. For the same reason, one person's experience or one school's problems aren't sufficient for a conclusion about many others unless you can establish that the experience or problems are typical in some significant way.

If you decide that you cannot cite enough representative examples to support your point, reexamine your thesis. Rather than switching to a new topic, you may be able to revise your thesis so that it claims no more than your examples can support. After all, the only way your paper will be convincing is if your readers feel that your examples and your claim about your topic correspond—that your thesis is supported by your examples and that your examples fairly represent the breadth of your topic.

STRUCTURING AN EXEMPLIFICATION ESSAY

Essays organized around examples usually follow a straightforward pattern. The introduction includes the thesis, which is supported by examples in the body of the essay. Each middle paragraph develops a separate example, an aspect of an extended example, or a point illustrated by several brief examples. The conclusion restates the thesis and reinforces the main idea of the essay. Of course, this pattern is arbitrary and need not be followed rigidly. At times, variations are advisable, even necessary. For instance, beginning your paper with a striking example might stimulate your readers' interest and curiosity; ending with one might vividly reinforce your thesis.

Exemplification presents one special organizational problem. In an essay of this type, a large number of examples is not unusual. If these examples are not handled properly, your paper could become a thesis followed by a list or by ten or fifteen very brief paragraphs. As you might imagine, this would result in a choppy, confused paper likely to lose your readers in the tangle of examples. One way to avoid this confusion is to select your best examples for full development in separate paragraphs and to drop the others. Another way is to categorize your examples and present them in the body of your essay in groups rather than individually. (Chapter 8 thoroughly discusses this process of classification.) By grouping several related examples in a single paragraph, you can replace choppiness with unity. Such an arrangement is illustrated by the following outline for a paper evaluating the nursing care at a local hospital. Notice how well the author groups his examples under four general categories: private rooms, semiprivate rooms, emergency wards, and outpatient clinics.

¶1   Introduction—thesis: The quality of nursing care at Albert Einstein Hospital is excellent.
¶2   Private rooms
Example 1: Responsiveness
Example 2: Good bedside care
Example 3: Effective rapport established

¶3   Semiprivate rooms
    Example 4: Small ratio of nurses to patients
    Example 5: Efficient use of time
    Example 6: Patient-centered care
¶4   Emergency wards
    Example 7: Adequate staffing
    Example 8: Satisfactory working relation between doctors and nurses
    Example 9: Nurses circulating among patients in the waiting room
¶5   Outpatient clinics
    Example 10: Nurses preparing patients
    Example 11: Nurses assisting during treatment
    Example 12: Nurses instructing patients after treatment
¶6   Conclusion—restatement of thesis

Example papers are frequently used in nonacademic writing situations; fiscal reports, memos, progress reports, and proposals can be organized this way. One of the more important uses you may make of the example pattern is in applying for a job. Your letter of application to a prospective employer is usually a variation of this form.

2432 Oak Drive

Reston, Virginia 22090

February 17, 1980

Mr. R. W. Weaver

Product Safety Division

General Motors Company

Detroit, Michigan 48202

Dear Mr. Weaver:

Opening   I have learned of your opening for a product
safety engineer both from your advertisement in the
February Journal of Product Safety Engineering and
from my work-study advisor, Dr. Jerome Weishoff. As
you know, Dr. Weishoff has worked as a consultant to
your division, and he has inspired much of my

Thesis enthusiasm about my field and about this opportunity to work on your research team. I am confident that my education and experience have prepared me to join General Motors as a product safety engineer.

Brief examples At present I am a senior at Drexel University where I am majoring in electrical engineering. Throughout my academic career I have maintained a 3.65 average and have been on the dean's list every quarter but one. In addition, I have been active in the campus community as junior class president and in my professional field as secretary of the product safety engineering society.

Brief examples My theoretical background corresponds to the criteria mentioned in your advertisement. Besides my electrical engineering program, which emphasized solid-state circuitry, I have taken two advanced physics classes. Moreover, through my computer courses, including systems programming, I have acquired a working knowledge of Cobol and Fortran.

Major example I spent my work-study periods working in the product safety division of the Budd Company in Philadelphia. During this time, I worked closely with my supervisor, Norman Gainor, manager of the product safety division. Our special projects included a study of circuit failure in subway cars.

Closing I have enclosed a résumé and will be available to discuss my qualifications any time after graduation on March 17. I am looking forward to meeting with you, and I hope to hear from you soon.

Sincerely,

Doris J. Miller

Points for Special Attention

Organization.   The letter of application is a special use of exemplification. Its purpose is to convince a prospective employer that you will meet his or her company's needs. Often the letter is written in response to an advertisement in a newspaper or a journal and should address the specific points which the employer has outlined in the advertisement.

In this letter, Doris Miller's thesis is that her education and experience ideally suit her for the job for which she is applying. The body of her letter is divided into three categories: education, theoretical background, and work-study experience. Each of the body paragraphs has a clear purpose and function, and each contains specific examples which tell the prospective employer what qualifies Doris Miller to be a product safety engineer.

Arrangement of Points.   Miller arranges her points so that her letter builds up to her strongest one. She begins with her education, outlines her theoretical background, and goes on to discuss her experience. Although her education and academic record are important, in this case they are not as significant to an employer as her job experience. Because her practical knowledge directly relates to the practical position she wants, Miller considered this her strongest point and wisely chose to present it last.

Miller closes her letter with an understated, but definite, request for an interview. In it, she not only asserts her willingness to be interviewed but also gives the date after which she will be available. Because people remember best what they read last, a strong conclusion is as essential here as it is in other writing situations. In a letter of application, the most effective strategy is to end with a request for an interview.

Persuasive Examples.   In order to support a thesis convincingly, examples should convey specific information, not just judgments. Saying "I am a good student who works hard at her studies" means very little. It is better to say, as Doris Miller does, "Throughout my academic career, I have maintained a 3.65 average and have been on the dean's list every quarter but one." A letter of application should show a prospective employer how your strengths and background correspond to the employer's needs, and specific examples can help such a reader reach the proper conclusions.

The following essay, by Norman Provizor, illustrates a more traditional academic use of the example pattern. Written for an

English composition class, it answers the question, "Is there too much violence on children's television?"

SATURDAY MORNING VIOLENCE

Introduction   For the past five years, television networks have come under increasing attack for the violent programs that fill their schedules. Psychologists and communications experts have formulated scales to measure the carnage that comes into American homes daily. Sociologists have discussed the possible effects of this situation on the viewing public. One area that is currently receiving attention is children's television. As even a

Thesis   cursory glance at Saturday morning cartoon shows reveals, children are being exposed to a steady diet of violence that rivals that of the prime-time shows their parents so eagerly watch.

Brief examples   Children's cartoons have traditionally contained much violence, and this situation is something we have learned to accept as normal. Consider how much a part of our landscape the following situations are. The coyote chases the roadrunner and finds himself standing in midair over a deep chasm. For a fraction of a second he looks pathetically at the audience; then he plunges to the ground. Elmer Fudd puts his shotgun into a tree where Bugs Bunny is hiding. Bugs bends the barrel so that, when Elmer pulls the trigger, the gun discharges into his face. A dog chases Woody Woodpecker into a sawmill and, unable to stop, slides into the whirling blade of a circular saw. As the scene ends, the two halves of the dog fall to the ground with a clatter.

Major example   Where these so-called traditional cartoons

depict violence as an isolated occurrence, newer
cartoons portray it as a normal condition of life.
The "Godzilla Super—Ninety Show" is a good example
of this. Every Saturday morning, Godzilla, a
prehistoric dinosaur who appears when called by his
human companions, battles monsters that seem to
appear everywhere. Every week the plot stays the
same; only the monsters change. And every week the
message to the young viewers is the same: "Only by
violent action can the problems of the world be
solved." For it is only when Godzilla burns, tears,
crushes, drowns, or stamps his adversaries to death
that the status quo can be reestablished. There is
never an attempt by the human characters to help
themselves or to find a rational explanation for
what is happening to them.

Major example   Even more shocking is the violence depicted in
"Challenge of the Superfriends," a ninety—minute
cartoon extravaganza that is, as its title suggests,
a weekly battle between the Superfriends (the forces
of good) and the Hall of Doom (the forces of evil). In
this series, violence and evil are ever present,
threatening to overwhelm goodness and mercy. Each
week the Hall of Doom destroys cities, blows up
planets, or somehow alters the conditions of our
world. In one episode Lex Luthor, Superman's arch
enemy, designs a ray that can bore to the center of
the earth and release its molten iron core. As the
ray penetrates the earth's crust, New York crumbles,
London shakes, and a tidal wave rushes toward Japan.
Of course the superheroes manage to set everything
right, but the precocious child viewers of the show
must know, even though it isn't shown, that many
people are killed when the buildings fall and the
tidal wave hits.

**Conclusion
(restatement of
thesis)**
Violence on Saturday morning children's television is the rule rather than the exception. There are few shows (other than those on public television) that attempt to go beyond the simplistic formulas that cartoons follow. As a result, our children are being shown that violence is superior to reason and that conflict and threats of violent death are acceptable conditions for existence. Perhaps the recently convened government commission to study violence will put an end to this situation, but until it does we parents will have to shudder every time our children sit down in front of the television for a Saturday morning of fun.

Points for Special Attention

Organization.   In his introduction, Norman Provizor establishes the context of his remarks: television networks have come under attack; psychologists, communications experts, and sociologists have studied violence on television. He then states his thesis that Saturday morning television exposes children to a high level of violence.

In the body of his essay, Provizor presents the examples that support his thesis. In the second paragraph, he begins with examples of what he calls traditional children's cartoons, those like "The Roadrunner," "Bugs Bunny," and "Woody Woodpecker" that, although violent, are restricted in scope. Provizor then gives examples of contemporary cartoons. In the third paragraph he uses the "Godzilla Super-Ninety Show" to illustrate his assertion that newer cartoons portray violence as a normal condition of life. The fourth paragraph presents "Challenge of the Superfriends" to exemplify the extent to which violence pervades children's programs.

In his conclusion, Provizor sums up the points he has made. He says that violence is the rule on Saturday mornings and that children are being shown that conflict and threats of violent death are acceptable conditions for existence. He ends his essay with an emphatic statement: parents will shudder every time their children watch Saturday morning television.

Enough Examples.   Certainly no single example, no matter how graphic, could adequately support the thesis of this essay. In order to establish that children's television is violent, Provizor has to use a number of examples. As a consequence, he presents three brief examples in the second paragraph and a more extensive example in each of the remaining body paragraphs.

Not only does Norman Provizor present several examples, but he is careful to ensure that they illustrate the full range of his subject. He draws from traditional cartoons as well as newer ones, and he presents the plots of these cartoons in enough detail to make them clear to his readers. He also makes sure that his examples are representative, that they are typical of Saturday morning cartoons. (As it happens, the "Godzilla Super-Ninety Show" and "Challenge of the Superfriends" were the top two shows when Provizor wrote his essay.)

Effective Examples.   All of the examples Provizor offers support his thesis. While developing five examples, he never loses sight of his main idea. Each paragraph in the body of his essay directly addresses one aspect of his thesis. His essay does not wander or get bogged down in needlessly long plot summaries or irrelevant digressions.

The selections that appear in this chapter all depend on exemplification to explain and clarify, to add interest, or to persuade. Some essays use a single extended example; others use a series of briefer illustrations.

The Ethics of Living Jim Crow
RICHARD WRIGHT

Richard Wright was a black writer whose work powerfully expresses what it was like for him to grow up black in America. The brief, informal essay which follows is an excerpt from Wright's autobiographical Black Boy, *first published in 1937. In this selection, Wright presents a single, emotionally moving example to support his implied thesis.*

My first lesson in how to live as a Negro came when I was quite small. We were living in Arkansas. Our house stood behind the railroad tracks. Its skimpy yard was paved with black cinders. Nothing green ever grew in that yard. The only touch of green we could see was far away, beyond the tracks, over where the white folks lived. But cinders were good enough for me and I never missed the green growing things. And anyhow cinders were fine weapons. You could always have a nice hot war with huge black cinders. All you had to do was crouch behind the brick pillars of a house with your hands full of gritty ammunition. And the first woolly black head you saw pop out from behind another row of pillars was your target. You tried your very best to knock it off. It was great fun. 1

I never fully realized the appalling disadvantages of a cinder environment till one day the gang to which I belonged found itself engaged in a war with the white boys who lived beyond the tracks. As usual we laid down our cinder barrage, thinking that this would wipe the white boys out. But they replied with a steady bombardment of broken bottles. We doubled our cinder barrage, but they hid behind trees, hedges, and the sloping embankments of their lawns. Having no such fortifications, we retreated to the brick pillars of our homes. During the retreat a broken milk bottle caught me behind the ear, opening a deep gash which bled profusely. The sight of blood pouring over my face completely demoralized our ranks. My fellow-combatants left me standing paralyzed in the center of the yard and scurried for their homes. A kind neighbor saw me and rushed me to a doctor, who took three stitches in my neck. 2

I sat brooding on my front steps, nursing my wound and waiting for my mother to come from work. I felt that a grave injustice had been done me. It was all right to throw cinders. The greatest harm a cinder could do was leave a bruise. But broken bottles were dangerous; they left you cut, bleeding, and helpless. 3

When night fell, my mother came from the white folks' kitchen.   4
I raced down the street to meet her. I could just feel in my bones
that she would understand. I knew she would tell me exactly what
to do next time. I grabbed her hand and babbled out the whole
story. She examined my wound, then slapped me.

"How come yuh didn't hide?" she asked me. "How come yuh   5
awways fightin'?"

I was outraged and bawled. Between sobs I told her that I didn't   6
have any trees or hedges to hide behind. There wasn't a thing I
could have used as a trench. And you couldn't throw very far when
you were hiding behind the brick pillars of a house. She grabbed
a barrel stave, dragged me home, stripped me naked, and beat me
till I had a fever of one hundred and two. She would smack my
rump with the stave, and, while the skin was still smarting, impart
to me gems of Jim Crow wisdom. I was never to throw cinders any
more. I was never to fight any more wars. I was never, never, under
any conditions, to fight *white* folks again. And they were absolutely
right in clouting me with the broken milk bottle. Didn't I know she
was working hard every day in the hot kitchens of the white folks
to make money to take care of me? When was I ever going to learn
to be a good boy? She couldn't be bothered with my fights. She
finished by telling me that I ought to be thankful to God as long as
I lived that they didn't kill me.

All that night I was delirious and could not sleep. Each time I   7
closed my eyes I saw monstrous white faces suspended from the
ceiling, leering at me.

From that time on, the charm of my cinder yard was gone. The   8
green trees, the trimmed hedges, the cropped lawns grew very
meaningful, became a symbol. Even today when I think of white
folks, the hard, sharp outlines of white houses surrounded by trees,
lawns, and hedges are present somewhere in the background of my
mind. Through the years they grew into an overreaching symbol
of fear.

COMPREHENSION

1. In what kind of area did Richard Wright live as a boy? What are the
   "appalling disadvantages of a cinder environment" that Wright refers to?

2. What does Wright mean when he says, "From that time on, the charm of
   my cinder yard was gone"?

3. What do the green trees and lawns of "the white folks" come to mean to
   Wright?

4. What is the "Jim Crow" wisdom that Wright hears from his mother?

PURPOSE AND AUDIENCE

1. Do you think Wright was addressing his essay to a white or black audience? What evidence led you to your conclusion?

2. Do you suppose Wright's purpose in writing this essay was to inform or to persuade? Why do you think so?

3. What is Wright's implied thesis?

STYLE AND STRUCTURE

1. The only time that Wright includes dialogue in his essay in when his mother speaks. What, if anything, does this add to his example? Do you think he should have used more dialogue? Why or why not?

2. Notice how many times Wright refers to the colors white, black, and green in his essay. What do you think is the reason for this repetition?

3. Wright uses convincing detail in this essay, but he does not present detailed physical descriptions of any of the people he mentions. Why do you think he chose not to do so?

4. What words and phrases does the author use to convey the passage of time?

5. Notice how the conclusion completes the essay's frame by referring back to the cinder yard mentioned at the beginning. What effect does this frame create? How does it help the reader understand the meaning of the essay?

6. In the longer chapter of which this is a part, Wright presents several other incidents that also teach him about Jim Crow behavior. Why did he choose to support his thesis with a few extended examples like this one instead of many shorter ones?

WRITING WORKSHOP

1. Write an essay about a time in your life when you learned a painful lesson. Use an extended example to support your thesis.

2. Write an essay about your own experiences with prejudice or discrimination. Use these experiences as examples to support your thesis.

The Peter Principle
LAWRENCE J. PETER AND RAYMOND HULL

*Lawrence J. Peter is a professor of education at the University of
Southern California, and Raymond Hull is a writer and dramatist.
Together they wrote* The Peter Principle, *a book that so dramatically
analyzed American organizations that its title has been absorbed into
our language. This selection, the first chapter of* The Peter Principle,
presents the book's thesis along with several supporting examples.

When I was a boy I was taught that the men upstairs knew what   1
they were doing. I was told, "Peter, the more you know, the further
you go." So I stayed in school until I graduated from college and
then went forth into the world clutching firmly these ideas and my
new teaching certificate. During the first year of teaching I was
upset to find that a number of teachers, school principals, super-
visors and superintendents appeared to be unaware of their professional responsibilities and incompetent in executing their duties.
For example my principal's main concerns were that all window
shades be at the same level, that classrooms should be quiet and
that no one step on or near the rose beds. The superintendent's
main concerns were that no minority group, no matter how fanatical,
should ever be offended and that all official forms be submitted on
time. The children's education appeared farthest from the admin-
istrator's mind.

At first I thought this was a special weakness of the school system   2
in which I taught so I applied for certification in another province.
I filled out the special forms, enclosed the required documents and
complied willingly with all the red tape. Several weeks later, back
came my application and all the documents!

No, there was nothing wrong with my credentials; the forms   3
were correctly filled out; an official departmental stamp showed
that they had been received in good order. But an accompanying
letter said, "The new regulations require that such forms cannot be
accepted by the Department of Education unless they have been
registered at the Post Office to ensure safe delivery. Will you please
remail the forms to the Department, making sure to register them
this time?"

I began to suspect that the local school system did not have a   4
monopoly on incompetence.

As I looked further afield, I saw that every organization contained   5
a number of persons who could not do their jobs.

A UNIVERSAL PHENOMENON

Occupational incompetence is everywhere. Have you noticed it? 6
Probably we all have noticed it.

We see indecisive politicians posing as resolute statesmen and 7
the "authoritative source" who blames his misinformation on
"situational imponderables." Limitless are the public servants who
are indolent and insolent; military commanders whose behavioral
timidity belies their dreadnought rhetoric, and governors whose
innate servility prevents their actually governing. In our sophistication, we virtually shrug aside the immoral cleric, corrupt judge,
incoherent attorney, author who cannot write and English teacher
who cannot spell. At universities we see proclamations authored
by administrators whose own office communications are hopelessly
muddled, and droning lectures from inaudible or incomprehensible
instructors.

Seeing incompetence at all levels of every hierarchy—political, 8
legal, educational and industrial—I hypothesized that the cause
was some inherent feature of the rules governing the placement of
employees. Thus began my serious study of the ways in which
employees move upward through a hierarchy, and of what happens
to them after promotion.

For my scientific data hundreds of case histories were collected. 9
Here are three typical examples.

Municipal Government File, Case No. 17 J. S. Minion* was a 10
maintenance foreman in the public works department of Excelsior
City. He was a favorite of the senior officials at City Hall. They all
praised his unfailing affability.

"I like Minion," said the superintendent of works. "He has good 11
judgment and is always pleasant and agreeable."

This behavior was appropriate for Minion's position: he was not 12
supposed to make policy, so he had no need to disagree with his
superiors.

The superintendent of works retired and Minion succeeded him. 13
Minion continued to agree with everyone. He passed to his foreman
every suggestion that came from above. The resulting conflicts in
policy, and the continual changing of plans, soon demoralized the
department. Complaints poured in from the Mayor and other
officials, from taxpayers and from the maintenance-workers' union.

Minion still says "Yes" to everyone, and carries messages briskly 14
back and forth between his superiors and his subordinates. Nom-

*Some names have been changed, in order to protect the guilty.

inally a superintendent, he actually does the work of a messenger.
The maintenance department regularly exceeds its budget, yet fails
to fulfill its program of work. In short, Minion, a competent foreman,
became an incompetent superintendent.

Service Industries File, Case No. 3   E. Tinker was exceptionally   15
zealous and intelligent as an apprentice at G. Reece Auto Repair
Inc., and soon rose to journeyman mechanic. In this job he showed
outstanding ability in diagnosing obscure faults, and endless patience in correcting them. He was promoted to foreman of the
repair shop.

But here his love of things mechanical and his perfectionism   16
become liabilities. He will undertake any job that he thinks looks
interesting, no matter how busy the shop may be. "We'll work it
in somehow," he says.

He will not let a job go until he is fully satisfied with it.   17

He meddles constantly. He is seldom to be found at his desk. He   18
is usually up to his elbows in a dismantled motor and while the
man who should be doing the work stands watching, other workmen
sit around waiting to be assigned new tasks. As a result the shop
is always overcrowded with work, always in a muddle, and delivery
times are often missed.

Tinker cannot understand that the average customer cares little   19
about perfection—he wants his car back on time! He cannot
understand that most of his men are less interested in motors than
in their pay checks. So Tinker cannot get on with his customers or
with his subordinates. He was a competent mechanic, but is now
an incompetent foreman.

Military File, Case No. 8   Consider the case of the late renowned   20
General A. Goodwin. His hearty, informal manner, his racy style
of speech, his scorn for petty regulations and his undoubted
personal bravery made him the idol of his men. He led them to
many well-deserved victories.

When Goodwin was promoted to field marshal he had to deal,   21
not with ordinary soldiers, but with politicians and allied gener-
alissimos.

He would not conform to the necessary protocol. He could not   22
turn his tongue to the conventional courtesies and flatteries. He
quarreled with all the dignitaries and took to lying for days at a
time, drunk and sulking, in his trailer. The conduct of the war
slipped out of his hands into those of his subordinates. He had
been promoted to a position that he was incompetent to fill.

AN IMPORTANT CLUE!

In time I saw that all such cases had a common feature. The 23
employee had been promoted from a position of competence to a
position of incompetence. I saw that, sooner or later, this could
happen to every employee in every hierarchy.

Hypothetical Case File, Case No. 1   Suppose you own a pill-rolling 24
factory, Perfect Pill Incorporated. Your foreman pill roller dies of
a perforated ulcer. You need a replacement. You naturally look
among your rank-and-file pill rollers.

Miss Oval, Mrs. Cylinder, Mr. Ellipse and Mr. Cube all show 25
various degrees of incompetence. They will naturally be ineligible
for promotion. You will choose—other things being equal—your
most competent pill roller, Mr. Sphere, and promote him to foreman.

Now suppose Mr. Sphere proves competent as foreman. Later, 26
when your general foreman, Legree, moves up to Works Manager,
Sphere will be eligible to take his place.

If, on the other hand, Sphere is an incompetent foreman, he will 27
get no more promotion. He has reached what I call his "level of
incompetence." He will stay there till the end of his career.

Some employees, like Ellipse and Cube, reach a level of incom- 28
petence in the lowest grade and are never promoted. Some, like
Sphere (assuming he is not a satisfactory foreman), reach it after
one promotion.

E. Tinker, the automobile repair-shop foreman, reached his level 29
of incompetence on the third stage of the hierarchy. General
Goodwin reached his level of incompetence at the very top of the
hierarchy.

So my analysis of hundreds of cases of occupational incompetence 30
led me on to formulate *The Peter Principle*:

In a Hierarchy Every Employee Tends
to Rise to His Level of Incompetence

A NEW SCIENCE!

Having formulated the Principle, I discovered that I had inadver- 31
tently founded a new science, hierarchiology, the study of hierarchies.

The term "hierarchy" was originally used to describe the system 32
of church government by priests graded into ranks. The contemporary meaning includes any organization whose members or
employees are arranged in order of rank, grade or class.

Hierarchiology, although a relatively recent discipline, appears   33
to have great applicability to the fields of public and private
administration.

THIS MEANS YOU!

My Principle is the key to an understanding of all hierarchal   34
systems, and therefore to an understanding of the whole structure
of civilization. A few eccentrics try to avoid getting involved with
hierarchies, but everyone in business, industry, trade-unionism,
politics, government, the armed forces, religion and education is
so involved. All of them are controlled by the Peter Principle.

Many of them, to be sure, may win a promotion or two, moving   35
from one level of competence to a higher level of competence. But
competence in that new position qualifies them for still another
promotion. For each individual, for *you*, for *me*, the final promotion
is from a level of competence to a level of incompetence.*

So, given enough time—and assuming the existence of enough   36
ranks in the hierarchy—each employee rises to, and remains at, his
level of incompetence. Peter's Corollary states:

In time, every post tends to be occupied by an employee who is   37
incompetent to carry out its duties.

WHO TURNS THE WHEELS?

You will rarely find, of course, a system in which *every* employee   38
has reached his level of incompetence. In most instances, something
is being done to further the ostensible purposes for which the
hierarchy exists.

Work is accomplished by those employees who have not yet   39
reached their level of incompetence.

COMPREHENSION

1. What things disillusioned Lawrence Peter during his first year of teaching?

2. What did Peter find out about organizations?

3. What is the Peter Principle? What happens when an employee reaches his "level of incompetence"?

*The phenomena of "percussive sublimation" (commonly referred to as "being kicked upstairs") and of "the lateral arabesque" are not, as the casual observer might think, exceptions to the Principle. They are only pseudo-promotions. . . .

4. What does Peter mean by *hierarchiology?* How did it lead him to the Peter Principle?

5. If the Peter Principle operates in hierarchies, who does the work?

PURPOSE AND AUDIENCE

1. Is this essay aimed at a general or a specialized audience? What led you to your conclusion?

2. What is Lawrence Peter's thesis?

3. The author places his thesis after the examples. Why does he wait so long to state it?

4. Does Peter give any indication of the purpose and occasion of this essay? If so, where?

STYLE AND STRUCTURE

1. Why does the author begin the essay with an example? Why does he present a series of brief examples before introducing the "typical case histories"?

2. Why does Peter says he collected hundreds of case histories for data? Why are the three case histories analyzed here typical?

3. Do you find the organization of this essay satisfactory? How else could the points be arranged?

4. In many places, Peter seems to exaggerate. For example, he says, "My Principle is the key ... to an understanding of the whole structure of civilization." Why does he do this? What is gained or lost by this tactic?

WRITING WORKSHOP

1. Does Lawrence Peter overstate his case? Write a letter to him in the form of an example essay pointing out the weaknesses of his position.

2. Study a school, business, or organization with which you are familiar. Write an example essay showing how the Peter Principle applies.

3. Do you know someone who has progressed to the highest level of his or her incompetence? Write an example essay showing how the Peter Principle applies.

Truth and Consequences
NORA EPHRON

Nora Ephron is a journalist who has worked for the New York Post,
New York *magazine, and* Esquire. *She is also the author of* Crazy Salad
and Scribble, Scribble, *two collections of essays about contemporary
society. The following selection, from* Crazy Salad, *makes its point
through three well-chosen examples, each presented in narrative form.*

I read something in a reporting piece years ago that made a 1
profound impression on me. The way I remember the incident
(which probably has almost nothing to do with what actually
happened) is this: a group of pathetically naïve out-of-towners are
in New York for a week and want very much to go to Coney Island.
They go to Times Square to take the subway, but instead of taking
the train to Brooklyn, they take an uptown train to the Bronx. And
what knocked me out about that incident was that the reporter
involved had been cool enough and detached enough and professional enough and (I could not help thinking) cruel enough to let
this hopeless group take the wrong train. I could never have done
it. And when I read the article, I was disturbed and sorry that I
could not; the story is a whole lot better when they take the wrong
train.

When I first read that, I was a newspaper reporter, and I still had 2
some illusions about objectivity—and certainly about that thing
that has come to be known as participatory journalism; I believed
that reporters had no business getting really involved in what they
were writing about. Which did not seem to me to be a problem at
the time. A good part of the reason I became a newspaper reporter
was that I was much too cynical and detached to become involved
in anything; I was temperamentally suited to be a witness to events.
Or so I told myself.

Years pass, and it is 1972 and I am at the Democratic Convention 3
in Miami attending a rump, half-secret meeting: a group of Betty
Friedan's followers are trying to organize a drive to make Shirley
Chisholm Vice-President. Friedan is not here, but Jacqui Ceballos,
a leader in N.O.W., *is,* and it is instantly apparent to the journalists
in the room that she does not know what she is talking about. It is
Monday afternoon and she is telling the group of partisans assembled in this dingy hotel room that petitions supporting Chisholm's

Vice-Presidential candidacy must be in at the National Committee by Tuesday afternoon. But the President won't be nominated until Wednesday night; clearly the Vice-Presidential petitions do not have to be filed until the next day. I am supposed to be a reporter here and let things happen. I am supposed to let them take the wrong train. But I can't, and my hand is up, and I am saying that they must be wrong, they must have gotten the wrong information, there's no need to rush the petitions, they can't be due until Thursday. Afterward, I walk out onto Collins Avenue with a fellow journalist/feminist who has managed to keep her mouth shut. "I guess I got a little carried away in there," I say guiltily. "I guess you did," she replies. (The next night, at the convention debate on abortion, there are women reporters so passionately involved in the issue that they are lobbying the delegates. I feel slightly less guilty. But not much.)

To give you another example, a book comes in for review. I am on the list now, The Woman List, and the books come in all the time. Novels by women. Nonfiction books about women and the women's movement. The apparently endless number of movement-oriented and movement-inspired anthologies on feminism; the even more endless number of anthologies on the role of the family or the future of the family or the decline of the family. I take up a book, a book I think might make a column. It is *Women and Madness*, by Phyllis Chesler. I agree with the book politically. What Chesler is saying is that the psychological profession has always applied a double standard when dealing with women; that psychological definitions of madness have been dictated by what men believe women's role ought to be; and this is wrong. Right on, Phyllis. But here is the book: it is badly written and self-indulgent, and the research seems to me to be full of holes. If I say this, though, I will hurt the book politically, provide a way for people who want to dismiss Chesler's conclusions to ignore them entirely. On the other hand, if I fail to say that there are problems with the book, I'm applying a double standard of my own, treating works that are important to the movement differently from others: babying them, tending to gloss over their faults, gentling the author as if she and her book were somehow incapable of withstanding a single carping clause. *Her heart is in the right place; why knock her when there are so many truly evil books around?* This is what is known in the women's movement as sisterhood, and it is good politics, I suppose, but it doesn't make for good criticism. Or honesty. Or the truth. (Furthermore, it is every bit as condescending as the sort of criticism men apply to books about women these days—that unconsciously patronizing tone that treats books by and about women as some sort of sub-genre of literature, outside the mainstream, not quite relevant, interesting really, how-these-women-do-go-on-and-we - really - must - try - to - understand - what - they - are - getting - at - what-ever-it-is.)

I will tell you one more story to the point—though this one is 5 not about me. A year and a half ago, some women from the Los Angeles Self-Help Clinic came to New York to demonstrate do-it-yourself gynecology and performed an abortion onstage using a controversial device called the Karman cannula. Subsequently, the woman on whom the abortion had been performed developed a serious infection and had to go into the hospital for a D and C.[1] One of the reporters covering the story, a feminist, found out about the infection, but she decided not to make the fact public, because she thought that to do so might hurt the self-help movement. When I heard about it, I was appalled; I was more appalled when I realized that I understood why she had done it.

But I cannot excuse that kind of self-censorship, either in that 6 reporter or in myself. I think that many of us in this awkward position worry too much about what the movement will think and how what we write will affect the movement. In fact, the movement is nothing more than an amorphous blob of individual women and groups, most of whom disagree with each other. In fact, no amount of criticism of the movement will stop its forward momentum. In fact, I am intelligent enough to know that nothing I write really matters in any significant way to any of it. And knowing all this, I worry. I am a writer. I am a feminist. When I manage, from time to time, to overcome my political leanings and get at the truth, I feel a little better. And then I worry some more.

COMPREHENSION

1. What point is Nora Ephron making with the story about the group who took the wrong subway?

2. How does Ephron feel about reporters getting personally involved in their subjects? Where in her essay does she give you this information?

3. Why did Ephron become a reporter?

4. What was Ephron's criticism of Jacqui Ceballos during the Democratic Convention?

[1] Dilation and curettage: enlargement of the cervical canal and scraping of the uterine wall.

5. What is Ephron's opinion of *Women and Madness*? How does her assessment of the book create a conflict for her?

6. Why was Ephron "appalled" when she realized why another reporter had suppressed facts about the demonstration by the women from the Self-Help Clinic?

PURPOSE AND AUDIENCE

1. Why does Ephron state her thesis at the end of the essay? Would it have been better placed at the beginning? Why or why not?

2. Is Ephron trying to present herself as a reporter, a feminist, or an observer? Why does she use phrases like *right on* and *what knocked me out*?

3. At whom is Ephron aiming her essay—feminists, reporters, women, or a general audience? Explain.

STYLE AND STRUCTURE

1. How does the story of the people taking the wrong subway draw the other examples together? By what means does Ephron carry the theme of this example through the entire essay?

2. Why does Ephron make a point of saying the third example "is not about me"?

3. How does Ephron create smooth transitions from one example to another? Are three examples enough to support her thesis? Why or why not?

4. Look carefully at the verb tenses Ephron uses in her essay. How can you account for two of the examples being in the present tense and one in the past tense?

5. Paragraph 4 features a parenthetical digression. Why does Ephron include this sentence in parentheses in her essay? How can you explain the unconventional structure of the sentence?

6. Why does Ephron end her essay with "and then I worry some more"?

WRITING WORKSHOP

1. Write an example essay about a conflict you have had between your loyalty to a group and your loyalty to your own ideals.

2. Write an example essay in which you discuss how your desire to succeed conflicts with your desire to stick strictly to the truth, or to use common sense, or to help someone.

3. Should a reporter ever get involved in what he or she is writing about? If so, when? Write an example essay presenting your position.

On Being the Right Size
J. B. S. HALDANE

J. B. S. Haldane was a scientist best known for his work in genetics. In this essay, he focuses on scale to illustrate how science can change the way we look at things. He uses a number of arresting examples to support his thesis. This essay first appeared in Haldane's 1928 book, Possible Worlds.

The most obvious differences between different animals are differ- 1
ences of size, but for some reason the zoologists have paid singularly little attention to them. In a large textbook of zoology before me I find no indication that the eagle is larger than the sparrow, or the hippopotamus bigger than the hare, though some gruding admissions are made in the case of the mouse and the whale. But yet it is easy to show that a hare could not be as large as a hippopotamus, or a whale as small as a herring. For every type of animal there is a most convenient size, and a large change in size inevitably carries with it a change of form.

Let us take the most obvious of possible cases, and consider a 2
giant man sixty feet high—about the height of Giant Pope and Giant Pagan in the illustrated *Pilgrim's Progress* of my childhood. These monsters were not only ten times as high as Christian, but ten times as wide and ten times as thick, so that their total weight was a thousand times his, or about eighty to ninety tons. Unfortunately the cross sections of their bones were only a hundred times those of Christian, so that every square inch of giant bone had to support ten times the weight borne by a square inch of human bone. As the human thigh-bone breaks under about ten times the human weight, Pope and Pagan would have broken their thighs every time they took a step. This was doubtless why they were sitting down in the picture I remember. But it lessens one's respect for Christian and Jack the Giant Killer.

To turn to zoology, suppose that a gazelle, a graceful little 3
creature with long thin legs, is to become large; it will break its bones unless it does one of two things. It may make its legs short and thick, like the rhinoceros, so that every pound of weight has still about the same area of bone to support it. Or it can compress its body and stretch out its legs obliquely to gain stability, like the giraffe. I mention these two beasts because they happen to belong to the same order as the gazelle, and both are quite successful mechanically, being remarkably fast runners.

Gravity, a mere nuisance to Christian, was a terror to Pope,   4
Pagan, and Despair. To the mouse and any smaller animal it
presents practically no dangers. You can drop a mouse down a
thousand-yard mine shaft; and, on arriving at the bottom, it gets a
slight shock and walks away, provided that the ground is fairly soft.
A rat is killed, a man is broken, a horse splashes. For the resistance
presented to movement by the air is proportional to the surface of
the moving object. Divide an animal's length, breadth, and height
each by ten; its weight is reduced to a thousandth, but its surface
only to a hundredth. So the resistance to falling in the case of the
small animal is relatively ten times greater than the driving force.

An insect, therefore, is not afraid of gravity; it can fall without   5
danger, and can cling to the ceiling with remarkably little trouble.
It can go in for elegant and fantastic forms of support like that of
the daddy-longlegs. But there is a force which is as formidable to
an insect as gravitation to a mammal. This is surface tension. A man
coming out of a bath carries with him a film of water of about one-
fiftieth of an inch in thickness. This weighs roughly a pound. A wet
mouse has to carry about its own weight of water. A wet fly has to
lift many times its own weight and, as everyone knows, a fly once
wetted by water or any other liquid is in a very serious position
indeed. An insect going for a drink is in as great danger as a man
leaning out over a precipice in search of food. If it once falls into
the grip of the surface tension of the water—that is to say, gets
wet—it is likely to remain so until it drowns. A few insects, such
as water-beetles, contrive to be unwettable; the majority keep well
away from their drink by means of a long proboscis.

Of course tall land animals have other difficulties. They have to   6
pump their blood to greater heights than a man, and, therefore,
require a larger blood pressure and tougher blood-vessels. A great
many men die from burst arteries, especially in the brain, and this
danger is presumably still greater for an elephant or a giraffe. But
animals of all kinds find difficulties in size for the following reason.
A typical small animal, say a microscopic worm or rotifer, has a
smooth skin through which all the oxygen it requires can soak in,
a straight gut with sufficient surface to absorb its food, and a single
kidney. Increase its dimensions tenfold in every direction, and its
weight is increased a thousand times, so that if it is to use its
muscles as efficiently as its miniature counterpart, it will need a
thousand times as much food and oxygen per day and will excrete
a thousand times as much of waste products.

Now if its shape is unaltered its surface will be increased only   7
a hundredfold, and ten times as much oxygen must enter per minute

through each square millimetre of skin, ten times as much food through each square millimetre of intestine. When a limit is reached to their absorptive powers their surface has to be increased by some special device. For example, a part of the skin may be drawn out into tufts to make gills or pushed in to make lungs, thus increasing the oxygen-absorbing surface in proportion to the animal's bulk. A man, for example, has a hundred square yards of lung. Similarly, the gut, instead of being smooth and straight, becomes coiled and develops a velvety surface, and other organs increase in complication. The higher animals are not larger than the lower because they are more complicated. They are more complicated because they are larger. Just the same is true of plants. The simplest plants, such as the green algae growing in stagnant water or on the bark of trees, are mere round cells. The higher plants increase their surface by putting out leaves and roots. Comparative anatomy is largely the story of the struggle to increase surface in proportion to volume.

Some of the methods of increasing the surface are useful up to a point, but not capable of a very wide adaptation. For example, while vertebrates carry the oxygen from the gills or lungs all over the body in the blood, insects take air directly to every part of their body by tiny blind tubes called tracheae which open to the surface at many different points. Now, although by their breathing movements they can renew the air in the outer part of the tracheal system, the oxygen has to penetrate the finer branches by means of diffusion. Gases can diffuse easily through very small distances, not many times larger than the average length travelled by a gas molecule between collisions with other molecules. But when such vast journeys—from the point of view of a molecule—as a quarter of an inch have to be made, the process becomes slow. So the portions of an insect's body more than a quarter of an inch from the air would always be short of oxygen. In consequence hardly any insects are much more than half an inch thick. Land crabs are built on the same general plan as insects, but are much clumsier. Yet like ourselves they carry oxygen around in their blood, and are therefore able to grow far larger than any insects. If the insects had hit on a plan for driving air through their tissues instead of letting it soak in, they might well have become as large as lobsters, though other considerations would have prevented them from becoming as large as man.

Exactly the same difficulties attach to flying. It is an elementary principle of aeronautics that the minimum speed needed to keep an aeroplane of a given shape in the air varies as the square root of its length. If its linear dimensions are increased four times, it must fly twice as fast. Now the power needed for the minimum speed increases more rapidly than the weight of the machine. So the larger aeroplane, which weighs sixty-four times as much as the smaller, needs one hundred and twenty-eight times its horsepower to keep up. Applying the same principle to the birds, we find that the limit to their size is soon reached. An angel whose muscles developed no more power weight for weight than those of an eagle or a pigeon would require a breast projecting for about four feet to house the muscles engaged in working its wings, while to econo-mize in weight, its legs would have to be reduced to mere stilts. Actually a large bird such as an eagle or kite does not keep in the air mainly by moving its wings. It is generally to be seen soaring, that is to say balanced on a rising column of air. And even soaring becomes more and more difficult with increasing size. Were this not the case eagles might be as large as tigers and as formidable to man as hostile aeroplanes.

But it is time that we pass to some of the advantages of size. One [10] of the most obvious is that it enables one to keep warm. All warm-blooded animals at rest lose the same amount of heat from a unit area of skin, for which purpose they need a food-supply proportional to their surface and not to their weight. Five thousand mice weigh as much as a man. Their combined surface and food or oxygen consumption are about seventeen times a man's. In fact a mouse eats about one quarter its own weight of food every day, which is mainly used in keeping it warm. For the same reason small animals cannot live in cold countries. In the arctic regions there are no reptiles or amphibians, and no small mammals. The smallest mammal in Spitzbergen is the fox. The small birds fly away in winter, while the insects die, though their eggs can survive six months or more of frost. The most successful mammals are bears, seals, and walruses.

Similarly, the eye is a rather inefficient organ until it reaches a [11] large size. The back of the human eye on which an image of the outside world is thrown, and which corresponds to the film of a camera, is composed of a mosaic of "rods and cones" whose diameter is little more than a length of an average light wave. Each eye has about a half a million, and for two objects to be distinguish-able their images must fall on separate rods or cones. It is obvious that with fewer but larger rods and cones we should see less distinctly. If they were twice as broad two points would have to be twice as far apart before we could distinguish them at a given distance. But if their size were diminished and their number increased we should see no better. For it is impossible to form a definite image smaller than a wave-length of light. Hence a mouse's eye is not a small-scale model of a human eye. Its rods and cones are not much smaller than ours, and therefore there are far fewer of them. A mouse could not distinguish one human face from another six feet away. In order that they should be of any use at all the eyes of small animals have to be much larger in proportion to their bodies than our own. Large animals on the other hand only require relatively small eyes, and those of the whale and elephant are little larger than our own.

For rather more recondite reasons the same general principle   12
holds true of the brain. If we compare the brain-weights of a set of very similar animals such as the cat, cheetah, leopard, and tiger, we find that as we quadruple the body-weight the brain-weight is only doubled. The larger animal with proportionately larger bones can economize on brain, eyes, and certain other organs.

Such are a very few of the considerations which show that for   13
every type of animal there is an optimum size. Yet although Galileo demonstrated the contrary more than three hundred years ago, people still believe that if a flea were as large as a man it could jump a thousand feet into the air. As a matter of fact the height to which an animal can jump is more nearly independent of its size than proportional to it. A flea can jump about two feet, a man about five. To jump a given height, if we neglect the resistance of air, requires an expenditure of energy proportional to the jumper's weight. But if the jumping muscles form a constant fraction of the animal's body, the energy developed per ounce of muscle is independent of the size, provided it can be developed quickly enough in the small animal. As a matter of fact an insect's muscles, although they can contract more quickly than our own, appear to be less efficient; as otherwise a flea or grasshopper could rise six feet into the air.

COMPREHENSION

1. According to Haldane, what does a large change in size inevitably result in for every animal?

2. What kind of changes must occur in an animal's form as it becomes larger? What happens if these changes don't occur?

3. What does Haldane mean when he says, "Gravity, a mere nuisance to Christian, was a terror to Pope, Pagan, and Despair"?

4. What difficulties do tall animals have that short animals don't?

5. What advantages do tall animals have that short animals don't?

PURPOSE AND AUDIENCE

1. This essay is aimed at a nontechnical audience. What assumptions does Haldane make about them? What concessions has he made to his audience?

2. Why does Haldane explicitly state his thesis?

STYLE AND STRUCTURE

1. How does Haldane group his examples?

2. Does the order of his examples affect Haldane's argument? Why or why not?

3. Why does Haldane mention the Giant Pope, the Giant Pagan, and the normal sized Christian from the illustrated version of *Pilgrim's Progress*? Would the essay have been better without these references? Explain.

4. How effective is Haldane's conclusion? Why does he end with another example?

WRITING WORKSHOP

1. Write an essay in which you discuss the advantages or disadvantages of being short or tall. Use several examples to support your thesis.

2. Choose a science-fiction movie you have seen in which a normal-sized animal suddenly grew into a monster. Using Haldane's discussion as reference material (with a footnote), write an essay in which you establish the impossibility of the giant creature.

3. Write an essay which has this thesis: "Although giants stride through the pages of countless fairy tales, in real life they would probably be sickly creatures." If you want more information than Haldane provides, go to the library and read the section on giants in Leslie Fiedler's *Freaks*. (Again, footnote this source in your essay.)

5

Process

WHAT IS PROCESS?

A process essay explains the steps or stages in doing something. As we mentioned in chapter 2, process is closely related to narrative since both present events in chronological order. Unlike a narrative that tells a story, however, a process essay details a particular series of events that could be duplicated with the same outcome. Because these events form a sequence, often with a fixed order, clarity is extremely important in process writing. Whether your reader is actually to perform the process or simply to understand how it takes place, your paper must make clear the exact order of the individual steps as well as their relationships to each other and to the process as a whole. Therefore, not only must there be clear, logical transitions between the steps in a process, but the steps must be presented in *strict* chronological order—that is, in the order of performance. Unlike narratives, then, process essays do not use flashbacks or otherwise experiment with time order.

Instructions and Process Explanations

The two basic kinds of process writing fulfill different purposes: instructions tell the reader how to do something, and explanations tell the reader how something is or was done. Instructions have many practical uses. A recipe, a handout about using your library's card catalog, or an operating manual for your car or your stereo are all written in the form of instructions. Instructions usually use the present tense and, like commands, the imperative mood: "Disconnect the system, and check the . . ." Occasionally, instructions are written in the future tense and the second person (*you*), speaking directly to readers about their anticipated actions: "Next, you will

135

turn the knob and adjust the . . ." Thus, both tense and mood suit the purpose of instructions, enabling the readers to follow along and perform the process themselves.

On the other hand, the purpose of a process explanation is to help the reader understand the steps of a procedure although they may not duplicate that process themselves. Thus, explanation essays can examine anything from how the first heart transplant was performed to how Michelangelo went about painting the ceiling of the Sistine Chapel. A process explanation may employ the first person (*I, we*) or the third (*he, she, it, they*), the past tense or the present. Since its readers need to understand, not perform, the process, the explanation does not use the second person (*you*) or the imperative mood characteristic of instructions. The style of a process explanation will vary with the writer's purpose and the regularity with which the process is or was performed. The chart below suggests some of the options available to you.

	First Person	*Third Person*
Present	"After I pin the pattern to the fabric, I cut it out with a sharp pair of scissors." (habitual process performed by the writer)	"After the photographer places the chemicals in the tray . . ." (habitual process performed by someone other than the writer)
Past	"After I pinned the pattern to the fabric . . ." (process performed in the past by the writer)	"When the mixture was cool, he added . . ." (process performed in the past by someone other than the writer)

Uses of Process Essays

Both instructions and process explanations are used in academic writing, and either can occur as the structural pattern for a relatively small part of a longer paper or for an entire piece of writing. For example, in a biology term paper on genetic engineering, you might devote a short section to an explanation of the process of amniocentesis; in an editorial on the negative side of fraternity life, you might decide to summarize briefly the process of pledging. On the other hand, an entire paper can be organized around a process pattern. In a political science paper you might fully re-create the course of an important legislative or judicial decision; in an English essay, you might trace the developmental steps through which a fictional character reached new insight; on a finance midterm, you might review the procedure for approving a commercial loan.

Process writing sometimes is used to persuade and at other times is used simply to present information. Thus, if its purpose is persuasive, a process paper may have a strong thesis like "Applying for public assistance is a needlessly complex process that discourages many potential recipients" or "The process of slaughtering baby seals is inhumane and sadistic." An informative process essay, on the other hand, may simply have a unifying idea like "Making lasagne consists of five basic steps" or "An appendectomy is a relatively routine surgical procedure."

STRUCTURING A PROCESS ESSAY

Like most other essays, a full-length process essay usually consists of three main sections. The introduction names the process and indicates why, and under what circumstances, it is performed. This section may also include information about materials or preliminary preparations. It may view the process as a whole, perhaps even listing its major stages. If the paper has a thesis, it too is stated in the introduction. Many process essays, however, have at their core nothing more debatable than "Typing your own blood is an easy procedure." Still, every process essay should have a clear unifying idea that gives readers a sense of what the process is and why it is performed. This unifying idea organizes the paper so it holds the readers' interest more effectively than an essay without a clear purpose.

To develop the thesis or the unifying idea, each paragraph in the body of the essay treats one major stage of the procedure. Each stage may group several steps, depending on the nature and complexity of the process. These steps are presented in chronological order, interrupted only for essential definitions and advice. Every step must be included and must appear in its proper place. Throughout the body of a process essay, transitional words and phrases are necessary so that each step, each stage, and each paragraph lead logically to the next. Transitions like *after this, next, then,* and *when you have finished* establish sequential and chronological relationships that help the reader follow the process. Particular words, however, should not be repeated so often that they become boring.

Finally, if the paper has a thesis, the conclusion may restate it. Otherwise, the conclusion may briefly review the procedure's major stages. Such an ending is especially useful if the paper has outlined a technical process which may seem complicated to the lay reader or if the procedure has been very long or complex. Whether or not the conclusion reviews the stages for the reader, it always summarizes the results of the process and explains their significance.

Designing a thorough, coherent process essay is not easy. It requires that you have a clear purpose before you begin and that you constantly consider your reader's needs. When necessary, you must explain the reasons for performing the steps, describe unfamiliar materials or equipment, define uncommon terms, and warn the reader about possible snags during the process. Sometimes you may even need to include illustrations. Besides complete information, your reader needs a clear and consistent discussion without ambiguities or surprising shifts. Thus, you should avoid unnecessary changes in tense, person, voice, and mood. Similarly, you should include appropriate articles (*a, an,* and *the*) so that your discussion moves smoothly like an essay, not abruptly like a cookbook. Careful attention to your essay's consistency as well as its overall structure will ensure that your reader understands your process explanations and instructions.

Let's suppose that you intend to use an extended explanation of a process as the pattern of development for a literature paper. You plan to follow a character from one significant event to another in order to show how he reaches an important turning point in his life. After brainstorming, you formulate your thesis statement: "In *The Red Badge of Courage,* Stephen Crane develops the theme of initiation by having the main character, Henry Fleming, progress through a series of stages which bring him to manhood." You then plan your essay, an extended account of the process by which Henry Fleming becomes a man, and prepare this outline:

¶1   Introduction—including thesis and outline of novel's setting and conflict.

¶2   First stage in process—uncertainty: Henry is dazed, confused, and naive; he knows little of war firsthand and uneasily awaits his first battle.

¶3   Second stage in process—fear: Henry feels fear and briefly considers desertion when he sees a dead soldier. He worries about his performance under fire.

¶4   Third stage in process—panic leading to guilt: Henry flees from battle. Later, alone in the forest, he feels a false peace, followed by remorse.

¶5   Fourth stage in process—longing for a wound: When the

other soldiers talk about their wounds, Henry's guilt increases. He longs for a wound to absolve his guilt.

¶6   Fifth stage in process—return to his regiment: By claiming he's been wounded by a cannonball, Henry's pride in himself is restored. He considers himself a "man of experience."

¶7   Sixth and final stage in process—challenge and triumph: Henry is tested and shows courage; he feels camaraderie with his fellow soldiers. "He felt a quiet manhood. . . . He was a man."

¶8   Conclusion—summary of stages and restatement of thesis.

This essay, when completed, will not be a mere plot summary or a critical book review; rather, it will be a persuasive essay that uses an account of a process to support its thesis. Because it is organized as a process explanation, the paper will do more than narrate the events in Henry Fleming's life; instead, it will consider the significance of each stage in Henry's development and assess the relationship of each stage to the others.

The following student essays, Scott Blackman's set of instructions for typing your own blood and S. Scott Wisneski's explanation of the process of orienteering, illustrate the two types of process essays.

TYPING YOUR OWN BLOOD

Introduction   Typing your own blood is often used as an
                                  introductory laboratory exercise. Even if you do not
                                  wish to learn your blood type, the exercise is useful
Unifying   because it familiarizes you with some simple
idea   laboratory techniques, illustrates the use of basic
                                  equipment, and prepares you to follow the stages of
                                  an orderly scientific procedure.

Materials   In order to type your own blood, you need the
                                  following equipment: alcohol—soaked cotton balls; a
                                  sterile lancet; a small test tube containing 1 ml. of
                                  saline solution; anti—A, anti—B, and anti—Rh serums
                                  with individual eye droppers; two microscope
                                  slides; a grease pencil; a Pasteur pipette; three
                                  applicator sticks; and a warm fluorescent light or
                                  other low—heat source.

First stage of process   With the grease pencil, label one slide Rh, and place this slide under the low—heat source. Divide your cool slide into two equal portions, labeling one side A and the other B. Apply one drop of anti—A serum to slide A, one drop of anti—B to slide B, and one drop of anti—Rh to the warm Rh slide.

Second stage of process   Use an alcohol—soaked cotton ball to swab your middle or ring finger, and allow the excess alcohol to evaporate. After opening the sterile lancet, prick the sterile finger once, approximately one—quarter inch beyond the end of the fingernail. Now, collect several drops of blood in the test tube containing the saline solution, and mix the solution. In the meantime, hold another sterile cotton ball over the cut to allow the blood to clot.

Third stage of process   Next, using the Pasteur pipette, transfer one drop of the saline solution containing the blood to each of the anti—A, anti—B, and anti—Rh serums, using a separate applicator stick to mix each. After two or three minutes, clumping should have appeared in one or all of the areas. A—clumping denotes A—type blood, B—clumping indicates B—type blood, A— and B—clumping signifies AB blood, and no clumping denotes O blood. Rh—clumping means that your blood is Rh positive; the absence of Rh—clumping indicates that you have Rh—negative blood.

Conclusion   By following the simple steps outlined above, you will learn much that will be of practical value in your future scientific explorations. As an added bonus, you will also learn your blood type.

Points for Special Attention

Structure.   Scott Blackman's instructions are so clear that they would make sense without the introductory and concluding paragraphs. Although the paper would then lack a unifying idea, it would still be a good example of process writing—a chronological presentation of a set of steps to be performed, preceded by a precise list of necessary materials. The introduction and conclusion, however, introduce and reinforce the reasons why the process is being carried out.

Purpose and Style. This set of instructions, written by Blackman for an introductory course in animal biology, has two purposes. It serves as a review exercise for the student author, and it provides other students with all the information they need to duplicate the process. Because it presents instructions rather than an extended explanation of a process, it is written in the second person and in the present tense, with the verbs in the form of commands. These commands, however, are not choppy or abrupt because the instructions include smooth transitions as well as appropriate articles and pronouns.

In contrast to "Typing Your Own Blood," the next essay is a process explanation.

ORIENTEERING

Introduction   Orienteering is like a treasure hunt. It is a
competitive race that involves navigating cross
country over unfamiliar terrain with a map and
compass in order to locate markers. The object of the
sport is to find as many markers as possible in the
shortest period of time, but outstanding physical
ability is not necessarily the determining factor in
winning. Those who are not strong or athletic may
still do well. The race does require speed,
accuracy, and mental decisiveness, and I admit that
these requirements intimidated me before I tried it.

Thesis   But despite my initial reluctance to try
orienteering, I now realize that it's a terrific way
to combine physical and mental exercise with fun.

Preparation for   The first time I tried orienteering, I needed
process   some basic education. As a competitor, I learned the
proper way to use a compass and map to help me find my

way through an unfamiliar area. I was pleased to find that my previous experience in hiking and hunting helped me at this stage, as it did during the race itself. Once I had my training, I was ready to compete.

First stage of process

Each time I begin the now—familiar process, I am first given a map, a compass, and a red pencil. (I bring a watch and a plastic bag in which to store the map.) Next, I consult a master map which shows the locations of the markers. Like the other players, I copy these locations onto my map with the red pencil as quickly as possible because by this time we are already being timed.

Second stage of process

Then, the race begins. All around me, the other competitors plan the easiest and quickest route to each point, being careful not to pick a route which will tire them out halfway through the race. I try to do the same. As I follow my route from marker to marker, I make sure to record the letter written on each one to prove I have reached that spot. The race ends when we all return to the starting point.

Third stage of process

The winner is decided by a group of judges, with the player who has successfully navigated to all markers in the shortest time declared the event's winner. Sometimes, there may be team scores, and the team with the lowest combined time wins. Now that I have been involved in orienteering for two years, I've been on a few of those winning teams.

Conclusion (restatement of thesis)

Orienteering has developed slowly in this country, but it is gaining popularity. And I found that once the basics of the sport are examined, it's best learned by doing. I tried it; I enjoyed it; and now I'm addicted to it. I've also introduced many of my friends to orienteering, and it's turned out to be one of the most enjoyable activities I've ever tried.

Points for Special Attention

Structure.   Although S. Scott Wisneski's paper, written for an English composition course, is an informal discussion of a process rather than a complex explanation, it nevertheless begins conventionally by listing necessary materials, naming and defining the process, and stating the thesis. The second paragraph outlines further preparation for the process: learning some general principles of orienteering and training with the necessary tools. Subsequent paragraphs present the stages in the process itself. The last paragraph sums up and restates the thesis.

Purpose and Style.   In his essay, Wisneski is trying to persuade his readers to try orienteering. As a consequence, he presents all the steps in the process so they seem simple and enjoyable. If he had written instructions rather than an explanation, the author would have given more specific detail and broken each stage into discrete steps so that his readers could duplicate the process themselves.

Throughout the paper, words and phrases like "first," "next," "by this time," "then," and "as I follow my route" help the reader to understand the steps in the process without difficulty. Finally, Wisneski uses the first person and present tense to describe the most important stages of a process he performs often.

In each of the essays that follow, process is the dominant pattern of development. The purposes of these essays, however, vary considerably. In the first selection, "Applying an Antique Finish," the purpose is to instruct the reader about how to perform the process; in "How Dictionaries Are Made" and "An Amish Wedding," the purpose is to explain the process for the reader. In "My First Conk" and "The Embalming of Mr. Jones," the authors have strongly persuasive purposes. Although not all these selections have implied or stated theses, each has a clear unifying idea.

Applying an Antique Finish
BERNARD GLADSTONE

The New York Times Complete Manual of Home Repair, from which this essay comes, is an aid for the do-it-yourself enthusiast. It presents in clear, logical fashion all the information homeowners need to perform household repairs on their own. Selections in the book originally appeared in the home improvement column of the New York Times, *a newspaper whose readers are well read and well informed. Bernard Gladstone, who wrote "Applying an Antique Finish" as a set of instructions rather than a process explanation, is very much aware of that audience's needs.*

Homeowners interested in refinishing an old chest, table or similar piece of furniture can most easily solve their problem by giving the piece an "antique" finish. This popular finish blends with almost any decorative scheme, and it has three definite advantages: 1

First, it does not require that the old finish be removed. Second, it can be applied over any type of paintable surface, regardless of whether it now has a "natural" or painted finish and regardless of whether it is wood or metal. Third, this type of finish requires no unusual skills, so it can be easily applied by any home handyman or handywoman. 2

Though there are many variations in shading, and many different methods of achieving it, basically all antique finishes consist of a white or colored ground coat which has one or more "glaze" colors rubbed over it to give a translucent, two-tone color effect. The top color is often a dark brown, muddy-colored glaze which when rubbed over white will make it look yellowed and aged (hence the term "antique white"). However, variations on this effect can be achieved by wiping on other colors, including tints such as pink, pale blue or gold. 3

Before starting the refinishing job, remove as much ornamental hardware as possible and make all necessary repairs by tightening loose joints, gluing down loose veneer, filling in open cracks and holes, and sanding down all rough spots. Remove wax, polish and dirt and dull the shine on the old finish (if any remains) by wiping the entire piece down with a prepared surface conditioner or "liquid sandpaper" of the type which is sold in most paint stores. If one of these is not available, the surface can be conditioned by washing with a strong detergent, then rubbing with fine sandpaper. 4

After the piece has been repaired, cleaned and dulled down   5
where necessary, it is ready for its base coat of paint. Use a satin-
finish enamel, and brush on smoothly with a clean brush. Allow
this to dry for at least 24 hours, then brush on a second coat of the
same material. It is a good idea to brush the paint onto several
scrap pieces of wood so that tests can be made on these to determine
the effect desired before working on the actual piece.

The last coat should be allowed to harden for at least two or   6
three days before the antique glaze is applied over it. To mix the
glaze, a thick, creamy liquid called glazing liquid should be
purchased. Into this is added some raw umber or burnt umber
(these are painters' tinting colors). A little turpentine is also added
to bring the liquid to a thinner brushing consistency. Raw umber
will give a muddy, grayish effect; burnt umber will give a warmer,
more brownish effect.

The exact proportions to be used in mixing this glaze will vary   7
with the effect desired and can be determined only by experimentation beforehand on scrap pieces. As a starting point, try adding
about 1 teaspoonful of the paste colorant to ½ pint of the glaze coat.
Thin this with about 10% turpentine, adding more if necessary to
achieve easier spreading.

If the glaze coat, or glazing liquid, cannot be purchased locally,   8
an oil called flatting oil can be used. This is thinner in consistency
and a little more difficult to handle since it may show a tendency
to run together and will not "stay put" as readily. Very little or no
turpentine should be added if flatting oil is used.

The antique glaze is applied over the white paint by brushing   9
it on sparingly. A wad of cheesecloth (bunched up, not folded) is
then used to wipe most of it off. The depth of color can be varied
by rubbing off more or less of the glaze and by rubbing in straight
lines as well as with a circular motion. Experiment first on the
scrap pieces to help decide on the method to be used. Rub with
more pressure in the center of each panel and less pressure around
the edges. This gives a lighter effect in the center while permitting
the edges to gradually blend in with a darker shading. Pat lightly
with the cheesecloth to eliminate sharp lines and distinct variations
in shading.

Once the desired color and effect have been achieved, the entire   10
piece is then antiqued or glazed (complete one side, or panel, at
a time). Brush on the glaze coat, wait a minute or two, then wipe
off with the cheesecloth. To achieve the most realistic effect, allow
the dark glaze to remain almost full strength in the bottom of

carvings or grooves, and wipe off down to the original color on all high spots.

Allow the finished piece to dry for at least 24 hours, then brush on a coat of clear, dull varnish to protect the finish. On dresser tops, table tops and other surfaces that will receive hard wear, a second coat of varnish is advisable after the first coat has thoroughly dried.   11

COMPREHENSION

1. Gladstone does not include a formal list of materials in his instructions. What would such a list include?

2. What preliminary work is necessary before the actual antiquing process begins? What are the individual stages in the process itself?

3. About how long does the process take?

PURPOSE AND AUDIENCE

1. Although this selection doesn't present an arguable thesis, it does have a clear statement of purpose. Where is this located?

2. Gladstone is writing with a very definite idea of his audience's needs and interests. Would you say he is writing for a beginner or an experienced craftsperson? How do you know?

3. Why does Gladstone list the advantages of antiquing?

4. Why do you think Gladstone chose to write this as a set of instructions rather than as a process explanation?

STYLE AND STRUCTURE

1. What tense is this piece written in? Are most of the sentences statements or commands?

2. Gladstone sometimes uses the passive voice. Locate several examples of the passive voice and rewrite each in the active voice. (For instance, "the surface can be conditioned" becomes "you can condition the surface.")

3. Gladstone pauses in his explanation several times to insert cautionary phrases. Find some of these warnings and explain why they appear where they do instead of grouped together at the beginning.

4. This selection ends rather abruptly. Why do you think it lacks a formal conclusion? Suggest a sentence or two that might be added to create a more graceful ending. Do you think your expanded conclusion strengthens the piece? Why or why not?

5. In the book from which this essay was taken, two illustrations show the application of the ground color and the glaze. Do you think such illustrations would make Gladstone's process easier to follow? Why or why not?

WRITING WORKSHOP

1. Write a set of instructions for an activity. Select something you understand well, such as procedures for your hobby or your job or directions for a game or sport.

2. Rewrite your set of instructions (see the question above) as a process explanation.

How Dictionaries Are Made
S. I. HAYAKAWA

In writing about the process of compiling a dictionary, S. I. Hayakawa also says a good deal about a dictionary's purpose in our society. Hayakawa, a noted semanticist, condenses this long and complex process into a few simple stages to make it accessible to his readers. His process explanation, although brief, does explicitly state an arguable thesis.

It is widely believed that every word has a correct meaning, that 1
we learn these meanings principally from teachers and grammarians (except that most of the time we don't bother to, so that we ordinarily speak "sloppy English"), and that dictionaries and grammars are the supreme authority in matters of meaning and usage. Few people ask by what authority the writers of dictionaries and grammars say what they say. I once got into a dispute with an Englishwoman over the pronunciation of a word and offered to look it up in the dictionary. The Englishwoman said firmly, "What for? I am English. I was born and brought up in England. The way I speak *is* English." Such self-assurance about one's own language is not uncommon among the English. In the United States, however, anyone who is willing to quarrel with the dictionary is regarded as either eccentric or mad.

Let us see how dictionaries are made and how the editors arrive 2
at definitions. What follows applies, incidentally, only to those dictionary offices where first-hand, original research goes on—not those in which editors simply copy existing dictionaries. The task of writing a dictionary begins with reading vast amounts of the literature of the period or subject that the dictionary is to cover. As the editors read, they copy on cards every interesting or rare word, every unusual or peculiar occurrence of a common word, a large number of common words in their ordinary uses, and also the sentences in which each of these words appears, thus:

> pail
> The dairy *pails* bring home increase of milk
> Keats, *Endymion*
> I, 44–45

That is to say, the context of each word is collected, along with the word itself. For a really big job of dictionary-writing, such as the *Oxford English Dictionary* (usually bound in about twenty-five volumes), millions of such cards are collected, and the task of editing occupies decades. As the cards are collected, they are alphabetized and sorted. When the sorting is completed, there will be for each word anywhere from two or three to several hundred illustrative quotations, each on its card.

To define a word, then, the dictionary-editor places before him the stack of cards illustrating that word; each of the cards represents an actual use of the word by a writer of some literary or historical importance. He reads the cards carefully, discards some, rereads the rest, and divides up the stack according to what he thinks are the several senses of the word. Finally, he writes his definitions, following the hard-and-fast rule that each definition *must* be based on what the quotations in front of him reveal about the meaning of the word. The editor cannot be influenced by what *he* thinks a given word *ought* to mean. He must work according to the cards or not at all.

The writing of a dictionary, therefore, is not a task of setting up authoritative statements about the "true meanings" of words, but a task of *recording*, to the best of one's ability, what various words *have meant* to authors in the distant or immediate past. *The writer of a dictionary is a historian, not a lawgiver.* If, for example, we had been writing a dictionary in 1890, or even as late as 1919, we could have said that the word "broadcast" means "to scatter" (seed, for example), but we could not have decreed that from 1921 on, the most common meaning of the word should become "to disseminate audible messages, etc., by radio transmission." To regard the dictionary as an "authority," therefore, is to credit the dictionary-writer with gifts of prophecy which neither he nor anyone else possesses. In choosing our words when we speak or write, we can be *guided* by the historical record afforded us by the dictionary, but we cannot be *bound* by it, because new situations, new experiences, new inventions, new feelings are always compelling us to give new uses to old words. Looking under a "hood," we should ordinarily have found, five hundred years ago, a monk; today, we find a motorcar engine.[1]

[1] *Webster's Third New International Dictionary* lists the word "hood" also as a shortened form of "hoodlum."

The time that elapsed between *Webster's Second Edition* (1934) and the *Third* (1961) indicates the enormous amount of reading and labor entailed in the preparation of a really thorough dictionary of a language as rapidly changing and as rich in vocabulary as English.

COMPREHENSION

1. What are the major stages of the process Hayakawa outlines?

2. How does Hayakawa say the meaning of the word *broadcast* has changed? How can you account for this change in meaning? What other words can you think of whose meanings have changed?

3. What does Hayakawa mean, in paragraph 5, when he says, *"The writer of a dictionary is a historian, not a lawgiver"?*

PURPOSE AND AUDIENCE

1. What kind of audience do you think Hayakawa is addressing here? How can you tell?

2. Hayakawa writes his process explanation in order to correct a common misconception about how dictionaries are made. What is this misconception, and how does he correct it in his thesis?

3. Why do you think Hayakawa decided to write this as a process explanation rather than as a set of instructions?

4. In paragraph 5, why do you think Hayakawa has placed the words *true meanings* in quotation marks?

5. In this brief essay, Hayakawa is writing to inform, to persuade, and to entertain. In what ways does he achieve each of these goals?

STYLE AND STRUCTURE

1. What constitutes the actual process explanation in this essay? What else does Hayakawa include? Why?

2. Although many process explanations are written in the past tense, this is written in the present. What do you think is the reason for this?

3. Why does Hayakawa present a visual illustration of one of the steps in the process he describes?

WRITING WORKSHOP

1. In this selection, Hayakawa has simplified a complex task. Write a process essay which simplifies this same task even further, aiming at an elementary school audience. Be sure to use many examples and detailed explanations.

2. Write a process essay explaining how you went about putting together a collection, a scrapbook, or an album of some kind. Be sure your essay makes clear why you collected or compiled your materials.

My First Conk
MALCOLM X

This selection is from The Autobiography of Malcolm X, *the life story of a black leader as dictated to Alex Haley. The autobiography relates Malcolm X's rise from poverty to national prominence as a lecturer and religious leader. In the course of his life (he was assassinated in 1964), Malcolm X served as everything from a numbers runner to a Pullman porter to a disciple of Elijah Muhammad, and his life story covers these diverse periods. "My First Conk" explains a ritual procedure that was part of his young manhood and also reflects his adult view of the process. The excerpt begins as an autobiographical narrative, goes on to explain a process, and ends on a strongly persuasive note.*

Shorty soon decided that my hair was finally long enough to be   1
conked. He had promised to school me in how to beat the barbershops' three- and four-dollar price by making up congolene, and then conking ourselves.

I took the little list of ingredients he had printed out for me, and   2
went to a grocery store, where I got a can of Red Devil lye, two eggs, and two medium-sized white potatoes. Then at a drugstore near the poolroom, I asked for a large jar of vaseline, a large bar of soap, a large-toothed comb and a fine-toothed comb, one of those rubber hoses with a metal spray-head, a rubber apron and a pair of gloves.

"Going to lay on that first conk?" the drugstore man asked me.   3
I proudly told him, grinning, "Right!"

Shorty paid six dollars a week for a room in his cousin's shabby   4
apartment. His cousin wasn't at home. "It's like the pad's mine, he spends so much time with his woman," Shorty said. "Now, you watch me—"

He peeled the potatoes and thin-sliced them into a quart-sized   5
Mason fruit jar, then started stirring them with a wooden spoon as he gradually poured in a little over half the can of lye. "Never use a metal spoon; the lye will turn it black," he told me.

A jelly-like, starchy-looking glop resulted from the lye and   6
potatoes, and Shorty broke in the two eggs, stirring real fast—his own conk and dark face bent down close. The congolene turned pale-yellowish. "Feel the jar," Shorty said. I cupped my hand against the outside, and snatched it away. "Damn right, it's hot, that's the lye," he said. "So you know it's going to burn when I

comb it in—it burns bad. But the longer you can stand it, the straighter the hair."

He made me sit down, and he tied the string of the new rubber apron tightly around my neck, and combed up my bush of hair. Then, from the big vaseline jar, he took a handful and massaged it hard all through my hair and into the scalp. He also thickly vaselined my neck, ears and forehead. "When I get to washing out your head, be sure to tell me anywhere you feel any little stinging," Shorty warned me, washing his hands, then pulling on the rubber gloves, and tying on his own rubber apron. "You always got to remember that any congolene left in burns a sore into your head." 7

The congolene just felt warm when Shorty started combing it in. But then my head caught fire. 8

I gritted my teeth and tried to pull the sides of the kitchen table together. The comb felt as if it was raking my skin off. 9

My eyes watered, my nose was running. I couldn't stand it any longer; I bolted to the washbasin. I was cursing Shorty with every name I could think of when he got the spray going and started soap-lathering my head. 10

He lathered and spray-rinsed, lathered and spray-rinsed, maybe ten or twelve times, each time gradually closing the hot-water faucet, until the rinse was cold, and that helped some. 11

"You feel any stinging spots?" 12

"No," I managed to say. My knees were trembling. 13

"Sit back down, then. I think we got it all out okay." 14

The flame came back as Shorty, with a thick towel, started drying my head, rubbing hard. *"Easy, man, easy!"* I kept shouting. 15

"The first time's always worst. You get used to it better before long. You took it real good, homeboy. You got a good conk." 16

When Shorty let me stand up and see in the mirror, my hair hung down in limp, damp strings. My scalp still flamed, but not as badly; I could bear it. He draped the towel around my shoulders, over my rubber apron, and began again vaselining my hair. 17

I could feel him combing, straight back, first the big comb, then the fine-tooth one. 18

Then, he was using a razor, very delicately, on the back of my neck. Then, finally, shaping the sideburns. 19

My first view in the mirror blotted out the hurting. I'd seen some pretty conks, but when it's the first time, on your *own* head, the transformation, after the lifetime of kinks, is staggering. 20

The mirror reflected Shorty behind me. We both were grinning and sweating. And on top of my head was this thick, smooth sheen of shining red hair—real red—as straight as any white man's. 21

How ridiculous I was! Stupid enough to stand there simply lost 22
in admiration of my hair now looking "white," reflected in the
mirror in Shorty's room. I vowed that I'd never again be without
a conk, and I never was for many years.

This was my first really big step toward self-degradation: when 23
I endured all of that pain, literally burning my flesh to have it look
like a white man's hair. I had joined that multitude of Negro men
and women in America who are brainwashed into believing that
the black people are "inferior"—and white people "superior"—
that they will even violate and mutilate their God-created bodies
to try to look "pretty" by white standards.

Look around today, in every small town and big city, from two- 24
bit catfish and soda-pop joints into the "integrated" lobby of the
Waldorf-Astoria, and you'll see conks on black men. And you'll see
black women wearing these green and pink and purple and red
and platinum-blonde wigs. They're all more ridiculous than a
slapstick comedy. It makes you wonder if the Negro has completely
lost his sense of identity, lost touch with himself.

You'll see the conk worn by many, many so-called "upper class" 25
Negroes, and, as much as I hate to say it about them, on all too
many Negro entertainers. One of the reasons that I've especially
admired some of them, like Lionel Hampton and Sidney Poitier,
among others, is that they have kept their natural hair and fought
to the top. I admire any Negro man who has never had himself
conked, or who has had the sense to get rid of it—as I finally did.

I don't know which kind of self-defacing conk is the greater 26
shame—the one you'll see on the heads of the black so-called
"middle class" and "upper class," who ought to know better, or the
one you'll see on the heads of the poorest, most downtrodden,
ignorant black men. I mean the legal-minimum-wage ghetto-dwell-
ing kind of Negro, as I was when I got my first one. It's generally
among these poor fools that you'll see a black kerchief over the
man's head, like Aunt Jemima; he's trying to make his conk last
longer, between trips to the barbershop. Only for special occasions
is this kerchief-protected conk exposed—to show off how "sharp"
and "hip" its owner is. The ironic thing is that I have never heard
any woman, white or black, express any admiration for a conk. Of
course, any white woman with a black man isn't thinking about his
hair. But I don't see how on earth a black woman with any race
pride could walk down the street with any black man wearing a
conk—the emblem of his shame that he is black.

To my own shame, when I say all of this I'm talking first of all 27
about myself—because you can't show me any Negro who ever

conked more faithfully than I did. I'm speaking from personal experience when I say of any black man who conks today, or any white-wigged black woman, that if they gave the brains in their heads just half as much attention as they do their hair, they would be a thousand times better off.

COMPREHENSION

1. What is a conk? Why did Malcolm X want to get his hair conked? What did a conk symbolize to him at first? What did it symbolize at the time he wrote about it?

2. List the materials Shorty asked Malcolm X to buy. Is the purpose of each explained? If so, where?

3. Outline the major stages in the procedure Malcolm X describes. Are they in chronological order? Which, if any, are out of place?

PURPOSE AND AUDIENCE

1. Why does Malcolm X write this selection as a process explanation instead of a set of instructions?

2. This process explanation has a definite thesis that makes its purpose clear. What is this thesis?

3. *The Autobiography of Malcolm X* was published in 1964, when many blacks got their hair straightened regularly. Is the thesis of the selection still appropriate today?

4. Why does Malcolm X include so many references to the pain and discomfort he endured as part of the process?

5. What is the relationship between Malcolm X's personal narrative and the universal statement he makes about conking in this selection?

STYLE AND STRUCTURE

1. Identify some of the transitional words Malcolm X uses to move from step to step.

2. Only about half of this selection is devoted to the process explanation. Where does the process begin? Where does it end?

3. How does the use of dialogue strenghten the process explanation? How does it strenghten Malcolm X's thesis?

WRITING WORKSHOP

1. Write a process explanation of an unpleasant ritual you have gone through in order to conform to a standard of physical beauty determined by society. (You might consider such procedures as shaving or getting a permanent wave).

2. Rewrite Malcolm X's process explanation as he might have described it when he still thought of it as a desirable process, worth all the trouble. Include all his steps, but change his thesis and slant your writing to make conking sound painless and simple.

An Amish Wedding

JOHN HOSTETLER

*John Hostetler is a historian who is an expert on Amish culture. In
this selection, he describes the process by which an Amish couple
arranges and celebrates a traditional wedding. The Amish, who
maintain their small, rural communities within our highly industrial-
ized society, place great importance on cultural stability and resist
change in customs and practices. "An Amish Wedding" clearly illustrates this loyalty to a fixed order. Note that Hostetler's process
explanation is considerably more formal then the three previous
selections in this chapter.*

A wedding in Amish life is an elaborate affair, for the whole 1
community has a stake in marriage. For the community it means a
new home, another place to have preaching when the couple is
located on the farm, and another family to raise children in the
Amish way. Marriage also means that the young couple is ready to
part with their juvenile and sometimes wild behavior and to settle
down to keeping the faith in a mature way. For the couple itself
marriage is a rite of passage marking the passing from youth into
the age of adult responsibility.

Amish courtship is secretive, and the community at large is not 2
to know about an intended wedding until the couple is "published"
in church, usually two Sundays before the wedding. Signs of an
approaching wedding, however, provide occasion for joking and
teasing. Since there is nothing among the Amish that corresponds
to the engagement, other signs of preparation become indicative of
a potential marriage. An overabundance of celery in the garden of
a home containing a potential bride is said to be one such sign,
since large quantities are used at weddings. Another cue may be
efforts on the part of the father of the potential bridegroom to
obtain an extra farm, or to remodel a vacant dwelling on one of his
own farms.

Weddings are traditionally held in November and December, 3
since this is a time when the work year allows community-wide
participation. The great amount of preparation requires that weddings be held during the week, usually on a Thursday, or on
Tuesday if there are conflicting dates with other marriages. Second
marriages or those involving older persons may be held anytime
during the year and often do not involve such elaborate preparations.

Shortly before a young man wishes to be married he approaches 4
the deacon or a minister of his choosing and makes known his

desire. The official then becomes the *Schteckleimann* or go-be-tween. His task is to go secretly, usually after dark, to the home of the bridegroom's fiancée and verify her wishes for marriage and to obtain the consent of her parents. Of course the girl and her parents have by this time already given informal consent, so that the duty of the intermediary is little more than a formality.

The deacon reports his findings to the bishop who announces or   5
"publishes" the intent of the couple at the next preaching service. The bridegroom-to-be, who is always present at this service, leaves immediately after the important announcement, just before the last hymn is sung. He hitches his horse and is off to the home of his fiancée, where she is awaiting the news that they have been "published."

After being "published" the bridegroom lives at the bride's   6
home until the wedding day. They are busy during this time with the innumerable preparations that must be made. Walnuts and hickory nuts need to be cracked, floors scrubbed, furniture moved, silverware polished, and dishes borrowed.

The bridegroom's first assignment is to invite personally all of   7
the wedding guests. He sets out in his buggy early Monday morning to invite two hundred or more friends, relatives, and neighbors agreed upon informally by the parents of the couple. No wedding invitations are mailed. Invitations include entire families, or certain members of the family, such as the husband or wife only. Children are specifically mentioned if they are invited. Some are invited only for the evening. Honorary invitations are extended to uncles, aunts, and neighbors to serve as cooks. Both men and their wives serve in this capacity. The parents of the bridal party decide who shall be invited to the wedding and who shall have special honors in serving the meal.

Wedding customs vary from one ceremonial and ecological   8
community to another, especially in menu, physical arrangements, and whether games are played. The following are observations made by the writer at a wedding in central Pennsylvania.

Large-scale preparations began on the day before the wedding.   9
The cooks, married couples numbering thirty persons in all, began to arrive at the bride's home at seven o'clock in the morning. Custom requires that the bridegroom cut off the heads of the fowl. Men picked the chickens, ducks, and turkeys. The women washed and dressed them. The women prepared the dressing, stuffed the fowl, washed dishes, baked quantities of pies, peeled two bushels of potatoes, and cracked nuts. The men cleaned celery, supplied plenty of hot water from large kettles, emptied garbage, and

constructed temporary tables for the main rooms in the house. These tables, made of wide pine boards and trestles, were placed around three sides of the living room. Two tables were in the kitchen and one in the bedroom, making the equivalent of about six tables with a total seating capacity of one hundred. The dressed, stuffed fowl were placed in the large outside bake oven on the evening before the wedding.

The wedding day itself was a great occasion not only for the bride and bridegroom, but for the kinship community and guests, especially the young people. Before daylight on the day of the wedding the bride and bridegroom and their two attending couples went to a neighbor's place a mile from the bride's home where the preaching and ceremony were to take place. A usual four-hour preaching service was held for the event, lasting from nine in the morning to one o'clock in the afternoon. This service was open to the public, but was attended chiefly by those who were invited to the wedding.   10

As wedding guests arrived for the service the bridal party was already sitting in the front row. When the house was filled, the ministers proceeded to the council room and the bride and groom followed. Here they were given private instructions concerning the duties of marriage, while the assembly below sang wedding hymns (*Ausbund,* selections 97, 69, 131). Upon returning to the assembly the bridal party (holding hands) took their special seats near the ministers' row, the three young men facing their partners. Their clothes were new, but typical of their regular Sunday garb. The main sermon delivered by the bishop focused on marriages in the Old Testament: the story of Adam and Eve, the wickedness of mankind after the flood in that "they took them wives of all which they chose," the uprightness of Noah's household in not intermarrying with unbelievers, the story of Isaac and Rebecca, and the adulterous plight of Solomon. The sermon was concluded with a rehearsal of the story of Tobias (from the Apocrypha) and how he got his wife. Two passages of Scripture were read with little comment.   11

Near the hour of twelve noon and at the end of his long sermon, the bishop asked the couple to come forward if it was still their desire to be united in matrimony. The ceremony was completed without the aid of a book or written notes. It consisted of a few questions and responses and concluded with the bishop placing his hands on the clasped hands of the couple as he pronounced a blessing upon them.   12

COMPREHENSION

1. Why is a wedding such an important event in Amish culture?

2. Why are weddings most often held in the winter and on weekdays?

3. In what specific ways are an Amish courtship and wedding different from most other modern American ones?

PURPOSE AND AUDIENCE

1. This selection does not have a thesis statement. What do you think Hostetler's purpose in writing it was?

2. How knowledgeable does Hostetler expect his audience to be about Amish customs? How can you tell?

3. Why do you supose Hostetler chose to explain a typical wedding objectively rather than to present a more subjective account that included his opinions and emotions?

STYLE AND STRUCTURE

1. Although the process is explained in the present tense at first, Hostetler switches to the past tense at the beginning of paragraph 9. How can you account for this shift in verb tense?

2. What function does paragraph 8 serve in this selection?

3. The selection is divided into two parts: wedding plans and the wedding day itself. Into what other stages could the process be broken down?

4. Although Hostetler presents an extremely detailed explanation of the courtship and marriage rituals, his account is not particularized. Does the absence of physical descriptions, dialogue, and names of real people detract from the selection's effectiveness? Why or why not?

WRITING WORKSHOP

1. Write a process essay that explains how a wedding is organized and celebrated in your culture or how another ritual takes place, such as a baptism, a confirmation, a bar mitzvah or bas mitzvah, or a funeral. Make sure you include all the major stages in the process.

2. Write a process essay that explains a personal ritual observed by your family or by you. Be certain to include the main stages in the process as well as its function or significance.

The Embalming of Mr. Jones
JESSICA MITFORD

This essay, an excerpt from Jessica Mitford's The American Way of Death, *painstakingly and ironically describes the dual process of embalming and restoring a cadaver. Her book, a scathing criticism of the funeral industry, sharpened public scrutiny of the way funerals are handled and prompted many angry responses from morticians. Notice as you read how Mitford's meticulous use of detail supports her thesis.*

Embalming is indeed a most extraordinary procedure, and one 1 must wonder at the docility of Americans who each year pay hundreds of millions of dollars for its perpetuation, blissfully ignorant of what it is all about, what is done, how it is done. Not one in ten thousand has any idea of what actually takes place. Books on the subject are extremely hard to come by. They are not to be found in most libraries or bookshops.

In an era when huge television audiences watch surgical oper- 2 ations in the comfort of their living rooms, when, thanks to the animated cartoon, the geography of the digestive system has become familiar territory even to the nursery school set, in a land where the satisfaction of curiosity about almost all matters is a national pastime, the secrecy surrounding embalming can, surely, hardly be attributed to the inherent gruesomeness of the subject. Custom in this regard has within this century suffered a complete reversal. In the early days of American embalming, when it was performed in the home of the deceased, it was almost mandatory for some relative to stay by the embalmer's side and witness the procedure. Today, family members who might wish to be in attendance would certainly be dissuaded by the funeral director. All others, except apprentices, are excluded by law from the preparation room.

A close look at what does actually take place may explain in 3 large measure the undertaker's intractable reticence concerning a procedure that has become his major *raison d'être.* Is it possible he fears that public information about embalming might lead patrons to wonder if they really want this service? If the funeral men are loath to discuss the subject outside the trade, the reader may, understandably, be equally loath to go on reading at this point. For those who have the stomach for it, let us part the formaldehyde curtain. . . .

160

The body is first laid out in the undertaker's morgue—or rather, 4
Mr. Jones is reposing in the preparation room—to be readied to bid
the world farewell.

The preparation room in any of the better funeral establishments 5
has the tiled and sterile look of a surgery, and indeed the embalmer–restorative artist who does his chores there is beginning to
adopt the term "dermasurgeon" (appropriately corrupted by some
mortician-writers as "demisurgeon") to describe his calling. His
equipment, consisting of scalpels, scissors, augers, forceps, clamps,
needles, pumps, tubes, bowls and basins, is crudely imitative of
the surgeon's as is his technique, acquired in a nine- or twelve-
month post-high-school course in an embalming school. He is
supplied by an advanced chemical industry with a bewildering
array of fluids, sprays, pastes, oils, powders, creams, to fix or soften
tissue, shrink or distend it as needed, dry it here, restore the
moisture there. There are cosmetics, waxes and paints to fill and
cover features, even plaster of Paris to replace entire limbs. There
are ingenious aids to prop and stabilize the cadaver: a Vari-Pose
Head Rest, the Edwards Arm and Hand Positioner, the Repose
Block (to support the shoulders during the embalming), and the
Throop Foot Positioner, which resembles an old-fashioned stocks.

Mr. John H. Eckels, president of the Eckels College of Mortuary 6
Science, thus describes the first part of the embalming procedure:
"In the hands of a skilled practitioner, this work may be done in
a comparatively short time and without mutilating the body other
than by slight incision—so slight that it scarcely would cause
serious inconvenience if made upon a living person. It is necessary
to remove all the blood, and doing this not only helps in the
disinfecting, but removes the principal cause of disfigurements due
to discoloration."

Another textbook discusses the all-important time element: "The 7
earlier this is done, the better, for every hour that elapses between
death and embalming will add to the problems and complications
encountered. . . ." Just how soon should one get going on the
embalming? The author tells us, "On the basis of such scanty
information made available to this profession through its rudimentary and haphazard system of technical research, we must conclude
that the best results are to be obtained if the subject is embalmed
before life is completely extinct—that is, before cellular death has
occurred. In the average case, this would mean within an hour
after somatic death." For those who feel that there is something a
little rudimentary, not to say haphazard, about this advice, a
comforting thought is offered by another writer. Speaking of fears

entertained in early days of premature burial, he points out, "One of the effects of embalming by chemical injection, however, has been to dispel fears of live burial." How true; once the blood is removed, chances of live burial are indeed remote.

To return to Mr. Jones, the blood is drained out through the veins and replaced by embalming fluid pumped in through the arteries. As noted in *The Principles and Practices of Embalming,* "every operator has a favorite injection and drainage point—a fact which becomes a handicap only if he fails or refuses to foresake his favorites when conditions demand it." Typical favorites are the carotid artery, femoral artery, jugular vein, subclavian vein. There are various choices of embalming fluid. If Flextone is used, it will produce a "mild, flexible rigidity. The skin retains a velvety softness, the tissues are rubbery and pliable. Ideal for women and children." It may be blended with B. and G. Products Company's Lyf-Lyk tint, which is guaranteed to reproduce "nature's own skin texture . . . the velvety appearance of living tissue." Suntone comes in three separate tints: Suntan; Special Cosmetic Tint, a pink shade "especially indicated for young female subjects"; and Regular Cosmetic Tint, moderately pink.

About three to six gallons of a dyed and perfumed solution of formaldehyde, glycerin, borax, phenol, alcohol and water is soon circulating through Mr. Jones, whose mouth has been sewn together with a "needle directed upward between the upper lip and gum and brought out through the left nostril," with the corners raised slightly "for a more pleasant expression." If he should be buck-toothed, his teeth are cleaned with Bon Ami and coated with colorless nail polish. His eyes, meanwhile, are closed with flesh-tinted eye caps and eye cement.

The next step is to have at Mr. Jones with a thing called a trocar. This is a long, hollow needle attached to a tube. It is jabbed into the abdomen, poked around the entrails and chest cavity, the contents of which are pumped out and replaced with "cavity fluid." This done, and the hole in the abdomen sewed up, Mr. Jones's face is heavily creamed (to protect the skin from burns which may be caused by leakage of the chemicals), and he is covered with a sheet and left unmolested for a while. But not for long—there is more, much more, in store for him. He has been embalmed, but not yet restored, and the best time to start the restorative work is eight to ten hours after embalming, when the tissues have become firm and dry.

The object of all this attention to the corpse, it must be remembered, is to make it presentable for viewing in an attitude of healthy repose. "Our customs require the presentation of our dead in the semblance of normality . . . unmarred by the ravages of illness, disease or mutilation," says Mr. J. Sheridan Mayer in his *Restorative Art*. This is rather a large order since few people die in the full bloom of health, unravaged by illness and unmarked by some disfigurement. The funeral industry is equal to the challenge: "In some cases the gruesome appearance of a mutilated or disease-ridden subject may be quite discouraging. The task of restoration may seem impossible and shake the confidence of the embalmer. This is the time for intestinal fortitude and determination. Once the formative work is begun and affected tissues are cleaned or removed, all doubts of success vanish. It is surprising and gratifying to discover the results which may be obtained."

The embalmer, having allowed an appropriate interval to elapse, returns to the attack, but now he brings into play the skill and equipment of sculptor and cosmetician. Is a hand missing? Casting one in plaster of Paris is a simple matter. "For replacement purposes, only a cast of the back of the hand is necessary; this is within the ability of the average operator and is quite adequate." If a lip or two, a nose or an ear should be missing, the embalmer has at hand a variety of restorative waxes with which to model replacements. Pores and skin texture are simulated by stippling with a little brush, and over this cosmetics are laid on. Head off? Decapitation cases are rather routinely handled. Ragged edges are trimmed, and head joined to torso with a series of splints, wires and sutures. It is a good idea to have a little something at the neck—a scarf or high collar—when time for viewing comes. Swollen mouth? Cut out tissue as needed from inside the lips. If too much is removed, the surface contour can easily be restored by padding with cotton. Swollen necks and cheeks are reduced by removing tissue through vertical incisions made down each side of the neck. "When the deceased is casketed, the pillow will hide the suture incisions . . . as an extra precaution against leakage, the suture may be painted with liquid sealer." [12]

The opposite condition is more likely to be present itself—that of emaciation. His hypodermic syringe now loaded with massage cream, the embalmer seeks out and fills the hollowed and sunken areas by injection. In this procedure the backs of the hands and fingers and the under-chin area should not be neglected. [13]

Positioning the lips is a problem that recurrently challenges the ingenuity of the embalmer. Closed too tightly, they tend to give a stern, even disapproving expression. Ideally, embalmers feel, the lips should give the impression of being ever so slightly parted, the [14] upper lip protruding slightly for a more youthful appearance. This takes some engineering, however, as the lips tend to drift apart. Lip drift can sometimes be remedied by pushing one or two straight pins through the inner margin of the lower lip and then inserting them between the two front upper teeth. If Mr. Jones happens to have no teeth, the pins can just as easily be anchored in his Armstrong Face Former and Denture Replacer. Another method to maintain lip closure is to dislocate the lower jaw, which is then held in its new position by a wire run through holes which have been drilled through the upper jaws at the midline. As the French are fond of saying, *il faut souffrir pour être belle.*[1]

If Mr. Jones has died of jaundice, the embalming fluid will very   15
likely turn him green. Does this deter the embalmer? Not if he has intestinal fortitude. Masking pastes and cosmetics are heavily laid on, burial garments and casket interiors are color-correlated with particular care, and Jones is displayed beneath rose-colored lights. Friends will say, "How *well* he looks." Death by carbon monoxide, on the other hand, can be rather a good thing from the embalmer's viewpoint: "One advantage is the fact that this type of discoloration is an exaggerated form of a natural pink coloration." This is nice because the healthy glow is already present and needs but little attention.

The patching and filling completed, Mr. Jones is now shaved,   16
washed and dressed. Cream-based cosmetic, available in pink, flesh, suntan, brunette and blonde, is applied to his hands and face, his hair is shampooed and combed (and, in the case of Mrs. Jones, set), his hands manicured. For the horny-handed son of toil special care must be taken; cream should be applied to remove ingrained grime, and the nails cleaned. "If he were not in the habit of having them manicured in life, trimming and shaping is advised for better appearance—never questioned by kin."

Jones is now ready for casketing (this is the present participle   17
of the verb "to casket"). In this operation his right shoulder should be depressed slightly "to turn the body a bit to the right and soften the appearance of lying flat on the back." Positioning the hands is a matter of importance, and special rubber positioning blocks may be used. The hands should be cupped slightly for a more lifelike, relaxed appearance. Proper placement of the body requires a delicate sense of balance. It should lie as high as possible in the casket, yet not so high that the lid, when lowered, will hit the nose.

---

[1]It is necessary to suffer in order to be beautiful.—EDS.

On the other hand, we are cautioned, placing the body too low "creates the impression that the body is in a box."

Jones is next wheeled into the appointed slumber room where   18
a few last touches may be added—his favorite pipe placed in his hand or, if he was a great reader, a book propped into position. (In the case of little Master Jones a Teddy bear may be clutched.) Here he will hold open house for a few days, visiting hours 10 A.M. to 9 P.M.

COMPREHENSION

1. How, according to Mitford, has the public's knowledge of embalming changed? How does she explain this change?

2. To what other professionals does Mitford liken the embalmer? Are these analogies flattering or critical? Explain.

3. What are the major stages of the process of embalming and restoration?

PURPOSE AND AUDIENCE

1. Mitford has a very definite purpose here; she has written this piece to convince her audience of something. What is her thesis?

2. Does Mitford expect her audience to agree with her thesis? How can you tell?

3. In her most recent book, Mitford refers to herself as a muckraker, one who informs the public of misconduct. Does she achieve this status here? Cite specific examples.

4. Why do you suppose Mitford names the cadaver Mr. Jones?

STYLE AND STRUCTURE

1. Identify the stylistic features that distinguish this process explanation from a set of instructions.

2. In this selection, as in most process essays, a list of necessary materials precedes the procedure. What additional details does Mitford include in her list in paragraph 5? How do these additions affect the reader?

3. Throughout this essay, Mitford uses extensive detail to convey her attitude without directly stating it. Give some examples of this technique.

4. Go through the essay and locate the author's remarks about the language of embalming. How are these comments about euphemisms, newly coined words, and other aspects of the language consistent with Mitford's thesis?

5. Throughout the essay, Mitford quotes a series of experts. How does she use their remarks to support her thesis?

6. What phrases signal Mitford's transitions between stages?

WRITING WORKSHOP

1. Rewrite this process explanation as a set of instructions, condensing it so that your essay is about five hundred words long. Unlike Mitford, keep your essay objective; organize it around a unifying idea rather than an arguable thesis statement.

2. In the role of a funeral director, write a letter to Mitford in which you take issue with her essay. Explain the practice of embalming as necessary and practical. Design your process explanation, unlike Mitford's, to defend the practice.

6

Cause and Effect

WHAT IS CAUSE AND EFFECT?

In cause and effect writing, you try to trace causes or predict effects or do both. Like narrative and process, cause and effect considers events in sequence. Here, however, the purpose is not to tell a story or to outline the steps in a procedure. Instead, it is to analyze causal relationships among those events by investigating which events produce or are produced by others. For this reason, the sequence of events does not necessarily follow chronological order.

Cause and effect relationships can be complex and subtle. Sometimes, in fact, many different causes can be responsible for one effect. A couple about to divorce might cite money problems, religious differences, and a poor sex life as causes leading up to their decision to separate.

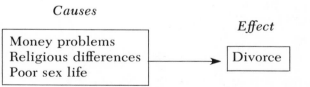

Similarly, many different effects can be produced by one cause. A hurricane, for instance, can cause property damage, injuries, and deaths.

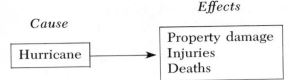

As you examine situations that seem suited to cause and effect analysis, you will discover that most complex situations have numerous causes producing many different effects. The following situations illustrate some possible cause and effect relationships:

1. During the last fifteen years, the college board scores of entering freshmen have been steadily declining. Since this decline coincides with the rise of television and since students are reading less and watching television more, many educators have concluded that television watching has led to lower board scores.
2. Before World War II, oral history—the systematic collection and preservation of dictated memoirs—was a method seldom used by researchers. In the postwar period, however, the development of the tape recorder has encouraged widespread use of oral history.
3. A professional basketball team, recently stocked with the best players money can buy, has had a miserable season. Since the individual players are talented and since they were successful under other coaches, fans blame the current coach for the team's losing streak and demand his ouster.

This chart summarizes the cause and effect relationships involved in these three situations:

Effect	Suspected Cause
Decline in college board scores	Television
Widespread use of oral history	Tape recorder
Team's losing streak	Coach

Since none of these suspected causes can be scientifically verified, we can probably never know for sure the extent of the cause and effect relationships between the coach and the team's disastrous season, the tape recorder and oral history, and television and college board scores. We can speculate about the validity of these connections, but we must consider other possibilities as well. Although each of these cause and effect relationships *seems* perfectly reasonable, other causes *could* have been responsible for the same effects:

1. Perhaps the generally open atmosphere of the late 1960s and early 1970s and the tendency of high schools to move away from required courses led to the decline in board scores.
2. Perhaps concern about the decreased availability of personal memoirs like diaries and journals encouraged the development of oral history.
3. Perhaps the individual players' inability to mesh well as a team is responsible for the losing streak.

Just as these other causes could have produced the same three effects, so the original suspected causes could have produced other results.

1. Increased television watching could have made college students better observers and listeners, although less responsive to the written questions on the college boards.
2. The development of the tape recorder could have interested people in the technology of the future rather than in the events of the past and present.
3. The coach could actually have kept the team from total collapse by mediating disputes among the players.

In each of these three situations, more than one cause and more than one result may be involved. To give your readers a complete analysis, you should try to consider all causes and effects, not just the most obvious ones or the first ones you think of.

Immediate and Remote Causes

Once you have decided that a cause and effect pattern of development might be appropriate for a topic, you need to distinguish between the easily seen and understood *immediate* causes and the less obvious but still important *remote* causes. As the circumstances surrounding two actual events reveal, both immediate and remote causes may be crucial for an accurate causal analysis.

During the winter of 1977–1978, an abnormally large amount of snow accumulated on the roof of the Civic Center Auditorium in Hartford, Connecticut. When the roof fell in, newspapers reported that the weight of the snow had caused the collapse. Clearly, the immediate cause of the cave-in was the accumulated snow. But insurance investigators had to search for other causes, the remote causes not so readily perceived. Perhaps the design of the roof was a remote, or less immediately evident, cause of the collapse. Perhaps the materials used in the roof's construction were partly to blame. Maybe maintenance crews had not done their jobs properly, or necessary repairs had not been made. Besides the snow, any or all of these less apparent but possibly critical factors might have contributed to the disaster. If you were the insurance investigator reporting on the causes of this event, you would want to assess all possible contributing factors rather than just the most obvious. If you did not consider the remote as well as the immediate causes, you might reach an oversimplified or false conclusion.

In the spring of 1968, Martin Luther King, Jr., was shot and killed. During the next few nights, civil disturbances broke out in New York City, Washington, D.C., and many other cities. Although the media cited the assassination of Dr. King as the cause of the unrest, it soon became apparent that his death had been the immediate precipitating cause of these disturbances, but that other frustrations and disappointments of life in the inner cities had been important remote causes. If you were a city official writing a report about these disturbances, your failure to perceive the underlying remote causes might lead you to make inappropriate recommendations on how to avoid such demonstrations in the future.

This diagram outlines the cause and effect relationships in the two situations summarized above.

Effect	Immediate Cause	Possible Remote Causes
Roof collapse	Weight of snow	Roof design Roof materials Improper maintenance Repairs not made
Civil disturbances	King's death	Tensions of inner city life, including unemployment, crime, poor health care, and poverty

Primary and Secondary Causes

A cause is classified as immediate or remote depending on how closely it precedes an effect and how easily it is recognized. In addition, a cause can be considered *primary* or *secondary* depending on its importance for explaining an effect. Let's look again at the examples of the Hartford roof collapse and the civil disturbances following the death of Martin Luther King, Jr. Most people agreed that the snow was the immediate, or most obviously perceived, cause of the roof collapse. Further investigation, however, revealed that it was not the weight of the snow but the design of the roof that was the primary, or most significant, cause of the disaster. Similarly, when the confusion following the assassination died down, it became clear that Dr. King's death, while surely precipitating the civil unrest, was by no means its primary cause. In fact, something far more subtle—racial discrimination—was later determined to be the primary cause. In other words, discrimination, though a remote cause, was the primary cause; Dr. King's death, though immediate, was secondary.

Effect	Primary Cause	Secondary Cause
Roof collapse	Roof design	Weight of snow
Civil disturbances	Racial discrimination	King's death

This distinction between the primary or most important cause and the secondary or less important cause is useful for planning a cause and effect paper. When you can identify the primary cause, you can emphasize it in your paper and play down the less important causes. If you properly weight each factor in your essay, your readers will more easily understand the logic of the relationships you are examining.

Post Hoc Reasoning

When developing a cause and effect paper, you must be certain that your conclusions are logical. Simply because event A precedes event B, you must not assume that event A has caused event B. This illogical assumption, called *post hoc* reasoning, equates a chronological sequence with causality. When you revise a cause and effect paper, make sure you have not confused words like *because, therefore,* and *consequently*—words that show a causal relationship—with words like *subsequently, later,* and *afterward*—words that show a chronological relationship.

Another recent event illustrates the power of *post hoc* reasoning. During the summer of 1976, the American Legion decided to hold its annual convention in Philadelphia, choosing that city because it had enough hotel rooms and because it was the headquarters for the United States bicentennial celebration. Subsequently, 180 legionnaires who had attended the convention came down with a mysterious viruslike infection, dubbed "Legionnaire's disease," and 29 died as a result. Investigators noted that virtually all of those who became ill had been staying at the Bellevue Stratford hotel. Adverse publicity caused business at the hotel to decline drastically, and in 1977 the hotel closed. Soon afterward it was sold.

This account suggests certain obvious cause and effect relationships:

Effect	Cause
Convention held in Philadelphia	Hotel rooms available Bicentennial city
Deaths	"Legionnaire's disease"
Hotel closed and sold	Bad publicity

Other cause and effect relationships may also exist (for instance, the cause of the disease might be a virus). This chart, however, represents the only relationships actually confirmed by the information in the paragraph. But what actually caused the bad publicity? It wasn't just that people who had stayed in the hotel died; rather, it was that the public assumed a cause and effect relationship before one was proved to exist. Although scientists have now discovered a valid cause and effect relationship between the Bellevue Stratford and Legionnaire's disease (bacteria responsible for the disease were found in the hotel's air-conditioning system), it was neither logical nor fair to *assume* that such a relationship existed before all other possible causes had been eliminated and before clear, irrefutable evidence was found to support the connection.

The Causal Chain

Sometimes an effect can also be a cause. This is true in a causal chain, where A causes B, B causes C, C causes D, and so on.

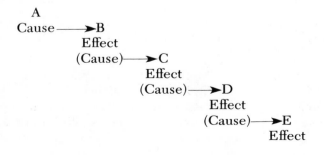

If your analysis of a situation reveals a causal chain, this discovery can be useful in your writing. The very operation of a causal chain suggests an organizational pattern for a paper. In addition, following the chain automatically keeps you from discussing links out of their logical order.

Here is a simple example of a causal chain: A judge wakes up one morning in a bad mood because his bed is lumpy and his arthritis is acting up. In court that morning, he gives a first offender an unusually stiff sentence. The convict, bitter at his punishment, sets his mattress on fire, and the fumes kill several of his fellow inmates. The wife of one of these inmates becomes mentally ill as a result of her husband's death, and her two children are placed in foster homes when she is institutionalized.

The causal chain, in which the result of one action is the cause of another, has led the judge's restless night to cause two children to be deprived of their parents. Leaving out any link in the chain, or putting any link in improper order, destroys the logic and continuity of the chain. The causal chain is common in academic subjects from economics to physics; perhaps the best example is a nuclear reaction.

Being able to perceive and analyze cause and effect relationships; to distinguish causes from effects and recognize causal chains; and to sort out immediate from remote, primary from secondary, and logical from illogical causes are all skills that will help you write. Understanding the nature of the cause and effect relationship will help you to decide when to use this pattern to structure a paper or a report.

STRUCTURING A CAUSE AND EFFECT ESSAY

After you have thought about the cause and effect relationships of your topic, you are ready to plan your paper. You have two basic options: to find causes or to predict effects. (Sometimes, of course, you may do both in one essay.) Often, your assigned topic will tell you which of these options to use. Here are a few likely topics for cause and effect treatment:

To find causes
{
Discuss the causes of World War I. (history exam)

Discuss the factors that contribute to the declining population of state mental hospitals. (social work paper)
}

To predict
effects
{
Outline the probable positive effects of moving
elementary school children from a highly structured classroom to a relatively open classroom.
(education paper)

Assess the economic implications of national
health insurance. (economics exam)

It is certainly possible to plan a cause and effect essay around
a unifying idea rather than an arguable thesis. For instance, on an
economics exam, your response to "Discuss the major effects of the
Vietnam War on the United States economy" could be a straightforward presentation of factual information, an attempt to inform
your readers and not to persuade them. However, like nearly every
paper or exam you write in college, your answer is more likely to
take a position in a thesis statement and then defend that position.
In fact, cause and effect analysis often requires judging and weight-
ing factors, and your assessment of the relative significance of
causes or effects may generate a thesis. Thus, when you plan your
essay, you will want to formulate your thesis statement as you settle
on the specific causes or effects you will discuss. This thesis
statement should tell your readers three things: the points you will
consider, the position you will take, and whether you will be
finding causes or predicting effects. Your thesis may also indicate
explicitly or implicitly the cause or effect you consider to be most
important and the order in which you will treat your points.

Finding Causes

Let's suppose you are planning the social work paper mentioned
above. ("Discuss the factors that contribute to the declining population of state mental hospitals.") Your assignment specifies an
effect—the declining population of state mental hospitals—and asks
you to discuss possible causes. Some causes might be:

- An increasing acceptance of mental illness in our society
- Prohibitive costs of in-patient care
- Increasing numbers of mental health professionals, thus facil-
  itating treatment outside the hospital

Many health professionals, however, feel that the most important
factor is the development and use of psychotropic drugs, like
thorazine, that have an altering effect on the mind. To emphasize

this cause in your paper, you could construct the following thesis statement:

Less important causes	Although society's increasing acceptance of the mentally ill, the high cost of in-patient care, and the rise in the number of health professionals have all been influential in reducing the population of state hospitals, the most important cause of this reduction is the development and use of psychotropic drugs.
Effect	
Most important cause	

This thesis statement fully prepares your readers for your essay. It identifies the causes you will consider, and it also reveals your position—your assessment of the relative significance of these causes. It states the less important causes first and indicates their secondary importance by *although*. Similarly, in the body of your essay the least important causes would be considered first so that the essay could gradually build up to the most convincing material, the information that is likely to have the greatest impact on the reader. An outline for your paper might look like this:

¶1   Introduction—including thesis that identifies the effect and its causes

¶2   First cause: Increased acceptance of the mentally ill

¶3   Second cause: High cost of in-patient care

¶4   Third cause: Rise in the number of health professionals

¶5   Fourth cause: Development and use of psychotropic drugs (the most important cause)

¶6   Conclusion and summary

Predicting Effects

Let's suppose you were planning the education paper mentioned earlier. ("Outline the probable positive effects of moving elementary school children from a highly structured classroom to a relatively open classroom.") You would use a procedure similar to the one above to predict effects rather than find causes. After brainstorming and deciding which specific points to discuss, you might formulate this thesis statement:

Cause	Moving children from a highly structured classroom to a relatively open one is likely to encourage more independent play, more flexibility in forming friendship groups, and ultimately more creativity.
Effects	

This thesis statement clearly spells out your position by telling the reader the three main points your essay will consider; it also specifies that these points are effects of the open classroom. After introducing the cause, your essay would treat these three effects in the order in which they are presented in the thesis statement, building up to the most important point. An outline of your paper might look like this:

¶1 Introduction—including thesis that identifies the cause and its effects
¶2 First effect: More independent play
¶3 Second effect: More flexible friendship groups
¶4 Third effect: More creativity (the most important effect)
¶5 Conclusion and summary

Sometimes you will be asked to discuss *both* causes and effects. The following take-home midterm, written for a history class, analyzes some of the causes and effects of the Irish potato famine that occurred between 1847 and 1849. Notice how the student writer, Evelyn Pellicane, concentrates on causes but goes on to discuss briefly the effects of this tragedy, just as the exam question directs.

Question: The 1840s was a volatile decade in Europe. Choose one social, political, or economic event that occurred during those years, analyze its causes, and briefly note how the event influenced later developments in European history.

THE IRISH FAMINE, 1845–1849

Thesis
    The Irish famine, which brought hardship and tragedy to Ireland during the 1840s, was caused and prolonged by four basic factors: the failure of the potato crop, the landlord—tenant system, errors in government policy, and the long—standing prejudice of the British toward Ireland.

First cause
    The immediate cause of the famine was the failure of the potato crop. In 1845, potato disease struck the crop, and potatoes rotted in the ground. The 1846 crop also failed, and before long people were eating weeds. The 1847 crop was healthy, but there weren't

enough potatoes to go around, and in 1848 the blight
struck again, leading to more and more evictions of
tenants by landlords.

Second cause   The tenants' position on the land had never been
very secure. Most had no leases and could be turned
out by their landlords at any time. If a tenant owed
rent, he was evicted—or, worse, put in prison,
leaving his family to starve. The threat of prison
caused many tenants to leave their land; those who
could leave Ireland did so, sometimes with money
provided by their landlords. Some landlords did try
to take care of their tenants, but most did not. Many
were absentee landlords who spent their rent money
abroad.

Third cause   Government policy errors, while not an immediate
cause of the famine, played an important role in
creating an unstable economy and perpetuating
starvation. In 1846, the government decided not to
continue selling corn, as it had during the first
year of the famine, claiming that low-cost purchases
of corn by Ireland had paralyzed British trade by
interfering with free enterprise. Thus, 1846 saw a
starving population, angry demonstrations, and
panic; even those with money were unable to buy food.
Still the government insisted that, if it sent food
to Ireland, prices would rise in the rest of the
United Kingdom and that this would be unfair to hard-
working English and Scots. As a result, no food was
sent. Throughout the years of the famine, the
British government aggravated an already grave
situation: they did nothing to improve agricultural
operations, to help people adjust to another crop,
to distribute seeds, or to reorder the landlord-
tenant system which made the tenants' position so
insecure.

Fourth cause   At the root of this poor government was the long–
standing British prejudice against the Irish.
Hostility between the two countries went back some
six hundred years, and the British were simply not
about to inconvenience themselves to save the Irish.
When the Irish so desperately needed grain to
replace the damaged potatoes, it was clear that
grain had to be imported from England. However, this
meant that the Corn Laws, which had been enacted to
keep the price of British corn high by taxing
imported grain, had to be repealed. The British were
unwilling to repeal the Corn Laws. Even when they did
supply corn meal, they made no attempt to explain to
the Irish how to cook this unfamiliar food. Moreover,
the British government was determined to make
Ireland pay for its own poor, and so it forced the
collection of taxes. Since many landlords just did
not have the tax money, they were forced to evict
their tenants. The British government's callous and
indifferent treatment of the Irish has been called
genocide.

Effects   As a result of this devastating famine, the
population of Ireland was reduced from about nine
million to about six and one–half million. During
the famine years, men roamed the streets looking for
work, begging when they found none. Epidemics of
"famine fever" and dysentery reduced the population
drastically. The most important historical result
of the famine, however, was the massive emigration
to the United States, Canada, and Great Britain of
poor, unskilled people who had to struggle to fit
into a skilled economy and who brought with them a
deep–seated hatred of the British. (This same hatred
remained strong in Ireland itself—–so strong that at
the time of World War II, Ireland, then independent,

remained neutral rather than coming to England's aid.) Irish immigrants faced slums, fever epidemics, joblessness, and hostility—even anti-Catholic and anti-Irish riots—in Boston, New York, London, Glasgow, and Quebec. In Ireland itself, poverty and discontent continued, and by 1848 those emigrating from Ireland included a more highly skilled class of farmer, the ones Ireland needed to recover and to survive.

Conclusion (restatement of thesis)   The Irish famine, one of the great tragedies of the nineteenth century, was a natural disaster compounded by the insensitivity of the British government and the archaic agricultural system of Ireland. While the deaths that resulted depleted Ireland's resources even more, the men and women who emigrated to other countries permanently enriched those nations.

Points for Special Attention

Answering an Exam Question. Before planning and writing her answer, Evelyn Pellicane carefully studied the exam question. She noted that it asks for both causes and effects but that its wording directs her to spend more time on causes ("analyze") than on effects ("briefly note"). Consequently, she divides her discussion in accord with these directions and is careful to indicate *explicitly* which are the causes ("government policy . . . played an important role") and which are the results ("The most important historical result . . ."").

The student author of this essay has obviously been influenced by outside sources; the ideas in the essay are not completely her own. Because this is an exam, however, and because the instructor is aware that the student has based her essay on class notes and assigned readings, she does not have to acknowledge her sources.

Structure. This is a relatively long essay; if it were not so clearly organized, it would be difficult to follow. Because the essay is to focus primarily on causes, Pellicane first introduces the effect—the famine itself—and then considers its causes. After she has examined the causes in the order in which they were set forth in the opening paragraph, she moves on to the results of the famine. She devotes one paragraph to her introduction and one to each cause; she sums up the effects or results in a separate paragraph and devotes the final paragraph to her conclusion. (Depending on a given paper's length and complexity, of course, more—or less—than one paragraph may be devoted to each cause or effect.) An outline for her paper might have looked like this:

¶1   Introduction—including thesis
¶2   First cause: Failure of the potato crop
¶3   Second cause: The landlord-tenant system
¶4   Third cause: Errors in government policy
¶5   Fourth cause: British prejudice
¶6   Results of the famine
¶7   Conclusion

Since the author of this paper feels that all the causes are very important and that they interconnect, they are not presented strictly in order of increasing importance. Instead, she begins with the immediate cause of the famine—the failure of the potato crop—and then digs more deeply until she arrives at the most remote cause, British prejudice.

Cause and Effect Relationships.   The cause and effect relationships in this essay are both subtle and complex; Pellicane considers a series of interconnected relationships and a number of causal chains. Throughout the essay, many words suggest cause and effect connections: *so, therefore, because, as a result, since, led to, brought about, caused,* and the like. These are the most effective transitions for such an essay.

All the selections that follow focus on cause and effect relationships. Some selections stress causes; others emphasize effects. As these essays illustrate, the cause and effect pattern is so versatile that it may be used to examine topics as dissimilar as anthropology, transportation, and sports.

The Telephone
JOHN BROOKS

The cause and effect pattern of development is frequently employed by writers who consider important historical changes. Since technology has transformed our lives, it is only natural for us to speculate about the nature and scope of these changes. In this brief excerpt from his book Telephone: The First Hundred Years, *John Brooks considers the effects, both positive and negative, of the telephone on our lives.*

What has the telephone done to us, or for us, in the hundred years 1
of its existence? A few effects suggest themselves at once. It has saved lives by getting rapid word of illness, injury, or famine from remote places. By joining with the elevator to make possible the multistory residence or office building, it has made possible—for better or worse—the modern city. By bringing about a quantum leap in the speed and ease with which information moves from place to place, it has greatly accelerated the rate of scientific and technological change and growth in industry. Beyond doubt it has crippled if not killed the ancient art of letter writing. It has made living alone possible for persons with normal social impulses; by so doing, it has played a role in one of the greatest social changes of this century, the breakup of the multigenerational household. It has made the waging of war chillingly more efficient than formerly. Perhaps (though not provably) it has prevented wars that might have arisen out of international misunderstanding caused by written communication. Or perhaps—again not provably—by magnifying and extending irrational personal conflicts based on voice contact, it has caused wars. Certainly it has extended the scope of human conflicts, since it impartially disseminates the useful knowedge of scientists and the babble of bores, the affection of the affectionate and the malice of the malicious.

But the question remains unanswered. The obvious effects just 2
cited seem inadequate, mechanistic; they only scratch the surface. Perhaps the crucial effects are evanescent and unmeasurable. Use of the telephone involves personal risk because it involves exposure; for some, to be "hung up on" is among the worst of fears; others dream of a ringing telephone and wake up with a pounding heart. The telephone's actual ring—more, perhaps, than any other sound in our daily lives—evokes hope, relief, fear, anxiety, joy, according to our expectations. The telephone is our nerve-end to society.

In some ways it is in itself a thing of paradox. In one sense a   3
metaphor for the times it helped create, in another sense the
telephone is their polar opposite. It is small and gentle—relying on
low voltages and miniature parts—in times of hugeness and violence. It is basically simple in times of complexity. It is so nearly
human, recreating voices so faithfully that friends or lovers need
not identify themselves by name even when talking across oceans,
that to ask its effects on human life may seem hardly more fruitful
than to ask the effect of the hand or the foot. The Canadian
philosopher Marshall McLuhan—one of the few who have ad-
dressed themselves to these questions—was perhaps not far from
the mark when he spoke of the telephone as creating "a kind of
extra-sensory perception."

COMPREHENSION

1. What are some of the positive effects of the telephone that Brooks
   mentions? What are some negative results?

2. Brooks suggests other crucial effects the telephone may possibly have
   had. What are they? Can you think of any others?

3. How does using the telephone involve "personal risk"?

4. What emotions does Brooks say the telephone's ring may evoke?

5. A paradox is a seeming contradiction that is somehow true. How is the
   telephone "a thing of paradox"?

PURPOSE AND AUDIENCE

1. In one sentence, state the essay's thesis. Why doesn't Brooks include
   such a thesis statement?

2. This excerpt appears at the beginning of a complete book about the
   telephone. What does this tell you about the author's probable purpose in
   writing these paragraphs? How well do you think he has achieved this
   purpose?

3. Brooks uses the first-person plural *us* in this essay instead of speaking
   either just about himself or about people in general. Why do you think he
   does this?

STYLE AND STRUCTURE

1. The essay begins with a question. Would a direct statement be more
   effective as an introduction? Explain.

2. How does the phrasing of the opening question prepare us to accept Brooks's thesis?

3. How does the first sentence in paragraph 2 serve as a transition between paragraphs?

4. Identify the phrases in this essay that explicitly point to the cause and effect connections.

5. Brooks ends his brief introduction to the effects of the telephone with a quotation. Do you think this is an effective conclusion? Explain.

WRITING WORKSHOP

1. Consider a machine that has had a significant effect on your life, such as the television, the duplicating machine, the pocket calculator, the radio, the typewriter, or the electric light. Write an essay whose first sentence is modeled on this essay's opening: "What has _____ done to us, or for us, in the _____ years of its existence?"

2. Write an essay about the effects of the telephone for an audience of school children. You may include some of Brooks's points, but you will have to simplify his explanations considerably.

Who Killed the Bog Men of Denmark? And Why?
MAURICE SHADBOLT

Mystery stories and archaeological explorations both seek to unearth causes which can explain perplexing situations. This selection combines archaeology and mystery to determine why a group of men died some two thousand years ago. To explain this puzzle, Maurice Shadbolt examines the direct and indirect causes of the deaths of the ancient bog men of Denmark.

Every year in the Danish town of Silkeborg, thousands of visitors file past the face of a murder victim. No one will ever know his name. It is enough to know that 2000 years ago he was as human as ourselves. That face has moved men and women to poetry, and to tears. 1

Last summer I journeyed to the lake-girt Danish town and, peering at that face behind glass in a modest museum, I felt awe—for his every wrinkle and whisker tell a vivid and terrible tale from Denmark's distant past. The rope which choked off the man's breath is still around his neck. Yet it is a perplexingly peaceful face, inscrutable, one to haunt the imagination. 2

This strangest of ancient murder mysteries began 27 years ago, on May 8, 1950, when two brothers, Emil and Viggo Højgaard, were digging peat in Tollund Fen, near Silkeborg. Their spring sowing finished, the brothers were storing up the umber-brown peat for their kitchen range, and for warmth in the winter to come. It was a peaceful task on a sunny morning. Snipe called from the aspens and firs fringing the dank bowl of the fen, where only heather and coarse grass grew. Then, at a depth of nine feet, their spades suddenly struck something. 3

They were gazing, with fright and fascination, at a face underfoot. The corpse was naked but for a skin cap, resting on its side as if asleep, arms and legs bent. The face was gentle, with eyes closed and lips lightly pursed. There was stubble on the chin. The bewildered brothers called the Silkeborg police. 4

Quick to the scene, the police did not recognize the man as anyone listed missing. Shrewdly guessing the brothers might have blundered into a black hole in Europe's past, the police called in archeologists. 5

Enter Prof. Peter Glob, a distinguished scholar from nearby 6
Aarhus University, who carefully dislodged a lump of peat from
beside the dead man's head. A rope made of two twisted hide
thongs encircled his neck. He had been strangled or hanged. But
when, and by whom? Glob ordered a box to be built about the
corpse and the peat in which it lay, so nothing might be disturbed.

Next day, the box, weighing nearly a ton, was manhandled out 7
of the bog onto a horse-drawn cart, on its way for examination at
Copenhagen's National Museum. One of Glob's helpers collapsed
and died with the huge effort. It seemed a dark omen, as if some
old god were claiming a modern man in place of a man from the
past.

Bog bodies were nothing new—since records have been kept, 8
Denmark's bogs have surrendered no fewer than 400—and the
preservative qualities of the humic acid in peat have long been
known. But not until the 19th century did scientists and historians
begin to glimpse the finds and understand that the bodies belonged
to remote, murky recesses of European prehistory. None survived
long: the corpses were either buried again or crumbled quickly
with exposure to light and air.

When peat-digging was revived during and after World War II, 9
bodies were unearthed in abundance—first in 1942 at Store Arden,
then in 1946, 1947 and 1948 at Borre Fen. Artifacts found beside
them positively identified them as people of Denmark's Early Iron
Age, from 400 B.C. to A.D. 400. None, then, was less than 1500
years old, and some were probably much older. The first of the
Borre Fen finds—a full-grown male—was to prove especially significant: Borre Fen man, too, had died violently, with a noose about
his neck, strangled or hanged. And his last meal had consisted of
grain.

Peter Glob, alongside his artist father (a portraitist and distin- 10
guished amateur archeologist), had been digging into Denmark's
dim past since he was a mere eight years old. For him, the Tollund
man, who had by far the best-preserved head to survive from
antiquity, was a supreme challenge. Since 1936, Glob had been
living imaginatively with the pagan hunters and farmers of 2000
years ago, fossicking among their corroded artifacts, foraging among
the foundations of their simple villages; he knew their habits, the
rhythms of their lives. Suddenly, here was a man of that very time.
"Majesty and gentleness," he recalls, "seemed to stamp his features
as they did when he was alive." What was this enigmatic face trying
to tell him?

Glob was intrigued by the fact that so many of the people found 11

in bogs had died violently: strangled or hanged, throats slit, heads
battered. Perhaps they had been travelers set upon by brigands, or
executed criminals. But there might be a different explanation.
These murder victims all belonged to the Danish Iron Age. If they
were to be explained away as victims of robber bands, there should
be a much greater spread in time—into other ages. Nor would
executed criminals all have had so many common traits.

Glob considered the body with care. X rays of Tollund man's   12
vertebrae, taken to determine whether he had been strangled or
hanged, produced inconclusive results. The condition of the wisdom teeth suggested a man well over 20 years old. An autopsy
revealed that the heart, lungs and liver were well preserved; most
important, the alimentary canal was undisturbed, containing the
dead man's last meal—a 2000-year-old gruel of hand-milled grains
and seeds: barley, linseed, flaxseed, knotgrass, among others.
Knowledge of prehistoric agriculture made it possible to determine
that the man had lived in the first 200 years A.D. The mixture of
grains and seeds suggested a meal prepared in winter or early
spring.

Since Iron Age men were not vegetarians, why were there no   13
traces of meat? Glob also marveled that the man's hands and feet
were soft; he appeared to have done little or no heavy labor in his
lifetime. Possibly, then, he was high-ranking in Iron Age society.

Then, on April 26, 1952, peat-digging villagers from Grauballe,   14
11 miles east of Tollund, turned up a second spectacularly well-
preserved body, and again Glob was fast to the scene. Unmistakably
another murder victim, this discovery was, unlike Tollund man, far
from serene. The man's throat had been slashed savagely from ear
to ear. His face was twisted with terror, and his lips were parted
with a centuries-silenced cry of pain.

Glob swiftly removed the body—still imbedded in a great block   15
of peat—for preservation and study. Carbon-dating of body tissue
proved Grauballe man to be about 1650 years old, a contemporary
of Constantine the Great. Grauballe man was in extraordinary
condition; his fingerprints and footprints came up clearly. Tallish
and dark-haired, Grauballe man, like Tollund man, had never done
any heavy manual work. He had been slain in his late 30s. Another
similarity came to light when Grauballe man's last meal was
analyzed: it had been eaten immediately before death and, like
Tollund man's, like Borre Fen man's too, it was a gruel of grains
and seeds, a meal of winter, or early spring. All three had perished
in a similar season.

Who had killed these men of the bogs? Why in winter, or early   16 spring? Why should they—apparently—have led privileged lives? And why the same kind of meals before their sudden ends?

The bodies had told Glob all they could. Now he turned to one 17 of his favorite sources—the Roman historian Tacitus. Nearly 2000 years ago Tacitus recorded the oral traditions of Germanic tribes who inhabited northwest Europe. Tacitus' account of these wild, brave and generous blue-eyed people often shed light into dark corners of Denmark's past. Glob found these lines: "At a time laid down in the distant past, all peoples that are related by blood meet in a sacred wood. Here they celebrate their barbarous rites with a human sacrifice."

Elsewhere, Tacitus wrote: "These people are distinguished by 18 a common worship of Nerthus, or Mother Earth. They believe that she interests herself in human affairs." Tacitus confirmed early spring as a time among the Germanic tribes for offerings and human sacrifice. They were asking the goddess to hasten the coming of spring, and the summer harvest. Men chosen for sacrifice might well have been given a symbolic meal, made up of plant seeds, before being consecrated through death to the goddess—thus explaining the absence of meat. The sacrificial men, with their delicate features, neat hands and feet, might have been persons of high rank chosen by lot for sacrifice, or priests, ritually married to Nerthus.

Tacitus supplied another essential clue: the symbol of Nerthus, 19 he recorded, was a twisted metal "torque," or neck ring, worn by the living to honor the goddess. The leather nooses about the necks of Tollund man and the body from Borre Fen and some earlier bodies were replicas of those neck rings. Glob concluded that it was Nerthus—Mother Earth herself—who had preserved her victims perfectly in her peaty bosom long after those who had fed them into the bogs were dust.

Peter Glob was satisfied. He had found the killer and identified 20 the victims. The centuries-old mystery of Denmark's bog bodies was no more.

COMPREHENSION

1. Identify at least one *result* of each of the following: the Højgaard brothers discover a body; the box containing the body is moved; the humic acid in peat has preservative qualities; peat digging is revived after World War II.

2. Identify at least one *cause* of each of the following: the man's hands and

feet are soft; his last meal was grain; he died a violent death; he wears a rope around his neck.

3. From what different sources do the clues about the bog man's murder come?

PURPOSE AND AUDIENCE

1. This essay originally appeared in *The Reader's Digest,* a magazine that prints selections likely to interest a wide general audience. In what ways does this selection qualify?

2. This essay has no arguable thesis. What, then, is the author's purpose in writing the essay?

STYLE AND STRUCTURE

1. In what ways is the structure of this essay similar to that of a modern mystery story? Identify the detective, the clues, and the background research. How is it different from a mystery story?

2. Are the style and structure of this essay different from those of a newspaper account? If so, how?

3. The author begins in the first person as if to make himself a part of the story he is relating. Do you think his brief appearance adds to or detracts from the essay's effectiveness? Why?

4. The author begins in the present tense and then uses flashbacks. How would the impact of the essay change if the author had used strict chronological order?

5. Several quotations appear in this essay. Are these direct quotations more convincing than the author's paraphrases would be? Why or why not?

WRITING WORKSHOP

1. Write a biographical sketch of the man the Højgaard brothers discovered, establishing the causes of his death.

2. Write an editorial for the Silkeborg daily newspaper in which you discuss the benefits and drawbacks for the town of the bog man's discovery.

3. Write an essay unraveling a mystery in your own life; for instance, explain the causes of a friend's strange actions or the reasons your family settled where it did years (or generations) ago.

Who Killed Benny Paret?

NORMAN COUSINS

Like the preceding selection about the bog men of Denmark, this essay investigates the cause of a man's death. Its purpose, however, is strongly persuasive. In answering the question posed by his essay's title, Norman Cousins takes a strong stand against violence in sports.

Sometime about 1935 or 1936 I had an interview with Mike Jacobs, the prize-fight promoter. I was a fledgling reporter at that time; my beat was education but during the vacation season I found myself on varied assignments, all the way from ship news to sports reporting. In this way I found myself sitting opposite the most powerful figure in the boxing world.

There was nothing spectacular in Mr. Jacobs' manner or appearance; but when he spoke about prize fights, he was no longer a bland little man but a colossus who sounded the way Napoleon must have sounded when he reviewed a battle. You knew you were listening to Number One. His saying something made it true.

We discussed what to him was the only important element in successful promoting—how to please the crowd. So far as he was concerned, there was no mystery to it. You put killers in the ring and the people filled your arena. You hire boxing artists—men who are adroit at feinting, parrying, weaving, jabbing, and dancing, but who don't pack dynamite in their fists—and you wind up counting your empty seats. So you searched for the killers and sluggers and maulers—fellows who could hit with the force of a baseball bat.

I asked Mr. Jacobs if he was speaking literally when he said people came out to see the killer.

"They don't come out to see a tea party," he said evenly. "They come out to see the knockout. They come out to see a man hurt. If they think anything else, they're kidding themselves."

Recently, a young man by the name of Benny Paret was killed in the ring. The killing was seen by millions; it was on television. In the twelfth round, he was hit hard in the head several times, went down, was counted out, and never came out of the coma.

The Paret fight produced a flurry of investigations. Governor Rockefeller was shocked by what happened and appointed a committee to assess the responsibility. The New York State Boxing Commission decided to find out what was wrong. The District

189

Attorney's office expressed its concern. One question that was solemnly studied in all three probes concerned the action of the referee. Did he act in time to stop the fight? Another question had to do with the role of the examining doctors who certified the physical fitness of the fighters before the bout. Still another question involved Mr. Paret's manager; did he rush his boy into the fight without adequate time to recuperate from the previous one?

In short, the investigators looked into every possible cause 8 except the real one. Benny Paret was killed because the human fist delivers enough impact, when directed against the head, to produce a massive hemorrhage in the brain. The human brain is the most delicate and complex mechanism in all creation. It has a lacework of millions of highly fragile nerve connections. Nature attempts to protect this exquisitely intricate machinery by encasing it in a hard shell. Fortunately, the shell is thick enough to withstand a great deal of pounding. Nature, however, can protect man against everything except man himself. Not every blow to the head will kill a man—but there is always the risk of concussion and damage to the brain. A prize fighter may be able to survive even repeated brain concussions and go on fighting, but the damage to his brain may be permanent.

In any event, it is futile to investigate the referee's role and seek 9 to determine whether he should have intervened to stop the fight earlier. That is not where the primary responsibility lies. The primary responsibility lies with the people who pay to see a man hurt. The referee who stops a fight too soon from the crowd's viewpoint can expect to be booed. The crowd wants the knockout; it wants to see a man stretched out on the canvas. This is the supreme moment in boxing. It is nonsense to talk about prize fighting as a test of boxing skills. No crowd was ever brought to its feet screaming and cheering at the sight of two men beautifully dodging and weaving out of each other's jabs. The time the crowd comes alive is when a man is hit hard over the heart or the head, when his mouthpiece flies out, when the blood squirts out of his nose or eyes, when he wobbles under the attack and his pursuer continues to smash at him with pole-axe impact.

Don't blame it on the referee. Don't even blame it on the fight 10 managers. Put the blame where it belongs—on the prevailing mores that regard prize fighting as a perfectly proper enterprise and vehicle of entertainment. No one doubts that many people enjoy prize fighting and will miss it if it should be thrown out. And that is precisely the point.

COMPREHENSION

1. Why, according to Mike Jacobs, do people come to see a prizefight? Does Cousins agree with him?

2. What were the official responses to Paret's death?

3. What was the immediate cause of Paret's death? What remote causes did the investigators consider? What, according to Cousins, is the primary cause? (That is, where does the "primary responsibility" lie?)

4. Why does Cousins feel that "it is futile to investigate the referee's role"?

5. Cousins ends his essay with "And that is precisely the point." What is the "point" to which he refers?

PURPOSE AND AUDIENCE

1. This persuasive essay has a strong thesis. What is it?

2. This essay appeared on May 5, 1962, a month after Paret died. What do you suppose its impact was on its audience? Is the impact the same today, or has it changed?

3. Why does Cousins present information about Mike Jacobs in the first two paragraphs?

4. At whom is this essay aimed—boxing enthusiasts, sports writers, or a general audience? What led you to your conclusion?

5. Does Cousins expect his audience to agree with his thesis? How does he try to win their sympathy for his position?

STYLE AND STRUCTURE

1. The essay begins with a brief narrative describing a meeting between Cousins and Mike Jacobs. Where does this narrative introduction end?

2. Once Paret's death is mentioned and the persuasive portion of the essay begins, the introductory narrative never resumes. Why not? Do you think this weakens the essay? Explain.

3. Sort out the complex cause and effect relationships discussed in paragraph 9.

4. Look at the last two sentences in paragraph 9. How does the contrast between them advance the essay's thesis?

5. What strategy does Cousins use in his conclusion? Is it effective? Explain.

WRITING WORKSHOP

1. Write a cause and effect essay examining how the demands of the public affect a professional sport. (You might examine violence in hockey or football, for example, or the ways in which an individual player cultivates an image for the fans.)

2. Write a cause and effect essay about a time when you did something you felt was dishonest or unwise in response to peer pressure. Be sure to identify the causes for your actions.

Riding on Air
ARTHUR C. CLARKE

Arthur C. Clarke, a prolific writer well known for his science-fiction pieces, turns to scientific fact here. Clarke's speculation about the future, in both his fiction and his nonfiction, often uses cause and effect reasoning. In "Riding on Air," he uses such reasoning to advance an intriguing suggestion about our transportation system.

Our century has seen two great revolutions in transport, each of which has changed the very pattern of human society. The automobile and the airplane have created a world that no man of a hundred years ago could have conceived in his wildest dreams. Yet both are now being challenged by something so new that it does not even have a name—something that may make the future as strange and alien to us as our world of superhighways and giant airports would be to a man from 1890. For this third revolution may bring about the passing of the wheel, our faithful servant since the dawn of history.

In many countries—the United States, England, the U.S.S.R., Switzerland, and doubtless elsewhere—major engineering efforts are now in progress to develop vehicles which literally float on air. The pioneering Saunders-Roe SR-N1 "Hovercraft" led to the 160-ton SR-N4's, which have ferried thousands of passengers across the English Channel, and far larger models are on the drawing board. They all depend for their operation on what is known as "Ground Effect," and for this reason have been called Ground Effect Machines or G.E.M.'s.

Although G.E.M.'s, since they support themselves by downward blasts of air, have a superficial resemblance to helicopters, they operate on quite different principles. If you are content to float only a few inches from the ground, you can support, *for the same horsepower*, many times the load that a helicopter can lift into the open sky. You can demonstrate this in your own home by an extremely simple experiment.

Suspend an electric fan in the middle of the room, so that it is free to move back and forth; then switch it on. You will find that the fan recoils a quarter of an inch or so, owing to the blast of air it produces. The thrust is not very great, yet this is the effect which drives all our airplanes and helicopters through the sky.

Now take the same fan and hang it facing the wall, as close to it

1

2

3

4

5

as the wire guard will allow you. This time, when you switch it on, you will find that the recoil is two or three times greater than before, because some of the air blast is being trapped as a kind of cushion between the fan and the wall. The more effective the trapping, the bigger the recoil. If you fitted a shroud or cowling round the fan to prevent the air from spilling out in all directions, the kick would increase still further.

This tells us what we must do if we wish to ride on a cushion   6
of air. Visualize a flat surface, and a slightly hollowed plate lying on top of it—such as a saucer, face downward. If we could blow into the saucer with sufficient force, it would rise until the air spilled out round the rim, and would remain floating a fraction of an inch above the ground.

In the right circumstances, even a small quantity of air can   7
produce a remarkable amount of lift. The scientists of the European Centre for Nuclear Research (CERN) recently put this effect to good use. They were confronted with the problem of moving equipment weighing up to three hundred tons—and, even trickier, of positioning it in the laboratory to within a fraction of a millimeter.

So they used saucer-shaped steel discs, about a yard across, with   8
rubber gaskets around the edges. When air at a pressure of seventy pounds per square inch is blown into such a pad, it can lift ten or twenty tons with ease. Equally important, there is so little friction that you can push the load around the lab with your fingers.

It is obvious that industry and heavy engineering will find many   9
uses for these floating saucers, and one trivial but amusing application of them has already entered the home. There is now a vacuum cleaner on the market that drifts effortlessly above the carpet, supported on its own exhaust, so that the busy housewife can get back to the TV set that vital few seconds earlier.

But what has all this got to do, you may wonder, with general   10
transportation? There are not many road surfaces as smooth as laboratory floors, or even dining-room carpets, so it would hardly seem that the good old-fashioned wheel has much to worry about.

However, this is a shortsighted view, as the scientists who started   11
looking into the theory of the ground effect soon discovered. Although the small-scale devices just mentioned will operate only on smooth, flat surfaces, when they are built in larger sizes the situation is completely different—and fraught with excitement to the transportation engineer.

For the bigger you make your G.E.M., the higher it will ride off   12
the ground and, therefore, the rougher the terrain it can cross. The Saunders-Roe SR-N1 skimmed along at a maximum altitude of

fifteen inches, but its larger successors will float at shoulder height on the invisible cushion formed by their curtains of downward-moving air.

Because they have no physical contact with the surface beneath them, G.E.M.'s can travel with equal ease over ice, snow, sand, plowed fields, swamps, molten lava—you name it, the G.E.M. can cross it. All other transport vehicles are specialized beasts, able to tackle only one or two kinds of terrain; and nothing has yet been invented that can travel swiftly and smoothly over a single one of the surfaces just mentioned. But to the G.E.M. they are all alike—*and a superhighway is no better.*

It takes some time to grasp this idea, and to realize that the immense networks of roads upon which two generations of mankind have spent a substantial fraction of their wealth may soon become obsolete. Traffic lanes of a sort would still be needed, of course, to keep vehicles out of residential areas, and to avoid the chaos that would result if every driver took the straightest line to his destination that geography allowed. But they need no longer be paved—they would merely be graded, so that they were clear of obstacles more than, say, six inches high. They would not even have to be laid on good foundations, for the weight of a G.E.M. is spread over several square yards, not concentrated at a few points of contact.

Today's turnpikes might well last for generations without any further maintenance if they had to carry only air-supported vehicles; the concrete could crack and become covered with moss—it would not matter in the least. There will clearly be enormous savings in road costs—amounting to billions a year—once we have abolished the wheel. But there will be a very difficult transition period before the characteristic road sign of the 1990's becomes universal: NO WHEELED VEHICLES ON THIS HIGHWAY.

Since the G.E.M.'s or aircars of the future need stick to the traffic lanes only when their drivers feel like it, the chief motoring offense at the turn of the century will not be speeding, but trespass. It is too much to expect that refugees from the cities, with the power to move like clouds over the length and breadth of the land, will refrain from entering and exploring any attractive piece of scenery that takes their fancy. Barbed-wire may make a second debut in the West as irate farmers try to keep weekenders from littering their land with picnic trash. Strategically placed rocks would be more effective, but they would have to be spaced close together, otherwise the invaders could slip between them.

There are few spots that a skillful aircar driver could not reach, and the breakdown vans of the future are going to receive S.O.S.

calls from families stranded in some very odd places. The Grand Canyon, for example—what a challenge that presents to the airborne motorist! It might even be possible to develop a specialized form of G.E.M. that could climb mountains; the driver could take his time—and throw out ground anchors if necessary—as he worked his way cautiously up the slanting surfaces of rock, snow, or ice. But this would, definitely, not be an operation for beginners.

If such ideas seem a little farfetched, that is because we still belong to the age of the wheel, and our minds cannot free themselves from its tyranny—perfectly summed up in the warning SOFT SHOULDERS. This is a phrase that will be meaningless to our grandchildren; to them, if a surface is reasonably plane, it will not matter whether it consists of concrete or quagmire.

It is only fair to point out that the large-scale use of private or family G.E.M.'s may not be a very practical proposition while we have to depend on the gasoline engine. Apart from the noise—and dust—it requires several hundred horsepower to produce speeds of only 60 m.p.h. Although there will certainly be great improvements in performance, it seems that at the present moment the smaller types of G.E.M. are of interest chiefly to the armed forces, farmers who have to deal with broken or flooded land, movie directors after unusual tracking shots, and similar specialized customers who can foot the gas bills.

But the gas engine is on its way out, as any petroleum geologist will assure you in his more unguarded moments. Before very much longer, out of sheer necessity, we must find some other source of power—perhaps a sophisticated type of electric battery, with at least a hundred times the capacity of today's clumsy monsters. Whatever the answer, within a few more decades there will be lightweight, long-endurance motors of some kind, ready to take over when the oil wells run dry. These will power the private aircars of the future, as the gasoline engine has driven the earth-bound automobiles of the past.

With the emancipation of traffic from the road, we will at last have achieved real mobility over the face of the Earth. The importance of this to Africa, Australia, South America, Antarctica, and all countries that lack (and now may never possess) well-developed highway systems can scarcely be overestimated. Pampas, steppes, veldt, prairies, snowfields, swamps, deserts—all will be able to carry heavy, high-speed traffic more smoothly, and perhaps more economically, than the finest roads that exist today. The opening up of the polar regions may well depend upon the speed with which freight-carrying G.E.M.'s are developed.

We will return to this subject later, but now it is time to go to   22
sea. For G.E.M.'s, of course, can travel with equal ease over land
or water. As they grow larger and faster, these sizeable vehicles
may have a revolutionary effect upon commerce, international
politics, and even the distribution of population. We do not need
any hypothetical new power plants to make them practical; when
we start thinking in terms of thousands of tons, today's gas turbines
are quite adequate and tomorrow's nuclear reactors will be even
better. As soon as we have gathered enough experience from the
present primitive models, we will be able to build giant, oceangoing
G.E.M.'s capable of carrying intercontinental cargoes at speeds of
at least a hundred miles an hour.

Unlike today's ships, the air-supported liners and freighters of   23
the next generation will be low, flat-bottomed vessels. They will
be extremely maneuverable—G.E.M.'s can move backward or
sideways simply by altering the direction of their air blasts—and
will normally float at an altitude of about ten feet. This will enable
them to skim smoothly over all but the very roughest seas. One
consequence of this is that they could be quite lightly constructed,
and would, therefore, be much more efficient than seaborne ships,
which must be built to withstand enormous stresses and strains.

Their speed would enable them to outrun or avoid all storms; in   24
any event, by the time they become operational the meteorological
satellites will have provided us with a worldwide weather service,
and every captain will know exactly what to expect during the few
hours he is at sea. In a hurricane, a large G.E.M. might even be
safer than a conventional ship of the same size, for it would be
above most of the wave action.

Because a "hovership" is completely indifferent to breakers,   25
reefs, and shoals, it could operate in waters where no other type of
marine craft could navigate. This may open up to commercial and
game fishermen thousands of square miles of absolutely virgin
territory, and may revolutionize the life of island communities. Vast
areas of the Great Barrier Reef—the 1,250-mile-long coral rampart
guarding the northeastern coast of Australia—are almost inacces-
sible except in a dead calm, and many of its smaller islands have
never been visited by man. A reliable G.E.M. bus service would,
alas, turn these minute pandanus-clad jewels into desirable housing
estates and holiday resorts.

As the G.E.M. is the most frictionless type of vehicle yet   26
invented, it can certainly travel much faster than any existing type
of marine craft, including 300 m.p.h. jetpropelled hydroplanes. This
suggests that the airlines may be in for some stiff competition, for

there are many passengers willing to spend days—but not weeks—at sea, especially if a smooth ride can be guaranteed. A vessel that could cruise at a modest 150 m.p.h. could get from London to New York in a day, thus neatly plugging the gap in the speed spectrum between the *Queen Mary* and the Boeing 747.

What makes the G.E.M. so attractive as a passenger vehicle is its built-in safety factor. When the engines of an airliner fail, or any major defect develops in the structure, there is little hope for those aboard. But almost anything could happen to a G.E.M., short of a head-on collision, and it would gently settle down onto its floats, without spilling a single drink in the bar. It would have no need for the immensely elaborate and expensive navigational and safety networks essential for air transport; in an emergency, the captain could always sit tight and think matters over, without worrying about his fuel reserve. From this point of view, G.E.M.'s seem to combine the best features of ships and aircraft, with remarkably few of their disadvantages.   27

The most shattering implications of G.E.M.'s do not, however, arise from their speed or their safety, but from the fact that they can ignore the divisions between land and sea. An oceangoing G.E.M. need not stop at the coastline; it can continue on inland with a supreme indifference to the great harbors and seaports that have been established by five thousand years of maritime commerce. (The SR-N1 has run up a beach with twenty fully armed Marines aboard; imagine what a fleet of such assault craft could have done on D-Day.)   28

Any stretch of coast that was not fronted by sheer cliffs would be an open door to G.E.M. freighters or liners. They could continue on inland with scarcely a pause for a thousand miles if need be, to deliver cargoes and passengers in the heart of a continent. All they would require would be fairly wide traffic lanes or throughways, clear of obstacles more than a yard or two in height; old railway tracks, of which there will be a good supply by the close of this century, will do excellently. And these lanes need not be dead ground, as are today's highways and railroads. They could be used for a wide variety of agricultural purposes—though not, it must be admitted, for the growing of wheat. The man-made gales would be a little too severe.   29

All this is very bad news for San Francisco, New Orleans, London, Los Angeles, Naples, Marseilles and any other seaport you care to name. But it is much worse news for Egypt and Panama.   30

Precisely. The "ships" of the future are not going to crawl along narrow ditches at five miles and a thousand dollars an hour, when   31 they can skim over land at twenty times the speed—*and can pick and choose their routes with almost the same freedom as in the open sea.*

The political consequences of this will be, to say the least,   32
extremely interesting. The entire Middle East situation would be
very different if Israel (or for that matter half a dozen other countries)
could put the Suez Canal permanently out of business merely by
offering unspoiled desert on highly competitive terms. And as for
Panama—I will leave that for the quiet contemplation of the United
States Navy and State Department.

It is an instructive and mind-stretching exercise to take a relief   33
map of the world, and to imagine where the G.E.M.'s trade routes
of the future will lie. Half a century from now, will Oklahoma City
be a greater port than Chicago? (Think of the millions of tons of
shipping that could maneuver on the Great Plains!) What is the
best way to take a 100-thousand-ton freighter through the Rockies,
the Andes, or the Himalayas? Will Switzerland become a major
shipbuilding nation? Will purely waterborne craft survive at all,
when land and ocean become a single continuum?

These are questions that we will soon have to answer. The   34
sudden and unexpected development of the G.E.M. requires us to
indulge in some particularly agile mental gymnastics; in our
preoccupation with cargoes hurled through the upper atmosphere
at the speed of sound, we have completely overlooked a major
revolution at sea level—one which may have brought us quite
literally to the end of the road.

COMPREHENSION

1. What are the advantages of the G.E.M.'s? What are the disadvantages?

2. List the effects Clarke feels the adoption of G.E.M.'s would have on our transportation system. Can you add others to his list?

3. Beyond transportation, Clarke speculates on the long-range social, economic, and political effects G.E.M.'s might have on countries around the world. List the ones he mentions. Which do you consider most significant?

PURPOSE AND AUDIENCE

1. Although Clarke is a respected scientist, this essay is not aimed at experts like himself. For whom is he writing? Point to specific passages that show what kind of readers he is addressing.

2. Clarke is writing this essay to inform, to entertain, and to persuade. Identify passages that serve each purpose.

3. What is Clarke's thesis in this essay?

STYLE AND STRUCTURE

1. Why does Clarke begin his essay by discussing the automobile and the airplane?

2. Clarke frequently addresses the reader as *you* and sometimes seems to be engaging in a dialogue with the reader. Why do you think he does this?

3. At one point, Clarke begins a new paragraph by announcing, "We will return to this subject later, but now it is time to go to sea." Can you suggest a more conventional transition? Which seems more effective? Why?

4. Why does Clarke ask questions in paragraph 33?

5. This selection includes a two-paragraph process explanation which is vital to the essay's development. What is the function of this process explanation?

WRITING WORKSHOP

1. Write a similar essay, as if you were speculating a century ago, about the airplane or the automobile.

2. Invent a new machine, and write an essay explaining the effects it will have on society.

3. Write an essay about the possible effects of eliminating some familiar and widely used invention.

Side Effects of Marathon Swimming
DIANA NYAD

In this excerpt from her autobiography, Other Shores, *Diana Nyad, a long-distance swimmer, talks about the unusual physical and mental side effects of marathon swimming. As you read, notice that some of the effects she describes also function as causes.*

Sometimes when I'm swimming, especially after a number of hours, I feel as though I am in the middle of a hallucination beyond my control. For many years, both during the hours of laps for sprint swimming and then during the long hours of continual swimming for the marathons, I had been experiencing what I considered to be very bizarre trips. I had gone through entire LSD trips without the drug (I took several acid trips to compare the experiences) while swimming, but I couldn't find another swimmer who was interpreting his experience in the same way. I had no reinforcement, no friend with whom to converse and learn. When I read the material of neurophysiologist John Lilly on sensory deprivation, I realized that what I had been going through on the long swims was the most successful experiment. 1

In the experimental sense, sensory deprivation means cutting off all the senses from outside stimulation and leaving the brain to its own devices. Lilly's method of doing this was to float for a number of hours in a large tank filled with an extremely dense solution so that the body would float very high. He would float on the surface with the room darkened or with dark goggles over his eyes. He discovered that if the water was kept at 93°F, he wouldn't be able to differentiate hot from cold, and his tactile sense wouldn't function. His hearing would disappear; his ears would be just under the surface and no sound waves were being produced in the tank. Lilly and hundreds of others (myself included) floated in his tanks for varying lengths of time, and each individual experienced the same phenomenon: When deprived of sensory stimulation, the brain is vitally active. Everyone who came out of the tanks said that he'd had very vivid daydreams and seemingly wild fantasies and everyone said that he felt rested. 2

Is this beginning to sound like self-hypnosis? Self-hypnosis becomes successful when you can entirely block out all outside stimuli and bring your mind to a pinpoint focus on one thought or one sensory image, such as a blinking light. When that pinpoint 3 focus is complete, the mind is free to travel and to remember and to imagine much better than when it is inhibited by the duties of ordinary sensory attention. And when the hypnotic trance is over, you feel as though your mind has been immensely creative at the same time that you feel wonderfully rested—just as floating in a sensory-deprivation tank produces many of the same effects as self-hypnosis.

This is where sports come in: Most require a concentrated focus   4
and a shutting out of outside stimuli. Aside from physical fitness, sociability and the particular pleasures that come with specific sports, many people participate in sports on a casual level for the mental freedom and relaxation they provide.

And on the higher levels, sports become a true meditation   5
ground. The beginning tennis player must constantly remind himself to "get the racket back, hit the ball in front of the body, put the body weight into the stroke." But the world-class player will undoubtedly play better if he can completely eliminate all outside stimuli, including his own conscious voice. When he sees the ball approaching over the net, his eyes focus on that spinning seam; he doesn't hear the crowd, he doesn't notice the heat, he just switches to automatic pilot and performs with the grace and speed of a cheetah. This is concentration, self-hypnosis—in effect, sensory deprivation. In tennis, the masters of concentration are Evert and Borg. It is always said that they never change expression; they apparently are not emotionally involved, which is another way of saying that their focus is so intense that it precludes other levels of awareness.

Sports such as tennis, football, skiing, and running are not cases   6
of strict sensory deprivation, however. Vision and hearing are necessary to perform well, which makes absolute sensory deprivation impossible. Marathon swimming, on the other hand, is the one sport where an absolute study of sensory deprivation can be made. It is the nature of the sport that the sensory functions cease to operate. It also lends itself to immediate and extreme self-hypnosis.

I wear a pair of plastic goggles and try very hard not to touch   7
them for the duration of the swim. The goggles fog over within just a few minutes after the start of the swim. I am breathing to my left, sixty times a minute, trying to catch a glimpse of my boat, and occasionally my trainer, through this seemingly dense fog. During the first few hours, when I am fresh, I can read short messages on the blackboard, and for a few hours after that, I can't read words but I can see the large numbers that tell me what hour I'm in.

Fatigue and the process of turning the head so many times a minute without ever focusing take their toll, and after approximately ten hours, I become almost blind. The only solution would be to take the goggles off, but my sight would still be extremely poor due to distortion, an experience much like what happens if you step out into the daylight after being enclosed in a pitch-black room for a number of hours. When I can no longer see while swimming, my trainer communicates with me by whistle. If I hear one long pull on the police whistle, I know I am veering too far to the right and I edge back toward the left. Two long pulls mean I must edge back toward the right; I am getting too close to the boat. Several short trills mean that I should stop and look to the boat for instruction. I may have swum too far ahead of the boat or am too far behind it; sometimes I am about to run into a dangerous piece of debris, or it is time to approach the boat for a feeding.

My hearing doesn't go completely, but it is 90 percent ineffectual.   8 I can usually hear the police whistle, although the crew often have to give me the signal a dozen times before I hear it and respond accordingly. Well into the swim, it is virtually impossible for me to discern words. If instruction is imperative, I try to raise the cap over my ears; the trainer has to yell at the top of his lungs, slowly and distinctly, and even then I am liable to catch only a couple of words. On the Lake Ontario swim, we hooked up giant speakers in hopes that I would be able to hear some music and ease my boredom. I never heard a note.

Because of visual and aural deprivation, all communication is   9 cut off. No outside stimulation can penetrate to the swimmer. Besides sight and hearing, other senses fail. The tactile sense is distorted because of the immersion time. Taste and smell are obliterated in the water. When I am in the middle of the swim, I would give anything for some outside stimulation of any sort. But when the swim is finally over, I realize that the fascinating mental process and the mental exhilaration would never have surfaced without the sensory deprivation.

To me, the long swims have become hypnotic sessions. My   10 memory delves back into my childhood, even to as early as two years old, to sift through events and reinterpret dialogue that I couldn't possibly remember when "conscious." My imagination flowers to the point that I am wonderfully entertained by the scenes I paint on my eyelids and I am sincerely frightened by the horrors I imagine myself to be confronting.

In most sports, it isn't easy to reach that point of pure focus   11 where all outside stimulation is blocked out. For me, it is so easy that it often becomes dangerous. My stroke has become automatic. If I'm cut off from any outside communication, if I don't have to think about swimming technique, if I'm not capable of focusing on any concrete subject (such as money) for more than thirty seconds, then how does my mind occupy itself? Left with such freedom, as on an acid trip, the mind does not restrict itself. Unlike an acid trip, there is no danger of drug abuse to the body and there would seemingly be no reason to stop the mind from going just as far as it wanted. The ideal situation, if letting the mind go was the sole interest, would be to swim for forty hours at a good pace, with no athletic objective, no one to beat, no record to break, no record to establish. It would be a much greater mind trip than floating in the deprivation tank, self-hypnosis or meditation. I have done all three; the mind will take a longer and richer voyage during the long swim. On the other hand, it seems so impractical to train like a bastard for years to be able to swim non-stop in open water for forty hours so that you can have a wild mind trip. I have compromised by setting athletic goals for myself while still being able to take the mind trip; the compromise is that I've had to come up with some technique to control the mind expansion so that I won't go too far away and render myself incapable of continuing to swim.

At first I tried singing songs to myself. Popular songs. Beatles. 12 Laura Nyro. But most of the time I was too delirious to remember the exact lyrics or to remember if I had sung one line twice or forgotten a line. And since the songs varied in cadence and rhythm, I was disturbed at not being able to syncopate my stroke with the song. Then I tried making up conversations among people, like I do at home. I would have party A speaking among parties B, C and D in an elaborate discussion about the beginning of the universe. Needless to say, this technique only contributed to my fantasy world instead of serving its intended purpose, which was to keep me in touch with reality as much as possible.

Counting was the answer. I made up counting goals, all of which 13 would ideally correspond to an hour of swimming. I could then come in for the feeding and start back swimming with a new counting goal in mind. Six hundred strokes. One hundred and fifty "Row, Row, Row Your Boats." Twenty-five "Frère Jacques" in sets of French, German and English. Ad infinitum. The counting acts as an hypnotic device in that the rhythmic counting over the hours lets the mind relax and dip further into fantasy. And the counting keeps my inner voice busy with some intelligible, conscious-world symbols so that I'm not so far gone as to be out of control. The counting helps me float in limbo between the unbearable sanity of knowing the exact extent of the pain I am feeling and the glorious insanity of a wild, safe LSD-type trip.

I always say that the experience of doing a marathon swim is   14 like spending six months on a shrink's couch. Due to the exhaustion and the hypnotic counting and stroking and the sensory deprivation effects, you have remembered so much and imagined so much and discovered so much about yourself and others that the whole psychological experience is very rich, rewarding and calming. Each decade of life usually brings with it more calm, more assurance of who you are and what you want. Each marathon swim seems to make you psychologically a decade older.

I don't mean to imply that the marathon swim is a pleasurable   15 mental experience as it is happening. The physical difficulties of the marathon prevent the mind expansion during the swim from being pure pleasure. The pleasure presents itself as an aftereffect when the extremity of physical stress is over.

I also don't mean to imply that every marathon swimmer derives   16 the same psychological benefits and pleasures from the long swim. It seems that I bring something to the sport, just as it brings something to me.

It was fascinating to me that I could break world records while   17 immersed in such a consuming fantasy world. After a couple of years on the pro circuit I began to notice a correlation between the two; my best races were those in which my fantasies were rich, intense and long-lasting. But how was it possible? How could my mind be in outer space, having forgotten who I was or what I was doing, while my body was stroking away at a world-class pace? Sometimes the screeching police whistle would shock me out of my dream world and I would be utterly amazed to discover that I was in the middle of some lake or ocean next to a boatload of frantic voices. As the brain quickly shifted back to the real world, I would be even more amazed to learn that I had swum another hour, it was time for another feeding, and I had moved up three positions in the race. I thought this was the unique case of marathon swimming, where being alert was not a prerequisite to success. But I found that the trick of taking the mind elsewhere to let the body perform without conscious interference was used with real results in other activities where sensory alertness is imperative. It's the step directly after pinpoint focus.

A general brain theory that has been suggested for centuries is   18 that the left side of the cerebral cortex is responsible for concrete, verbal, rational behavior while the right side controls abstract, conceptual behavior. Intellect versus intuition. And "versus" is precisely right. It seems that we are not very successful in working both sides simultaneously. If the left side is active balancing a complicated mathematical equation, the right side is basically dormant; if the right side is busy choreographing a ballet, the left side takes a nap.

These are blatantly layman's terms; the process is much more complicated. I have a theory, however, that stems from this idea of the right side resting while the left side worked and vice versa. It seems to me that if you could get them to operate simultaneously more often, you would tap a greater percentage of the brain's potential and you might experience a unique sensation. After all, I believe this is what happens during a marathon swim.

19

COMPREHENSION

1. List the *physical* side effects of marathon swimming. Now, list the *mental* side effects. What is the relationship between physical and mental effects?

2. What methods does Nyad use to keep in touch with reality? What methods do her crew members use to help her?

3. Nyad believes that the left brain and the right brain work together during a marathon swim. How does her essay demonstrate that this cooperation takes place?

PURPOSE AND AUDIENCE

1. This essay appeared in *Glamour* magazine, which is primarily aimed at the fashion- and beauty-conscious young woman. Why might its subject matter appeal to *Glamour*'s readers?

2. What do you suppose is Nyad's primary motive for writing about the side effects of marathon swimming? What does she want her audience to feel?

3. Why does Nyad mention LSD? Why does she introduce John Lilly's experiments?

4. Does this essay have an explicitly stated thesis? If so, what is it? If not, write a sentence that could serve as the essay's thesis.

STYLE AND STRUCTURE

1. Throughout the essay, Nyad uses the technique of analogy, comparing what happens to her when she swims with what happens during other experiences. Name some analogies she uses. Why do you think she uses this technique?

2. The first section of this essay includes two definitions. Identify these definitions, and explain why they are necessary. Are there any other terms that might have been defined?

3. Nyad's essay includes several sections of process explanation. Identify these passages, and explain why they are necessary.

4. Although this essay deals primarily with effects, it also describes a causal chain. Identify the elements of this chain.

5. How would the impact of this essay be different if it had been written in the third person by a scientist who had observed Nyad?

6. At the end of the essay, Nyad introduces a theory she has developed. Do you think this theory is reasonable? Does it constitute an appropriate conclusion? Why or why not?

WRITING WORKSHOP

1. Analyze an experience that required you to concentrate intensely. The experience could be related to physical exercise or sports, intellectual activity, or anything else you'd like. Write a cause and effect essay that explains the mental and physical consequences of that concentration.

2. Think of an activity in which you become so involved that it could almost have been considered an obsession (for example, applying to colleges, pledging a fraternity or sorority, earning money, dieting). Write a cause and effect essay in which you stress the motives that led to this intense involvement.

7

Comparison and Contrast

WHAT IS COMPARISON AND CONTRAST?

Imagine two photographs, one of a soldier returning from World War II and the other of a prisoner of war coming home from Vietnam. Individually, the photographs give us a lot of information. Each man is being greeted by his family, and each man, having been through a harrowing experience, is glad to be home. The style of dress shows that the first picture was taken in the late 1940s and the second in the early 1970s. But put these two photographs side by side, and you gain insights you could not get by looking at each picture separately. Now, your view of both pictures and your awareness of their similarities and differences enable you to make a statement about more than the individuals who fought in these wars. Despite the fact that these two soldiers are returning from very different wars—one a clear cut American victory, the other a long overdue withdrawal—both men are being welcomed joyously by their families. There are, as these pictures assert, human values that even war cannot overshadow.

We arrived at this conclusion by using a method of thinking called comparison and contrast. A *comparison* shows how two or more things or ideas are alike, and a *contrast* shows how they are different. To *compare and contrast* is to consider both similarities and differences.

Throughout our lives we are bombarded with countless bits of information from newspapers, television, radio, and personal experience: the police strike in Memphis; city workers walk out in

Philadelphia; the Senate debates government spending; a tax revolt succeeds in California. The list is endless. Yet somehow we must make sense of the jumbled facts and figures that surround us. One way we have of understanding information like this is to put it side by side with other data and then to compare and contrast. Do the police in Memphis have the same complaints as the city workers in Philadelphia? What are the differences between the two situations? Is the national debate on spending akin to the California debate on taxes? How do they differ? We make similar distinctions every day about matters that directly affect us. When we make personal decisions, we consider alternatives, asking ourselves whether one option seems better than another. Should I buy a car with manual or automatic transmission? What are the advantages and disadvantages of each? Should I major in history or business? What job opportunities will each major offer me? Should I register as a Democrat or a Republican, or should I join a smaller political party? What are the positions of each on government spending, welfare, and the Equal Rights Amendment?

Because this way of thinking is central to our understanding of the world, comparison and contrast is often required in papers and on essay examinations:

> Compare and contrast the attitudes toward science and technology expressed in Stanislaw Lem's *Solaris* and Isaac Asimov's *I, Robot*. (English)
>
> What are the similarities and differences between mitosis and meiosis? (biology)
>
> Discuss the relative advantages and disadvantages of establishing a partnership and incorporating. (business law)
>
> Discuss the advantages and disadvantages of heterogeneous pupil grouping. (education)

Uses of Comparison and Contrast

You aren't likely to sit down and say to yourself, "I think I'll write a comparison and contrast essay today. Now what shall I write about?" Usually you will use comparison and contrast because you have been told to or because you decide it suits your topic. In the questions above, for instance, the instructors have phrased their questions to tell students how to treat the material. When you read the questions, certain key words and phrases—*compare and contrast, similarities and differences, advantages and disadvantages*—indicate that you should use a comparison and contrast pattern to organize your essay. Also, the very nature of certain assignments requires this pattern of development. If a student majoring in hospital management were told to evaluate two health delivery systems, he or she could best carry out the assignment using comparison and contrast. Nonacademic writing situations likewise call for this pattern. If a store manager were to recommend which of three lines of furniture should be dropped the following year, he or she would most likely submit a report in the form of comparison and contrast. Similarly, if a consulting firm were hired to study an urban police force to determine the relative performance of male and female officers, its final report would probably contain many comparison and contrast sections.

Basis of Comparison

Before you can compare or contrast two things, you must determine what elements they have in common. For example, although cats and dogs are very different pets, both can learn from their owners. Cats and dogs may be taught different behaviors in different ways, but these differences can be analyzed because both animals share a common element, that of being trainable. Without a common element, there would be no basis for analysis—that is, no basis of comparison.

In addition to being shared by both subjects, a basis of comparison should lead you, and thus your reader, beyond the obvious. For instance, at first the idea of a comparison and contrast essay on bees and people might seem absurd. After all, these two creatures differ in species, physical structure, and intelligence. Their differences are so obvious that an essay based on them would be pointless. But, with further analysis, you might decide there are quite a few similarities between the two. Both are social animals that live in complex social structures, and both have tasks to perform and roles to fulfill in their societies. Thus, you might write an essay on the common elements that seem most provocative—social structures and roles—rather than those elements that lead nowhere—species, physical structure, and intelligence. If you tried to compare bees and Volkswagens or humans and golf tees, however, you would run into trouble. Although some points of comparison could be found, they are forced and ill-founded. Little is gained from observing that both bees and Volkswagens travel great distances or that both people and tees are needed to play golf. Therefore, when you decide to use comparison and contrast, brainstorm to generate as many creative ideas as possible. Then critically review your ideas to make sure you have reasonable bases for comparison. The things you plan to compare and contrast must share some basis of comparison, and your analysis of their common elements must have some purpose.

Points for Discussion

Once you have decided that a sound basis of comparison exists, you should select your specific points for discussion. You do this just as you would for any other essay—with one crucial difference. You must discuss the same common elements for all subjects you are going to compare or contrast. For instance, if you were going to compare and contrast two novels, you could consider the following elements in *both* works:

Novel A	*Novel B*
Major characters	Major characters
Minor characters	Minor characters
Themes	Themes

A frequent error that you should avoid is to discuss different elements for each subject. Doing this obscures any basis of comparison that might exist. The two novels, for example, could not be meaningfully compared or contrasted if you discussed elements such as these:

Novel A	*Novel B*
Major characters	Plot
Minor characters	Author's life
Themes	Symbols

Thesis Statement

A comparison and contrast essay may be informational or judgmental. An informational essay simply presents two or more items side by side to illustrate their similarities or differences. It does not judge the relative merits of the items and often does not contain a thesis statement (although it always has a unifying idea). An essay in which you make judgments, on the other hand, always has a thesis. This thesis establishes the significance of the comparison or contrast and takes an arguable position on the relative merits of the items discussed. In a college paper that uses a comparison and contrast pattern, a thesis statement almost always strengthens the writing by clarifying its purpose.

As in all essays, your thesis statement should tell your readers what to expect in your essay. It should mention not only the subjects to be compared and contrasted but also the significance of the comparison. In addition, your thesis should indicate whether you will concentrate on similarities, differences, or both. The very structure of the sentence that states your thesis can help to show the focus of your essay. As the following sentences illustrate, a thesis statement can emphasize the central concern of the essay by stating it in the main, rather than the subordinate, clause of the sentence:

> Even though doctors and nurses perform distinctly different tasks at a hospital, their functions overlap in their contacts with patients.

> Although Melville's *Moby Dick* and London's *The Sea Wolf* are both about the sea, the major characters, minor characters, and themes of *Moby Dick* establish its superiority to *The Sea Wolf*.

The structure of the first sentence emphasizes similarities, and the structure of the second highlights differences. Moreover, both sentences establish the things to be compared or contrasted as well as the significance or purpose of the juxtaposition.

STRUCTURING A COMPARISON AND CONTRAST ESSAY

After you have established your basis of comparison, selected your points for discussion, and formulated your thesis statement, you are ready to organize your paper. Like every other type of essay examined in this book, a comparison and contrast essay has an introduction, several body paragraphs, and a conclusion. Within the body of your paper, there are two basic comparison and contrast patterns you can follow: you can discuss each subject separately, devoting one or more paragraphs to subject A and then the same number to subject B; or you can discuss one point of comparison in each section, making your points about subject A and subject B in turn. As you might expect, both organizational patterns have advantages and disadvantages that you should consider before you use them.

Subject-by-Subject Comparison

When you make a subject-by-subject comparison, you essentially write a separate essay about each subject, but you organize these miniature essays identically. In each, you use the *same basis of comparison* to select points about the subject, and you arrange these points in the same order. The following outline illustrates this procedure:

¶1 Introduction—thesis: Even though doctors and nurses perform distinctly different tasks at a hospital, their functions overlap in their contacts with patients.

¶2 Doctor's functions:
Teaching patients
Assessing patients
Dispensing medication

¶3 Nurse's functions:
Teaching patients
Assessing patients
Dispensing medication

¶4 Conclusion

Subject-by-subject comparison is usually used only for short papers. In longer papers, where many points are made about each subject, this organizational pattern puts too many demands upon your readers, requiring them to remember all your points throughout your paper. In addition, because of the size of each section, your paper may sound like two separate essays weakly connected by a transitional phrase. Instead, for longer or more complex papers, it is best to discuss each point of comparison for both subjects together, making your comparisons as you go along.

Point-by-Point Comparison

When you use a point-by-point comparison, your paper is organized around points of comparison instead of subjects. Each section discusses one element common to both subjects. Paragraph by paragraph, you first make a point about one subject, then follow it with a comparable point about the other. This alternating pattern continues throughout the body of your essay, until all your comparisons or contrasts have been made. The following outline illustrates a point-by-point comparison:

¶1 Introduction—thesis: Although Melville's *Moby Dick* and London's *The Sea Wolf* are both about the sea, the major characters, minor characters, and themes of *Moby Dick* establish its superiority to *The Sea Wolf*.

¶2–3   Major characters:
       The Sea Wolf
       Moby Dick
¶4–5   Minor Characters:
       The Sea Wolf
       Moby Dick
¶6–7   Themes:
       The Sea Wolf
       Moby Dick
¶8   Conclusion

Point-by-point comparison works best for long papers because your readers can see the comparisons or contrasts as they go along. For this reason it is generally easier to follow than subject-by-subject comparison. Readers do not have to wait several paragraphs to find out the differences between *Moby Dick* and *The Sea Wolf*. In addition, since each section of your paper makes these comparisons or contrasts for them, readers do not have to try to remember on page six what you said on page three.

In college you will often need to write comparison and contrast essays on midterm and final examinations. The following question, from a science-fiction final examination, is typical of the kind you will encounter:

Question: Choose any two of the books you have read this semester, and discuss how their views of the future differ. Account if you can for the differences you uncover.

Here is an answer to this question by a student, Jane Czerak:

Introduction   When science fiction discusses another world, it is actually discussing our world, and when science fiction discusses the future, it is actually discussing the present. Both Robert Heinlein's Starship Troopers and John Brunner's Stand on Zanzibar are near-future science fiction— supposedly set fifty years from the time they were written. Although these books are alike in some

Thesis (emphasizing differences)

ways, they differ in other ways that reflect the moods of the times in which they were written.

First subject (view of the future)

Starship Troopers takes place in a world that is substantially different from ours. Earth is the center of an empire that encompasses several of the outer planets. Space exploration has led to the colonization of a number of worlds and the inevitable alien encounter. Earth is locked in mortal combat with buglike aliens who are bent on appropriating the living space that people on earth need to survive. The result of this struggle is that the military has assumed great power. In order to obtain citizenship, a person must first serve in the armed forces. The vote is achieved only by those who have fought the bugs and survived.

First subject (reflection of the past)

In many ways, Starship Troopers reflects the times in which it was written. The 1950s was a decade in which the United States still had faith in military power and in its ability to police the world. Despite the example of Korea, America viewed its atomic arsenal as an umbrella that would protect it from harm. The world of Starship Troopers is one which faces an alien challenge. War is seen as an inevitable result of man's expansion, and only through struggle can man establish his right to survive. In this light, the bugs can be seen as symbols of all that threatened the United States throughout the 1950s.

Second subject (view of the future)

The world of Stand on Zanzibar is very much like ours today. The story takes place in the near future, and the first half of the book is set in New York City. Many of the problems that beset New York today are still present in the future, but they are even more severe. Because of overpopulation, living

space is at a premium, and people can afford
apartments only by sharing the expense with others.
Corporations have assumed great power and virtually
run the government. Every facet of life seems to be
permeated by television and advertising. People are
encouraged to buy as much as they can whenever they
can——this in spite of the fact that earth's
resources seem to be declining at an alarming rate.
In order to try to cope with this suicidal way of
life, most states have passed laws strictly limiting
people's right to bear children.

Second subject (reflection of the past)

Stand on Zanzibar was published in 1968 and very
accurately expresses the mood of those times.
Possibly because of the joint effects of the war in
Vietnam and the Johnson presidency, Americans were
examining their personal and national goals. The
population explosion, ecology, and corporate power
became topics of great interest. Brunner takes these
problems and examines what would happen if Americans
continued their present course of action. The result
is the world of Stand on Zanzibar where the United
States consumes most of the earth's resources and
continually searches our overextended planet for
more.

Conclusion

Although Starship Troopers and Stand on Zanzibar
were written only nine years apart, they
differ greatly in concept. Great changes took place
in the United States between 1959 and 1968, and these
books reflect the shifts in priorities and
consciousness that occurred. Using the near future
as settings for their works, Heinlein and Brunner

Restatement of thesis

create interesting and subtle works which
nonetheless are as different as the volatile times
in which they were written.

Points for Special Attention

Structure.   Jane Czerak chose to answer her examination question by using a subject-by-subject comparison. Although her discussion is somewhat involved, she actually makes only two major points about both books: that they treat the future in different ways and that this treatment reflects the times in which they were written. Because readers can easily keep these ideas in mind, a subject-by-subject discussion is a good strategy for Czerak to use. Of course, she could have used a point-by-point discussion and written an equally good paper. But because she was writing a midterm and time was important, she chose the strategy that would enable her to organize her essay most quickly and easily.

Transition.   Any comparison and contrast essay needs transition so that it flows smoothly. Without adequate transition, a point-by-point comparison can produce a series of choppy paragraphs, and a subject-by-subject comparison can read like two separate essays. In addition to connecting the sections of an essay, transitional words and phrases like the following, when used properly, can highlight similarities and differences for your reader:

> on the one hand . . . on the other hand . . .
> even though
> on the contrary
> in spite of
> although
> despite
> unlike
> both
> like
> likewise
> similarly

Jane Czerak could have used these phrases more often than she does, particularly when she shifts from her first subject to her second. By adding a transitional phrase to the following sentence, she not only could have emphasized the differences between the two books she is discussing but also could have improved the transition between the two sections of her paper:

> *without transition:*   The world of *Stand on Zanzibar* is very much like ours today.

with transition: Unlike Heinlein's future world, the world of *Stand on Zanzibar* is very much like ours today.

Topic Sentences. A topic sentence presents the main idea of a paragraph; often, it appears as the paragraph's first sentence. Like transitional phrases, topic sentences guide your reader through your paper. When reading a comparison and contrast essay, a reader can easily become lost in a jumble of points, especially if the paper is long and complex. Direct, clearly stated topic sentences act as guideposts, alerting your reader to the comparisons and contrasts you are making. Czerak's topic sentences are straightforward and reinforce the major points she is making about each book. And, as in any good comparison and contrast essay, each of the points discussed in part one of her paper is also discussed in part two. Notice how her topic sentences reinforce this balance:

Starship Troopers takes place in a world that is substantially different from ours.	The world of *Stand on Zanzibar* is very much like ours today.
In many ways, *Starship Troopers* reflects the times in which it was written.	*Stand on Zanzibar* was published in 1968 and very accurately expresses the mood of those times.

The selections that follow illustrate both point-by-point and subject-by-subject comparison. Moreover, each uses transitional elements and topic sentences to enhance clarity and to achieve balance between categories. Although they vary greatly in organization, length, and complexity, each reading selection is primarily concerned with the similarities and differences between its subjects.

Brother, Can You Spare a Dime?
E. Y. HARBURG AND JAY GORNEY

*Written in 1930, "Brother, Can You Spare a Dime?" became the unoffi-
cial theme song of America's depression years. This song establishes its
point-by-point comparison by ending each stanza with a refrain. Much
of its force comes from the vivid contrast between the wistful sentiment
at the beginning of each verse and the stark reality of the concluding
"Brother, can you spare a dime?" Although a song is not an essay, this
selection almost outlines how point-by-point comparison is organized.*

Once I built a railroad,
Made it run,—
Made it race against time,
Once I built a railroad,
Now it's done,—
Brother, can you spare a dime?   6

Once I built a tower,
To the sun,—
Brick and rivet and lime,
Once I built a tower,
Now it's done,—
Brother, can you spare a dime?   12

(Chorus): Once in khaki suits,
Gee we looked swell,
Full of that Yankee Doodle-de-dum.
Half a million boots went sloggin'
Through Hell,
I was the kid with the drum.   18

Say, don't you remember,
They called me Al,—
It was Al all the time,
Say, don't you remember,
I'm your Pal!—
Buddy, can you spare a dime?   24

COMPREHENSION

1. To what events in the past do the sections of the song beginning with *once* refer?

2. Who might the speaker be? Why is he asking for a dime? To whom is he talking?

3. What picture of the 1930s does this song paint?

4. What things are being contrasted in each stanza of this song?

PURPOSE AND AUDIENCE

1. What reaction do you think the songwriters expected from their song's original audience in the 1930s? Do you think the effect is similar today?

2. Although this selection is not an essay, it does have an implied thesis. What is that thesis?

3. E. Y. Harburg, who is now in his seventies, has updated his original lyrics to reflect our times. Here is the first stanza of his new version of the song:

> Once we had depression
> But with a dime,—
> A guy wasn't out of luck,
> Now we've got inflation,
> Drugs and crime,—
> Brother, can you spare a buck?

How does this compare to the original version? How have the expectations of Harburg's audience changed?

STYLE AND STRUCTURE

1. Repetition is usually important in popular songs. What words and phrases does this song repeat? What function do these repetitions serve?

2. In academic writing, clichés—tired, overused phrases like "race against time"—are discouraged, yet Harburg and Gorney use them in their song. Why do they do this? Can you find other clichés in the lyrics?

3. The song is written in the first person (*I, we*). How would its impact change if it employed the third person (*he, she, they*) instead?

4. Why do you suppose the lyricist uses *Buddy* instead of *Brother* in the song's last line?

5. Because this is a song, the lyricist had to alter normal sentence structure at times so the words would fit the music. What words have been omitted for this reason?

WRITING WORKSHOP

1. Write your own song lyrics comparing your childhood with your life now. After you finish, expand your lyrics into a comparison and contrast essay.

2. Imagine you are the speaker in "Brother, Can You Spare a Dime?" Choose one or two stanzas of the song, and use them as a topic outline as you write a comparison and contrast essay. Be inventive, and supply as many details as you can.

3. Look back at the updated lyrics in question 3 under "Purpose and Audience." Write a brief comparison and contrast essay about Harburg's attitudes toward the depression during the 1930s and his attitudes toward the present.

From Song to Sound: Bing and Elvis
RUSSELL BAKER

*Russell Baker writes a syndicated column which often treats contempo-
rary social and political issues in a humorous or satirical manner. This
column is a serious one, however, and comments on the differences
between two eras as well as two performers.*

1   The grieving for Elvis Presley and the commercial exploitation of
his death were still not ended when we heard of Bing Crosby's
death the other day. Here is a generational puzzle. Those of an age
to mourn Elvis must marvel that their elders could really have
cared about Bing, just as the Crosby generation a few weeks ago
wondered what all the to-do was about when Elvis died.

2   Each man was a mass culture hero to his generation, but it tells
us something of the difference between generations that each man's
admirers would be hard-pressed to understand why the other could
mean very much to his devotees.

3   There were similarities that ought to tell us something. Both
came from obscurity to national recognition while quite young and
became very rich. Both lacked formal music education and went on
to movie careers despite lack of acting skills. Both developed
distinctive musical styles which were originally scorned by critics
and subsequently studied as pioneer developments in the art of
popular song.

4   In short, each man's career followed the mythic rags-to-triumph
pattern in which adversity is conquered, detractors are given their
comeuppance and estates, fancy cars and world tours become the
reward of perseverance. Traditionally this was supposed to be the
history of the American business striver, but in our era of committee
capitalism it occurs most often in the mass entertainment field, and
so we look less and less to the board room for our heroes and more
and more to the microphone.

5   Both Crosby and Presley were creations of the microphone. It
made it possible for people with frail voices not only to be heard
beyond the third row but also to caress millions. Crosby was among
the first to understand that the microphone made it possible to sing
to multitudes by singing to a single person in a small room.

6   Presley cuddled his microphone like a lover. With Crosby the
microphone was usually concealed, but Presley brought it out on

stage, detached it from its fitting, stroked it, pressed it to his mouth.
It was a surrogate for his listener, and he made love to it un-
ashamedly.

The difference between Presley and Crosby, however, reflected 7
generational differences which spoke of changing values in American life. Crosby's music was soothing; Presley's was disturbing. It
is too easy to be glib about this, to say that Crosby was singing to,
first, Depression America and, then, to wartime America, and that
his audiences had all the disturbance they could handle in their
daily lives without buying more at the record shop and movie
theater.

Crosby's fans talk about how "relaxed" he was, how "natural," 8
how "casual and easy going." By the time Presley began causing
sensations, the entire country had become relaxed, casual and easy
going, and its younger people seemed to be tired of it, for Elvis's
act was anything but soothing and scarcely what a parent of that
placid age would have called "natural" for a young man.

Elvis was unseemly, loud, gaudy, sexual—that gyrating pelvis!— 9
in short, disturbing. He not only disturbed parents who thought
music by Crosby was soothing but also reminded their young that
they were full of the turmoil of youth and an appetite for excitement.
At a time when the country had a population coming of age with
no memory of troubled times, Presley spoke to a yearning for disturbance.

It probably helped that Elvis's music made Mom and Dad climb 10
the wall. In any case, people who admired Elvis never talk about
how relaxed and easy going he made them feel. They are more
likely to tell you he introduced them to something new and exciting.

To explain each man in terms of changes in economic and 11
political life probably oversimplifies the matter. Something in the
culture was also changing. Crosby's music, for example, paid great
attention to the importance of lyrics. The "message" of the song
was as essential to the audience as the tune. The words were
usually inane and witless, but Crosby—like Sinatra a little later—
made them vital. People remembered them, sang them. Words still
had meaning.

Although many of Presley's songs were highly lyrical, in most 12
it wasn't the words that moved audiences; it was the "sound." Rock
'n' roll, of which he was the great popularizer, was a "sound" event.
Song stopped being song and turned into "sound," at least until
the Beatles came along and solved the problem of making words
sing to the new beat.

Thus a group like the Rolling Stones, whose lyrics are often 13 elaborate, seems to the Crosby-tuned ear to be shouting only gibberish, a sort of accompanying background noise in a "sound" experience. The Crosby generation has trouble hearing rock because it makes the mistake of trying to understand the words. The Presley generation has trouble with Crosby because it finds the sound unstimulating and cannot be touched by the inanity of the words. The mutual deafness may be a measure of how far we have come from really troubled times and of how deeply we have come to mistrust the value of words.

COMPREHENSION

1. List the similarities between Crosby and Presley that Baker considers.

2. List the differences Baker notes between the two men.

3. How does Baker account for the differences?

4. What, according to Baker's essay, is the difference between *song* and *sound*?

5. What are some nonmusical examples of the "mutual deafness" Baker mentions in his final paragraph?

PURPOSE AND AUDIENCE

1. This column was printed in newspapers all over the country shortly after Bing Crosby died. How does its subject matter make it particularly appropriate for this diverse audience?

2. What is the essay's thesis?

3. At times, Baker seems to be guilty of making unsupported generalizations (for example, he assumes that his readers, like him, have "come to mistrust the value of words"). How do you suppose he expected his audience to react to such assumptions?

STYLE AND STRUCTURE

1. Baker considers both similarities and differences. Why does he deal with similarities first? What sentence signals his move from similarities to differences?

2. Which of the two patterns of organization (subject by subject or point by point) does Baker use here? Why? Could he have used the other pattern? Why or why not?

3. Paragraphs in this essay are relatively short because their length was determined by narrow newspaper columns. If you were typing this essay

on standard paper, would you combine any paragraphs or make any other changes in paragraphing? If so, where?

4. Can you tell by the essay's language whether Baker is a fan of Presley or Crosby or both? If so, how?

5. Baker uses the microphone to illustrate *both* similarities and differences. Could another symbol—the radio or phonograph, for instance—have been used as effectively? Why or why not?

WRITING WORKSHOP

1. Choose any two musicians or groups, and analyze their similarities and differences as performers.

2. Compare and contrast the lyrics of a Bing Crosby song with one sung by Elvis Presley.

3. Write an article for an Elvis Presley fan magazine in which you compare and contrast him with Bing Crosby. Use Baker's facts, but slant them to show Presley in a much more favorable light. If you can, supply additional information to supplement Baker's account.

4. Find news magazine accounts of Presley's and Crosby's funerals, and write an essay comparing and contrasting them.

Grant and Lee: A Study in Contrasts
BRUCE CATTON

Bruce Catton, reporter, historian, and Pulitzer Prize winner, was a recognized authority on the Civil War. This essay, which first appeared in a collection of historical essays called The American Story, *is tightly organized and has explicit topic sentences and transitions. Note that this "study in contrasts" identifies a number of important similarities between Ulysses S. Grant and Robert E. Lee.*

When Ulysses S. Grant and Robert E. Lee met in the parlor of a 1 modest house at Appomattox Court House, Virginia, on April 9, 1865, to work out the terms for the surrender of Lee's Army of Northern Virginia, a great chapter in American life came to a close, and a great new chapter began.

These men were bringing the Civil War to its virtual finish. To 2 be sure, other armies had yet to surrender, and for a few days the fugitive Confederate government would struggle desperately and vainly, trying to find some way to go on living now that its chief support was gone. But in effect it was all over when Grant and Lee signed the papers. And the little room where they wrote out the terms was the scene of one of the poignant, dramatic contrasts in American history.

They were two strong men, these oddly different generals, and 3 they represented the strengths of two conflicting currents that, through them, had come into final collision.

Back of Robert E. Lee was the notion that the old aristocratic 4 concept might somehow survive and be dominant in American life.

Lee was tidewater Virginia, and in his background were family, 5 culture, and tradition . . . the age of chivalry transplanted to a New World which was making its own legends and its own myths. He embodied a way of life that had come down through the age of knighthood and the English country squire. America was a land that was beginning all over again, dedicated to nothing much more complicated than the rather hazy belief that all men had equal rights and should have an equal chance in the world. In such a land Lee stood for the feeling that it was somehow of advantage to human society to have a pronounced inequality in the social structure. There should be a leisure class, backed by ownership of land; in turn, society itself should be keyed to the land as the chief source of wealth and influence. It would bring forth (according to this ideal) a class of men with a strong sense of obligation to the community; men who lived not to gain advantage for themselves, but to meet the solemn obligations which had been laid on them by the very fact that they were privileged. From them the country would gets its leadership; to them it could look for the higher values—of thought, of conduct, of personal deportment—to give it strength and virtue.

Lee embodied the noblest elements of this aristocratic ideal.   6
Through him, the landed nobility justified itself. For four years, the Southern states had fought a desperate war to uphold the ideals for which Lee stood. In the end, it almost seemed as if the Confederacy fought for Lee; as if he himself was the Confederacy ... the best thing that the way of life for which the Confederacy stood could ever have to offer. He had passed into legend before Appomattox. Thousands of tired, underfed, poorly clothed Confederate soldiers, long since past the simple enthusiasm of the early days of the struggle, somehow considered Lee the symbol of everything for which they had been willing to die. But they could not quite put this feeling into words. If the Lost Cause, sanctified by so much heroism and so many deaths, had a living justification, its justification was General Lee.

Grant, the son of a tanner on the Western frontier, was everything   7
Lee was not. He had come up the hard way and embodied nothing in particular except the eternal toughness and sinewy fiber of the men who grew up beyond the mountains. He was one of a body of men who owed reverence and obeisance to no one, who were self-reliant to a fault, who cared hardly anything for the past but who had a sharp eye for the future.

These frontier men were the precise opposites of the tidewater   8
aristocrats. Back of them, in the great surge that had taken people over the Alleghenies and into the opening Western country, there was a deep, implicit dissatisfaction with a past that had settled into grooves. They stood for democracy, not from any reasoned conclusion about the proper ordering of human society, but simply because they had grown up in the middle of democracy and knew how it worked. Their society might have privileges, but they would be privileges each man had won for himself. Forms and patterns meant nothing. No man was born to anything, except perhaps to a chance to show how far he could rise. Life was competition.

Yet along with this feeling had come a deep sense of belonging   9
to a national community. The Westerner who developed a farm, opened a shop, or set up in business as a trader, could hope to prosper only as his own community prospered—and his community

ran from the Atlantic to the Pacific and from Canada down to Mexico. If the land was settled, with towns and highways and accessible markets, he could better himself. He saw his fate in terms of the nation's own destiny. As its horizons expanded, so did his. He had, in other words, an acute dollars-and-cents stake in the continued growth and development of his country.

And that, perhaps, is where the contrast between Grant and Lee   10 becomes most striking. The Virginia aristocrat, inevitably, saw himself in relation to his own region. He lived in a static society which could endure almost anything except change. Instinctively, his first loyalty would go to the locality in which that society existed. He would fight to the limit of endurance to defend it, because in defending it he was defending everything that gave his own life its deepest meaning.

The Westerner, on the other hand, would fight with an equal   11 tenacity for the broader concept of society. He fought so because everything he lived by was tied to growth, expansion, and a constantly widening horizon. What he lived by would survive or fall with the nation itself. He could not possibly stand by unmoved in the face of an attempt to destroy the Union. He would combat it with everything he had, because he could only see it as an effort to cut the ground out from under his feet.

So Grant and Lee were in complete contrast, representing two   12 diametrically opposed elements in American life. Grant was the modern man emerging; beyond him, ready to come on the stage, was the great age of steel and machinery, of crowded cities and a restless burgeoning vitality. Lee might have ridden down from the old age of chivalry, lance in hand, silken banner fluttering over his head. Each man was the perfect champion of his cause, drawing both his strengths and his weaknesses from the people he led.

Yet it was not all contrast, after all. Different as they were—in   13 background, in personality, in underlying aspiration—these two great soldiers had much in common. Under everything else, they were marvelous fighters. Furthermore, their fighting qualities were really very much alike.

Each man had, to begin with, the great virtue of utter tenacity   14 and fidelity. Grant fought his way down the Mississippi Valley in spite of acute personal discouragement and profound military handicaps. Lee hung on in the trenches at Petersburg after hope itself had died. In each man there was an indomitable quality . . . the born fighter's refusal to give up as long as he can still remain on his feet and lift his two fists.

Daring and resourcefulness they had, too; the ability to think   15 faster and move faster than the enemy. These were the qualities which gave Lee the dazzling campaigns of Second Manassas and Chancellorsville and won Vicksburg for Grant.

Lastly, and perhaps greatest of all, there was the ability, at the end, to turn quickly from war to peace once the fighting was over. Out of the way these two men behaved at Appomattox came the possibility of a peace of reconciliation. It was a possibility not wholly realized, in the years to come, but which did, in the end, help the two sections to become one nation again . . . after a war whose bitterness might have seemed to make such a reunion wholly impossible. No part of either man's life became him more than the part he played in this brief meeting in the McLean house at Appomattox. Their behavior there put all succeeding generations of Americans in their debt. Two great Americans, Grant and Lee— very different, yet under everything very much alike. Their encounter at Appomattox was one of the great moments of American history.

16

COMPREHENSION

1. What took place at Appomattox Court House on April 9, 1865? Why did the meeting at Appomattox signal the closing of "a great chapter in American life"?

2. How does Robert E. Lee represent the old aristocracy?

3. How does Ulysses S. Grant represent Lee's opposite?

4. According to Catton, where is it that "the contrast between Grant and Lee becomes most striking"?

5. What similarities does Catton see between the two men?

PURPOSE AND AUDIENCE

1. Catton's purpose in contrasting Grant and Lee is to make a general statement about the differences between two currents in American history. Summarize these differences. Do you think they are valid today?

2. Is Catton's purpose in comparing Grant and Lee the same as his purpose in contrasting them? That is, do their similarities also make a statement about America? Explain.

3. State the essay's thesis in your own words.

4. Why do you suppose Catton provides the background for the meeting at Appomattox but presents no information about the dramatic meeting itself?

STYLE AND STRUCTURE

1. Does Catton use subject-by-subject or point-by-point comparison? Why do you think he chose the structure he did?

2. In this essay, topic sentences are extremely important and extremely helpful to the reader. Explain the functions of the following sentences: "Grant . . . was everything Lee was not" (paragraph 7); "So Grant and Lee were in complete contrast . . ." (paragraph 12); "Yet it was not all contrast, after all" (paragraph 13); "Lastly, and perhaps greatest of all . . ." (paragraph 16).

3. Catton carefully uses transitions in his essay. Identify the transitional words or expressions that link each paragraph to the preceding one.

4. Some of Catton's paragraphs (3, 4, 15) are only one or two sentences long. Others (5, 6, 16) are much longer. How can you explain such variation in paragraph length?

5. Most of this essay is devoted to the contrast between Grant and Lee. Where are their similarities mentioned? Why does Catton do this?

WRITING WORKSHOP

1. Write a similar "study in contrasts" about two people you know well—two teachers, your parents, two relatives, two friends—or about two fictional characters you are very familiar with.

2. Write a dialogue between two people you know that reveals their contrasting attitudes toward school, work, or any other subject.

Denotation and Connotation
LAURENCE PERRINE

Laurence Perrine, a veteran teacher and the author of many popular textbooks, undertakes in this essay to introduce the concept of multiple word meanings. The essay, from an introductory poetry text, distinguishes between the dictionary definition of a word and the very different meanings that same word may suggest or connote. Perrine abundantly uses concrete examples to support his point; as you read, notice how his illustrations make his comparisons easy to understand.

A primary distinction between the practical use of language and the literary use is that in literature, especially in poetry, a *fuller* use is made of individual words. To understand this, we need to examine the composition of a word. 1

The average word has three component parts: sound, denotation, and connotation. It begins as a combination of tones and noises, uttered by the lips, tongue, and throat, for which the written word is a notation. But it differs from a musical tone or a noise in that it has a meaning attached to it. The basic part of this meaning is its DENOTATION or denotations: that is, the dictionary meaning or meanings of the word. Beyond its denotations, a word may also have connotations. The CONNOTATIONS are what it suggests beyond what it expresses: its overtones of meaning. It acquires these connotations by its past history and associations, by the way and the circumstances in which it has been used. The word *home,* for instance, by denotation means only a place where one lives, but by connotation it suggests security, love, comfort, and family. The words *childlike* and *childish* both mean "characteristic of a child," but *childlike* suggests meekness, innocence, and wide-eyed wonder, while *childish* suggests pettiness, willfulness, and temper tantrums. If we name over a series of coins: *nickel, peso, lira, shilling, sen, doubloon,* the word *doubloon,* to four out of five readers, will immediately suggest pirates, though one will find nothing about pirates in looking up its meaning in the dictionary. Pirates are part of its connotation. 2

Connotation is very important to the poet, for it is one of the means by which he can concentrate or enrich his meaning—say more in fewer words. Consider, for instance, the following short poem: 3

THERE IS NO FRIGATE LIKE A BOOK

There is no frigate like a book
    To take us lands away,
Nor any coursers like a page
    Of prancing poetry:
This traverse may the poorest take
    Without oppress of toll;
How frugal is the chariot
    That bears the human soul!

Emily Dickinson (1830–1886)

In this poem Emily Dickinson is considering the power of a   4
book or of poetry to carry us away, to let us escape from our
immediate surroundings into a world of the imagination. To do this
she has compared literature to various means of transportation: a
boat, a team of horses, a wheeled land vehicle. But she has been
careful to choose kinds of transportation and names for them that
have romantic connotations. "Frigate" suggests exploration and
adventure; "coursers," beauty, spirit, and speed; "chariot," speed
and the ability to go through the air as well as on land. (Compare
"Swing Low, Sweet Chariot" and the myth of Phaethon, who tried
to drive the chariot of Apollo, and the famous painting of Aurora
with her horses, once hung in almost every school.) How much of
the meaning of the poem comes from this selection of vehicles and
words is apparent if we try to substitute for them, say, *steamship,
horses,* and *streetcar.*

Just as a word has a variety of connotations, so also it may have   5
more than one denotation. If we look up the word *spring* in the
dictionary, for instance, we will find that it has between twenty-
five and thirty distinguishable meanings: It may mean (1) a pounce
or leap, (2) a season of the year, (3) a natural source of water, (4) a
coiled elastic wire, etc. This variety of denotation, complicated by
additional tones of connotation, makes language confusing and
difficult to use. Any person using words must be careful to define
by context precisely the meanings that he wishes. But the difference
between the writer using language to communicate information
and the poet is this: the practical writer will always attempt to
confine his words to one meaning at a time; the poet will often take
advantage of the fact that the word has more than one meaning by
using it to mean more than one thing at the same time. Thus when
Edith Sitwell in one of her poems writes, "This is the time of the
wild spring and the mating of tigers," she uses the word *spring* to

denote both a season of the year and a sudden leap and she uses
tigers rather than *lambs* or *birds* because it has a connotation of
fierceness and wildness that the other two lack.

WHEN MY LOVE SWEARS THAT SHE IS MADE OF TRUTH

When my love swears that she is made of truth,
I do believe her, though I know she lies,
That she might think me some untutored youth,
Unlearnèd in the world's false subtleties.
Thus vainly thinking that she thinks me young,   5
Although she knows my days are past the best,
Simply I credit her false-speaking tongue;
On both sides thus is simple truth supprest.
But wherefore says she not she is unjust?°   unfaithful
And wherefore say not I that I am old?   10
Oh, love's best habit is in seeming trust,
And age in love loves not to have years told:
Therefore I lie with her and she with me,
And in our faults by lies we flattered be.

William Shakespeare (1564–1616)

A frequent misconception of poetic language is that the poet   6
seeks always the most beautiful or noble-sounding words. What he
really seeks are the most *meaningful* words, and these vary from
one context to another. Language has many levels and varieties,
and the poet may choose from them all. His words may be grandiose
or humble, fanciful or matter of fact, romantic or realistic, archaic
or modern, technical or everyday, monosyllabic or polysyllabic.
Usually his poem will be pitched pretty much in one key. The
words in Emily Dickinson's "There is no frigate like a book" and
those in Thomas Hardy's "The Man He Killed" . . . are chosen
from quite different areas of language, but each poet has chosen
the words most meaningful for his own poetic context. Sometimes
a poet may import a word from one level or area of language into
a poem composed mostly of words from a different level or area. If
he does this clumsily, the result will be incongruous and sloppy.
If he does it skillfully, the result will be a shock of surprise and an
increment of meaning for the reader. In fact, the many varieties of
language open to the poet provide his richest resource. His task is
one of constant exploration and discovery. He searches always for
the secret affinities of words that allow them to be brought together
with soft explosions of meaning.

THE NAKED AND THE NUDE

For me, the naked and the nude
(By lexicographers construed
As synonyms that should express
The same deficiency of dress
Or shelter) stand as wide apart   5
As love from lies, or truth from art.

Lovers without reproach will gaze
On bodies naked and ablaze;
The hippocratic eye will see
In nakedness, anatomy;   10
And naked shines the Goddess when
She mounts her lion among men.

The nude are bold, the nude are sly
To hold each treasonable eye.
While draping by a showman's trick   15
Their dishabille in rhetoric,
They grin a mock-religious grin
Of scorn at those of naked skin.

The naked, therefore, who compete
Against the nude may know defeat;   20
Yet when they both together tread
The briary pastures of the dead,
By Gorgons with long whips pursued,
How naked go the sometime nude!

Robert Graves (b. 1895)

The person using language to convey information is largely   7
indifferent to the sound of his words and is hampered by their
connotations and multiple denotations. He tries to confine each
word to a single exact meaning. He uses, one might say, a fraction
of the word and throws the rest away. The poet, on the other hand,
tries to use as much of the word as he can. He is interested in
sound and uses it to reinforce meaning. ... He is interested in
connotation and uses it to enrich and convey meaning. And he may
use more than one denotation.

The purest form of practical language is scientific language. The   8
scientist needs a precise language for conveying information precisely. The fact that words have multiple denotations and various
overtones of meaning is a hindrance to him in accomplishing his

purpose. His ideal language would be a language with a one-to-one correspondence between word and meaning; that is, every word would have one meaning only, and for every meaning there would be only one word. Since ordinary language does not fulfill these conditions, he has invented one that does. A statement in his language looks something like this:

$$SO_2 + H_2O = H_2SO_3$$

In such a statement the symbols are entirely unambiguous; they have been stripped of all connotation and of all denotations but one. The word *sulfurous,* if it occurred in poetry, might have all kinds of connotations: fire, smoke, brimstone, hell, damnation. But H_2SO_3 means one thing and one thing only: sulfurous acid.

The ambiguity and multiplicity of meanings possessed by words 9 are an obstacle to the scientist but a resource to the poet. Where the scientist wants singleness of meaning, the poet wants richness of meaning. Where the scientist requires and has invented a strictly one-dimensional language, in which every word is confined to one denotation, the poet needs a multidimensional language, and he creates it partly by using a multidimensional vocabulary, in which to the dimension of denotation he adds the dimensions of connotation and sound.

The poet, we may say, plays on a many-stringed instrument. And 10 he sounds more than one note at a time.

The first problem in reading poetry, therefore, or in reading any 11 kind of literature, is to develop a sense of language, a feeling for words. One needs to become acquainted with their shape, their color, and their flavor. There are two ways of doing this: extensive use of the dictionary and extensive reading.

COMPREHENSION

1. What does Perrine say is the difference between the practical use of language and the literary use of language?

2. Define *denotation* and *connotation.*

3. Why is connotation so important to the poet?

4. Explain what Perrine means when he says "a frequent misconception of poetic language is that the poet seeks always the most beautiful or noble-sounding words."

5. Differentiate between *poetic* and *scientific* uses of language.

PURPOSE AND AUDIENCE

1. This selection is from an introductory poetry text designed for college undergraduates. How can you tell it is not from an advanced text?

2. What is the purpose for which Perrine has written this chapter? That is, do you think he means to entertain, inform, or persuade? Explain.

3. Perrine gives many examples of poetic uses of language and few examples of scientific uses. Why does he do this?

STYLE AND STRUCTURE

1. Does Perrine use a subject-by-subject or point-by-point comparison?

2. What points does Perrine make about both denotation and connotation?

3. Identify the topic sentences, and show how they emphasize the main points of the essay.

4. Why does Perrine end with a discussion of *poetic* and *scientific* uses of language?

5. Which words reveal Perrine's attitude toward *poetic* and *scientific* language?

WRITING WORKSHOP

1. In a comparison and contrast essay, discuss the different denotations and connotations of one of the following word pairs.

gay–homosexual	letter carrier–mailman
girl–woman	average–mediocre
lady–woman	police officer–cop
Negro–black	alcoholic–drunk
mother–parent	mentally ill–crazy

2. Find descriptions of the same event in two different newspapers. Write a comparison and contrast essay concentrating on the denotations and connotations of the words used in the two stories.

Confessions of a Misspent Youth
MARA WOLYNSKI

*Mara Wolynski is a free-lance writer who attended a small private
school in New York City. In "Confessions of a Misspent Youth," she
contrasts her progressive education with the more basic education of
traditional schools. Wolynski does not use one of the two basic comparison and contrast patterns in her essay. In fact, much of her comparison
is implied rather than stated. As you read "Confessions of a Misspent
Youth," consider how she organized her essay and why she chose to
structure it as she did.*

The idea of permissive education appealed to my mother in 1956   1
when she was a Bohemian and I was four. In Greenwich Village,
she found a small private school whose beliefs were hers and
happily enrolled me. I know it was an act of motherly love but it
might have been the worst thing she ever did to me. This school—
I'll call it Sand and Sea—attracted other such parents, upper-
middle-class professionals who were determined not to have their
children pressured the way they had been. Sand and Sea was the
school without pain. And it was the kind of school that the back-to-
basics people rightly fear most. At Sand and Sea, I soon became an
exemplar of educational freedom—the freedom not to learn.

Sand and Sea was run by fifteen women and one man who taught   2
"science." They were decent people, some old, some young, and
all devoted to cultivating the innate creativity they were convinced
we had. There was a tremendous emphasis on the arts. We weren't
taught techniques, however, because any kind of organization
stunted creativity.

HAPPINESS AND HIEROGLYPHICS

We had certain hours allotted to various subjects but we were free   3
to dismiss anything that bored us. In fact, it was school policy that
we were forbidden to be bored or miserable or made to compete
with one another. There were no tests and no hard times. When I
was bored with math, I was excused and allowed to write short
stories in the library. The way we learned history was by trying to
re-create its least important elements. One year, we pounded corn,
made tepees, ate buffalo meat and learned two Indian words. That
was early American history. Another year we made elaborate

costumes, clay pots, and papier-mâché gods. That was Greek culture. Another year we were all maidens and knights in armor because it was time to learn about the Middle Ages. We drank our orange juice from tin-foil goblets but never found out what the Middle Ages were. They were just "The Middle Ages."

I knew that the Huns pegged their horses and drank a quart of blood before going to war but no one ever told us who the Huns were or why we should know who they were. And one year, the year of ancient Egypt, when we were building our pyramids, I did a thirty-foot-long mural for which I laboriously copied hieroglyphics onto the sheet of brown paper. But no one ever told me what they stood for. They were just there and beautiful. 4

IGNORANCE IS NOT BLISS

We spent great amounts of time being creative because we had been told by our incurably optimistic mentors that the way to be happy in life was to create. Thus, we didn't learn to read until we were in the third grade because early reading was thought to discourage creative spontaneity. The one thing they taught us very well was to hate intellectuality and anything connected with it. Accordingly, we were forced to be creative for nine years. And yet Sand and Sea has failed to turn out a good artist. What we did do was to continually form and re-form interpersonal relationships and that's what we thought learning was all about and we were happy. At ten, for example, most of us were functionally illiterate but we could tell that Raymond was "acting out" when, in the middle of what passed for English, he did the twist on top of his desk. Or that Nina was "introverted" because she always cowered in the corner. 5

When we finally were graduated from Canaan, however, all the happy little children fell down the hill. We felt a profound sense of abandonment. So did our parents. After all that tuition money, let alone the loving freedom, their children faced high school with all the glorious prospects of the poorest slum-school kids. And so it came to be. No matter what school we went to, *we* were the underachievers and the culturally disadvantaged. 6

For some of us, real life was too much—one of my oldest friends from Sand and Sea killed himself two years ago after flunking out of the worst high school in New York at twenty. Various others have put in time in mental institutions where they were free, once again, to create during occupational therapy. 7

During my own high-school years, the school psychologist was baffled by my lack of substantive knowledge. He suggested to my 8 mother that I be given a battery of psychological tests to find out why I was blocking out information. The thing was, I wasn't blocking because I had no information to block. Most of my Sand and Sea classmates were also enduring the same kinds of hardships that accompany severe handicaps. My own reading comprehension was in the lowest eighth percentile, not surprisingly. I was often asked by teachers how I had gotten into high school. However, I did manage to stumble *not only* through high school but also through college (first junior college—rejected by all four-year colleges—and then New York University), hating it all the way as I had been taught to. I am still amazed that I have a B.A., but think of it as a B.S.

THE LURE OF LEARNING

The parents of my former classmates can't figure out what went   9 wrong. They had sent in bright curious children and gotten back, nine years later, helpless adolescents. Some might say that those of us who freaked out would have freaked out anywhere, but when you see the same bizarre behavior pattern in succeeding graduating classes, you can draw certain terrifying conclusions.

Now I see my twelve-year-old brother (who is in a traditional   10 school) doing college-level math and I know that he knows more about many other things besides math than I do. And I also see traditional education working in the case of my fifteen-year-old brother (who was summarily yanked from Sand and Sea, by my reformed mother, when he was eight so that he wouldn't become like me). Now, after seven years of real education, he is making impressive film documentaries for a project on the Bicentennial. A better learning experience than playing Pilgrim for four and a half months, and Indian for four and a half months, which is how I imagine they spent this year at Sand and Sea.

And now I've come to see that the real job of school is to entice   11 the student into the web of knowledge and then, if he's not enticed, to drag him in. I wish I had been.

COMPREHENSION

1. Why was Sand and Sea "the kind of school that the back-to-basics people rightly fear most"?

2. What does Wolynski mean when she says that it was school policy that students were forbidden to be bored?

3. What is Wolynski's major criticism of Sand and Sea's emphasis on creativity? What was it that students actually learned?

4. Despite her criticism of the school, Wolynski says that students there were happy. Is this a contradiction?

5. What happened to the author after she graduated from Sand and Sea and attended a public school? Why does she refer to herself and her former classmates as "the culturally disadvantaged"?

PURPOSE AND AUDIENCE

1. In her thesis statement, Wolynski says that she was an example of "educational freedom—freedom not to learn." What does she mean?

2. Is this essay intended for an audience familiar with progressive or traditional education? How can you tell?

3. In paragraph 9 Wolynski admits that she could be accused of overstating her case. How effectively does she refute this charge?

4. Why does Wolynski bring her brothers into her discussion? What is the purpose of this tactic?

STYLE AND STRUCTURE

1. Why does Wolynski imply most of her points of contrast? What information does she expect her audience to provide?

2. What is the basis of contrast between these two types of education?

3. Most of the examples Wolynski uses to support her criticism of Sand and Sea concern the teaching of history. Should the author have provided examples of other subjects, or are the brief references to reading and English enough? Explain.

4. Comment on the effectiveness of Wolynski's conclusion. Does it accurately sum up her essay, or should she have emphasized other points?

WRITING WORKSHOP

1. Write an essay which compares or contrasts your education with Mara Wolynski's. Try to draw specific points of comparison or contrast wherever you can.

2. Write a comparison and contrast essay about one of your high school classes and one of the college classes you are in now.

3. If your education has included different kinds of schools or experiences, write an essay contrasting them. Be certain that your thesis, like Wolynski's, is clear.

8

Division and Classification

WHAT IS DIVISION AND CLASSIFICATION?

When we face a confusing world, we instinctively try to make sense out of it. We want to organize the things around us so we can understand and connect our different experiences. Moreover, we want to order both the things we observe and the things we do in order to uncover connections among these observations and actions. One way we do this is by placing things side by side, comparing and contrasting them. Another is by *dividing* a mass of information into groups and *classifying* individual bits of information into one group or another. Through this process of division and classification, we can arrange random ideas by putting scattered bits of information into useful, coherent order. By breaking a large group into smaller categories and by grouping separate items in larger categories, we identify relationships between the whole and its parts and bring to light similarities and differences among the parts themselves. Thus, the process of division and classification is as essential a way of thinking as comparison and contrast.

Because it is so fundamental, the process of division and classification has many applications. In countless practical situations, it brings order to chaos. Thus, department store managers direct merchandise to different departments, college catalog editors classify courses by subject matter, and dictionary writers use the letters of the alphabet to arrange words. Without such organization, merchandise might be anywhere in a store, psychology might follow American literature and precede advanced optics, and *aard-*

243

vark might appear next to *zebra*. Similarly, the editors of the Sunday newspaper might mix hockey scores with real estate ads rather than grouping their articles into sections for news, sports, classified ads, travel, entertainment, and comics. Tables of contents, supermarkets, biological hierarchies, libraries, and telephone books all reflect this dual process: the division of the whole into categories or sections and the assignment of each individual item to one of these groups.

When we began to write this book, for example, we were already sure of our organizing principle and we had made some preliminary decisions about which categories, or patterns of development, we would cover. We could also, of course, have classified the selections according to the kind of writing (such as essay, newspaper article, or poem) or according to the length, subject matter, degree of difficulty, or any other principle. We decided, however, that our divisions would represent the structural patterns of writing that parallel ways of organizing thoughts and ideas: cause and effect, definition, comparison and contrast, and so forth. As we collected interesting reading selections, we classified each one into one category: the one that represented the essay's dominant pattern of development. This process of dividing and classifying made our work—and makes yours—much simpler.

In fact, besides following our classification system, you have already invented your own. Each time you have sorted and grouped your ideas after brainstorming, you have applied this procedure. When you brainstorm, as chapter 1 explains, you first consider your larger topic, listing all the related points you can think of. Next, you *divide* your topic into logical categories and *classify* the items on your list into one category or another, perhaps narrowing, expanding, or eliminating some categories—or some points—as you go along. This picking and choosing, sorting and grouping reduces your material until it is manageable and eventually generates your thesis and the main points of your essay.

Uses of Division and Classification

The pattern of division and classification is the obvious choice for certain assignments. When you must assess various investment strategies for your finance course, you naturally turn to division. If your English literature term paper is to include Mark Twain's letters, travel books, essays, and autobiographical writings, classification is the logical method to organize your material and structure your paper. For other assignments, you might use division and classification to group types of medication, describe the federal separation of powers, or categorize anything from political theories to figures of speech. Sometimes you will organize an entire paper around classification and division; at other times, the pattern of classification and division will structure only part of a longer paper.

STRUCTURING A DIVISION AND CLASSIFICATION ESSAY

Once you decide to use classification and division as your pattern of development, you need to plan your essay. If your topic consists of many individual items that you want to group, your main task will be to classify. If your topic consists of a large group that you want to partition, your main task will be to divide. Often you will use both perspectives to be certain that your analysis is complete. Regardless of your initial vantage point, your result will be the same—a system that categorizes the members of a group.

This system must be logical and consistent. Just as a clear basis of comparison determines the points in a comparison and contrast essay, so a principle of classification determines the system you use to categorize items in division and classification. Of course, every group of people, things, or ideas can be divided in many ways. A group of students, for example, can be categorized by sex, age, or major. Automobiles can be classed by year, color, or gas mileage. Textbooks can be grouped by cost, weight, or quality. Your purpose in classifying, however, determines which principle you use. When you are in line at the bookstore with only twenty dollars, the cost of different books may be your only principle of selection. As you carry your books across campus, however, weight may matter more. Finally, as you study and read, the quality of your books may be paramount. Similarly, when you organize an essay, your principle of classification is determined by your writing situation—your assignment, your purpose, your audience, and your special knowledge and interests.

Although any group can be categorized in many ways, only one principle of classification should be used at a given time. Otherwise, you confuse your reader by mixing up different kinds of categories. In addition, your principle should so clearly define your categories that they are mutually exclusive. After all, a classification system is useless if an item might fit anywhere. Instead, each item should fit only one category, and every item should fit somewhere. Then, your classification system is coherent, consistent, and thorough.

Once you define your principle, apply it to your topic, and derive your categories, you should plan their discussion in your essay. Just as a comparison and contrast essay makes comparable points about its subjects, so your classification essay should treat all categories similarly. When you discuss comparable points for each, you ensure that your reader sees your distinctions among categories and understands your definition of each category.

Finally, arrange your categories in some logical order, preferably so that one leads to the next and the least important yields to the most important. Such an order ensures that your reader sees how the categories relate and how significant each is. Whatever this order, it should correspond with your unifying idea or support your thesis since that establishes the relative value of your categories.

Like other essays, the division and classification essay does not necessarily have a thesis. Even if it is merely expository, however, it must have a unifying idea, usually an enumeration of the categories into which your subject is divided or classified. But in most academic situations, your essay needs a thesis if it is to communicate more than simple information, if it is to convince your readers that your categories are significant and that their relationships to each other and to the whole subject are logical. Enumerating different kinds of investments, for instance, would be pointless if you did not evaluate the strengths and weaknesses of each and then make recommendations based on your assessment. Similarly, your term paper about Twain's nonfiction would accomplish nothing if it merely classified his writings. Instead, your arrangement into categories should communicate your position about these works to your reader, perhaps demonstrating that some types of Twain's nonfiction deserve higher public regard.

Once your topic is thoroughly analyzed and your thesis or unifying idea is formulated, you should plan your division and classification paper around the same three major sections that other essays have. Your introduction should orient the reader by mentioning your topic, the principle by which your material is divided and classified, and the individual categories the group is divided into. If your paper has a thesis, it, too, should be stated in the introduction. Once your readers have this information, they can easily follow your paper as it develops. In subsequent paragraphs, you should treat the categories one by one in the order in which your introduction presents them. Finally, your conclusion should restate your thesis, summing up the points you made about your categories.

Dividing a Topic

Let's suppose that you are planning a paper on investments for your finance course. You want to discuss different types of investments, so you plan to use division—the process of breaking a group into categories—to analyze your topic. Based on your preliminary research, you decide to concentrate on the categories of investments usually considered by a new investor with a moderate income, namely stocks, bonds, and real estate:

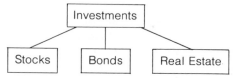

Based on this division, you formulate your thesis: "Carefully selected stocks, bonds, and real estate are all sound investments, but the beginner would be best advised to invest in bonds."

You realize that the body of your essay should devote a paragraph or two to each category in turn, examining the same aspects of each type of investment so that their relative merits are clear. If you consider stability, ease of liquidation, and potential for long-term growth for stocks, you know you should consider the same points—and no others—for bonds and real estate. If you change considerations, your classification will be unbalanced, and your readers will be confused.

If you were assigned a long paper, you would repeat the process of division for each of your main categories. By subdividing, you could distinguish between common and preferred stocks, municipal and corporate bonds, and commercial and residential real estate. For a short paper, however, such subdivision would not be practical. Instead, you would have to concentrate on more general distinctions between broader categories or limit your topic to one subdivision. You might outline such a short paper on investments like this:

¶1   Introduction—thesis: Carefully selected stocks, bonds, and real estate are all sound investments, but the beginner would be best advised to invest in bonds.
¶2   First category: Advantages and disadvantages of stocks.
¶3   Second category: Advantages and disadvantages of real estate.
¶4   Third category: Advantages and disadvantages of bonds, emphasizing advantages.
¶5   Conclusion, including restatement of thesis.

Classifying Information

When you plan a paper such as the essay on investments, your main task is division. For other topics, however, your main task is classification—assigning individual items to their proper categories. Let's suppose that you are preparing a comprehensive term paper for an American literature course on Mark Twain's relatively unexplored works. You have already limited your topic to nonfiction works, and you have read *Roughing It, Life on the Mississippi,* and *The Innocents Abroad.* Besides these books derived from his experiences, you have read his autobiography. This, in turn, led you to some of his correspondence and his essays. You realize that the works you have studied can easily be classified as four different types of Twain's nonfiction: travel books, essays, letters, and autobiography. Your classification system seems an obvious way to organize Twain's nonfiction, but you know that you need a strong thesis statement so that your paper does more than just list his works. You decide that you want to persuade the reader to reconsider the reputations of some of these works, and you formulate this thesis: "Although the popular travel books are the best known of Mark Twain's nonfiction works, his essays, his letters, and particularly his autobiography deserve equal attention." You might diagram your classification like this:

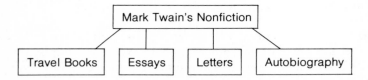

Then you might expand this classification diagram into an outline:

I. Introduction—thesis: Although the popular travel books are the best known of Mark Twain's nonfiction works, his essays, his letters, and particularly his autobiography deserve equal attention.

II. Travel books
   A. *Roughing It*
   B. *The Innocents Abroad*
   C. *Life on the Mississippi*

III. Essays
   A. "Fenimore Cooper's Literary Offenses"
   B. "How To Tell A Story"
   C. "The Awful German Language"

IV. Letters
   A. To W. D. Howells
   B. To his family

V. Autobiography

VI. Conclusion, including restatement of thesis

Since this topic outline represents a long term paper, each of the outline's divisions or subdivisions might require several paragraphs.

Once your term paper is finished, you are confident that it will be clear and persuasive despite its length because you have carefully considered each of the characteristics of an effective division and classification analysis. First of all, you applied only *one* principle of classification when you grouped Twain's nonfiction works according to their literary genres. Of course, you selected this system rather than another—for example, theme, subject matter, stage in his career, or contemporary critical reception—because it suited your purpose. In fact, if you had written your term paper for a political science course, you might even have examined Twain as a social critic by classifying his works according to the amount or kind of political commentary in each. Your system, however, was most appropriate for your writing situation.

Given the group of works you classified, your system was logical. If you had divided Twain's works into novels, essays, short stories, letters, and political works, for instance, you would have mixed two principles of classification, genre and content. As a result, a highly political novel like *The Gilded Age* would have fit more than one category. Likewise, had you left out essays as a category, for instance, you could not have classified several significant works of nonfiction, thus undermining your essay's thesis.

In addition, you arranged your categories so they would support your thesis. Since you challenged the dominance of Twain's travel books, you discussed them briefly early in your paper. Similarly, the autobiography made your best case for the merit of the other nonfiction works and thus was most effective placed last. Of course, you could have arranged your categories in several other orders, such as shorter to longer works or least to most popular, depending on the details of your argument.

Finally, you are certain that you have treated your categories comparably. In fact, you verified this by underlining each point in your rough draft and cross-checking the order of points from category to category. You knew your case would be weakened if you inadvertently skipped style in your discussion of Twain's letters after you had included it for every other category. This omission might lead your readers to suspect either that you could not discuss this point because you had not done enough research on the letters or that you had ignored the point because the style of his letters did not measure up somehow. Your careful organization, however, prevented such questions by your reader.

The following student essay, written by Linda Mauro for an

exam in American government, is structured according to the pattern of division and classification. It divides a whole, the federal government, into categories based on a constitutional principle.

Question: By enumerating the duties of each of the three branches of the federal government, explain the constitutional theory of separation of powers.

SEPARATION OF POWERS: HOW IT WORKS

Introduction and unifying idea

The United States Constitution established a system of separation of powers so that no one branch of government would be too powerful. Under this system, each of the three branches—executive, legislative, and judicial—has a separate function, and each acts to check and balance the workings of the others.

First category

The executive power of government is vested in the president. The president serves as commander in chief of the armed forces. He has the power to make treaties with foreign nations and to appoint ambassadors, Supreme Court justices, cabinet members, and other officials, subject to the approval of Congress. He can also fill vacancies that may occur in Congress due to deaths or resignations. The Constitution also specifies that the president give regular state of the union messages. Finally, as the nation's chief executive officer, the president serves many ceremonial functions, receiving and visiting heads of state and other foreign dignitaries.

Second category

The legislative branch of government includes the two houses of Congress: the Senate and the House of Representatives. The Senate has the power to remove officials from office by impeachment. Either house of Congress may introduce bills, which must be passed by both houses and approved by the president

before they become law. (Bills which involve raising
revenue must originate in the House.) Congress has
many other powers specified by the Constitution,
among them the powers to collect taxes, establish
post offices, grant patents and copyrights, borrow
money, regulate commerce with other countries, coin
money and punish counterfeiting, establish
naturalization laws, raise and fund armed forces,
and declare war.

Third category   The most important part of the judicial branch of
government is the Supreme Court. The judicial
branch, which also includes the United States
Superior Court and, in fact, the entire federal
court system, is empowered to rule on all laws of the
federal government. Specific examples might be
suits in which the United States is a party, cases
involving ambassadors, disputes between two states,
and cases of treason.

Conclusion   Later constitutional amendments and court
decisions have redefined and reinterpreted the
powers of all three branches of government, but the
principle of separation of powers remains.

Points for Special Attention

Answering an Exam Question. As was mentioned in chapter 1, an
important part of writing an essay is making sure you understand
the assignment. This exam question does *not* ask the student to
evaluate the system or to compare it to any other; it simply asks for
an explanation. Since Linda Mauro knew that the system depends
on three components—the executive, legislative, and judicial
branches of government—she immediately decided to use division
to structure her essay. Since the question asks for an enumeration,
not an evaluation or interpretation, she did not waste time volunteering unnecessary information.

Thesis Statement. Mauro's essay objectively discusses the three
branches of government. It does not—and, given the exam question,

should not—take a position on the relative merits of the three branches. Consequently, it has no thesis. It does, however, express a unifying idea in the first paragraph.

Organization.   The question itself, which asked students to explain the whole by reviewing its parts, made division and classification the logical organizational pattern. Each of the three paragraphs in the body of the essay relates the functions of one branch of government. Mauro does not feel that any one branch is more significant or stronger than any other; in fact, their relative equality is the point of the system. Thus, she has no particular reason for ordering her body paragraphs as she does. Her decision is purely arbitrary.

Transition Between Categories.   In each body paragraph, Mauro clearly announces every new category of government in the first sentence. Because of these topic sentences, a reader knows which branch of government will be considered in the paragraph. These sentences serve as transitions, marking the shifts from category to category. A longer essay or a less familiar classification system might require additional transitions to show the relationships among parts or between a part and the whole. Words such as *first, next, then, finally, like, unlike,* and *besides,* as well as comparatives (*more, less*) and superlatives (*most, least*), can reveal these connections.

Parallel Treatment of Categories.   Since the three branches of government have different responsibilities, Mauro could not treat identical points for each. She could not, for instance, note the influence each branch has on the armed forces or on impeachment proceedings because these items simply do not apply to all branches. She did, however, follow her principle of classification and provide comparable information—their constitutional duties—for each.

Conclusion.   The essay ends with a brief conclusion, a one sentence summary rather than a complete paragraph. This would not usually be sufficient for a full-length essay, but it is adequate during an exam when time is limited. In this writing situation, the audience—the course instructor—is more interested in a clear arrangement of relevant information in the body of the essay than in a fully developed conclusion.

This more technical student paper, written for an advanced pharmacology course, uses a complex division and classification structure. The student first divides depression into three categories in order to assess different kinds of drug therapy. He also classifies the drugs used to treat depression. Both sections provide essential information and prepare the reader to understand and accept the essay's implied thesis. Both advance the paper's purpose, warning consumers against a certain type of drug and advising that only patients suffering from certain kinds of depression use it.

TREATMENT OF DEPRESSION: A NOTE OF CAUTION
TO THE CONSUMER

Introduction

Depression is a well-recognized problem in American society, and most persons will admit to having felt depressed at one time or another. In the overwhelming majority of instances, such a feeling is not indicative of any true disorder. Problems arise, however, when the depression becomes so severe or prolonged as to produce a noticeable change in a person's lifestyle and behavior.

Categories of depression

Three very general categories of depression have been identified and may, under certain conditions, warrant the use of antidepressant drugs. First, exogenous depressions are those in which an individual reacts inordinately to some precipitating situation, such as the death of a loved one or a major business failure. Exaggerated reactions, usually occurring in persons with neurotic tendencies, may be prolonged and incapacitating. Next, other persons seem to have been depressed all of their lives, and their self-esteem is chronically rock bottom. As these individuals find little joy in social interaction, they generally avoid contact with other people. Such depression is most often seen in alcoholics, narcotic addicts, and persons with sociopathic behavior patterns. In the last group, depressive symptoms have a definite onset, but an external precipitating factor cannot be identified. This endogenous depression, which occurs more frequently in the elderly, is characterized by marked apathy, lack of energy, feelings of guilt and worthlessness, early–morning awakening, and decreased appetite.

First category of drugs

Drugs available for the treatment of depression fall into two major categories. The first are the tricyclic antidepressants. While several drugs are included in this category (common trade names include Tofranil, Norpramin, Pertofrane, Elavil, Aventyl, Vivactil, and Sinequan), there are no major differences in effectiveness. Side effects are generally not severe and may include drowsiness, dryness of the mouth, and excessive sweating.

Second category of drugs

The other major class of antidepressants are the monoamine oxidase inhibitors (abbreviated MAO inhibitors). Two of these drugs, isocarboxazid (Marplan) and phenelzine (Nardil), are chemically related. The other one, tranylcypromine (Parnate), is chemically distinct. These drugs are less consistently effective and more potentially toxic than the tricyclics. Some of the side effects of the MAO inhibitors include agitation, hallucinations, a severe hepatitislike reaction, and high blood pressure.

The blood–pressure–elevating effect is probably the basis for considerable sentiment against the MAO inhibitors, and rightfully so. These drugs may interact with many of the ingredients in nonprescription cold products to produce a dangerous elevation of blood pressure.

Additionally, the depressed person should not take an MAO inhibitor simultaneously with a tricyclic. Mania and convulsions may result if these two drugs are combined.

One of the greatest dangers associated with the MAO inhibitors revolves around the effects of certain foods. Common food products—especially aged cheeses but also sour cream, chianti, sherry, beer, pickled herring, chocolate, yeast, broad beans, canned figs, raisins, chicken livers, and meat prepared with tenderizers—contain a chemical (tyramine) which may react with the MAO inhibitor to produce a severe attack of high blood pressure usually accompanied by a splitting headache and, possibly, confusion. Brain hemorrhage has even been reported in some cases, but usually these individuals already had some previous defect in the blood vessels of the brain.

While all of the MAO inhibitors should be viewed with skepticism because of their potential to produce dangerous elevations in blood pressure in association with certain foods, tranylcypromine has most frequently been incriminated in causing these reactions. Indeed, the potential hazard of this drug should not be underestimated, especially if the user is not hospitalized and cannot therefore be closely watched by skilled medical personnel. In 1964 the safety of tranylcypromine was so severely questioned that it was removed from the market by the Food and Drug Administration. Now the drug has returned with the warning that its use should be limited to hospitalized or closely supervised patients who have not responded to other antidepressant therapy.

Conclusion   If you do not fall into one of the categories
                      stated above and your physician has prescribed
                      tranylcypromine (Parnate), it would be best to
                      discuss with him your concern about this drug. If
                      your physician is unaware of the potential dangers
                      of tranylcypromine, ask him to consult with your
                      pharmacist. This professional will be able to
                      provide complete information about the effects of
                      tranylcypromine taken with certain foods and
                      medications.

Points for Special Attention

Parallel Treatment of Categories.   This essay discusses kinds of
depression and kinds of drugs used to treat depression. Each
category is clearly described and mutually exclusive; no category
of depression or of drug is omitted. Each category is also treated
equally. Each kind of depression, for example, is described in
terms of its causes, its symptoms, and the kinds of people likely to
suffer from it; each category includes all these points and no others.
Similarly, both kinds of drugs are considered only in terms of the
chemical similarities among the drugs in each category and the
side effects associated with each group.

Structure.   Patrick Knight's essay illustrates how useful the division
and classification pattern can be as part of an essay. His essay's
complex structure may be outlined like this:

¶1   Introduction
¶2   Categories of depression
¶3   First category of drug therapy for depression (tricyclic
      antidepressants)
¶4   Second category of drug therapy for depression (MAO
      inhibitors)
¶5   Side effects of MAO inhibitors in general
¶6   Side effects of MAO inhibitors in combination with certain
      foods
¶7   Hazards of a particular MAO inhibitor (tranylcypromine)
¶8   Conclusion and recommendations to the reader

Purpose and Audience. Patrick Knight's essay does not have a stated thesis. Implied throughout is the warning that, although severe depression can be treated with drugs, MAO inhibitors can have dangerous side effects and should be used with caution. This implied thesis gives coherence to the essay and underlies every paragraph.

Although most of Knight's paper concentrates on the negative side effects of the MAO inhibitors, both of the division and classification analyses that introduce the essay have important functions. The essay's purpose is to warn certain categories of people about certain kinds of drugs. Ultimately, the paper focuses on one subcategory of MAO inhibitor, tranylcypromine. Here, classification is the means by which Knight narrows his subject from depression, to treatment of depression, to treatment of depression with any of the MAO inhibitors, and finally to treatment of depression with tranylcypromine.

Each of the essays that follow uses division and classification as its pattern of development. In some cases, this pattern is used to explain ideas; in others, it is used to persuade the reader of something.

The Life Stream
LOUIS FAUGERES BISHOP

Because the division and classification pattern is precise and can encompass and relate many details, it is particularly well suited to scientific exposition. Here, Louis Faugeres Bishop organizes his discussion according to this pattern: he divides blood into its components and describes the smaller elements of those components in some detail. Notice, however, that his treatment of the different components of blood is not always parallel.

Under the microscope we can see that [blood] is composed of a 1 watery fluid called plasma, in which certain formed elements are suspended. The formed elements are different types of cells—red blood cells, white blood cells and platelets.

The red blood cells are the most numerous of the formed 2 elements. There are normally about 5,000,000 in each cubic millimeter of blood in men and about 4,500,000 in women during the child bearing years. Each cell is about $1/3500$ of an inch in diameter. Normally the cells are in the form of disks, both sides of which are concave.

Red blood cells are developed in the red marrow, found in the 3 ends of the long bones and throughout the interior of flat bones, such as the vertebrae and ribs. The cells have definite nuclei in the early stages of their formation; in man and in other mammals the nuclei are lost by the time the cells have become mature and before they are released into the blood stream.

Each mature red blood cell has a structural framework called the 4 stroma, which is made up chiefly of proteins and fatty materials. It forms a mesh extending into the interior of the cell; it gives the cell its shape and flexibility. The most important chemical substance in the cell is hemoglobin, which causes blood to have a red color. Hemoglobin is composed of an iron-containing pigment called heme and a protein called globin; there are about four parts of heme to ninety-six parts of globin. In man the normal amount of hemoglobin is 14 to 15.6 grams per 100 cubic centimeters of blood; in woman it is 11 to 14 grams.

Hemoglobin combines with oxygen in the lungs after air has 5 been inhaled; the resulting compound is called oxyhemoglobin. When the red blood cells later make their way to other parts of the body deficient in oxygen, the oxygen in the compound breaks its bonds and makes its way by diffusion to the tissues of the oxygen-poor areas. Thus the red blood cells draw oxygen from the lungs, transport it in the blood stream and release it to the tissues as needed.

The white blood cells are the body's military force, attacking 6 disease organisms such as staphylococci, streptococci and menin-gococci. These cells are far less numerous than the red variety; the proportion of white to red under normal conditions is 1 to 400 or 500. The white cells are semitransparent bodies. They differ from red cells in several important respects; among other things, they contain no hemoglobin and they always have nuclei.

There are several easily distinguished varieties of white cells: 7 neutrophils, lymphocytes, basophils, eosinophils and monocytes. Neutrophils, basophils and eosinophils are formed in the bone marrow. Lymphocytes are made in the lymphatic tissues; mono-cytes, in the reticulo-endothelial system.

The neutrophils are by far the most numerous of the white blood 8 cells, making up from 65 to 70 per cent of the total. They derive their name from the fact that they readily take the color of a neutral dye. These cells are about half as large again as red blood cells.

Platelets are tiny circular or oval disks, which are derived from 9 certain giant cells in the bone marrow, called megakaryocytes. Their number ranges from 200,000 per cubic millimeter to 500,000 or more. The platelets, which are much smaller than the blood cells, serve several useful purposes. When they disintegrate, they liberate a substance called thrombokinase or thromboplastin, which is vital in the blood-clotting process. They also help to plug leaks in the tiny blood vessels called capillaries.

The plasma is the watery part of the blood, making up from 50 10 to 60 per cent of the total. It is a clear yellow fluid, serving as a vehicle for the transportation of red blood cells, white blood cells, platelets and various substances necessary for the vital functioning of the body cells, for clotting and for the defense of the body against disease. After clotting occurs, a straw-colored fluid called serum is left; this retains its liquid form indefinitely.

About 90 per cent of plasma is water, in which a great variety of 11 substances are held in suspension or in solution. These include proteins, such as fibrinogen, albumin and the globulins, and also sugar, fat and inorganic salts derived from food or from the storage depots of the body. Plasma contains urea, uric acid, creatine and other products of the breakdown of proteins. There are enzymes, such as adrenal hormones, thyroxine and insulin, derived from the glands of internal secretion. There are also various gases: oxygen and nitrogen, diffused into the blood from the lungs; and carbon dioxide, diffused into the blood from the tissues.

COMPREHENSION

1. What are the three principal components of blood? Briefly outline the origin, appearance, and function of each.

2. What is the most important substance in red blood cells? Why?

3. What are some ways in which the different varieties of white blood cells may be classified? Why are they called "the body's military force"?

4. What is the relationship between plasma and the other components of blood?

PURPOSE AND AUDIENCE

1. This selection is from *The Book of Popular Science*. How can you tell it is aimed at a popular audience rather than scientists? In what respects might it be difficult for the reader who had no scientific background?

2. The first two sentences of this essay state its unifying idea, but it has no arguable thesis. Why not?

3. If the excerpt's purpose is not to persuade, what is it?

STYLE AND STRUCTURE

1. What determines the order in which Bishop introduces the components of blood? Could the order be changed? If so, would other changes be necessary?

2. Good division and classification essays are supposed to treat each category equally, but Bishop's essay does not always do this. Why not? Why is certain information provided for some categories but not for others?

3. How does the author let you know when a new category is being introduced?

4. Because this is an excerpt from a longer essay, it ends rather abruptly. Does this hurt the selection in any way? If so, how? If not, why not?

WRITING WORKSHOP

1. Write a brief essay on the composition of blood for an elementary school

audience. Be sure to define unfamiliar words (or use familiar ones or analogies); include simple drawings if you think they will help.

2. Write a division and classification essay about your extended family tree. Begin with your family as a whole, and divide and subdivide it into its component parts. You may include a drawing of the tree if you wish.

Faces in the Crowd

This essay, from Time *magazine, follows the division and classification pattern perfectly. It divides rock music audiences into five types. Then each category is discussed separately and completely in terms of the same points. Because this essay classifies people, however, it is, to some extent, creating stereotypes.*

Who's playing at the local rock palace? One way to find out is to look at the marquee. Another, says California Promoter Steve Wolf, is to watch the crowd strolling—or floating, in the case of heavy grass consumers—through the door. "Audiences resemble the groups they come to see," says Wolf. Those words are reckless understatements.

No one who has ever mixed with a San Francisco psychedelic-style concert crowd is likely to forget the experience. Going to see the Boz Scaggs, Grace Slick, or Hot Tuna? Better take ear muffs and a flak jacket. Psychedelic rock crowds can be hostile collections of spacy Vietvets still suffering from post-Viet Nam syndrome, pimply feminists in granny glasses, and young high school dropouts. Bottles and firecrackers spin through the air. At a Grateful Dead concert, usually a four- or five-hour affair, the typical freak is a blend of drug hunger, male lonerism, and musical knowledgeability. He will attend somnolently to the music (probably after swilling a bottle of wine), sway ecstatically forward toward the performers. In contrast, the audience for Balladeer James Taylor, or the country-rock group Poco, whose music has crisp pattern and infectious surfaces, has a well-scrubbed look and an enraptured response to the music.

Of course, when hallowed groups like the Rolling Stones, the Who, or Bob Dylan make one of their infrequent appearances, categories crumble; everybody comes, just like the World Series. Still, it is possible to define five general types of audience on the basis of dress, manner, consumption, age and music taste. The categories:

Heavy Metal. So named because of the massive banks of amplifiers, drums and loudspeakers employed by Grand Funk, Led Zeppelin, Black Sabbath and Blue Oyster Cult. The music is pure buzz— heavy, simplistic blues played at maximum volume and wallowed in mostly by young teen-agers just experimenting with marijuana, the lingua franca of rock, and perhaps hard drugs too.

This audience can be trouble for concert-hall managers. Says Cleveland Promoter Jules Belkin, "They are up on the seats boogieing and running around the hall." Dress ranges from scruffy jeans to $200 velveteen jackets. The girls may come in couples to ogle, say, at topless Mark Farner of Grand Funk. Then there are the brassy groupies with their stevedore vocabularies who haughtily flaunt their backstage passes. The boys come in gangs and do what gangs do—fling lighted matches, fight the bouncers, sometimes toss empty wine bottles. Vomiting from too much beer or wine is a status symbol. If these kids do not have tickets, they break in. A heavy security force, sometimes including local police, is *de rigueur* at most rock concerts.

The Listeners.   Performing groups that attract this crowd include the Moody Blues, Yes, Weather Report and The Eleventh House. The music is predominantly classical or jazz rock. The Listeners tend to be Heavy Metal graduates—youths ranging in age into the early 20's, who know and care about musicianship. Sedated by grass, Seconals, and Quaaludes, they tend to applaud rather than scream their approval.

Squeaky Cleans.   A description used by Singer Bette Midler to characterize fans of the soft, often poetic songs of such bards as Cat Stevens, James Taylor, Joni Mitchell, Melanie. This is an orderly dating crowd in its late teens and early 20's who are interested in love songs. Girls generally outnumber the boys by 2 to 1. Melanie's ethereal fans tend to invade the stage, only to sit quietly at her feet, perhaps lighting candles. Mitchell's following emulates her. "Since Joni started wearing gowns," says Wolf, "the girls have started wearing dresses and makeup."

Glitter Trippers.   Glitter stars do not seem so much to have created their fandom as to have been created by it. The fastest-growing audience in rock dotes on the finery of such brocade-, sequin-, mascara-, and rouge-wearing performers as Todd Rundgren, Suzi Quatro, Alice Cooper, and the New York Dolls. Occasionally a glitter singer like England's bisexual David Bowie is actually good. Mostly, though, admits the Dolls' David Johansen, "the whole glitter trip is just jive." A concert can also be simply an excuse for youngsters to come out for a reasonably harmless masquerade party.

The kids go on parade to show off their white tuxedos and top hats, feather boas, and of course glitter, lavishly applied to face and body.

The Evening-Outers.   These are the young marrieds, who, says one   9
New York promoter, "are dressed to the nines, and smoke where they're supposed to." As mellowed graduates of the 1960's rock revolution, they will naturally show up to hear the Stones or Dylan, but mostly they turn out for the Carpenters, or the Fifth Dimension. Promoters like the Evening-Outers because they spend money generously at the concession bars.

Begun by the Beatles a decade ago, the rock revolution suc-   10
ceeded beyond everyone's wildest dreams. Rock defined an emerging segment of America, financed a counterculture, and spawned a $2 billion industry. Its principal gift to those who were young in the 1960's was to provide a common means of expression—a common music, a common language, even a kind of cathartic theater in which a Janis Joplin assumed almost mythic dimensions as a tragic heroine and Dylan strolled the stage like an Orpheus. It is no secret that rock's classic era is gone forever, along with the social bonds that nurtured it. The current fragmentation of the rock audience certifies that. In fairness, it must be added that it also signifies a diversity of personal taste and music style unknown previously in American pop music. If rock can be described as being in a somewhat self-expressive romantic era, can its neoclassic period—or a pop Stravinsky—be far behind?

COMPREHENSION

1. What characteristics does the author say will be considered for each of the five groups? Is this promise kept?

2. The author says more about Heavy Metal than any of the other four categories. Why?

3. List the rock groups the author mentions. Which are still popular? Do they have anything in common that might explain their continued popularity?

PURPOSE AND AUDIENCE

1. What is the thesis of this essay? Where does it appear?

2. The last paragraph makes a statement about rock music in general which reveals why the author used the pattern of division and classification. What is that statement?

3. This essay appeared in *Time* magazine, a general interest news magazine with a largely middle-class readership. Many of these readers would not be admirers of the rock groups described here. What then is the author's purpose in writing this essay?

STYLE AND STRUCTURE

1. The essay opens with a question. Do you think this is an effective technique for this essay? Why or why not?

2. What are the categories identified here? On what basis are they classified?

3. How are the categories set off in the text of the article? How effective is this technique? Could the categories have been just as easily identified without it? Explain.

4. Outline or diagram the categories and subcategories presented in the essay.

5. Several quotations are included in this essay. Why do you think the author includes them? Is this purpose successfully achieved?

6. Are the categories listed in this essay mutually exclusive? Why or why not?

WRITING WORKSHOP

1. Since rock music changes so rapidly, this essay, which appeared June 26, 1974, is already somewhat dated. Write an updated version of the essay, substituting your own categories of rock groups and audiences.

2. Write an essay in which you classify different reactions to a particular song, movie, or television program. Be certain that your categories support a thesis.

3. Write a classification and division essay that categorizes performers and audiences at an event other than a rock concert. Be certain that your categories support a thesis.

Sex Bias in Textbooks
LENORE J. WEITZMAN AND DIANE RIZZO

Although male and female roles have changed in nearly every area of our lives, corresponding changes have not always occurred in the depiction of those roles in books written for children. Lenore J. Weitzman and Diane Rizzo find this particularly disturbing because of the profound influence these books have on their readers. Notice how the authors analyze statistical data to draw conclusions and how they organize those data into categories.

Textbooks have always been a cornerstone of our education system. Although the main function of textbooks is to convey specific information, textbooks also provide the child with ethical and moral values. Thus, at the same time that a child is learning history or math, he or she is also learning what is good, desirable, just.   1

This second type of information—which sociologists refer to as the "latent content" of textbooks—provides standards for how men, women, boys, and girls should act. This latent content was the focus of research we carried on for the last three years. During that time, we have analyzed the latent content of the most widely used textbook series in the United States in each of five subject areas: science, arithmetic, reading, spelling, and social studies. (A grant from the Rockefeller Family Fund supported the research.) Through computer analysis, we obtained data on the sex, age, racial distribution, and activities of the textbook characters by grade level and subject area.   2

This article will summarize the ways in which the two sexes are portrayed and the type of behavior encouraged for each.   3.

Sex Distribution. Since women comprise 51 percent of the U.S. population, one might expect half the people in textbook illustrations to be females. However, males overwhelmingly predominate in all series: Females are only 31 percent of the total, while males are 69 percent. Of over 8,000 pictures analyzed, more than 5,500 are of males. Girl students using these books are likely to feel excluded.   4

Sex Differences by Grade Level. The percentage of females varies by grade level. In all series combined, females comprise a third of   5

266

the illustrations at the second grade level, but only a fifth of the total on the sixth grade level. In other words, by the sixth grade, there are four pictures of males for every picture of a female. This contrast is vividly illustrated in the accompanying figure. Thus, as the textbooks increase in sophistication, women become less numerous and, by implication, less significant as role models.

This decline in female role models makes it harder for a girl 6
student to identify with the textbook characters and thus may make it harder for her to assimilate the lesson. Covertly, she is being told that she, a female, is less important as the textbook world shifts to the world of adults—to the world of men.

This declining representation of females is particularly striking 7
in some of the series. For example, in the second grade spelling series, 43 percent of the illustrations are of females, but in the sixth grade series, the percentage has declined to a mere 15 percent.

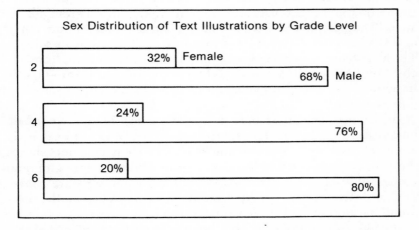

Sex Differences in Activities.   The pictures of children show three 8
striking differences between the boys and girls. First, boys are portrayed as active, skillful, and adventuresome; girls are typically shown as passive—as watching and waiting for boys.

Second, while boys are depicted as intelligent and as mastering 9
work-related skills, girls are shown engaging in domestic activities or in grooming themselves, trying on clothes, and shopping. Third, girls are depicted as affectionate, nurturing, and emotional, but boys almost never embrace or cry. Thus, the young boy is taught that to be manly he must control his emotions. In the same way that girls are constrained by images which stereotype them as pretty and passive, boys are constrained by images which stereotype them

as strong and unemotional. The textbooks thereby encourage both sexes to limit their development.

Adult men and women in textbooks are even more sex-stereo- [10] typed. While only a few women are shown outside the home, men are portrayed in over 150 occupational roles. A young boy is told he can be anything from a laborer to a doctor. He is encouraged to imagine himself in a wide variety of roles and both to dream about and plan his occupational future.

In contrast, the future for young girls seems preordained: Almost [11] all adult women in textbooks are housewives. In reality, however, 9 out of 10 women in our society will work at some point in their lives. By ignoring women workers, the textbooks fail to provide the necessary occupational role models for girls and thus unnecessarily restrict future horizons.

Sex Differences in Subject Areas.   There are systematic differences [12] in the treatment that girls and women receive in different subject areas. The percentage of females in illustrations varies from a high of 33 percent in social studies to a low of 26 percent in science. These subject differences are important in understanding why children like certain subjects and want to major in them—or why, in contrast, they feel unwelcome because of the covert messages they receive.

In science, the most male-oriented series, 74 percent of the [13] pictures are of males. The science texts seem to imply that the world of science is a masculine domain. When boys are shown, they are actively involved in experiment—looking through micro-scopes and pouring chemicals. In contrast, when girls are shown, they observe the boys' experiments. The epitome of the male prototype in science is the astronaut. But only boys are pictured as astronauts and, in the text, only boys are told to imagine that they can explore the moon.

In mathematics textbooks, many problems are based on sex- [14] sterotyped roles, with men earning money and women dividing pies. Further, despite the Equal Pay Act of 1963, we found math problems in which girls were paid less than boys for the same work. (It would be hard to imagine a textbook publisher allowing an example in which a black child is paid less than a white child.)

In the reading series, story titles provide a good indicator of the [15] relative importance of males and females. Boys predominate in every grade. The series examined had 102 stories about boys and only 35 about girls.

Even the female heroines reinforce traditional female roles. For [16] example, Kirsten, the heroine of a third grade story, wins over the girls who have rejected her by making Danish cookies and having the most popular booth at the school fair. The moral in this story is that girls can succeed by cooking and serving. But Kirsten slights herself and the very skill that had earned her favor when she says, "It's easy; even I can do it, and you know how stupid I am." Thus, even when girls succeed, they tend to deprecate themselves. In contrast, boys show a great deal of confidence and pride.

Both the reading and spelling series demonstrate a surprising   17
amount of antagonism and hostility toward females. In the spelling series, female characters are yelled at and pushed around. In the reading series, they are shown as stupid and clumsy three times as frequently as males.

In social studies, the best series studied, women were often   18
skillful and important. Here, mothers play a crucial role in passing on their cultural tradition to their daughters. Although we applaud these positive pictures of women, it should be noted that mothers in the series teach only their daughters, not their sons. Similarly, fathers teach only sons. Thus, traditional sex roles are perpetuated. Today, boys need to learn to manage in the home and to be parents, and girls need to learn about vocations and the outdoors. Textbooks could expand rather than contract children's potential.

Although this series has the largest percentage of females in   19
pictures, still 2 out of 3 are pictures of males. Women are in the section on the home but are absent from the sections on history, government, and society.

After studying these textbooks for three years, one cannot help   20
but conclude that children are being warped by the latent messages in them. We urge teachers to examine the textbooks they use and to check the ways in which sex roles are stereotyped. Only teachers can change the impact that these books will have on our young people and on the next generation of adults. Teachers can tell their girl students about the world and the real options they have in it. Teachers can encourage them to dream and can help them plan.

What is sorely lacking in textbooks and thus desperately needed   21
in the classroom is a new image of adult women and a wide range of adult role models for young girls. Girls—and boys too—should learn about the history of women in this country, about suffrage and the current women's liberation movement, and about female heroines of our country and the world. What a difference it would make if young girls could point to adult women with pride and feel that they themselves have an exciting life ahead.

While we must all create pressure to change the textbooks, in   22
the meantime, it is up to teachers to counteract the latent messages
in them and to create positive images of adult women in the minds
of students.

COMPREHENSION

1. What information are the authors classifying in this essay?

2. How does the percentage of females in textbook illustrations vary according to grade level?

3. What are the three differences between illustrations of boys and girls in activities?

4. How do the social studies texts differ from the others Weitzman and Rizzo examined?

5. What recommendations do the authors make at the end of the essay? Can you make these recommendations more specific than they do?

PURPOSE AND AUDIENCE

1. This essay is written to convince. What is its thesis? Where is this position stated?

2. This article appeared in 1975 in a journal aimed at teachers. Would it also be appropriate for a P.T.A. periodical? for a magazine whose readers are primarily homemakers? Explain.

STYLE AND STRUCTURE

1. The first two paragraphs of this essay contain an unusual amount of information for an introduction to a brief essay. Is all the information necessary? Why or why not?

2. What is the function of the essay's brief third paragraph? Is it necessary? Should it have been developed further? Explain.

3. When the authors consider sex differences by grade level, they use a bar graph as an illustration. Do you find the graph helpful or intrusive? Why?

4. Would you find the section on sex differences in activities more helpful if some actual textbook pictures had been included, or do you consider the section convincing as it is? Explain.

5. The section developed in paragraphs 12 through 19 has several subdivisions. On what basis are these subdivisions made?

WRITING WORKSHOP

1. Write an essay in which you classify your own textbooks according to a principle of your choice. You might classify them according to level of difficulty, subject matter, format, approach, attitude toward the reader, or whatever. Be sure to specify the features of each category you set up and establish categories that support a thesis.

2. Think about some of the books you liked when you were a child. Write a short classification essay examining the different roles assigned in them to women (or to men).

Friends, Good Friends—and Such Good Friends

JUDITH VIORST

Judith Viorst writes a regular column in Redbook, *a magazine aimed at young, married women. This essay first appeared as one of those columns. Viorst concentrates on family and other personal relationships and is known for her collections of light verse as well as her informal essays like this one.*

Women are friends, I once would have said, when they totally love and support and trust each other, and bare to each other the secrets of their souls, and run—no questions asked—to help each other, and tell harsh truths to each other (no, you can't wear that dress unless you lose ten pounds first) when harsh truths must be told. 1

Women are friends, I once would have said, when they share the same affection for Ingmar Bergman, plus train rides, cats, warm rain, charades, Camus, and hate with equal ardor Newark and Brussels sprouts and Lawrence Welk and camping. 2

In other words, I once would have said that a friend is a friend all the way, but now I believe that's a narrow point of view. For the friendships I have and the friendships I see are conducted at many levels of intensity, serve many different functions, meet different needs and range from those as all-the-way as the friendship of the soul sisters mentioned above to that of the most nonchalant and casual playmates. 3

Consider these varieties of friendship: 4

1. Convenience friends. These are the women with whom, if our paths weren't crossing all the time, we'd have no particular reason to be friends: a next-door neighbor, a woman in our car pool, the mother of one of our children's closest friends or maybe some mommy with whom we serve juice and cookies each week at the Glenwood Co-op Nursery. 5

Convenience friends are convenient indeed. They'll lend us their cups and silverware for a party. They'll drive our kids to soccer when we're sick. They'll take us to pick up our car when we need a lift to the garage. They'll even take our cats when we go on vacation. As we will for them. 6

But we don't, with convenience friends, ever come too close or 7 tell too much; we maintain our public face and emotional distance. "Which means," says Elaine, "that I'll talk about being overweight but not about being depressed. Which means I'll admit being mad but not blind with rage. Which means that I might say that we're pinched this month but never that I'm worried sick over money."

But which doesn't mean that there isn't sufficient value to be found in these friendships of mutual aid, in convenience friends. 8

2. Special-interest friends. These friendships aren't intimate, and they needn't involve kids or silverware or cats. Their value lies in some interest jointly shared. And so we may have an office friend or a yoga friend or a tennis friend or a friend from the Women's Democratic Club. 9

"I've got one woman friend," says Joyce, "who likes, as I do, to take psychology courses. Which makes it nice for me—and nice for her. It's fun to go with someone you know and it's fun to discuss what you've learned, driving back from the classes." And for the most part, she says, that's all they discuss. 10

"I'd say that what we're doing is *doing* together, not being together," Suzanne says of her Tuesday-doubles friends. "It's mainly a tennis relationship, but we play together well. And I guess we all need to have a couple of playmates." ' 11

I agree. 12

My playmate is a shopping friend, a woman of marvelous taste, a woman who knows exactly *where* to buy *what*, and furthermore is a woman who always knows beyond a doubt what one ought to be buying. I don't have the time to keep up with what's new in eyeshadow, hemlines and shoes and whether the smock look is in or finished already. But since (oh, shame!) I care a lot about eyeshadow, hemlines and shoes, and since I don't *want* to wear smocks if the smock look is finished, I'm very glad to have a shopping friend. 13

3. Historical friends. We all have a friend who knew us when ... maybe way back in Miss Meltzer's second grade, when our family lived in that three-room flat in Brooklyn, when our dad was out of work for seven months, when our brother Allie got in that fight where they had to call the police, when our sister married the endodontist from Yonkers and when, the morning after we lost our virginity, she was the first, the only, friend we told. 14

The years have gone by and we've gone separate ways and we've little in common now, but we're still an intimate part of each other's past. And so whenever we go to Detroit we always go to visit this friend of our girlhood. Who knows how we looked before our teeth were straightened. Who knows how we talked before our voice got 15 un-Brooklyned. Who knows what we ate before we learned about artichokes. And who, by her presence, puts us in touch with an earlier part of ourself, a part of ourself it's important never to lose.

"What this friend means to me and what I mean to her," says 16 Grace, "is having a sister without sibling rivalry. We know the texture of each other's lives. She remembers my grandmother's cabbage soup. I remember the way her uncle played the piano. There's simply no other friend who remembers those things."

4. Crossroads friends. Like historical friends, our crossroads 17 friends are important for *what was*—for the friendship we shared at a crucial, now past, time of life. A time, perhaps, when we roomed in college together; or worked as eager young singles in the Big City together; or went together, as my friend Elizabeth and I did, through pregnancy, birth and that scary first year of new motherhood.

Crossroads friends forge powerful links, links strong enough to 18 endure with not much more contact than once-a-year letters at Christmas. And out of respect for those crossroads years, for those dramas and dreams we once shared, we will always be friends.

5. Cross-generational friends. Historical friends and crossroads 19 friends seem to maintain a special kind of intimacy—dormant but always ready to be revived—and though we may rarely meet, whenever we do connect, it's personal and intense. Another kind of intimacy exists in the friendships that form across generations in what one woman calls her daughter-mother and her mother-daughter relationships.

Evelyn's friend is her mother's age—"but I share so much more 20 than I ever could with my mother"—a woman she talks to of music, of books and of life. "What I get from her is the benefit of her experience. What she gets—and enjoys—from me is a youthful perspective. It's a pleasure for both of us."

I have in my own life a precious friend, a woman of 65 who has 21 lived very hard, who is wise, who listens well; who has been where I am and can help me understand it; and who represents not only an ultimate ideal mother to me but also the person I'd like to be when I grow up.

In our daughter role we tend to do more than our share of self- 22 revelation; in our mother role we tend to receive what's revealed. It's another kind of pleasure—playing wise mother to a questing younger person. It's another very lovely kind of friendship.

6. Part-of-a-couple friends. Some of the women we call our 23 friends we never see alone—we see them as part of a couple at couples' parties. And though we share interests in many things and

respect each other's views, we aren't moved to deepen the relationship. Whatever the reason, a lack of time or—and this is more likely—a lack of chemistry, our friendship remains in the context of a group. But the fact that our feeling on seeing each other is always, "I'm *so* glad she's here" and the fact that we spend half the evening talking together says that this too, in its own way, counts as a friendship.

(Other part-of-a-couple friends are the friends that came with   24
the marriage, and some of these are friends we could live without. But sometimes, alas, she married our husband's best friend; and sometimes, alas, she *is* our husband's best friend. And so we find ourself dealing with her, somewhat against our will, in a spirit of what I'll call *reluctant* friendship.)

7. Men who are friends. I wanted to write just of women friends,   25
but the women I've talked to won't let me—they say I must mention man-woman friendships too. For these friendships can be just as close and as dear as those that we form with women. Listen to Lucy's description of one such friendship:

"We've found we have things to talk about that are different   26
from what he talks about with my husband and different from what I talk about with his wife. So sometimes we call on the phone or meet for lunch. There are similar intellectual interests—we always pass on to each other the books that we love—but there's also something tender and caring too."

In a couple of crises, Lucy says, "he offered himself, for talking   27
and for helping. And when someone died in his family he wanted me there. The sexual, flirty part of our friendship is very small, but *some*—just enough to make it fun and different." She thinks—and I agree—that the sexual part, though small, is always *some*, is always there when a man and a woman are friends.

It's only in the past few years that I've made friends with men,   28
in the sense of a friendship that's *mine*, not just part of two couples. And achieving with them the ease and the trust I've found with women friends has value indeed. Under the dryer at home last week, putting on mascara and rouge, I comfortably sat and talked with a fellow named Peter. Peter, I finally decided, could handle the shock of me minus mascara under the dryer. Because we care for each other. Because we're friends.

8. There are medium friends, and pretty good friends, and very   29
good friends indeed, and these friendships are defined by their level of intimacy. And what we'll reveal at each of these levels of intimacy is calibrated with care. We might tell a medium friend, for example, that yesterday we had a fight with our husband. And we

might tell a pretty good friend that this fight with our husband made us so mad that we slept on the couch. And we might tell a very good friend that the reason we got so mad in that fight that we slept on the couch had something to do with that girl who works in his office. But it's only to our very best friends that we're willing to tell all, to tell what's going on with that girl in his office.

The best of friends, I still believe, totally love and support and   30
trust each other, and bare to each other the secrets of their souls, and run—no questions asked—to help each other, and tell harsh truths to each other when they must be told.

But we needn't agree about everything (only 12-year-old girl   31
friends agree about *everything*) to tolerate each other's point of view. To accept without judgment. To give and to take without ever keeping score. And to *be* there, as I am for them and as they are for me, to comfort our sorrows, to celebrate our joys.

COMPREHENSION

1. In her first three paragraphs, Viorst refutes her own previously held assumptions about friends. What are these assumptions? With what is she replacing them?

2. What does Viorst mean when she says that with convenience friends we keep our public face and emotional distance?

3. What does Viorst mean in paragraph 24 by "a reluctant friendship"?

4. What distinguishes medium, pretty good, and best friends?

PURPOSE AND AUDIENCE

1. Viorst wrote this article for an audience she knows and understands well. Does she expect this audience to be in agreement with her? How can you tell?

2. Does this article have a thesis? If so, what is it?

3. This essay, although it was written by a woman and is aimed at an audience of women, presents stereotypes about the female sex. Identify some of these stereotypes, and note any that some women might object to.

4. In paragraph 28, why does Viorst say, "It's only in the past few years that I've made friends with men"?

STYLE AND STRUCTURE

1. Why do you think Viorst selected division and classification as her essay's pattern of development? Could she have expressed the same ideas in an essay structured according to a different pattern? Explain.

2. Throughout the essay Viorst refers to many of her own friends by name and even quotes them. Why do you think she does this?

3. Although Viorst begins the essay in the first person singular (*I, my*), later she alternates between the first person singular and the first person plural (*we, our*). How do you account for this?

4. Although this is a classification essay, Viorst also uses narrative and definition. Where does she use each?

5. As is often the case, classification in this essay involves comparison and contrast. Explain.

6. Many times Viorst repeats a word or phrase to emphasize a point, to show a relationship between two pieces of information, or to act as a transition. An example is "I once would have said" in paragraphs 2 and 3. Find other examples of such repetition, and explain in each case why it is used.

7. Where does Viorst introduce the actual classification? Where does she complete her classification and begin her conclusion?

WRITING WORKSHOP

1. Classify your own friends (male or female) in a similar essay. You may borrow Viorst's categories or devise your own.

2. If you have one good friend who serves many purposes for you, apply several of Viorst's categories to your friend. In a brief division and classification essay, show how your friend is many different things to you.

Reports, Inferences, Judgments
S. I. HAYAKAWA

The well-known semanticist S. I. Hayakawa has a great interest in words and their meanings. He believes that seemingly minor differences in meaning sometimes can be tremendously important; for this reason, we must choose our words carefully. Here, Hayakawa distinguishes three words which are frequently confused and thus classifies statements into three distinct types. He makes the differences among his categories clear with many vivid examples and precise definitions.

For the purposes of the interchange of information, the basic symbolic act is the *report* of what we have seen, heard, or felt: "There is a ditch on each side of the road." "You can get those at Smith's Hardware Store for $2.75." "There aren't any fish on that side of the lake, but there are on this side." Then there are reports of reports: "The longest waterfall in the world is Victoria Falls in Rhodesia." "The Battle of Hastings took place in 1066." "The papers say that there was a smash-up on Highway 41 near Evansville." Reports adhere to the following rules: first, they are *capable of verification;* second, they *exclude,* as far as possible, *inferences* and *judgments.* (These terms will be defined later.)

VERIFIABILITY

Reports are verifiable. We may not always be able to verify them ourselves, since we cannot track down the evidence for every piece of history we know, nor can we all go to Evansville to see the remains of the smash-up before they are cleared away. But if we are roughly agreed upon the names of things, upon what constitutes a "foot," "yard," "bushel," "kilogram," "meter," and so on, and upon how to measure time, there is relatively little danger of our misunderstanding each other. Even in a world such as we have today, in which everybody seems to be quarreling with everybody else, *we still to a surprising degree trust each other's reports.* We ask directions of total strangers when we are traveling. We follow directions on road signs without being suspicious of the people who put them up. We read books of information about science, mathematics, automotive engineering, travel, geography, the history of costume, and other such factual matters, and we usually assume that the author is doing his best to tell us as truly as he can what he knows. And we are safe in so assuming most of the time. With the interest given today to the discussion of biased newspapers, propagandists, and the general untrustworthiness of many of the communications we receive, we are likely to forget that we still have an enormous amount of reliable information available and that deliberate misinformation, except in warfare, is still more the exception than the rule. The desire for self-preservation that compelled men to evolve means for the exchange of information also compels them to regard the giving of false information as profoundly reprehensible.

At its highest development, the language of reports is the language of science. By "highest development" we mean greatest general usefulness. Presbyterian and Catholic, workingman and capitalist, East German and West German *agree* on the meanings of such symbols as $2 \times 2 = 4$, *100° C, HNO₃, 3:35* A.M., *1940* A.D., *1,000 kilowatts, Quercus agrifolia,* and so on. But how, it may be asked, can there be agreement about even this much among people who disagree about political philosophies, ethical ideas, religious beliefs, and the survival of my business versus the survival of yours? The answer is that circumstances *compel men to agree,* whether they wish to or not. If, for example, there were a dozen different religious sects in the United States, each insisting on its own way of naming the time of the day and the days of the year, the mere necessity of having a dozen different calendars, a dozen different kinds of watches, and a dozen sets of schedules for business hours, trains, and television programs, to say nothing of the effort that would be required for translating terms from one nomenclature to another, would make life as we know it impossible.[1]

The language of reports, then, including the more accurate

---

[1] According to information supplied by the Association of American Railroads, "Before 1883 there were nearly 100 different time zones in the United States. It wasn't until November 18 of that year that . . . a system of standard time was adopted here and in Canada. Before then there was nothing but local or 'solar' time. . . . The Pennsylvania Railroad in the East used Philadelphia time, which was five minutes slower than New York time and five minutes faster than Baltimore time. The Baltimore & Ohio used Baltimore time for trains running out of Baltimore, Columbus time for Ohio, Vincennes (Indiana) time for those going out of Cincinnati. . . . When it was noon in Chicago, it was 12:31 in Pittsburgh, 12:24 in Cleveland, 12:17 in Toledo, 12:13 in Cincinnati, 12:09 in Louisville, 12:07 in Indianapolis, 11:50 in St. Louis, 11:48 in Dubuque, 11:39 in St. Paul, and 11:27 in Omaha. There were 27 local time zones in Michigan alone. . . . A person traveling from Eastport, Maine, to San Francisco, if he wanted always to have the right railroad time and get off at the right place, had to twist the hands of his watch 20 times en route." Chicago *Daily News* (September 29, 1948).

reports of science, is "map" language, and because it gives us reasonably accurate representations of the "territory," it enables us to get work done. Such language may often be dull reading: one does not usually read logarithmic tables or telephone directories for entertainment. But we could not get along without it. There are numberless occasions in the talking and writing we do in everyday life that *require that we state things in such a way that everybody will be able to understand and agree with our formulation.*

INFERENCES

... An inference, as we shall use the term, is a *statement about*   5 *the unknown made on the basis of the known.* We may *infer* from the material and cut of a woman's clothes her wealth or social position; we may *infer* from the character of the ruins the origin of the fire that destroyed the building; we may *infer* from a man's calloused hands the nature of his occupation; we may *infer* from a senator's vote on an armaments bill his attitude toward Russia; we may *infer* from the structure of the land the path of a prehistoric glacier; we may *infer* from a halo on an unexposed photographic plate its past proximity to radioactive materials; we may *infer* from the sound of an engine the condition of its connecting rods. Inferences may be carefully or carelessly made. They may be made on the basis of a broad background of previous experience with the subject matter or with no experience at all. For example, the inferences a good mechanic can make about the internal condition of a motor by listening to it are often startlingly accurate, while the inferences made by an amateur (if he tries to make any) may be entirely wrong. But the common characteristic of inferences is that they are statements about matters which are not directly known, made on the basis of what has been observed.[2]

The avoidance of inferences ... requires that we make no   6 guesses as to what is going on in other people's minds. When we say, "He was angry," we are not reporting; we are making an inference from such observable facts as the following: "He pounded his fist on the table; he swore; he threw the telephone directory at his stenographer." In this particular example, the inference appears

[2] The behaviorist school of psychology tries to avoid inferences about what is going on in other people's minds by describing only external behavior. A famous joke about behaviorism goes: Two behaviorists meet on the street. The first says, "You're fine. How am I?"

to be safe; nevertheless, it is important to remember, especially for the purposes of training oneself, that it is an inference. Such expressions as "He thought a lot of himself," "He was scared of girls," "He has an inferiority complex," made on the basis of casual observation, and "What Russia really wants to do is to establish a communist world dictatorship," made on the basis of casual reading, are highly inferential. We should keep in mind their inferential character and . . . should substitute for them such statements as "He rarely spoke to subordinates in the plant," "I saw him at a party, and he never danced except when one of the girls asked him to," "He wouldn't apply for the scholarship, although I believe he could have won it easily," and "The Russian delegation to the United Nations has asked for *A, B,* and *C.* Last year they voted against *M* and *N* and voted for *X* and *Y.* On the basis of facts such as these, the newspaper I read makes the inference that what Russia really wants is to establish a communist world dictatorship. I agree."

Even when we exercise every caution to avoid inferences and   7 to report only what we see and experience, we all remain prone to error, since the making of inferences is a quick, almost automatic process. We may watch a car weaving as it goes down the road and say, "Look at that *drunken driver*," although what we see is only the *irregular motion of the car*. I once saw a man leave a dollar at a lunch counter and hurry out. Just as I was wondering why anyone should leave so generous a tip in so modest an establishment, the waitress came, picked up the dollar, put it in the cash register as she punched up ninety cents, and put a dime in her pocket. In other words, my description to myself of the event, "a dollar tip," turned out to be not a report but an inference.

All this is not to say that we should never make inferences. The   8 inability to make inferences is itself a sign of mental disorder. For example, the speech therapist Laura L. Lee writes, "The aphasic [brain-damaged] adult with whom I worked had great difficulty in making inferences about a picture I showed her. She could tell me what was happening at the moment in the picture, but could not tell me what might have happened just before the picture or just afterwards."[3] Hence the question is not whether or not we make inferences; the question is whether or not we are aware of the inferences we make.

[3] "Brain Damage and the Process of Abstracting: A Problem in Language Learning," *ETC.: A Review of General Semantics,* XVI (1959), 154–62.

Report	Can be verified or disproved
Inference	A statement about the unknown made on the basis of the known
Judgment	An expression of the writer's approval or disapproval

JUDGMENTS

... By judgments, we shall mean *all expressions of the writer's* 9
*approval or disapproval of the occurrences, persons, or objects he
is describing.* For example, a report cannot say, "It was a wonderful
car," but must say something like this: "It has been driven 50,000
miles and has never required any repairs." Again, statements such
as "Jack lied to us" must be suppressed in favor of the more
verifiable statement, "Jack told us he didn't have the keys to his car
with him. However, when he pulled a handkerchief out of his
pocket a few minutes later, a bunch of car keys fell out." Also a
report may not say, "The senator was stubborn, defiant, and
uncooperative," or "The senator courageously stood by his principles"; it must say instead, "The senator's vote was the only one
against the bill."

Many people regard statements such as the following as state- 10
ments of "fact": "Jack *lied* to us," "Jerry is a *thief*," "Tommy is
clever." As ordinarily employed, however, the word "lied" involves
first an inference (that Jack knew otherwise and deliberately
misstated the facts) and second a judgment (that the speaker
disapproves of what he has inferred that Jack did). In the other two
instances, we may substitute such expressions as, "Jerry was
convicted of theft and served two years at Waupun," and "Tommy
plays the violin, leads his class in school, and is captain of the
debating team." After all, to say of a man that he is a "thief" is to
say in effect, "He has stolen *and will steal again*"—which is more
of a prediction than a report. Even to say, "He has stolen," is to
make an inference (and simultaneously to pass a judgment) on an
act about which there may be difference of opinion among those
who have examined the evidence upon which the conviction was
obtained. But to say that he was "convicted of theft" is to make a
statement capable of being agreed upon through verification in
court and prison records.

Scientific verifiability rests upon the external observation of 11
facts, not upon the heaping up of judgments. If one person says,
"Peter is a deadbeat," and another says, "I think so too," the

statement has not been verified. In court cases, considerable trouble is sometimes caused by witnesses who cannot distinguish their judgments from the facts upon which those judgments are based. Cross-examinations under these circumstances go something like this:

> WITNESS: That dirty double-crosser Jacobs ratted on me.
> DEFENSE ATTORNEY: Your honor, I object.
> JUDGE: Objection sustained. (Witness's remark is stricken from the record.) Now, try to tell the court exactly what happened.
> WITNESS: He double-crossed me, the dirty, lying rat!
> DEFENSE ATTORNEY: Your honor, I object!
> JUDGE: Objection sustained. (Witness's remark is again stricken from the record.) Will the witness try to stick to the facts.
> WITNESS: But I'm telling you the facts, your honor. He did double-cross me.

This can continue indefinitely unless the cross-examiner exercises some ingenuity in order to get at the facts behind the judgment. To the witness it is a "fact" that he was "double-crossed." Often patient questioning is required before the factual bases of the judgment are revealed.

Many words, of course, simultaneously convey a report and a   12
judgment on the fact reported. . . . For the purposes of a report as here defined, these should be avoided. Instead of "sneaked in," one might say "entered quietly"; instead of "politician," "congress-man" or "alderman" or "candidate for office"; instead of "bureau-crat," "public official"; instead of "tramp," "homeless unem-ployed"; instead of "dictatorial set-up," "centralized authority"; instead of "crackpot," "holder of nonconformist views." A news-paper reporter, for example, is not permitted to write, "A crowd of suckers came to listen to Senator Smith last evening in that rickety firetrap and ex-dive that disfigures the south edge of town." Instead he says, "Between 75 and 100 people heard an address last evening by Senator Smith at the Evergreen Gardens near the South Side city limits."

COMPREHENSION

1. What is the basic difference between reports on the one hand and inferences and judgments on the other?

2. What everyday examples of reports does Hayakawa mention?

3. Why, according to Hayakawa, couldn't we get along without reports?

4. Define *inference* and *judgment,* and give two of your own examples of each.

5. Why do you think Hayakawa considers the distinction between reports, inferences, and judgments so important?

PURPOSE AND AUDIENCE

1. Is the primary purpose of Hayakawa's essay to entertain, to inform, or to persuade? Explain.

2. Does this essay have an explicitly stated thesis? If so, where is it?

3. Why does Hayakawa use *we* rather than *I* or *one* throughout the essay?

STYLE AND STRUCTURE

1. After Hayakawa defines *inference,* he follows with a sentence that presents a series of examples. How does the structure of that sentence clarify his definition?

2. This essay specifically exemplifies each kind of statement the author examines. Why is such evidence particularly important in an essay on this subject?

3. What is the purpose of the hypothetical conversation in paragraph 11? Does it effectively serve this purpose?

4. Why does Hayakawa include additional information in footnotes instead of integrating it into the body of his essay? Is all the footnoted information necessary?

WRITING WORKSHOP

1. Select a fairly long newspaper story on a topic that interests you. Classify its information as reports, inferences, and judgments. Then write a division and classification essay about what you discover.

2. Study a picture in a newspaper or magazine carefully. Decide which of your observations about it are facts, which are inferences, and which are judgments. Write a division and classification paper explaining your decisions.

9

Definition

WHAT IS DEFINITION?

Any time you take an exam you are likely to encounter questions that require definitions. You might be asked to define *behaviorism,* tell what a *cell* is, explain the meaning of the literary term *naturalism,* include a clear, comprehensive definition of *mitosis* in your answer, or define *authority.* Such exam questions can't always be answered in one or two sentences. They call for definitions that might require several paragraphs.

Such extended definitions are useful for many academic assignments besides exams. A thoughtful definition can clarify precise scientific terms as well as more general concepts from any course. Definitions can explain abstractions like *freedom* or controversial terms like *right to life* or slang terms whose meanings may vary from locale to locale or change as time passes. In some situations, a specific definition can be essential because a term has more than one meaning, because you are using it in an uncommon way, or because you suspect the term is unfamiliar to your readers.

Although the extended definition essays considered in this section are long, many of them also contain shorter definitions like those in the dictionary. Furthermore, papers often incorporate brief definitions of terms to clarify points or establish basic information that equips the reader to follow the rest of the discussion. Whether it appears in another kind of essay or acts as a center for an extended definition, the dictionary or brief formal definition establishes the essential meaning of a term.

Formal or Dictionary Definitions

Thumb through any dictionary, and you will see pages of words followed by definitions. These definitions all follow a standard

285

three-part structure: first the term to be defined, then the general class it is a part of, and finally the qualities that differentiate it from the other terms in the same class.

Term	Class	Differentiation
Behaviorism	is a theory	that regards the objective facts of a subject's actions as the only valid basis for psychological study.
A cell	is a unit of protoplasm	with a nucleus, cytoplasm, and an enclosing membrane.
Naturalism	is a literary movement	whose original adherents believed that writers should treat life with scientific objectivity.
Mitosis	is the process	of nuclear division of cells, consisting of prophase, metaphase, anaphase, and telophase.
Authority	is power	that has been legitimized.

Often such short definitions provide necessary information in essays planned around other patterns of development. Sometimes such definitions are part of longer definition essays. There they can introduce the extended definition, establish the essay's unifying idea or thesis, or define other essential terms. All definitions, regardless of length and context, include the three components that pinpoint what something is and what it is not.

Extended or Essay-Length Definitions

An extended definition includes the basic parts of a formal definition—the term, its class, and its distinguishing characteristics. Beyond these essentials, an extended definition does not follow a set pattern. Instead, it adapts whatever techniques best suit the term being defined and the writing situation. In fact, any of the essay patterns explored in this book can be used to structure a definition essay. Usually, you can select an appropriate pattern after considering the term or subject you wish to define as well as your purpose and writing situation. Sometimes, as you brainstorm, jotting down your ideas about the term or subject, a pattern will naturally suggest itself. Other times, working out the term's formal definition will suggest distinctions or illustrations around which a pattern can grow. For example, the formal definitions of the five terms discussed earlier might be extended using different patterns of development.

1. To define *behaviorism*, you could give examples. You could expand your formal definition with carefully chosen cases that exemplify behaviorist assumptions and methods, thus showing how this theory applies in different situations. Through these examples, your reader could see exactly how this psychological approach works and what it can and can't account for.

2. When definining a *cell*, you could use description. You could tell your reader what the various parts of a cell look like. Concentrating on the cell membrane, cytoplasm, and nucleus, you could detail each structure's appearance and function. With these clear descriptions, your reader is equipped to visualize the whole cell and understand its workings.

3. An extended definition of *naturalism* could employ a comparison and contrast structure. Since naturalism is one of several major movements in American literature, you could show how it differs from other literary movements like romanticism or realism. To clarify your definition, you could compare and contrast quotations and situations from several naturalistic works with those from works by romantic or realistic writers. Thus, a reader could see both the abstract theory of the naturalists and their practice in contrast to the theory and practice of other writers.

4. A definition of *mitosis* could be organized as a process. You could explain the four stages of mitosis, making sure that you point out the transition from one phase to another. By tracing the process from stage to stage for the reader, you could be certain that this type of cell division is clearly defined.

5. Finally, you could define *authority* using division and classification. Based on Max Weber's model, you could break the term into kinds of authority: traditional authority, charismatic authority, and legal-bureaucratic authority. Then, through parallel discussions explaining how each type of authority is legitimized, you could analyze and clarify this very broad term for your reader.

Each of these patterns of development helps define by emphasizing a central, essential characteristic of the subject. Naturally, other options are also available. Cause and effect or narration can be used to structure definition papers, as can any combination of patterns. Additionally, a few techniques are unique to definition:

- You can define a term by using *synonyms*.
- You can define a term by using *negation* (telling what it is *not*)

• You can define a term by using *enumeration* (listing its characteristics)

Although your definitions and definition essays may take many forms, you should be certain that they are clear and that they actually define. You should be sure you have a true definition, not just a descriptive statement such as "Happiness is a pizza and a sixpack." Likewise, repetition is not definition, so don't include the term you are defining in your definition. Explaining that "abstract art is a school of artists whose works are abstract" clarifies nothing for your reader. Finally, define as precisely as possible. Name the class of the term you are defining, stating, for example, that "mitosis is a process" rather than "mitosis is when a cell divides." Further, define this class as narrowly and as accurately as possible. Be specific when you differentiate your term from other members of its narrowed class. Only careful attention to the language and structure of your definition can ensure that your meaning will be clear to your reader.

STRUCTURING A DEFINITION ESSAY

Like any other paper, a definition essay should have an introduction with a thesis, a body, and a conclusion. Although a dictionary definition is not arguable, an extended definition can be. It may show the term being defined in a special light determined by your attitude toward the subject, by your purpose in defining the term, and by your audience. Thus, your extended definition paper about literary naturalism could argue that this movement was a logical outgrowth of nineteenth-century science and industry. And your essay defining the cell could maintain that the complexities of this unit of protoplasm probably will never be fully understood. Such a thesis provides a center for a definition essay and makes it more than just a catalog of facts.

Let's suppose that you are assigned a short paper in your introductory psychology course. You decide to define *behaviorism*. Since this is still a somewhat controversial theory, you decide that your best strategy is to supplement a formal definition with examples showing how behaviorist assumptions and methods are applied in specific situations. (Your class notes and your textbook include many such illustrations.) These examples will support your thesis that behaviorism is a valid approach for treating certain psychological dysfunctions. In combination, your examples will define *behaviorism* as it is understood today.

An outline for your essay might look like this:

¶1   Introduction—thesis: For modern psychologists, behaviorism has evolved into a valid approach for treating a wide variety of psychological dysfunctions

¶2   Background: An introductory definition of behaviorism, including its origins and evolution

¶3   First example: The use of behaviorism to help psychotics function in an institutional setting

¶4   Second example: The use of behaviorism to treat neurotic behavior such as chronic anxiety, a phobia, or a pattern of destructive acts

¶5   Third example: The use of behaviorism to treat normal but antisocial or undesirable behavior such as heavy smoking or overeating

¶6   Conclusion—restatement of thesis

Notice how the three examples in the body of this paper define behaviorism in a way that a formal definition could not. The complexity, the detail, and the breadth of this paper could not be duplicated by a one- or two-sentence definition.

The following student essay, written by Pat Good for an art history course, defines a controversial artistic movement. Using information from her class notes, Good presents the thesis that dadaism was not a short-lived eccentric fad but a significant creative movement.

THE DADA SPIRIT

Introduction	The dada movement is defined in <u>Webster's</u> <u>New</u>
Formal definition	<u>Collegiate</u> <u>Dictionary</u> as "a movement in art and literature based on deliberate irrationality and negation of traditional artistic values." In fact,
Negation	the word <u>dada</u> is often assumed to be synonymous with antiart and nihilism. This assumption ignores both
Thesis	that one of the purposes of this movement, like any other such movement, was to produce art and also that there was a very positive side to its seemingly negative form of expression.

Class of term

Background

Differentiation of term

.

Contrast

Comparison

.

Contrast

Example

One characteristic of any new movement in art or literature is reaction against forms which have been established in the past. These forms are questioned and explored, and, when found to be no longer adequate, they are replaced with something new. The one major difference between dada and other artistic movements was that the dadaist attacks on all traditional values, not merely artistic ones, were more severe and involved shock tactics aimed not only at existing art forms but at the bourgeoisie, who thought art was synonymous with good taste. But simply to call dada the "negation of traditional artistic values," as some critics do, ignores the creative force behind this movement.

Like any other artistic movement, the dada movement was intent more on keeping the creative force alive than on destroying anything. It just happened that the dadaists believed that to acquire a set form, a trademark, or any identifiable characteristics was a sign that the creative impulse was dying. They felt that, in order for their art to be constantly alive, it had to be constantly changing. This constant flux caused much contradiction within the movement itself. But these contradictions were themselves part of the movement. The ideas of two artists could be totally dissimilar and even contradictory, but if these ideas were personal and disconnected from any preconceived values, then they were dada. Thus, the importance of dada was not in any method or form but in the direct and individual statement.

Up until the time of the movement, much art had been based on some type of representation. Marcel Duchamp was one who refuted this principle and some of his own past work by inventing the ready—made. The ready—made was an object, often commercially made, which he extracted directly from his environment and elevated to the position of art. He simply took a bottle rack and called it "A Bottle Rack." He reversed the usual order of the procedure, and, instead of making his work of art imitative, he made the thing itself the work of art. The irony and rebelliousness of Duchamp's acts contain the spirit of dada. But the ready—made could not be called a typical example of dada because there really could be no typical example. After Duchamp made the ready—made, no one else could make another one. Each artist had to invent his own vital form of expression.

Conclusion (restatement of thesis)   Often the dada movement is seen by critics only as something which set out to destroy existing art forms and social values without offering other forms or values to replace them. This view ignores the fact that the aspirations of the dadaists were some of the most idealistic ever. They wanted to assert the independent spirit and the freedom of the artist. That they remained as unstructured as possible in trying to do this should not be passed off as simply "deliberate irrationality and the negation of traditional artistic values." After all, the ground they cleared made it possible for future artists to confront the twentieth century, perceiving it in new ways and representing it in new forms.

Points for Special Attention

Topic. *Dada* is a term that is perfectly suited to an extended definition. It can't be defined adequately with a synonym because there really is no equivalent term. Besides, *dada* is a term unfamiliar to many, and so a paper that offers a definition is likely to arouse a reader's curiosity.

Formal Definition.   This student essay begins somewhat conventionally with a dictionary excerpt which provides a clear, three-part definition. This can be a dreary opening and can even be misleading if the dictionary is seen simply as an authority. But Pat Good, acknowledging the inadequacy of that definition, proceeds to do something less conventional: she refutes the commonly held assumption that dada is an antiart movement. In doing so, she more fully defines the term, enlarging the formal definition she gives at the beginning.

Thesis.   Good's defense of dada as a positive, valuable artistic movement gives an argumentative slant to her paper, and this serves as her thesis. Without such a thesis, her essay would not have the solidarity and structure it now possesses.

Development.   Good uses familiar techniques to compose her extended definition of dada. She begins her definition with negation, stating what dada is not; she then presents some necessary background about art movements, comparing and contrasting dada with other movements to make some distinctions that are critical to her definition. Next, she explains the rationale behind dada, telling what the movement really stands for. In the fourth paragraph she offers an extended example of dada, Duchamp's ready-made. Each of these techniques contributes to the effectiveness of her definition.

No one pattern is more appropriate than another for a definition paper. In fact, combining several patterns may most effectively define the significant aspects of your term. Your choice of pattern should evolve naturally from your knowledge of your material, your purpose, and the needs of your audience. The essays that follow, which range from the informal to the technical, employ exemplification, comparison and contrast, narration, and other methods of developing extended definitions.

The Astonishing Talmud
LEO ROSTEN

*In this short definition essay, Leo Rosten, best known for his light,
humorous fiction, turns to a more serious topic. Using various patterns
of development and sprinkling numerous quotations throughout, Rosten
introduces a term with which many of his readers may be unfamiliar.
In defining the Talmud, Rosten also presents historical and practical
information about the Jewish religion and its ethics, laws, and rituals.*

Ask your most learned friends where the following sagacities 1
originated:

"All's well that ends well." (Shakespeare, of course.) 2

"A man betrays his character through three things: his tipping, 3
his tippling and his temper." (Oscar Wilde? Or was it Voltaire?)

"Give every man the benefit of the doubt." (Cicero? Oliver 4
Wendell Holmes?)

"A dream uninterpreted is like a letter unopened." (Surely 5
Sigmund Freud?)

It may surprise you to learn that each of these aphorisms comes 6
from the Talmud.* And I am willing to wager that 95 percent of our
best-educated Americans cannot tell you what is meant by the
"Talmud"—though it is one of the main sources for what we know
about Judaism in the pre-Christian era, and the reservoir from
which all of Judaism, Christianity and Islam drew their basic moral
code, many of their articles of faith, and the foundations of their
theology.

Examples? Take these flashing insights into the enduring areas 7
of human concern, all in the Talmud:

Ethics: "What is hateful to you, never do to a fellow man: that 8
is the whole Law—all the rest is commentary."

Adam: "Why did God create only one man? So that thereafter 9
no one could say, 'My ancestors were nobler than yours,' or that
virtue and vice are inherited, or that some races are better than
others. . . . And to teach us that whoever destroys a single life is as
guilty as though he had destroyed the entire world; and that
whoever saves one life earns as much merit as if he had saved the
whole world."

* The Talmudic sages left many writings not included in the Talmud itself but later
compiled to form a group of volumes called the "Midrash." In this article, I use the
"Talmud" in its broader sense to include the Midrash.

Women: "The Lord did not create woman from man's head, so   10
that he can command her; nor from man's foot, so that she would
be his slave. God made Eve from Adam's side so that woman will
always be nearest man's heart. . . . Be careful not to make a woman
weep: God counts her tears."

Children: "Never threaten a child: either punish him or forgive   11
him. . . . If you must strike a child, use a string."

Law: "For capital crimes, a majority of one judge may acquit,   12
but only a majority of two can convict. . . . Judges who sentence a
man to death may not eat or drink for the next 24 hours."

Truth: "If you add to the truth, you subtract from it."   13

Conduct: "When the wise get angry, they lose their wis-   14
dom. . . . Better embarrassment in this world than shame in the
world to come."

Worry: "Don't worry too much about tomorrow: who knows what   15
may befall you today?"

Now I must apologize. Have I given you the impression that the   16
Talmud is a fascinating succession of noble ideas and scintillating
epigrams? Alas, not so. The ideas *are* majestic, the reasoning is
subtle and sublime, the aphorisms are superb. But they are buried
in a text that is ensnarled in archaic technicalities, pedantic
digressions, quaint superstitions, exasperating *pilpul* (hair-splitting)
and obsessiveness about matters which today seem as irrelevant as
the size of Nebuchadnezzar's tonsils. The analyses remind me of
medieval arguments over the number of angels who can sit on the
point of a needle.

But we must not forget that the problems with which the great   17
Talmudists—rabbis and philosophers, judges and scholars—wres-
tled were anything but remote or absurd to *them*. They were trying
to clarify what God meant by every word, phrase, metaphor,
injunction or prohibition in the Pentateuch, or Torah (Genesis,
Exodus, Leviticus, Numbers, Deuteronomy). To the Hebrew sages,
their work was sanctified and imperative.

They were not trying to produce a work of art. They were   18
hammering out a code of faith, laws and ethics—binding on their
leaders no less than on their children—about the intricacies of
religion: rituals of worship; obligations of marriage; conditions
under which obedience to, or rebellion against, alien rulers must
be observed; circumstances under which ransom must be paid
(women took precedence over men) or apostates ostracized; oblig-
atory kindness due orphans and widows, animals or slaves—in
short, the sacred responsibilities of men and women to God, to

THE ASTONISHING TALMUD **295**

each other and to the community. Thus the Talmud may be described as a combination of all the papal bulls, the American Constitution, the Napoleonic Code, and the collected reasonings and decisions of our Supreme Court. We shall see how many scholars and centuries it took to complete so monumental a task.

The Talmud is not, as many think, the Torah, the first five books 19 of the Old Testament, which ancient Hebrews called "the Books of Moses" or "the Law of Moses." The Talmud is a massive compilation of 63 massektoth ("little books"). These are transcripts of symposiums that went on, by some estimates, for 1200 years— from the fifth century before the Christian era to the eighth century A.D. More than 2000 scholar-rabbi-sages conducted these debates, which were held in the great academies of the Holy Land and of Babylon. To these centers of scholarship came the most brilliant and erudite sages, and the most complex correspondence from rabbis and rabbinical courts in other parts of the world. Each land produced its own Talmud, but it is the Babylonian work we call *the* Talmud. It is more than three times as long and has been preserved in toto: the century-earlier Jerusalem Talmud was not.

The Talmud is meant to be studied, not merely read. It is an 20 almanac, a casebook, a reference encyclopedia. (An English-language translation runs to 35 volumes.) While it revolves around the commanding questions about the human condition, the debates and commentaries (and the omnibus commentaries *upon* commentaries) also concern the less lofty, ranging from adultery to agriculture (how should Egyptian beans be planted?); from admonitions about personal hygiene to the treatment of wizards; from Satan to pedagogy ("No more than 25 children shall be in a class"); from the merciful slaughter of livestock to rules governing mourning and penance; from every variety of sin to that salvation promised by the appearance of the Messiah. No topic is absent; the most majestic wisdom accompanies the most mundane preoccupations.

But if there is one theme in the tumultuous pages of the Talmud, 21 I think it is this: Every Jew must devote himself to endless acts of compassion. For as the Talmud observes, "The Torah begins with acts of loving and ends with kindness; it begins with God clothing Adam and Eve, and ends with God burying Moses. . . . The beginning and end of the Torah is performing acts of loving-kindness."

I have always cherished this passage: "When my time comes to 22 die," said the frog, "I shall go down to the sea, there to be swallowed by one of its creatures. For in that way, even my death will be an act of kindness."

The Talmud was for centuries known to the Christian world only   23
in random and garbled extracts. It was damned and outlawed and
torn to shreds or cast into flames—in Paris, Rome, Toledo, Constantinople—by churchmen and emperors, from Justinian down to
the Nazis and other fanatics in our midst.

Still, the Talmud was constantly studied and discussed by every   24
male Jew (and aristocratic females), as it is today by "practicing"
Jews in every land on earth. Tremendous importance and *mitzvahs*
(good deeds) have always been associated with reading a portion
of the Torah or Talmud every day, especially on the Sabbath. To
do so was and is to earn a "portion of bliss" in the world to come.

In Jerusalem and in Córdoba, Bombay, Kobe, Khartoum or Kiev,   25
wherever Jews landed after the Diaspora (dispersion after the
banishments from their Holy Land), the little shops, marketplaces,
country fairs contained the spectacle of merchants, cobblers, la-
borers, draymen, bakers and barbers poring over the *Pirke Aboth*
(Ethics of the Fathers), the most beloved Talmud section.

Down the centuries Jewish communities rang with the impas-   26
sioned disputes of those exploring the grandeur of God's message
and the complexities of Biblical exegesis. "Learning is achieved
only in the company of others," says the Talmud. In 1887, the small
town of Kroze, Poland (now Kražiai, Lithuania), sheltered but
200 Jewish families; yet these families formed nine permanent
study groups, employed ten male and two female teachers and
could boast two full-time bookbinders and repairers. It is no wonder
that Mohammed called the Jews "the People of the Book."

The Talmud is celebrated as a treasury of parables, fables and   27
anecdotes of great insight and power. They are not meant to
entertain, please note. They are vehicles for instruction, arresting
ways of driving home a moral. I give you my favorite:

"In a harbor, two ships sailed: one setting forth on a voyage, the   28
other coming home to port. Everyone cheered the ship going out,
but the ship sailing in was scarcely noticed. To this, a wise man
said: 'Do not rejoice over a ship setting out to sea, for you cannot
know what terrible storms it may encounter, and what fearful
dangers it may have to endure. Rejoice rather over the ship that has
safely reached port and brings its passengers home in peace.'

"And this is the way of the world: When a child is born, all   29
rejoice; when someone dies, all weep. We should do the opposite.
For no one can tell what trials and travails await a newborn child;
but when a mortal dies in peace, we should rejoice, for he has
completed a long journey, and there is no greater boon than to
leave this world with the imperishable crown of a good name."

COMPREHENSION

1. Does a formal definition of the Talmud appear anywhere in the essay? If so, where? If not, provide one.

2. How does the Talmud reflect the laws, rituals, and ethics of Judaism? Give specific examples.

3. What, according to Rosten, is the Talmud's major theme? What passage does he offer as an illustration of this theme? What other topics does the Talmud deal with?

4. What does Rosten think is the real purpose of the Talmud's parables?

PURPOSE AND AUDIENCE

1. This essay was written for *The Reader's Digest.* Do you think its tone is appropriate for this general interest magazine, which is widely read by Christians as well as Jews? Why or why not?

2. Does this essay include an explicit thesis? If so, where? If not, suggest a thesis for the essay.

3. Where is Rosten trying to entertain? to inform? to persuade? Which of these do you think is his primary purpose? Explain.

STYLE AND STRUCTURE

1. Why do you think Rosten begins his essay with a series of quotations? How does the use of quotations throughout his article strengthen his definition?

2. What patterns of development does Rosten use to define the Talmud? What other patterns might he have used?

3. Why does the title call the Talmud "astonishing"? Do you think this claim is supported in the essay? Explain.

4. Find in the essay examples of the following techniques characteristic of definition: definition by negation, explanation of the term's origins, and definition by analogy.

5. What technique does Rosten use to define briefly words or phrases he thinks his audience may be unfamiliar with? Are there additional words or phrases you think he should have defined? Which ones? Look them up in a dictionary, and write brief definitions for them similar to Rosten's.

6. Rosten concludes with his favorite anecdote. Is this anecdote an effective conclusion? Why or why not?

WRITING WORKSHOP

1. Choose a significant document or ritual that is part of your own religious or cultural heritage. Define it, using any pattern or combination of patterns you choose, but include a formal definition somewhere in your essay. Assume your readers are not familiar with the term you are defining.

2. With Rosten's article as source material, write a simple definition of the Talmud, using a series of examples to structure your essay. Imagine that your audience is a group of Jewish school children.

A Definition of Technical Writing
PATRICK M. KELLEY AND ROGER E. MASSE

This essay, first published in a journal for teachers of technical writing, explains the process of introducing the term technical writing *to a class of beginning students. In addition, the essay presents a clear, detailed definition of the term. Notice how Patrick M. Kelley and Roger E. Masse, instructors of technical writing at New Mexico State University, bring in literary as well as scientific sources to advance their definition.*

What is technical writing? That question is likely to be the first 1 question asked of a professor by students in a first course in technical writing. In English 218, Technical Writing, the first course at New Mexico State University, we anticipate the question by devoting our first class to a definition.

We begin our definition of technical writing with an illustration 2 of non-technical writing. Stanza one of Shelley's "To a Skylark" is not technical writing.

> Hail to thee, blithe Spirit!
> Bird thou never wert,
> That from Heaven, or near it,
> Pourest thy full heart
> In profuse strains of unpremeditated art.[1]

We ask our students to consider first the subject of this piece of 3 non-technical writing. Although Shelley's subject is the skylark of the title, that skylark is not the skylark of the science of ornithology. It is, instead, more a spirit than a skylark. In line 1, Shelley addresses the skylark as a "blithe Spirit." In line 2, he states that the skylark never was a bird. And in lines 3–5, he suggests that the skylark is an angel, or almost an angel, singing angelically "from Heaven, or near it." The subject then, as treated here, is not scientific, unless angelology is a science.

We ask students to consider second the writer's purpose. Shel- 4 ley's purpose is to move the reader. His purpose is to make the reader sense the beauty of the song of the skylark, the "profuse strains of unpremeditated art" that pour from its "full heart."

And we ask students to consider third the writer's attitude. 5 Shelley's attitude is subjective. He, himself, is moved by the beauty of the song of the skylark, moved enough, at least, that he writes the poem.

A contrasting illustration of technical writing allows us to con-   6
tinue our definition. The entry "Skylark" in *The Audubon Illustrated Handbook of American Birds* by Edgar M. Reilly, Jr., is
technical writing.

SKYLARK (*Alauda arvensis*)
Appearance: Between Robin and House Sparrow in size (7-7½ in.).
The Skylark is brown above, streaked with black and darker brown;
the tail has 2 white outer tail feathers on each side. The breast and
flanks are light buffy brown, streaked and spotted with dark brown,
and the rest of the underparts are white. The bill, legs, and feet are
yellowish, and the eyes dark brown.

Voice: The song, which has been the subject of much poetry, is
delivered while the bird is poised on pulsing wings well above the
ground; it is a long, beautiful song, replete with trills and cadenzas
at a rather high pitch. Its note outside the courtship season is a loud,
clear, bubbly chir-r-r-up.

Range and status: Native of Europe, n. and c. Asia, and n. Africa.
Introduced and established in Hawaii and on Vancouver I., B.C.,
where it is resident; not successful on Long I., N.Y., where it was
last recorded in 1913. Locally common.

Habitat: Open fields and cultivated land.

Seasonal movements: None in America.

Biology: Nest: A grass-lined hollow on ground in fields. Eggs: 3–4;
whitish ground color nearly hidden by spots of brown and gray.
Incubation: 11–12 days; 13–14 in incubator. Age at 1st flight: 9–10
days. Food: Weed seeds and grain; almost 50% insects and small
invertebrates.

Suggested reading: G. D. Sprot, "Notes on the Introduced Skylark
in the Victorian District of Vancouver Island," *Condor*, vol. 39, pp.
24–30, 1937.[2]

We ask students to consider first, in contrast, the subject of this   7
piece of technical writing. Reilly's subject is no spirit, but the
feathers-and-blood skylark. It is the skylark of the science of
ornithology, with its scientific name, *Alauda arvensis.*

We ask them to consider second, in contrast, the writer's purpose.   8
Reilly's purpose is not to move the reader, but to inform him. His
purpose is to inform the reader of the "Appearance," "Voice,"
"Range and status," "Habitat," "Seasonal movements," and "Biology" of the skylark. He even informs the reader of "Suggested
reading" for more information on the skylark.

And we ask them to consider third, again in contrast, the writer's   9
attitude. Reilly's attitude is not subjective, but objective. He
presents the facts about the skylark as they are, unaffected by his
own thoughts and feelings about skylarks. That the skylark is, in
appearance, "Between Robin and House Sparrow in size (7–7½
in.)" is a fact, objectively presented. And the rest of the entry
consists of facts objectively presented, except for one word. The
exception, which students are quick to note themselves, is the word
"beautiful" in the section on "Voice." That the song of the skylark
is "beautiful" is Reilly's opinion. It is not a fact.

Despite Reilly's slip into the subjectivity of non-technical writ-   10
ing, his "Skylark," especially as it contrasts with Shelley's "To a
Skylark," gives meaning to our definition of technical writing:

> Technical Writing is writing about a subject in the pure sciences or
> the applied sciences in which the writer informs the reader through
> an objective presentation of facts.

For students, of course, the definition needs further definition.   11
The *pure sciences* we define as those sciences in which knowledge
is sought for its own sake. Mathematics, the physical sciences, and
the biological sciences are pure sciences, as are, arguably, some of
the social sciences. The *applied sciences* we define as those sciences
in which knowledge from the pure sciences is used. Agriculture,
engineering, and medicine are applied sciences. Writing about any
subject within any of these sciences, we tell our students, is
technical writing.

That is, such writing is technical writing if in it the writer *informs*   12
the reader. The purpose of science is to know. (In fact, the word
science is derived from the Latin *scire*, "to know.") The purpose
of the technical writer is to let his reader know of the knowledge
discovered in the pure sciences and of the use of that knowledge
in the applied sciences. Thus, we tell students, writing about a
subject in the sciences in which the writer informs the reader is
technical writing.

That is, such writing is technical writing if in it the writer   13
informs through an objective presentation of facts. *Objective* refers
to a state of mind. If a writer is objective, he is free from any bias
toward his subject. If he writes objectively, he presents the facts
as they are, unaffected by his thoughts and feelings about them.
These *facts* are pieces of information that can be verified objectively. In other words, they are pieces of information that can be
proved accurate by simple experience or by scientific observation
and experimentation.

To clinch our definition, we conclude with another pair of   14
contrasting illustrations. The illustration of non-technical writing
is from Melville's classification of whales in Chapter XXXII,
"Cetology," of *Moby-Dick*. Melville's subject in the illustration,
the narwhale, is part of the pure science of cetology. But, as we ask
our students to note, instead of informing the reader through an
objective presentation of facts about the narwhale, Melville entertains the reader through a subjective presentation of his opinions,
the salty opinions of old salts, and a phallic joke.

Melville begins as follows: 15

> (*Narwhale*) that is, *Nostril whale.*—Another instance of a curiously
> named whale, so named I suppose from his peculiar horn being
> originally mistaken for a peaked nose. The creature is some sixteen
> feet in length, while its horn averages five feet, though some exceed
> ten, and even attain to fifteen feet. Strictly speaking, this horn is but
> a lengthened tusk, growing out from the jaw in a line a little depressed
> from the horizontal. But it is only found on the sinister side, which
> has an ill-effect, giving its owner something analogous to the aspect
> of a clumsy left-handed man. What precise purpose this ivory horn
> or lance answers, it would be hard to say. It does not seem to be used
> like the blade of the sword-fish and bill-fish; though some sailors tell
> me that the Narwhale employs it for a rake in turning over the bottom
> of the sea for food. Charley Coffin said it was used for an ice-piercer;
> for the Narwhale, rising to the surface of the Polar Sea, and finding
> it sheeted with ice, thrusts his horn up, and so breaks through. But
> you cannot prove either of these surmises to be correct. My own
> opinion is, that however this one-sided horn may really be used by
> the Narwhale—however that may be—it would certainly be very
> convenient to him for a folder in reading pamphlets.[3]

Melville begins his description of the narwhale not with its   16
scientific name, but with a nickname, "Nostril whale." He presents
his opinion of the name: the whale "is curiously named" because
of its "peculiar horn." Melville then presents facts about the length
of the whale and its tusk. But, with the facts, he also presents the
opinions of some sailors and his own salty opinion that the tusk of
the narwhale "would certainly be very convenient to him for a
folder in reading pamphlets." Such writing may entertain the
reader, but it does not inform him of the purpose of the tusk.

In the next part of the passage, Melville continues to entertain   17
with an elaborate phallic joke at the expense of both the narwhale
and "Queen Bess":

> Narwhale I have heard called the Tusked whale, the Horned whale,
> and the Unicorn whale. He is certainly a curious example of the

Unicornism to be found in almost every kingdom of animated nature.
. . . Originally it [the tusk] was in itself accounted an object of great
curiosity. Black Letter tells me that Sir Martin Frobisher on his
return from that voyage, when Queen Bess did gallantly wave her
jewelled hand to him from a window of Greenwich Palace, as his
bold ship sailed down the Thames; "when Sir Martin returned from
that voyage," saith Black Letter, "on bended knees he presented to
her highness a prodigious long horn of the Narwhale, which for a
long period after hung in the castle at Windsor." An Irish author
avers that the Earl of Leicester, on bended knees, did likewise
present to her highness another horn, pertaining to a land beast of
the unicorn nature.[4]

The phallic joke entertains the reader, unless he is a prude; but it
does nothing to inform him about the narwhale.

Melville ends the description of the narwhale with a presentation   18
of facts into which he interjects his opinions:

The Narwhale has a very picturesque, leopard-like look, being of a
milk-white ground color, dotted with round and oblong spots of
black. His oil is very superior, clear and fine; but there is little of it,
and he is seldom hunted. He is mostly found in the circumpolar
seas.[5]

All that Melville writes of the appearance of the narwhale is fact,   19
but that the whale is "very picturesque" is his opinion. Likewise,
all that Melville writes of the oil of the narwhale is fact, but that
the oil is "very superior" is his opinion. Only in the last sentence
on the habitat of the narwhale does Melville inform the reader
through an objective presentation of facts. Only there, we suggest
to students, is the writing technical writing.

In contrast, all of the writing is technical writing in the following   20
illustration. This illustration, also a description of the narwhale, is
from *The Whale,* Chapter 3, "The Different Kinds of Cetaceans,"
by Dr. Leonard Harrison Matthews and Dr. Age Jonsgard. Matthews
and Jonsgard consistently inform the reader through an objective
presentation of facts. And again we ask students to note the contrast.

Matthews and Jonsgard begin with a classification of the narwhale   21
and a description of the suborder:

A. *SUBORDER:* Toothed cetaceans (*Odontoceti*) The toothed cetaceans are the second of the two suborders of cetaceans. They
are all provided with teeth, the number of which, however, varies.
Female beaked whales even look toothless because the pair of
teeth present in the lower jaw is unusually hidden in the gum.
Apart from the sperm whale, the giant among the toothed ceta-

ceans, most of them are small. As compared to whalebone whales
the size of the head and mouth is small. All toothed cetaceans
have five digits in the flipper, a single blowhole and all but one
an asymmetrical skull. With very few exceptions, males grow
bigger—in some species considerably bigger—than the females.
They feed on fish, mainly small shoalfish, and some species also
eat squid.

B. *FAMILY:* Ocean Dolphins (*Delphinidae*) . . .
C. *SUBFAMILY:* Monodontinae . . .[6]

Two genera belong to the subfamily, each of which includes only
one species: *Delphinapterus,* the white whale, and *Monodon,* the
narwhale.

To describe the suborder, Matthews and Jonsgard present known   22
facts unaffected by their thoughts and feelings. They inform the
reader of the suborder, family, subfamily, and genus of the narwhale.
They inform him of the cetaceans' teeth, relative size, flippers,
blowholes, skulls, and diets. Nowhere in the description do Matthews and Jonsgard present their opinions.

After describing the suborder, Matthews and Jonsgard describe   23
the narwhale itself:

The narwhal (*M. monoceros*), which may reach a length of about
fifteen feet, is closely akin to the white whale. Its most distinctive
feature is the spirally twisted tusk which may extend eight feet
outwards from the front of the head of the male.

The tusk is the left one of two teeth in the upper jaw; very
occasionally the right tooth grows out as a tusk so that the animal has
two tusks. The rudimentary teeth are present in the female but they
do not grow into tusks.

The color of the older animals is gray-white with darkish spots on
the back. The distribution of the narwhal is confined to the Arctic
areas of the North Atlantic Ocean. Stragglers may also occur in boreal
waters.[7]

Here again Matthews and Jonsgard consistently inform through   24
an objective presentation of facts. After stating the scientific name
of the narwhale, they present facts about its length, tusk, color, and
distribution. They present no opinions of these facts. Even when
they state that the tusk of the narwhale is "its most distinctive
feature," they do not present an opinion because the tusk is, in
fact, the most distinctive feature of the narwhale, a feature so
distinctive that it is the basis for the scientific name, *M. monoceros.*

The narwhale is a scientific subject, whether it is described in   25
Moby-Dick or *The Whale.* But whereas Melville's writing is non-

technical, Matthews and Jonsgard's writing is technical. Their description of the narwhale fulfills our definition of technical writing as writing about a subject in the pure sciences or the applied sciences in which the writer informs the reader through an objective presentation of facts.

NOTES

[1] Percy Bysshe Shelley, "To a Skylark," *The Norton Anthology of Poetry*, ed. Arthur M. Eastman (New York: W. W. Norton & Company, 1970), p. 660.

[2] Edgar M. Reilly, Jr., *The Audubon Illustrated Handbook of American Birds* (New York: McGraw-Hill Book Company, 1968), pp. 299–300.

[3] Herman Melville, *Moby-Dick* (New York: W. W. Norton & Company, 1967), pp. 124–125.

[4] Melville, p. 125.

[5] Melville, p. 125.

[6] Dr. Leonard H. Matthews and Dr. Age Jonsgard, *The Whale* (New York: Simon and Schuster, 1968), p. 74.

[7] Matthews and Jonsgard, pp. 77–78.

COMPREHENSION

1. What is Kelley and Masse's formal definition of technical writing?

2. Identify the subject of each of the four excerpts this article discusses and the purpose and attitude of each writer.

3. What characteristics of the Shelley poem disqualify it as a piece of technical writing?

4. Why is the Melville selection not technical writing?

PURPOSE AND AUDIENCE

1. The authors are explicitly addressing their ideas to other college professors. Why, then, is their essay written on a level that is relatively simple and easy to understand?

2. This essay does not have a thesis. Why not?

STYLE AND STRUCTURE

1. What is the major pattern of development the authors use to define technical writing? What other methods do they use?

2. The authors could have defined technical writing without using the Shelley poem or the Melville excerpt. How might they then have changed their treatment of the Reilly and the Matthews and Jonsgard selections?

3. Why do the authors present two pairs of excerpts (Shelley with Reilly; Melville with Matthews and Jonsgard) to make their point? Would one have been enough? Why or why not?

4. The conclusion refers only to the second pair of excerpts. Would it have been more effective if it summed up both? Explain.

WRITING WORKSHOP

1. Choose a subject that can be defined in both technical and nontechnical terms. Using exemplification as your pattern of development, use the two different approaches to define your subject.

2. Write an extended definition of technical writing, structuring your essay by means of exemplification.

3. Imagine you are working for a company that markets ingenious ideas and inventions. Write a definition of one of your products for your technical division. Then, write a second definition for your sales department.

New Superstitions for Old
MARGARET MEAD

*Margaret Mead was perhaps the best-known American social scientist
of her time. Her 1928 book,* Coming of Age in Samoa, *became a best-
seller, popularizing anthropology and encouraging wide interest in the
field. In forty-one other books, and in numerous speeches, articles, and
magazine columns, Mead spoke out on social and ethical issues. In this
essay, she tackles a characteristically controversial subject—superstition.*

Once in a while there is a day when everything seems to run
smoothly and even the riskiest venture comes out exactly right.
You exclaim, "This is my lucky day!" Then as an afterthought you
say, "Knock on wood!" Of course, you do not really believe that
knocking on wood will ward off danger. Still, boasting about your
own good luck gives you a slightly uneasy feeling—and you carry
out the little protective ritual. If someone challenged you at that
moment, you would probably say, "Oh, that's nothing. Just an old
superstition." 1

But when you come to think about it, what is superstition? 2

In the contemporary world most people treat old folk beliefs as 3
superstitions—the belief, for instance, that there are lucky and
unlucky days or numbers, that future events can be read from
omens, that there are protective charms or that what happens can
be influenced by casting spells. We have excluded magic from our
current world view, for we know that natural events have natural
causes.

In a religious context, where truths cannot be demonstrated, we 4
accept them as a matter of faith. Superstitions, however, belong to
the category of beliefs, practices and ways of thinking that have
been discarded because they are inconsistent with scientific knowledge. It is easy to say that other people are superstitious because
they believe what we regard to be untrue. "Superstition" used in
that sense is a derogatory term for the beliefs of other people that
we do not share. But there is more to it than that. For superstitions
lead a kind of half life in a twilight world where, sometimes, we
partly suspend our disbelief and act as if magic worked.

Actually, almost every day, even in the most sophisticated home, 5
something is likely to happen that evokes the memory of some old
folk belief. The salt spills. A knife falls to the floor. Your nose

tickles. Then perhaps, with a slightly embarrassed smile, the person who spilled the salt tosses a pinch over his left shoulder. Or someone recites the old rhyme, "Knife falls, gentleman calls." Or as you rub your nose you think, That means a letter. I wonder who's writing? No one takes these small responses very seriously or gives them more than a passing thought. Sometimes people will preface one of these ritual acts—walking around instead of under a ladder or hastily closing an umbrella that has been opened inside a house—with such remarks as "I remember my great-aunt used to . . ." or "Germans used to say you ought not . . ." And then, having placed the belief at some distance away in time or space, they carry out the ritual.

Everyone also remembers a few of the observances of child- 6
hood—wishing on the first star; looking at the new moon over the right shoulder; avoiding the cracks in the sidewalk on the way to school while chanting, "Step on a crack, break your mother's back"; wishing on white horses, on loads of hay, on covered bridges, on red cars; saying quickly, "Bread-and-butter" when a post or a tree separated you from the friend you were walking with. The adult may not actually recite the formula "Star light, star bright . . ." and may not quite turn to look at the new moon, but his mood is tempered by a little of the old thrill that came when the observance was still freighted with magic.

Superstition can also be used with another meaning. When I 7
discuss the religious beliefs of other peoples, especially primitive peoples, I am often asked, "Do they really have a religion, or is it all just superstition?" The point of contrast here is not between a scientific and a magical view of the world but between the clear, theologically defensible religious beliefs of members of civilized societies and what we regard as the false and childish views of the heathen who "bow down to wood and stone." Within the civilized religions, however, where membership includes believers who are educated and urbane and others who are ignorant and simple, one always finds traditions and practices that the more sophisticated will dismiss offhand as "just superstition" but that guide the steps of those who live by older ways. Mostly these are very ancient beliefs, some handed on from one religion to another and carried from country to country around the world.

Very commonly, people associate superstition with the past, with 8
very old ways of thinking that have been supplanted by modern knowledge. But new superstitions are continually coming into being and flourishing in our society. Listening to mothers in the park in the 1930's, one heard them say, "Now, don't you run out

into the sun, or Polio will get you." In the 1940's elderly people explained to one another in tones of resignation, "It was the Virus that got him down." And every year the cosmetics industry offers us new magic—cures for baldness, lotions that will give every woman radiant skin, hair coloring that will restore to the middle-aged the charm and romance of youth—results that are promised if we will just follow the simple directions. Families and individuals also have their cherished, private superstitions. You must leave by the back door when you are going on a journey, or you must wear a green dress when you are taking an examination. It is a kind of joke, of course, but it makes you feel safe.

These old half-beliefs and new half-beliefs reflect the keenness   9
of our wish to have something come true or to prevent something bad from happening. We do not always recognize new superstitions for what they are, and we still follow the old ones because someone's faith long ago matches our contemporary hopes and fears. In the past people "knew" that a black cat crossing one's path was a bad omen, and they turned back home. Today we are fearful of taking a journey and would give anything to turn back—and then we notice a black cat running across the road in front of us.

Child psychologists recognize the value of the toy a child holds   10
in his hand at bedtime. It is different from his thumb, with which he can close himself in from the rest of the world, and it is different from the real world, to which he is learning to relate himself. Psychologists call these toys—these furry animals and old, cozy baby blankets—"transitional objects"; that is, objects that help the child move back and forth between the exactions of everyday life and the world of wish and dream.

Superstitions have some of the qualities of these transitional   11
objects. They help people pass between the areas of life where what happens has to be accepted without proof and the areas where sequences of events are explicable in terms of cause and effect, based on knowledge. Bacteria and viruses that cause sickness have been identified; the cause of symptoms can be diagnosed and a rational course of treatment prescribed. Magical charms no longer are needed to treat the sick; modern medicine has brought the whole sequence of events into the secular world. But people often act as if this change had not taken place. Laymen still treat germs as if they were invisible, malign spirits, and physicians sometimes prescribe antibiotics as if they were magic substances.

Over time, more and more of life has become subject to the   12
controls of knowledge. However, this is never a one-way process. Scientific investigation is continually increasing our knowledge.

But if we are to make good use of this knowledge, we must not only rid our minds of old, superseded beliefs and fragments of magical practice, but also recognize new superstitions for what they are. Both are generated by our wishes, our fears and our feeling of helplessness in difficult situations.

Civilized peoples are not alone in having grasped the idea of superstitions—beliefs and practices that are superseded but that still may evoke the different worlds in which we live—the sacred, the secular and the scientific. They allow us to keep a private world also, where, smiling a little, we can banish danger with a gesture and summon luck with a rhyme, make the sun shine in spite of storm clouds, force the stranger to do our bidding, keep an enemy at bay and straighten the paths of those we love. 13

COMPREHENSION

1. What kinds of long-standing rituals does Mead consider to be superstitions? Can you think of others?

2. In what way are religion and superstition similar? How are they different?

3. Why does Mead say many superstitions have disappeared?

4. Why do we retain so many superstitions?

5. What are transitional objects? How does Mead relate them to superstitions?

PURPOSE AND AUDIENCE

1. This essay was originally published in 1966 in a magazine aimed at young mothers. In what way, if any, does Mead tailor her subject to fit her readers? How could she have increased the essay's relevance for this audience?

2. What is the thesis of Mead's essay? Where does it appear?

3. Can you determine Mead's attitude toward her subject? Does she feel that superstitions are silly or useful? Explain.

STYLE AND STRUCTURE

1. By what methods of development does Mead expand her definition of superstition? What other methods might she have used?

2. Where, if anywhere, does Mead formally define superstition? Define it in your own words.

3. How does the extended comparison between superstitions and a child's toy advance the essay's argument?

4. Mead opens her essay by directly addressing her readers and their superstitions; she uses this device later in the essay, too. What is the effect of this technique?

WRITING WORKSHOP

1. Write an extended definition of your own idea of superstition, using a series of examples to support your thesis.

2. Write a definition of superstition in which you use one extended example, perhaps a personal experience or observation, as the basis of your paper.

3. Mead's essay distinguishes between science and superstition, but perhaps this contrast is overstated. Are there any similarities? Write an essay in which you compare the two in order to define superstition as a form of primitive or unsophisticated science (or to define science as sophisticated superstition).

The Googol
EDWARD KASNER AND JAMES R. NEWMAN

This definition of a mathematical concept is an excerpt from an essay entitled "New Names for Old." In the essay, Edward Kasner and James R. Newman note that mathematics constantly inspires new words to name new ideas. Mathematics, however, tends to adopt names that are much simpler than those used in other sciences, to use "easy words for hard ideas." In this selection, Kasner and Newman define one of these simple words: the googol.

It was raining and the children were asked how many raindrops 1 would fall on New York. The highest answer was 100. They had never counted higher than 100 and what they meant to imply when they used that number was merely something very, very big—as big as they could imagine. They were asked how many raindrops hit the roof, and how many hit New York, and how many single raindrops hit all of New York in 24 hours. They soon got a notion of the bigness of these numbers even though they did not know the symbols for them. They were certain in a little while that the number of raindrops was a great deal bigger than a hundred. They were asked to think of the number of grains of sand on the beach at Coney Island and decided that the number of grains of sand and the number of raindrops were about the same. But the important thing is that they realized that the number was *finite, not infinite.* In this respect they showed their distinct superiority over many scientists who to this day use the word infinite when they mean some big number, like a billion billion.

Counting, something such scientists evidently do not realize, is 2 a precise operation.[1] It may be wonderful but there is nothing vague or mysterious about it. If you count something, the answer you get is either perfect or all wrong; there is no half way. It is very much like catching a train. You either catch it or you miss it, and if you miss it by a split second you might as well have come a week late. There is a famous quotation which illustrates this:

> Oh, the little more, and how much it is!
> And the little less, and what worlds away!

[1] No one would say that 1 + 1 is "about equal to 2." It is just as silly to say that a billion billion is not a finite number, simply because it is big. Any number which can be named or conceived of in terms of the integers is finite. *Infinite means something quite different.*

A big number is big, but it is definite and it is finite. Of course in poetry, the finite ends with about three thousand; any greater number is infinite. In many poems, the poet will talk to you about the infinite number of stars. But, if ever there was a hyperbole, this is it, for nobody, not even the poet, has ever seen more than three thousand stars on a clear night, without the aid of a telescope.

With the Hottentots, infinity begins at three.[2] Ask a Hottentot how many cows he owns, and if he has more than three he'll say "many." The number of raindrops falling on New York is also "many." It is a large finite number, but nowhere near infinity.

Now here is the name of a very large number: "Googol."[3] Most people would say, "A googol is so large that you cannot name it or talk about it; it is so large that it is infinite." Therefore, we shall talk about it, explain exactly what it is, and show that it belongs to the very same family as the number 1.

A googol is this number which one of the children in the kindergarten wrote on the blackboard:

10000000000000000000000000000000000000000000000000000
0000000000000000000000000000000000000000000000000.

The definition of a googol is: 1 followed by a hundred zeros. It was decided, after careful mathematical researches in the kindergarten, that the number of raindrops falling on New York in 24 hours, or even in a year or in a century, is much less than a googol. Indeed, the googol is a number just larger than the largest numbers that are used in physics or astronomy. All those numbers require less than a hundred zeros. This information is, of course, available to everyone, but seems to be a great secret in many scientific quarters.

A very distinguished scientific publication recently came forth with the revelation that the number of snow crystals necessary to form the ice age was a billion to the billionth power. This is very startling and also very silly. A billion to the billionth power looks like this:

$$1000000000^{1000000000}$$

A more reasonable estimate and a somewhat smaller number would be 10^{30}. As a matter of fact, it has been estimated that if the

[2] Although, in all fairness, it must be pointed out that some of the tribes of the Belgian Congo can count to a million and beyond.
[3] Not even approximately a Russian author.

entire universe, which you will concede is a trifle larger than the earth, were filled with protons and electrons, so that no vacant space remained, the total number of protons and electrons would be 10^{110} (i.e., 1 with 110 zeros after it). Unfortunately, as soon as people talk about large numbers, they run amuck. They seem to be under the impression that since zero equals nothing, they can add as many zeros to a number as they please with practically no serious consequences. We shall have to be a little more careful than that in talking about big numbers.

To return to Coney Island, the number of grains of sand on the beach is about 10^{20}, or more descriptively, 100000000000000000000. That is a large number, but not as large as the number mentioned by the divorcee in a recent divorce suit who had telephoned that she loved the man "a million billion billion times and eight times around the world." It was the largest number that she could conceive of, and shows the kind of thing that may be hatched in a love nest. 9

Though people do a great deal of talking, the total output since the beginning of gabble to the present day, including all baby talk, love songs, and Congressional debates, totals about 10^{16}. This is ten million billion. Contrary to popular belief, this is a larger number of words than is spoken at the average afternoon bridge. 10

A great deal of the veneration for the authority of the printed word would vanish if one were to calculate the number of words which have been printed since the Gutenberg Bible appeared. It is a number somewhat larger than 10^{16}. A recent popular historical novel alone accounts for the printing of several hundred billion words. 11

The largest number seen in finance (though new records are in the making) represents the amount of money in circulation in Germany at the peak of the inflation. It was less than a googol— merely 12

496,585,346,000,000,000,000.

A distinguished economist vouches for the accuracy of this figure. The number of marks in circulation was very nearly equal to the number of grains of sand on Coney Island beach.

The number of atoms of oxygen in the average thimble is a good deal larger. It would be represented by perhaps 1000000000000000000000000000. The number of electrons, in size exceedingly smaller than the atoms, is much more enormous. The number of electrons which pass through the filament of an ordinary fifty-watt electric lamp in a minute equals the number of drops of water that flow over Niagara Falls in a century. 13

One may also calculate the number of electrons, not only in the $\quad$ 14 average room, but over the whole earth, and out through the stars, the Milky Way, and all the nebulae. The reason for giving all these examples of very large numbers is to emphasize the fact that no matter how large the collection to be counted, a finite number will do the trick. Mathematics, to be sure, exhibits a great variety of infinite collections, but those encountered in nature, though sometimes very large, are all definitely finite. A celebrated scientist a few years ago stated in all seriousness that he believed that the number of pores (through which leaves breathe) of all the leaves, of all the trees in all the world, would certainly be infinite. Needless to say, he was not a mathematician. The number of electrons in a single leaf is much bigger than the number of pores of all the leaves of all the trees of all the world. And still the number of all the electrons in the entire universe can be found by means of the physics of Einstein. It is a good deal less than a googol—perhaps one with seventy-nine zeros, 10^{79}, as estimated by Eddington.

Words of wisdom are spoken by children at least as often as by $\quad$ 15 scientists. The name "googol" was invented by a child (Dr. Kasner's nine-year-old nephew) who was asked to think up a name for a very big number, namely, 1 with a hundred zeros after it. He was very certain that this number was not infinite, and therefore equally certain that it had to have a name. At the same time that he suggested "googol" he gave a name for a still larger number: "Googolplex." A googolplex is much larger than a googol, but is still finite, as the inventor of the name was quick to point out. It was first suggested that a googolplex should be 1, followed by writing zeros until you got tired. This is a description of what would happen if one actually tried to write a googolplex, but different people get tired at different times and it would never do to have Carnera a better mathematician than Dr. Einstein, simply because he had more endurance. The googolplex, then, is a specific finite number, with so many zeros after the 1 that the number of zeros is a googol. A googolplex is much bigger than a googol, much bigger even than a googol times a googol. A googol times a googol would be 1 with 200 zeros, whereas a googolplex is 1 with a googol of zeros. You will get some idea of the size of this very large but finite number from the fact that there would not be enough room to write it, if you went to the farthest star, touring all the nebulae and putting down zeros every inch of the way.

One might not believe that such a large number would ever $\quad$ 16 really have any application; but one who felt that way would not be a mathematician. A number as large as the googolplex might be of real use in problems of combination. This would be the type of problem in which it might come up scientifically:

Consider this book which is made up of carbon and nitrogen and 17 of other elements. The answer to the question, "How many atoms are there in this book?" would certainly be a finite number, even less than a googol. Now imagine that the book is held suspended by a string, the end of which you are holding. How long will it be necessary to wait before the book will jump up into your hand? Could it conceivably ever happen? One answer might be "No, it will never happen without some external force causing it to do so." But that is not correct. The right answer is that it will almost *certainly* happen *sometime* in less than a googolplex of years—perhaps tomorrow.

The explanation of this answer can be found in physical chem- 18 istry, statistical mechanics, the kinetic theory of gases, and the theory of probability. We cannot dispose of all these subjects in a few lines, but we will try. Molecules are always moving. Absolute rest of molecules would mean absolute zero degrees of temperature, and absolute zero degrees of temperature is not only nonexistent, but impossible to obtain. All the molecules of the surrounding air bombard the book. At present the bombardment from above and below is nearly the same and gravity keeps the book down. It is necessary to wait for the favorable moment when there happens to be an enormous number of molecules bombarding the book from below and very few from above. Then gravity will be overcome and the book will rise. It would be somewhat like the effect known in physics as the Brownian movement, which describes the behavior of small particles in a liquid as they dance about under the impact of molecules. It would be analogous to the Brownian movement on a vast scale.

But the probability that this will happen in the near future or, 19 for that matter, on any specific occasion that we might mention, is between $\frac{1}{googol}$ and $\frac{1}{googolplex}$. To be reasonably sure that the book will rise, we should have to wait between a googol and a googolplex of years.

When working with electrons or with problems of combination 20 like the one of the book, we need larger numbers than are usually talked about. It is for that reason that names like googol and googolplex, though they may appear to be mere jokes, have a real value. The names help to fix in our minds the fact that we are still dealing with finite numbers. To repeat, a googol is 10^{100}; a googolplex is 10 to the googol power, which may be written $10^{10^{100}} = 10^{googol}$.

We have seen that the number of years that one would have to 21
wait to see the miracle of the rising book would be less than a
googolplex. In that number of years the earth may well have become
a frozen planet as dead as the moon, or perhaps splintered to a
number of meteors and comets. The real miracle is not that the
book will rise, but that with the aid of mathematics, we can project
ourselves into the future and predict with accuracy *when* it will
probably rise, i.e., sometime between today and the year googolplex.

COMPREHENSION

1. What do the school children realize about numbers that many scientists
   do not? In what way is this distinction important to the essay's central
   premise?

2. What is a googol? How did the term originate? Why is this origin of
   significance in the article?

3. When telling of the scientist who believed the number of pores in all the
   world's leaves would be infinite, why do the authors say, "Needless to say,
   he was not a mathematician"?

4. What is a googolplex? Is it finite or infinite? How can you tell?

PURPOSE AND AUDIENCE

1. This essay is aimed not at mathematicians but at an audience with broad
   general knowledge. What demonstrates this?

2. This selection does not really take a stand about an arguable proposition.
   What, then, is the purpose of this definition? What might the authors hope
   to accomplish by defining the googol?

STYLE AND STRUCTURE

1. Throughout the essay, the authors keep their discussion on an everyday,
   nontechnical level. How do they do this?

2. What patterns of development do the authors use to define the googol?

3. Why do the authors introduce the googol before the googolplex?

4. Why do the authors use so many concrete examples of very large numbers
   (such as grains of sand and marks in circulation)?

5. Several footnotes appear in this selection. Why do the authors choose not
   to include this information in the text of the essay?

WRITING WORKSHOP

1. Using (and acknowledging) the authors' analogies, write an essay defining the googol for an audience of school children.

2. Invent a name for an object or concept that has not, to the best of your knowledge, been named before. Then write a definition of that term.

3. Each profession or occupation develops its own jargon. Write an essay about the jargon of a particular field, defining one term or several terms. Include an explanation of why they are used.

The Etymology of the International Insult
CHARLES F. BERLITZ

In this essay, which first appeared in 1970 in Penthouse *magazine,*
Charles Berlitz, founder of the famous Berlitz School of Languages,
tackles one area of language study: the racial slur. By presenting the
etymology, or origin, of some of the best-known insults, Berlitz shows
how senseless they are. At the same time, he defines the ethnic or racial
insult.

"What is a kike?" Disraeli once asked a small group of fellow   1
politicians. Then, as his audience shifted nervously, Queen Vic-
toria's great Jewish Prime Minister supplied the answer himself.
"A kike," he observed, "is a Jewish gentleman who has just left the
room."

The word kike is thought to have derived from the ending *-ki* or   2
-ky found in many names borne by the Jews of Eastern Europe. Or,
as Leo Rosten suggests, it may come from *kikel,* Yiddish for a circle,
the preferred mark for name signing by Jewish immigrants who
could not write. This was used instead of an X, which resembles
a cross. Kikel was not originally pejorative, but has become so
through use.

Yid, another word for Jew, has a distinguished historic origin,   3
coming from the German *Jude* (through the Russian *zhid*). *Jude*
itself derives from the tribe of Judah, a most honorable and ancient
appellation. The vulgar and opprobrious word "Sheeny" for Jew
is a real inversion, as it derives from *shaine* (Yiddish) or *schön*
(German), meaning "beautiful." How could beautiful be an insult?
The answer is that it all depends on the manner, tone or facial
expression or sneer (as our own Vice President[1] has trenchantly
observed) with which something is said. The opprobrious Mexican
word for an American—*gringo*—for example, is essentially simply
a sound echo of a song the American troops used to sing when the
Americans were invading Mexico—"Green Grow the Lilacs."
Therefore the Mexicans began to call the Americans something
equivalent to "los green-grows" which became Hispanized to
gringo. But from this innocent beginning to the unfriendly emphasis

[1] Spiro T. Agnew—EDS.

with which many Mexicans say *gringo* today there is a world of difference—almost a call to arms, with unforgettable memories of past real or fancied wrongs, including "lost" Texas and California.

The pejorative American word for Mexicans, Puerto Ricans, Cubans and other Spanish-speaking nationals is simply *spik*, excerpted from the useful expression "No esspick Englitch." Italians, whether in America or abroad, have been given other more picturesque appellations. *Wop,* an all-time pejorative favorite, is curiously not insulting at all by origin, as it means, in Neapolitan dialect, "handsome," "strong" or "good looking." Among the young Italian immigrants some of the stronger and more active—sometimes to the point of combat—were called *guappi,* from which the first syllable, "wop," attained an "immediate insult" status for all Italians.

"Guinea" comes from the days of the slave trade and is derived from the African word for West Africa. This "guinea" is the same word as the British unit of 21 shillings, somehow connected with African gold profits as well as New Guinea, which resembled Africa to its discoverers. Dark or swarthy Italians and sometimes Portuguese were called *Guineas* and this apparently spread to Italians of light complexion as well.

One of the epithets for Negroes has a curious and tragic historic origin, the memory of which is still haunting us. The word is "coons." It comes from *baracoes* (the o gives a nasal n sound in Portuguese), and refers to the slave pens or barracks (*"baracoons"*) in which the victims of the slave trade were kept while awaiting transshipment. Their descendants, in their present emphasizing of the term "black" over "Negro," may be in the process of upgrading the very word "black," so often used pejoratively, as in "blackhearted," "black arts," "black hand," etc. Even some African languages use "black" in a negative sense. In Hausa "to have a black stomach" means to be angry or unhappy.

The sub-Sahara African peoples, incidentally, do not think that they are black (which they are not, anyway). They consider themselves a healthy and attractive "people color," while whites to them look rather unhealthy and somewhat frightening. In any case, the efforts of African Americans to dignify the word "black" may eventually represent a semantic as well as a socio-racial triumph.

A common type of national insult is that of referring to nationalities by their food habits. Thus "Frogs" for the French and "Krauts" for the Germans are easily understandable, reflecting on the French addiction to *cuisses de grenouilles* (literally "thighs of frogs") and that of the Germans for various kinds of cabbage, hot or cold. The French call the Italians *"les macaronis"* while the German insult word for Italians is *Katzenfresser* (cateaters), an unjust accusation considering the hordes of cats among the Roman ruins fed by individual cat lovers—unless they are fattening them up? The insult word for an English person is "limey," referring to the limes distributed to seafaring Englishmen as an antiscurvy precaution in the days of sailing ships and long periods at sea.

At least one of these food descriptive appellations has attained a permanent status in English. The word "Eskimo" is not an Eskimo word at all but an Algonquin word unit meaning "eaters-of-flesh." The Eskimos naturally do not call themselves this in their own language but, with simple directness, use the word *Inuit*—"the men" or "the people."

Why is it an insult to call Chinese "Chinks"? Chink is most probably a contraction of the first syllables of *Chung-Kuo-Ren*— "Middle Country Person." In Chinese there is no special word for China, as the Chinese, being racially somewhat snobbish themselves (although *not* effete, according to recent reports), have for thousands of years considered their land to be the center or middle of the world. The key character for China is therefore the word *chung* or "middle" which, added to *kuo,* becomes "middle country" or "middle kingdom"—the complete Chinese expression for "China" being *Chung Hwa Min Kuo* ("Middle Flowery People's Country"). No matter how inoffensive the origin of "Chink" is, however, it is no longer advisable for everyday or anyday use now.

Jap, an insulting diminutive that figured in the last national U.S. election (though its use in the expression "fat Jap" was apparently meant to have an endearing quality by our Vice President), is a simple contraction of "Japan," which derives from the Chinese word for "sun." In fact the words "Jap" and "Nip" both mean the same thing. "Jap" comes from Chinese and "Nip" from Japanese in the following fashion: *Jihpen* means "sun origin" in Chinese, while *Nihon* (Nippon) gives a like meaning in Japanese, both indicating that Japan was where the sun rose. Europeans were first in contact with China, and so originally chose the Chinese name for Japan instead of the Japanese one.

The Chinese "insult" words for whites are based on the observations that they are *too* white and therefore look like ghosts or devils, *fan kuei* (ocean ghosts), or that their features are too sharp instead of being pleasantly flat, and that they have enormous noses, hence *ta-bee-tsu* (great-nosed ones). Differences in facial physiognomy have been fully reciprocated by whites in referring to Asians as "Slants" or "Slopes."

Greeks in ancient times had an insult word for foreigners too,   13
but one based on the sound of their language. This word is still
with us, though its original meaning has changed. The ancient
Greeks divided the world into Greeks and "Barbarians"—the latter
word coming from a description of the ridiculous language the
stranger was speaking. To the Greeks it sounded like the "baa-
baa" of a sheep—hence "Barbarians"!

The black peoples of South Africa are not today referred to as   14
Negro or Black but as Bantu—not in itself an insult but having
somewhat the same effect when you are the lowest man on the
totem pole. But the word means simply "the men," *ntu* signifying
"man" and *ba* being the plural prefix. This may have come from an
early encounter with explorers or missionaries when Central or
South Africans on being asked by whites who they were may have
replied simply "men"—with the implied though probably unspoken
follow-up question, "And who are you?"

This basic and ancient idea that one's group are the only people—   15
at least the only friendly or non-dangerous ones—is found among
many tribes throughout the world. The Navajo Indians call themselves *Diné*—"the people"—and qualify other tribes generally as
"the enemy." Therefore an Indian tribe to the north would simply
be called "the northern enemy," one to the east "the eastern
enemy," etc., and that would be the *only* name used for them.
These ancient customs, sanctified by time, of considering people
who differ in color, customs, physical characteristics and habits—
and by enlargement all strangers—as potential enemies is something mankind can no longer afford, even linguistically. Will man
ever be able to rise above using insult as a weapon? It may not be
possible to love your neighbor, but by understanding him one may
be able eventually to tolerate him. Meanwhile, if you stop calling
him names, he too may eventually learn to dislike *you* less.

COMPREHENSION

1. What are the origins of the pejorative words for Jews? for Spanish
speakers? for Italians? for Negroes?

2. Which ethnic slurs are derived from national eating habits? In what other
ways can origins of slurs be categorized?

3. If the origins of most of these expressions have no negative or insulting
associations, why do the expressions themselves have the power to
offend?

4. How does Berlitz support his claim that many, even most, nationalities are
snobbish, even chauvinistic?

PURPOSE AND AUDIENCE

1. In the opening anecdote, what did Disraeli mean by his answer? What effect was it calculated to have on his audience? What effect does Berlitz expect the narrative to have on the reader?

2. Berlitz's essay first appeared in *Penthouse* magazine, a publication for men. Do you think it interested readers who bought *Penthouse* expecting only articles and pictures about sex? Why or why not?

3. Berlitz wrote this essay in 1970. Is it more or less relevant today? Explain.

4. The essay is a strongly persuasive one, and yet the thesis is not revealed until the last paragraph. Do you think it should have been explicitly stated sooner? If so, where? If not, why not?

STYLE AND STRUCTURE

1. What pattern of development does Berlitz use to define the national insult? Do you think other methods might have been more effective? Explain.

2. Throughout the essay, Berlitz uses several different words to signify the negative connotation of the ethnic insult. *Pejorative* is one such word; name two others.

3. Most of the essay's paragraphs are unified by a central idea. Paragraph 8, for instance, is about names that are derived from food habits, and paragraph 11 is about the word *Jap.* Go through the essay, and identify each paragraph's central unifying principle. Does any paragraph lack one?

WRITING WORKSHOP

1. Write an essay defining a series of pejorative terms used to describe a group. The group may be determined by ethnic or racial ties, sexual preference, religion, intelligence, geographical area, physical handicap, or any other criteria. Develop your essay by exemplification.

2. Write an essay defining a slang term. In your extended definition, you may use examples (illustrating its usage), narrative (telling an anecdote involving the term), comparison and contrast (juxtaposing your term with similar ones), or any other patterns of development.

10

Argumentation

WHAT IS ARGUMENTATION?

All of us like a good argument. Long after we graduate, we remember the heated debates that took place in our college classrooms. We enjoy the confrontation of an intellectual argument that allows us to test our ideas and see how well they stand up. Not surprisingly, the first rules governing argumentation were formulated by the ancient Greeks for public speaking. As Aristotle pointed out, certain techniques are more effective than others in convincing an audience that an idea is worth accepting or at least considering. As you will see in this chapter, these techniques apply to writing as well as public speaking.

In your academic courses, two situations, both somewhat specialized, are likely to require an essay structured as a formal argument. The first, preparing a speech for a class in debating or public speaking, applies argumentative techniques just as the Greeks did originally. The second, writing an editorial for the school newspaper, applies argumentative techniques to writing. Although neither of these assignments is a standard part of the average student's curriculum, other writing situations, from English composition essays to research papers, may require that you advocate a change in procedures or policy, that you persuade someone that your views are valid, or that you convince someone to do something. Moreover, practice in constructing argumentative essays gives you skills applicable to many situations: assessing your audience, formulating a thesis, acknowledging opposing views, and using convincing arguments and reasons to support your position. In fact, many of the earlier essays in this book have had characteristics typical of argumentative essays. Most contain thesis statements, and all try to impress readers with the reasonableness of their positions. An argumentative essay, however, focuses on an issue and establishes the controversial nature of the topic. It tries to convince readers to change their ideas, opinions, and actions, and it appeals to reason through the logic of a well-structured argument.

Argumentative essays seldom depend upon a single pattern of development. Instead, writers use all the methods they can in order to convince their readers. As you will notice, each of the essays in this chapter combines various patterns of development. Within a single essay, a narrative paragraph may be followed by one that is descriptive and by still another that compares and contrasts. This variety, when carefully planned, allows a writer to incorporate every possible strategy to convince and motivate an audience.

Choosing a Topic

Choosing the right topic for an argumentative essay is important. It should be one that you care about, one in which you have an intellectual or emotional interest. But you should not let your involvement with your topic blind you to the strengths and weaknesses of your evidence. You should be willing, in advance, to look at your topic from as many different angles as you can so that you understand how a reader might feel and can build a persuasive case. If you think you cannot do this, then you should abandon your topic and pick another one that you can deal with more objectively.

Besides caring about your topic, you should be well informed about it. Opinion without evidence is not persuasive. In addition, you should select a limited issue, one narrow enough that it can be treated in a brief essay, or confine your discussion to a particular aspect of a broad issue. Finally, you should consider your purpose— what you expect your argument to accomplish and how you wish your audience to respond. If your topic is so far-reaching that you cannot specify what you want to persuade a reader to think and do or so idealistic that your expectations are impossible or unreasonable, your essay will not be effective.

Finding Something to Say

After deciding on a topic, you should gather as much relevant information as you can. First, brainstorm to think of experiences and examples that would support your thesis. If your topic is technical or demands specific knowledge, go to the library and use the card catalog, periodical indexes, and reference books to locate the information you need. You can also talk to people who are knowledgeable about your topic. Often fifteen minutes with an instructor yields a reading list that saves hours of research time.

When selecting and reviewing material, remember two things. First, read selections or consider positions that represent the full range of opinions on your subject, not just one side or another. Take pains to define points or to find articles or books that disagree with the position you plan to take. Then you will understand your opposition and be able to refute it effectively when you write your paper. Second, keep in mind the limits of your paper. You will need fewer facts and examples for a brief essay than you will for a term paper.

Audience

Before writing any essay, you should analyze the characteristics, values, and interests of your audience. When writing argumentative essays, however, certain questions require special attention. You need to assess what your readers like and dislike, what opinions they already have about your topic, and whether they should be considered hostile, neutral, or friendly. Each of these considerations influences your approach to your subject. Naturally, it would be relatively easy to convince college students that tuition should be lowered or instructors that salaries should be raised. You could be reasonably sure, in advance, that each group would be friendly and would agree with your position. But most argumentative essays are more difficult to write than these essays because you try to do more than just persuade people who already agree with your position. For example, you might face the challenge of convincing college students that tuition should be raised to pay for an increase in instructors' salaries or persuading instructors that they should forgo raises so that tuition can remain the same. Whether your readers are mildly sympathetic, neutral, or even hostile to your position, your job is to change their ideas so that they accord more closely with your own.

Your analysis of your audience is important because it determines the arguments and approach you use in your essay. If you were planning to convince students that tuition should be raised or instructors that salaries should be frozen, your appeals would consider different factors. To each group, you would want to seem reasonable by recognizing the validity of its position. At the same time, since you could assume that either instructors or students would be a hostile audience, you would appeal to each group with arguments that would override its particular objections. In either essay, your object would be to present your ideas fairly, acknowledge your opponent's possible objections, and refute them whenever you honestly can. No matter how logical your presentation is, it will not convince your readers if they feel that you are unreasonable. To appear reasonable to the students, you might grant that tuition is high but point out that the last tuition hike was three years ago and was only 10 percent. Then you could demonstrate that salaries have increased only 5 percent during each of the past five years despite an average 8.5 percent increase in the cost of living. When addressing the instructors, you might grant that their salaries have not kept up with inflation. Then you could go on to note that most of their students come from families whose incomes average $15,000 or $20,000 a year and whose budgets are already overburdened. Thus, although an increase in salaries would be desirable, it could have a disastrous effect. If the resultant tuition increase forced many students to drop out of school or transfer, some instructors might lose their jobs.

Fair and Unfair Persuasion

There are many ways to appeal to an audience. Unfortunately, not all of them are fair, logical, or reasonable. Every day, commercials persuade people to spend millions of dollars on various products. They tell us to buy certain toothpaste if we want to have sex appeal and to use a certain deodorant if we want to be popular, appealing, as many critics have pointed out, to our fears and desires. Likewise, political speakers may move people by playing on their prejudices and emotions, sometimes with appalling results as in the cases of Hitler and Mussolini. These appeals, although undeniably effective, often rely on trickery and subterfuge to achieve their ends. A good argumentative essay, however, should be more than an appeal to an audience's prejudices. Instead, it should rely on logic and reason.

To argue logically, an essay should be based on solid factual information. Readers respect a clearly reasoned argument that leads them from reliable evidence to a logical conclusion. If you find that the facts do not support your conclusion, you should consider the possibility that your position is weak or even wrong. Without strong evidence, your essay will not persuade an audience, regardless of your personal convictions.

In addition to presenting accurate and pertinent information, a fair argument maintains a reasonable tone. Besides taking account of its audience's viewpoint, it does not attack the character or intelligence of the opposition. In fact, such name-calling can backfire; your approach can turn a sympathetic audience against your position. On the other hand, an equitable argument may lead even a hostile reader to consider its merit.

Logical and Illogical Argument

Arguments depend on two forms of logic, induction and deduction. *Induction* proceeds from individual observations to a general conclusion, and *deduction* moves from a general premise or assumption to a specific conclusion.

When medical doctors examine a patient and, based on the symptoms, make a diagnosis, they use induction, and so do pollsters when they predict the outcome of an election on the basis of responses to a public opinion survey. Martin Luther King, Jr., relies upon induction in "Letter from Birmingham Jail" when he outlines the series of steps that led him to Birmingham, Alabama. Inductive essays use examples to establish valid conclusions and, like exemplification essays, should contain enough examples to justify their conclusions. In addition, these examples should be representative of the group to which they belong and should be drawn from reliable sources.

Deduction depends upon the syllogism, a three-part argument that consists of a major premise, a minor premise, and a conclusion that follows necessarily from these premises:

Major premise	All Olympic runners are strong.
Minor premise	John is an Olympic runner.
Conclusion	Therefore, John is strong.

Of course, no argumentative essay will be as simple as this, but its argument can be tested by being put in this three-part form. The Declaration of Independence offers an example:

Major premise	Tyrannical rulers deserve no loyalty.
Minor premise	King George is a tyrannical ruler.
Conclusion	Therefore, King George deserves no loyalty.

When a conclusion follows logically from the major and minor premises, the argument is said to be valid. If, however, there is a missing link or fallacy in the chain of reasoning, the argument is invalid and can seriously undermine your essay. Here are some common logical fallacies that you should watch out for.

Begging the Question.   The fallacy of begging the question results when a debatable premise is presented as if it were true.

> Atomic power is an unacceptable source of energy. The question, then, is what we can do to limit its use.

Atomic power may be a dangerous source of energy, but it does not necessarily follow that it is unacceptable. This argument begs the question by providing no evidence for this questionable statement.

Argument from Analogy.   This fallacy occurs when an argument uses analogy, a comparison of two unlike things, to prove a point. Although analogies can explain an abstract or unclear idea, they can never be used to prove anything.

> The overcrowded conditions in some parts of our city have forced people together like rats in a cage. Like rats, they will eventually turn upon each other, fighting and killing until a balance is restored. It is therefore necessary that we vote to appropriate funds to build low-cost housing.

Although low-cost housing may be desirable, an argument based solely on an analogy between people and rats is not valid. Simply because two things have some characteristics in common, it does not necessarily follow that they are alike in all respects.

Ad Hominem Argument.   An argument that commits this fallacy turns away from the facts of an issue and directs attention to the man (*ad hominem*) involved in the issue.

> The public should not take seriously Dr. Mason's plan for upgrading county health services. He is a reformed alcoholic, whose second wife recently divorced him.

This argument makes no attempt to refute Dr. Mason's plan but instead attacks Dr. Mason himself by introducing facts about his private life. It casts aspersions on the doctor's character and implies a relationship between his character and his ideas.

Post Hoc, Ergo Propter Hoc.   The *post hoc, ergo propter hoc* (after this, therefore because of this) fallacy occurs when an argument assumes that, because one event occurred prior to another event, the first event caused the second event.

> Throughout the early 1960s, America was able to hold its own in Vietnam. Then came the Beatles, peace demonstrators, and hippies. It is clear that these groups undermined our confidence in our nation's military superiority.

This argument asserts that the Beatles, peace demonstrators, and hippies were responsible for America's withdrawal from Vietnam. Using this kind of faulty reasoning, we could also say that the same was true for the Rolling Stones, the Black Panthers, Richard Nixon, or any other group or individual present before America began peace negotiations. In fact, every event is preceded by countless other events, and sequence alone can never prove causality. A valid argument must establish, not simply assume, a causal connection. (For a fuller discussion of this fallacy, see Chapter 6.)

STRUCTURING AN ARGUMENTATIVE ESSAY

Like the other essays you have been writing, argumentative essays have introductions, body paragraphs, and conclusions. In addition, they also use special strategies that ensure clarity and persuasiveness. As the essays for this chapter illustrate, a typical argumentative essay includes an introduction to the problem, an outline of alternative positions, a thesis stating the author's stand, supporting evidence for this position, refutation of opposing views, and a forceful conclusion that restates the thesis.

First of all, a writer usually introduces an argumentative essay by stating the problem or issue to be discussed. For example, Thomas Jefferson begins the Declaration of Independence by presenting the issue that the document addresses: the obligation of the people of the United States to tell the world why they must separate from Great Britain. Steven Muller, in "Our Youth Should Serve," introduces his essay by stating the problem with which he is concerned: in our society, young people are not able to develop a sense of purpose.

After presenting the problem, Muller, like many other writers of argumentative essays, outlines positions other than his own. Currently, he says, society offers young people two options after high school: they can go to work or to college. Neither choice provides them with outlets for their idealism or allows them to develop a sense of purpose.

Following the recognition of other positions comes the thesis, an exact and direct statement of the stand the essay will take. In Jefferson's case, his thesis is that, because of the tyranny of the British king, the United States must break away from Great Britain. In Muller's, it is that young people should be able to volunteer in peacetime to serve their country.

In the body of an argumentative essay, the writer offers the facts, examples, and reasons that support the main idea. In the Declaration of Independence, Jefferson lists twenty-eight examples of injustice endured by the American colonies. Muller outlines his plan for a youth corps in great detail, establishing, as he does so, the credibility of his idea.

In the process of supporting the argument, a writer must anticipate and refute possible criticisms of the position taken in the essay. Jefferson, for example, realizes that some might think his actions extreme, so he emphasizes that time and time again the colonists appealed to the British for redress. Muller directly considers several possible objections to his plan and gives reasons why these criticisms are unwarranted.

Finally, in most argumentative essays, the conclusion restates the thesis and reinforces it one final time. Since people remember best what they read last, a writer almost always makes sure that the conclusion contains a powerful statement calculated to stay with the reader. In his conclusion, Jefferson ends with a flourish: he speaks for the representatives of the states, appealing to God for divine guidance and explicitly dissolving all connections between Great Britain and America. In contrast, Muller's conclusion is more modest. In it, he reviews the benefits of his plan for a youth service corps and urges its serious consideration.

The following diagram outlines the structure for an argumentative essay:

Introduction:	Introduce the problem.
	Present other possible positions.
	State the thesis.
Body:	Offer facts, examples, data, and other information to support the thesis.
	Anticipate and refute possible criticisms.
Conclusion:	Restate the thesis.
	End with a forceful closing statement.

Let's suppose that your journalism instructor has given you the following assignment: "Select a controversial topic that interests you, and write a brief editorial. Direct your editorial to readers who do not share your views and try to convince them that your position is reasonable. Be sure to acknowledge the views your audience holds and to refute any criticisms of your argument that you can anticipate."

You are especially well informed about one local issue because you have just read a series of articles on it. A citizens' group has formed to lobby for a local ordinance that would authorize spending tax dollars for parochial and private schools in your community. Since you have also recently studied the constitutional doctrine of separation of church and state in your American history class, you know you could fairly and convincingly argue against the position taken by this group.

An outline of your essay might look like this:

¶1   Introduction of problem: Should public tax revenues be spent on aid to parochial and private schools?
Possible positions: Parochial and private school parents want the same financial support for their children's schools that public schools receive; some politicians suggest money go only for transportation or for textbooks; some people believe any aid at all violates the Constitution.
Thesis: Despite the pleas of citizens' groups like Private and Parochial School Parents United, using tax dollars to support nonpublic schools directly violates the United States Constitution.

¶2   Evidence: Quotation from the Constitution and general explanation of the principle of separation of church and state.

¶3   Evidence: Examples of recent court cases interpreting and applying this principle.

¶4   Local application of evidence: Interpretation of how the Constitution and the court cases apply to your community's situation.

¶5   Anticipation and refutation of criticisms: Response to the arguments by the citizens' group (for example, that *their* taxes support public schools).

¶6   Conclusion: Restatement of thesis and strong closing statement.

Of course, not every argumentative essay contains all the elements just discussed, but many do. Still, no pattern or strategy should be followed blindly. The material you are working with, your thesis, your purpose, the audience you are addressing, and the limitations of your assignment ultimately determine how you will structure your paper. The following student essay, written by Monica Borkowski for her composition class, does, however, illustrate all the standard techniques.

MEN AND EXTRAVAGANCE, OR HOW I LEARNED TO HATE
DIAMOND JIM BRADY

Introduction to the problem

We are all sure to have at least one acquaintance who is stingy, and we complain to all our friends about what a loser this miser is. Our complaints are justified, too, given the psychology of this affliction: the person who is retentive with money is likely to be equally stingy with love and attention. Since everyone desires a balanced give-and-take relationship, the flinty-souled miser is high on the list of undesirables.

But when we encounter the opposite—a spendthrift in all his glory—where are the complaints? Where is the Freudian diagnosis? We hear

Other possible positions

few downgrading remarks because we all love to see a fool and his money parted, especially if some of that money comes our way. This is particularly true when it comes to male-female relationships. Many women, for instance, are pleased to be in the company of a man who always grabs the tab, who drives suavely into a ten-dollar parking garage without complaint instead of cruising around, cursing and perspiring, before finding a dollar lot a mile away. How much a man spends on a woman <u>must</u> have something to do with how much he loves her, and besides, how can that wonderful feeling of being pampered be wrong?

I think it is time that we stop encouraging this distorted idea of masculinity (a woman who goes wild with money is hardly admired!) and give more credit

to a man of average income who is trying to behave
sensibly. I am referring to the man who picks up the
tab most times but not always, who takes some trouble
to buy gas from self—service stations and sometimes
shops at a discount menswear store. We are so
forthright in considering a stingy man a loser;

Thesis isn't it time to consider his opposite—the
compulsively extravagant male—as at least equally
undesirable?

Literary evidence   Just look at how our society teaches males that
extravagance is a positive characteristic. Scrooge,
the main character of Dickens's <u>A</u> <u>Christmas</u>
<u>Carol</u>, is portrayed as an evil man until he is
rehabilitated—meaning that he gives up his miserly
ways and freely distributes gifts and money on
Christmas day. This behavior, of course, is rewarded
when people change their opinions about him and
decide that perhaps he isn't such a bad person after
all.

Historical evidence   Diamond Jim Brady is another interesting
example. This individual was a financier who was
known for his extravagant taste in women and food. In
any given night, he would consume food enough to feed
at least ten of the many poor who roamed the streets
of late nineteenth—century New York. Yet, despite
his selfishness and infantile self—gratification,
Diamond Jim Brady's name has become a synonym for the
good life.

Personal evidence   In my own experience, as unpleasant as a stingy
man may be, his frugality is preferable to the
hypocrisy of the big spender. I say
<u>hypocrisy</u> because the spendthrift really

Anticipation and refutation of criticism   operates out of some insecurity and not out of
generosity or, as most women want to believe,
enchantment with them. Usually he is so worried

about his masculinity or lovableness or something
that he has to make a bigger impression than anyone
else. Vanity, not generosity or love, is his driving
force.

Additional personal evidence

This type of man, at least in my experience,
usually seems to revel in <u>owing</u> money too.
Carefully observe such men a while, and just listen
to them brag about how they would absolutely die
without their credit cards or how they probably owe
more banks and collection agencies than anyone else
they know. Just after a woman has seriously fallen
for a big spender and his flair for living, she
usually has to face the bitter reality that he is not
affluent or self-assured at all--just extravagantly
in hock!

Restatement of argument

Certainly the big spender might make a good date
for two or three nights, but as a serious lover,
husband, and father, he is a total disaster.

Points for Special Attention

Choosing the Topic.   Borkowski's paper illustrates that an argumentative essay does not have to be about a burning issue. It can be about anything debatable that you feel strongly about. Her choice of topic shows imagination and individuality. It enabled her to approach an often-discussed problem—sexual stereotypes—in an interesting and novel way.

Gathering Materials.   Borkowski most likely did not have to do much library research for this paper. Possibly she had to consult an encyclopedia to get information about Charles Dickens and Diamond Jim Brady, but she could have known about them from her history and English classes. However, this is not to say that Monica Borkowski's paper did not involve gathering ideas. Instead of doing library research, she had to spend a lot of time thinking of appropriate experiences and examples to support her assertions. Certainly, her audience would not accept her thesis without this detail. Even though most of her examples came from her own experience, she had to be sure that they were clear and to the point.

Audience.   The subject of this argumentative essay is not as controversial as abortion, gun control, or taxing churches, but it nonetheless provocatively challenges her audience's prevalent attitude. Monica Borkowski's main point is that society's positive view of the male spendthrift is inappropriate. By revealing the extravagant man to be selfish, insecure, infantile, and foolish, she challenges the opinions of many in her audience.

Borkowski treats her readers as if they disagreed with her point of view. She avoids name-calling and goes into great detail to support her assertions and convince her audience that what she says is true. In doing so, she relies primarily on images with which both she and her audience are familiar: the man who picks up checks, who spends his money freely, who is always ready with his credit card, and who, consequently, is always in debt. Since most of us know someone like this, her characterization rings true. In addition, she uses characters from literature and history to support her point that society encourages this type of behavior.

Organization.   Monica Borkowski uses all the elements discussed earlier in this chapter. She begins her essay by introducing the problem she is going to discuss, that spendthrifts are tolerated and even encouraged by society. She then outlines the various positions people take on this subject: that the big spender is a desirable alternative to the miser and that his extravagance is a measure of his love and affection. Her thesis is straightforward and clearly states her position on the issue: society should stop encouraging such extravagance in men. After all, she says, this characteristic is discouraged in women. Borkowski then goes on to offer the facts and examples that support her thesis. In her sixth paragraph, she anticipates a major criticism of her argument: that the big spender's generosity is his way of showing affection. She disagrees, maintaining that the compulsively extravagant male is actually vain and infantile. Although her conclusion is rather brief, it does reenforce this point and reiterate her main idea.

The five essays that follow represent a wide range of historical and topical perspectives; each, however, presents a formal argument to support a controversial thesis. As you read each essay, try to trace the characteristic strategies of the classic pattern for argument.

The Declaration of Independence
THOMAS JEFFERSON

*The Declaration of Independence challenges a basic assumption of the
age in which it was written—the divine right of kings. In order to
accomplish his ends, Thomas Jefferson followed many of the principles
of argumentative writing. Unlike many modern revolutionary manifes-
tos, the Declaration of Independence is a model of clarity and precision
that attempts to establish and support its thesis by means of irrefutable
logic and reason.*

When in the course of human events, it becomes necessary for one 1
people to dissolve the political bands which have connected them
with another, and to assume among the powers of the earth, the
separate and equal station to which the Laws of Nature and of
Nature's God entitle them, a decent respect to the opinions of
mankind requires that they should declare the causes which impel
them to the separation.

We hold these truths to be self-evident, that all men are created 2
equal, that they are endowed by their Creator with certain un-
alienable rights, that among these are life, liberty and the pursuit
of happiness. That to secure these rights, governments are instituted
among men, deriving their just powers from the consent of the
governed. That whenever any form of government becomes destructive of these ends, it is the right of the people to alter or to
abolish it, and to institute new government, laying its foundation
on such principles and organizing its powers in such form, as to
them shall seem most likely to effect their safety and happiness.
Prudence, indeed, will dictate that governments long established
should not be changed for light and transient causes; and accordingly all experience hath shown, that mankind are more disposed
to suffer, while evils are sufferable, than to right themselves by
abolishing the forms to which they are accustomed. But when a
long train of abuses and usurpations, pursuing invariably the same
object, evinces a design to reduce them under absolute despotism,
it is their right, it is their duty, to throw off such government, and
to provide new guards for their future security. Such has been the
patient sufferance of these Colonies; and such is now the necessity
which constrains them to alter their former systems of government.
The history of the present King of Great Britain is a history of

repeated injuries and usurpations, all having in direct object the establishment of an absolute tyranny over these States. To prove this, let facts be submitted to a candid world.

He has refused his assent to laws, the most wholesome and necessary for the public good.   3

He has forbidden his Governors to pass laws of immediate and pressing importance, unless suspended in their operation till his assent should be obtained; and when so suspended, he has utterly neglected to attend to them.   4

He has refused to pass other laws for the accommodation of large districts of people, unless those people would relinquish the right of representation in the legislature, a right inestimable to them and formidable to tyrants only.   5

He has called together legislative bodies at places unusual, uncomfortable, and distant from the depository of their public records, for the sole purpose of fatiguing them into compliance with his measures.   6

He has dissolved representative houses repeatedly, for opposing with manly firmness his invasions on the rights of the people.   7

He has refused for a long time, after such dissolutions, to cause others to be elected; whereby the legislative powers, incapable of annihilation, have returned to the people at large for their exercise; the State remaining in the meantime exposed to all the dangers of invasion from without and convulsions within.   8

He has endeavoured to prevent the population of these states; for that purpose obstructing the laws for naturalization of foreigners; refusing to pass others to encourage their migration hither, and raising the conditions of new appropriations of lands.   9

He has obstructed the administration of justice, by refusing his assent to laws for establishing judiciary powers.   10

He has made judges dependent on his will alone, for the tenure of their offices, and the amount and payment of their salaries.   11

He has erected a multitude of new offices, and sent hither swarms of officers to harass our people, and eat out their substance.   12

He has kept among us, in times of peace, standing armies without the consent of our legislatures.   13

He has affected to render the military independent of and superior to the civil power.   14

He has combined with others to subject us to a jurisdiction foreign to our constitution, and unacknowledged by our laws; giving his assent to their acts of pretended legislation: 15

For quartering large bodies of armed troops among us: 16

For protecting them, by a mock trial, from punishment for any   17 murders which they should commit on the inhabitants of these States:

For cutting off our trade with all parts of the world: 18

For imposing taxes on us without our consent: 19

For depriving us in many cases of the benefits of trial by jury: 20

For transporting us beyond seas to be tried for pretended   21
offences:

For abolishing the free system of English laws in a neighbouring   22
Province, establishing therein an arbitrary government, and enlarging its boundaries so as to render it at once an example and fit
instrument for introducing the same absolute rule into these
Colonies:

For taking away our Charters, abolishing our most valuable laws,   23
and altering fundamentally the forms of our governments:

For suspending our own legislatures, and declaring themselves   24
invested with power to legislate for us in all cases whatsoever.

He has abdicated government here, by declaring us out of his   25
protection and waging war against us.

He has plundered our seas, ravaged our coasts, burnt our towns,   26
and destroyed the lives of our people.

He is at this time transporting large armies of foreign mercenaries   27
to complete the works of death, desolation and tyranny, already
begun with circumstances of cruelty and perfidy scarcely paralleled
in the most barbarous ages, and totally unworthy the head of a
civilized nation.

He has constrained our fellow citizens taken captive on the high   28
seas to bear arms against their country, to become the executioners
of their friends and brethren, or to fall themselves by their hands.

He has excited domestic insurrections amongst us, and has   29
endeavoured to bring on the inhabitants of our frontiers, the
merciless Indian savages, whose known rule of warfare, is an
undistinguished destruction of all ages, sexes, and conditions.

In every stage of these oppressions we have petitioned for   30
redress in the most humble terms: our repeated petitions have been
answered only by repeated injury. A prince whose character is thus
marked by every act which may define a tyrant is unfit to be the
ruler of a free people.

Nor have we been wanting in attention to our British brethren.   31
We have warned them from time to time of attempts by their
legislature to extend an unwarrantable jurisdiction over us. We
have reminded them of the circumstances of our emigration and
settlement here. We have appealed to their native justice and
magnanimity, and we have conjured them by the ties of our common

kindred to disavow these usurpations, which would inevitably interrupt our connections and correspondence. They too have been deaf to the voice of justice and of consanguinity. We must, therefore, acquiesce in the necessity, which denounces our separation, and hold them, as we hold the rest of mankind, enemies in war, in peace friends.

We, therefore, the Representatives of the United States of America, in General Congress assembled, appealing to the Supreme Judge of the world for the rectitude of our intentions, do, in the name, and by authority of the good people of these Colonies, solemnly publish and declare, That these United Colonies are, and of right ought to be, Free and Independent States; that they are absolved from all allegiance to the British Crown, and that all political connection between them and the state of Great Britain, is and ought to be totally dissolved; and that as Free and Independent States, they have full power to levy war, conclude peace, contract alliances, establish commerce, and to do all other acts and things which Independent States may of right do. And for the support of this declaration, with a firm reliance on the protection of Divine Providence, we mutually pledge to each other our lives, our fortunes, and our sacred honor. 32

COMPREHENSION

1. What "truths" does Jefferson assert are "self-evident"?

2. What does Jefferson say is the source from which governments derive their powers?

3. What reasons does Jefferson give to support his premise that the United States should break away from Great Britain?

4. What conclusions about the British crown does Jefferson draw from the facts he presents?

PURPOSE AND AUDIENCE

1. What is the thesis of the Declaration of Independence?

2. The Declaration of Independence was written during a period now referred to as the Age of Reason. In what ways has Jefferson tried to make his document reasonable?

3. For what audience is the document intended?

4. How does Jefferson attempt to convince his audience that he is reasonable?

5. In paragraph 31, following the list of grievances, why does Jefferson address his "British brethren"?

STYLE AND STRUCTURE

1. Construct a topic outline of the Declaration of Independence.

2. Is the Declaration of Independence an example of inductive or deductive reasoning?

3. How does Jefferson create smooth and logical transitions from one paragraph to another?

4. Why does Jefferson list all of his twenty-eight grievances?

5. Jefferson begins the last paragraph of the Declaration of Independence with "We, therefore . . ." What clues about the intent of the document do these words give?

6. What particular words does Jefferson use that are rare today?

WRITING WORKSHOP

1. Write an argumentative essay from the point of view of King George III, and try to convince the colonists that they should not break away from Great Britain. If you can, refute several of the points Jefferson lists in the Declaration.

2. Following Jefferson's example, write a declaration of independence from your school, job, family, or any other institution with which you are connected.

3. Write an essay in which you state a grievance that you share with other members of some group, and then argue for the best way to eliminate it.

Our Youth Should Serve
STEVEN MULLER

*Steven Muller is the president of Johns Hopkins University. In "Our
Youth Should Serve," Muller argues strongly for the establishment of a
youth corps for which high school graduates could volunteer. The structure of this essay follows the traditional pattern for an argumentative
essay. Review the strategies listed earlier in the chapter before you read
this essay so you can identify each element as you come to it.*

Too many young men and women now leave school without a well-   1
developed sense of purpose. If they go right to work after high
school, many are not properly prepared for careers. But if they enter
college instead, many do not really know what to study or what to
do afterward. Our society does not seem to be doing much to
encourage and use the best instincts and talents of our young.

On the one hand, I see the growing problems of each year's new   2
generation of high-school graduates. After twelve years of school-
ing—and television—many of them want to participate actively in
society; but they face either a job with a limited future or more
years in educational institutions. Many are wonderfully idealistic:
they have talent and energy to offer, and they seek the meaning in
their lives that comes from giving of oneself to the common good.
But they feel almost rejected by a society that has too few jobs to
offer them and that asks nothing of them except to avoid trouble.
They want to be part of a new solution; instead society perceives
them as a problem. They seek a cause; but their elders preach only
self-advancement. They need experience on which to base choice;
yet society seems to put a premium on the earliest possible choice,
based inescapably on the least experience.

NECESSARY TASKS

On the other hand, I see an American society sadly in need of   3
social services that we can afford less and less at prevailing costs
of labor. Some tasks are necessary but constitute no career; they
should be carried out, but not as anyone's lifetime occupation. Our
democracy profoundly needs public spirit, but the economy of our
labor system primarily encourages self-interest. The Federal government spends billions on opportunity grants for post-secondary
education, but some of us wonder about money given on the basis

only of need. We ask the young to volunteer for national defense, but not for the improvement of our society. As public spirit and public services decline, so does the quality of life. So I ask myself why cannot we put it all together and ask our young people to volunteer in peacetime to serve America?

I recognize that at first mention, universal national youth service   4
may sound too much like compulsory military service or the Hitler Youth or the Komsomol. I do not believe it has to be like that at all. It need not require uniforms or camps, nor a vast new Federal bureaucracy, nor vast new public expenditures. And it should certainly not be compulsory.

A voluntary program of universal national youth service does of   5
course require compelling incentives. Two could be provided. Guaranteed job training would be one. Substantial Federal assis- tance toward post-secondary education would be the other. This would mean that today's complex measures of Federal aid to students would be ended, and that there would also be no need for tuition tax credits for post-secondary education. Instead, prospective students would *earn* their assistance for post-secondary education by volunteering for national service, and only those who earned assistance would receive it. Present Federal expenditures for the assistance of students in post-secondary education would be con- verted into a simple grant program, modeled on the post-World War II GI Bill of Rights.

VOLUNTEERS

But what, you say, would huge numbers of high-school graduates   6
do as volunteers in national service? They could be interns in public agencies, local, state and national. They could staff day-care programs, neighborhood health centers, centers to counsel and work with children; help to maintain public facilities, including highways, rail beds, waterways and airports; engage in neighbor- hood renewal projects, both physical and social. Some would elect military service, others the Peace Corps. Except for the latter two alternatives and others like them, they could live anywhere they pleased. They would not wear uniforms. They would be employed and supervised by people already employed locally in public- agency careers.

Volunteers would be paid only a subsistence wage, because they   7
would receive the benefits of job training (not necessarily confined to one task) as well as assistance toward post-secondary education if they were so motivated and qualified. If cheap mass housing for

some groups of volunteers were needed, supervised participants in the program could rebuild decayed dwellings in metropolitan areas.

All that might work. But perhaps an even more attractive version   8
of universal national youth service might include private industrial and commercial enterprise as well. A private employer would volunteer to select a stated number of volunteers. He would have their labor at the universally applied subsistence wage; in return he would offer guaranteed job training as well as the exact equivalent of what the Federal government would have to pay for assistance toward post-secondary education. The inclusion of volunteer private employers would greatly amplify job-training opportunities for the youth volunteers, and would greatly lessen the costs of the program in public funds.

DIRECT BENEFITS

The direct benefits of such a universal national-youth-service   9
program would be significant. Every young man and woman would face a meaningful role in society after high school. Everyone would receive job training, and the right to earn assistance toward post-secondary education. Those going on to post-secondary education would have their education interrupted by a constructive work experience. There is evidence that they would thereby become more highly motivated and successful students, particularly if their work experience related closely to subsequent vocational interests. Many participants might locate careers by means of their national-service assignments.

No union jobs need be lost, because skilled workers would be   10
needed to give job training. Many public services would be performed by cheap labor, but there would be no youth army. And the intangible, indirect benefits would be the greatest of all. Young people could regard themselves as more useful and needed. They could serve this country for a two-year period as volunteers, and *earn* job training and/or assistance toward post-secondary education. There is more self-esteem and motivation in earned than in unearned benefits. Universal national youth service may be no panacea. But in my opinion the idea merits serious and imaginative consideration.

COMPREHENSION

1. What two problems is Steven Muller addressing?

2. What possible objections does Muller refute?

3. What incentives to volunteer would young people have?

4. What two versions of his plan does Muller suggest?

5. What would be the direct benefits of his plan?

PURPOSE AND AUDIENCE

1. What is Steven Muller's thesis?

2. At what audience is Muller aiming his essay?

3. How might Muller's academic position influence his audience's response to his essay?

4. Why does Muller refer to young people as *they*? Would this approach appeal to an audience of college students?

STYLE AND STRUCTURE

1. Like the other writers whose essays appear in this section, Steven Muller uses more than one pattern of development. Identify at least three different patterns in his essay.

2. Why does Muller follow his thesis with a discussion of possible objections to it?

3. Are the objections Muller offers the most obvious ones? Why or why not? Can you think of others?

4. How does Muller support his assertions?

5. In spite of his concluding statements, could Muller be criticized for offering his plan as a panacea?

WRITING WORKSHOP

1. Write an argumentative essay against Steven Muller's plan. Refute as many of his points as you can.

2. Write an argumentative essay in which you discuss your own plan for giving high school graduates the sense of purpose Muller feels they lack.

3. Write an essay arguing that you and your peers already have goals and purpose. Use concrete examples from your own experience and observations as support.

The Case Against Man
ISAAC ASIMOV

Isaac Asimov is perhaps the best-known American science-fiction writer. His two most famous works, the Foundation Trilogy *and* I, Robot, *have been translated into many languages and have earned him an international reputation as a master of the genre. Recently, Asimov has turned from science-fiction to science writing. In "The Case Against Man," Asimov looks into the future to predict what the situation could be like if the increasing world population is not curbed. Notice how Asimov establishes the reasonableness of his position and how he presents his controversial thesis to his audience.*

The first mistake is to think of mankind as a thing in itself. It isn't. It is part of an intricate web of life. And we can't think even of life as a thing in itself. It isn't. It is part of the intricate structure of a planet bathed by energy from the Sun. 1

The Earth, in the nearly 5 billion years since it assumed approximately its present form, has undergone a vast evolution. When it first came into being, it very likely lacked what we would today call an ocean and an atmosphere. These were formed by the gradual outward movement of material as the solid interior settled together. 2

Nor were ocean, atmosphere, and solid crust independent of each other after formation. There is interaction always: evaporation, condensation, solution, weathering. Far within the solid crust there are slow, continuing changes, too, of which hot springs, volcanoes, and earthquakes are the more noticeable manifestations here on the surface. 3

Between 2 billion and 3 billion years ago, portions of the surface water, bathed by the energetic radiation from the Sun, developed complicated compounds in organization sufficiently versatile to qualify as what we call "life." Life forms have become more complex and more various ever since. 4

But the life forms are as much part of the structure of the Earth as any inanimate portion is. It is all an inseparable part of a whole. If any animal is isolated totally from other forms of life, then death by starvation will surely follow. If isolated from water, death by dehydration will follow even faster. If isolated from air, whether free or dissolved in water, death by asphyxiation will follow still faster. If isolated from the Sun, animals will survive for a time, but plants would die, and if all plants died, all animals would starve. 5

It works in reverse, too, for the inanimate portion of Earth is   6
shaped and molded by life. The nature of the atmosphere has been
changed by plant activity (which adds to the air the free oxygen it
could not otherwise retain). The soil is turned by earthworms,
while enormous ocean reefs are formed by coral.

The entire planet, plus solar energy, is one enormous intricately   7
interrelated system. The entire planet is a life form made up of
nonliving portions and a large variety of living portions (as our own
body is made up of nonliving crystals in bones and nonliving water
in blood, as well as of a large variety of living portions).

In fact, we can pursue the analogy. A man is composed of 50   8
trillion cells of a variety of types, all interrelated and interdepen-
dent. Loss of some of those cells, such as those making up an entire
leg, will seriously handicap all the rest of the organism: serious
damage to a relatively few cells in an organ, such as the heart or
kidneys, may end by killing all 50 trillion.

In the same way, on a planetary scale, the chopping down of an   9
entire forest may not threaten Earth's life in general, but it will
produce serious changes in the life forms of the region and even
in the nature of the water runoff and, therefore, in the details of
geological structure. A serious decline in the bee population will
affect the numbers of those plants that depend on bees for fertil-
ization, then the numbers of those animals that depend on those
particular bee-fertilized plants, and so on.

Or consider cell growth. Cells in those organs that suffer constant   10
wear and tear—as in the skin or in the intestinal lining—grow and
multiply all life long. Other cells, not so exposed, as in nerve and
muscle, do not multiply at all in the adult, under any circumstances.
Still other organs, ordinarily quiescent, as liver and bone, stand
ready to grow if that is necessary to replace damage. When the
proper repairs are made, growth stops.

In a much looser and more flexible way, the same is true of the   11
"planet organism" (which we study in the science called ecology).
If cougars grow too numerous, the deer they live on are decimated,
and some of the cougars die of starvation, so that their "proper
number" is restored. If too many cougars die, then the deer multiply
with particular rapidity, and cougars multiply quickly in turn, till
the additional predators bring down the number of deer again.
Barring interference from outside, the eaters and the eaten retain
their proper numbers, and both are the better for it. (If the cougars
are all killed off, deer would multiply to the point where they
destroy the plants they live off, and more would then die of
starvation than would have died of cougars.)

The neat economy of growth within an organism such as a human   12
being is sometimes—for what reason, we know not—disrupted, and
a group of cells begins growing without limit. This is the dread
disease of cancer, and unless that growing group of cells is somehow
stopped, the wild growth will throw all the body structure out of
true and end by killing the organism itself.

In ecology, the same would happen if, for some reason, one   13
particular type of organism began to multiply without limit, killing
its competitors and increasing its own food supply at the expense
of that of others. That, too, could end only in the destruction of the
larger system—most or all of life and even of certain aspects of the
inanimate environment.

And this is exactly what is happening at this moment. For   14
thousands of years, the single species Homo sapiens, to which you
and I have the dubious honor of belonging, has been increasing in
numbers. In the past couple of centuries, the rate of increase has
itself increased explosively.

At the time of Julius Caesar, when Earth's human population is   15
estimated to have been 150 million, that population was increasing
at a rate such that it would double in 1,000 years if that rate
remained steady. Today, with Earth's population estimated at about
4,000 million (26 times what it was in Caesar's time), it is increasing
at a rate which, if steady, will cause it to double in 35 years.

The present rate of increase of Earth's swarming human popu-   16
lation qualifies Homo sapiens as an ecological cancer, which will
destroy the ecology just as surely as any ordinary cancer would
destroy an organism.

The cure? Just what it is for any cancer. The cancerous growth   17
must somehow be stopped.

Of course, it will be. If we do nothing at all, the growth will stop,   18
as a cancerous growth in a man will stop if nothing is done. The
man dies and the cancer dies with him. And, analogously, the
ecology will die and man will die with it.

How can the human population explosion be stopped? By raising   19
the deathrate, or by lowering the birthrate. There are no other
alternatives. The deathrate will rise spontaneously and finally
catastrophically, if we do nothing—and that within a few decades.
To make the birthrate fall, somehow (almost *any* how, in fact), is
surely preferable, and that is therefore the first order of mankind's
business today.

Failing this, mankind would stand at the bar of abstract justice   20
(for there may be no posterity to judge) as the mass murderer of life
generally, his own included, and mass disrupter of the intricate

planetary development that made life in its present glory possible in the first place.

Am I too pessimistic? Can we allow the present rate of population   21
increase to continue indefinitely, or at least for a good long time? Can we count on science to develop methods for cleaning up as we pollute, for replacing wasted resources with substitutes, for finding new food, new materials, more and better life for our waxing numbers?

Impossible! If the numbers continue to wax at the present rate.   22

Let us begin with a few estimates (admittedly not precise, but   23
in the rough neighborhood of the truth).

The total mass of living objects on Earth is perhaps 20 trillion   24
tons. There is usually a balance between eaters and eaten that is about 1 to 10 in favor of the eaten. There would therefore be about 10 times as much plant life (the eaten) as animal life (the eaters) on Earth. There is, in other words, just a little under 2 trillion tons of animal life on Earth.

But this is all the animal life that can exist, given the present   25
quantity of plant life. If more animal life is somehow produced, it will strip down the plant life, reduce the food supply, and then enough animals will starve to restore the balance. If one species of animal life increases in mass, it can only be because other species correspondingly decrease. For every additional pound of human flesh on Earth, a pound of some other form of flesh must disappear.

The total mass of humanity now on Earth may be estimated at   26
about 200 million tons, or one ten-thousandth the mass of all animal life. If mankind increases in numbers ten thousandfold, then Homo sapiens will be, perforce, the *only* animal species alive on Earth. It will be a world without elephants or lions, without cats or dogs, without fish or lobsters, without worms or bugs. What's more, to support the mass of human life, all the plant world must be put to service. Only plants edible to man must remain, and only those plants most concentratedly edible and with minimum waste.

At the present moment, the average density of population of the   27
Earth's land surface is about 73 people per square mile. Increase that ten thousandfold and the average density will become 730,000 people per square mile, or more than seven times the density of the workday population of Manhattan. Even if we assume that mankind will somehow spread itself into vast cities floating on the ocean surface (or resting on the ocean floor), the average density of human life at the time when the last nonhuman animal must be

killed would be 310,000 people per square mile over all the world, land and sea alike, or a little better than three times the density of modern Manhattan at noon.

We have the vision, then, of high-rise apartments, higher and more thickly spaced than in Manhattan at present, spreading all over the world, across all the mountains, across the Sahara Desert, across Antarctica, across all the oceans; all with their load of humanity and with no other form of animal life beside. And on the roof of all those buildings are the algae farms, with little plant cells exposed to the Sun so that they might grow rapidly and, without waste, form protein for all the mighty population of 35 trillion human beings. 28

Is that tolerable? Even if science produced all the energy and materials mankind could want, kept them all fed with algae, all educated, all amused—is the planetary high-rise tolerable? 29

And if it were, can we double the population further in 35 more years? And then double it again in another 35 years? Where will the food come from? What will persuade the algae to multiply faster than the light energy they absorb makes possible? What will speed up the Sun to add the energy to make it possible? And if vast supplies of fusion energy are added to supplement the Sun, how will we get rid of the equally vast supplies of heat that will be produced? And after the icecaps are melted and the oceans boiled into steam, what? 30

Can we bleed off the mass of humanity to other worlds? Right now, the number of human beings on Earth is increasing by 80 million per year, and each year that number goes up by 1 and a fraction percent. Can we really suppose that we can send 80 million people per year to the Moon, Mars, and elsewhere, and engineer those worlds to support those people? And even so, merely remain in the same place ourselves? 31

No! Not the most optimistic visionary in the world could honestly convince himself that space travel is the solution to our population problem, if the present rate of increase is sustained. 32

But when will this planetary high-rise culture come about? How long will it take to increase Earth's population to that impossible point at the present doubling rate of once every 35 years? If it will take 1 million years or even 100,000, then, for goodness sake, let's not worry just yet. 33

Well, we don't have that kind of time. We will reach that dead end in no more than 460 years. 34

At the rate we are going, without birth control, then even if 35 science serves us in an absolutely ideal way, we will reach the planetary high-rise with no animals but man, with no plants but algae, with no room for even one more person, by A.D. 2430.

And if science serves us in less than an ideal way (as it certainly   36 will), the end will come sooner, much sooner, and mankind will start fading long, long before he is forced to construct that building that will cover all the Earth's surface.

So if birth control *must* come by A.D. 2430 at the very latest,   37 even in an ideal world of advancing science, let it come *now*, in heaven's name, while there are still oak trees in the world and daisies and tigers and butterflies, and while there is still open land and space, and before the cancer called man proves fatal to life and the planet.

COMPREHENSION

1. What does Asimov mean when he says, "The first mistake is to think of mankind as a thing in itself"?

2. To what disease does Asimov compare unrestrained population growth? Do you think this is a good comparison? Why or why not?

3. At what rate is the human population increasing?

4. What will happen if the present rate of population growth continues?

5. How can science and technology help the earth's population? Are there limits to this help?

PURPOSE AND AUDIENCE

1. Much of this essay is devoted to proving to the audience that a problem actually exists. Do you think this is necessary? Could Asimov have made his point in another way? Explain.

2. What assumption does Asimov make about his audience?

3. Where does Asimov state his thesis? Why does he wait so long to do so?

4. Where does Asimov anticipate his audience's objection to his position?

STYLE AND STRUCTURE

1. Is this essay primarily an example of inductive or deductive reasoning?

2. At several points in his essay, Asimov asks questions. What is the function of these questions?

3. Much of the force of this essay comes from the comparisons that Asimov uses to make his points clear to his readers. List the different comparisons Asimov uses. What do they have in common?

4. Do you think Asimov could be criticized for being an alarmist? Does he gain any advantage in taking an extreme position? Explain.

5. Asimov rarely talks about "our" population problem. Instead, he talks as if he were a visitor from another planet viewing an alien species: "earth's population," "life forms," and "Homo sapiens." Why does he do this?

6. The conclusion of this essay is a single sentence. What does Asimov gain or lose by this tactic?

7. How do the introduction and conclusion tie the essay together?

WRITING WORKSHOP

1. Write an argumentative essay in which you defend the thesis that, although the population increase is a cause for concern, it is not as serious as Asimov suggests. Refute specific points in his essay whenever possible.

2. Write an essay in which you argue for or against birth control. Since this is a controversial issue, be careful to respond to the sensitivities of your audience.

Letter from Birmingham Jail
MARTIN LUTHER KING, JR.

Martin Luther King, Jr., was the most influential voice of the civil rights movement from 1956, the year he led the Montgomery bus boycott, to 1968, the year he was assassinated. In 1963 he launched a campaign against segregation in Birmingham, Alabama, but he met fierce opposition from the police as well as from white moderates who saw him as dangerous. Arrested and jailed for eight days, King wrote his "Letter from Birmingham Jail" to white clergymen to explain his actions and to answer those who urged him to call off the demonstrations. Having much in common with the Declaration of Independence, the "Letter from Birmingham Jail" is a well-reasoned and extended defense of demonstrations and civil disobedience.

April 16, 1963

My Dear Fellow Clergymen:

While confined here in the Birmingham city jail, I came across 1 your recent statement calling my present activities "unwise and untimely." Seldom do I pause to answer criticism of my work and ideas. If I sought to answer all the criticisms that cross my desk, my secretaries would have little time for anything other than such correspondence in the course of the day, and I would have no time for constructive work. But since I feel that you are men of genuine good will and that your criticisms are sincerely set forth, I want to try to answer your statement in what I hope will be patient and reasonable terms.

I think I should indicate why I am here in Birmingham, since 2 you have been influenced by the view which argues against "outsiders coming in." I have the honor of serving as president of the Southern Christian Leadership Conference, an organization operating in every southern state, with headquarters in Atlanta, Georgia. We have some eighty-five affiliated organizations across the South, and one of them is the Alabama Christian Movement for Human Rights. Frequently we share staff, educational, and financial resources with our affiliates. Several months ago the affiliate here in Birmingham asked us to be on call to engage in a nonviolent direct-action program if such were deemed necessary. We readily consented, and when the hour came we lived up to our promise. So I, along with several members of my staff, am here because I was invited here. I am here because I have organizational ties here.

But more basically, I am in Birmingham because injustice is 3 here. Just as the prophets of the eighth century B.C. left their villages and carried their "thus saith the Lord" far beyond the boundaries of their home towns, and just as the Apostle Paul left his village of Tarsus and carried the gospel of Jesus Christ to the far corners of the Greco-Roman world, so am I compelled to carry the gospel of freedom beyond my own home town. Like Paul, I must constantly respond to the Macedonian call for aid.

Moreover, I am cognizant of the interrelatedness of all commu-   4
nities and states. I cannot sit idly by in Atlanta and not be concerned about what happens in Birmingham. Injustice anywhere is a threat to justice everywhere. We are caught in an inescapable network of mutuality, tied in a single garment of destiny. Whatever affects one directly, affects all indirectly. Never again can we afford to live with the narrow, provincial, "outside agitator" idea. Anyone who lives inside the United States can never be considered an outsider anywhere within its bounds.

You deplore the demonstrations taking place in Birmingham. But   5
your statement, I am sorry to say, fails to express a similar concern for the conditions that brought about the demonstrations. I am sure that none of you would want to rest content with the superficial kind of social analysis that deals merely with effects and does not grapple with underlying causes. It is unfortunate that demonstrations are taking place in Birmingham, but it is even more unfortunate that the city's white power structure left the Negro community with no alternative.

In any nonviolent campaign there are four basic steps: collection   6
of the facts to determine whether injustices exist; negotiation; self-purification; and direct action. We have gone through all these steps in Birmingham. There can be no gainsaying the fact that racial injustice engulfs this community. Birmingham is probably the most thoroughly segregated city in the United States. Its ugly record of brutality is widely known. Negroes have experienced grossly unjust treatment in courts. There have been more unsolved bombings of Negro homes and churches in Birmingham than in any other city in the nation. These are the hard, brutal facts of the case. On the basis of these conditions, Negro leaders sought to negotiate with the city fathers. But the latter consistently refused to engage in good-faith negotiation.

Then, last September, came the opportunity to talk with leaders   7
of Birmingham's economic community. In the course of the nego-tiations, certain promises were made by the merchants—for ex-ample, to remove the stores' humiliating racial signs. On the basis of these promises, the Reverend Fred Shuttlesworth and the leaders

of the Alabama Christian Movement for Human Rights agreed to a moratorium on all demonstrations. As the weeks and months went by, we realized that we were the victims of a broken promise. A few signs, briefly removed, returned; the others remained.

As in so many past experiences, our hopes had been blasted, and the shadow of deep disappointment settled upon us. We had no alternative except to prepare for direct action, whereby we would present our very bodies as means of laying our case before the conscience of the local and the national community. Mindful of the difficulties involved, we decided to undertake a process of self-purification. We began a series of workshops on nonviolence, and we repeatedly asked ourselves: "Are you able to accept blows without retaliating?" "Are you able to endure the ordeal of jail?" We decided to schedule our direct-action program for the Easter season, realizing that except for Christmas, this is the main shopping period of the year. Knowing that a strong economic-withdrawal program would be the by-product of direct action, we felt that this would be the best time to bring pressure to bear on the merchants for the needed change. 8

Then it occurred to us that Birmingham's mayoral election was coming up in March, and we speedily decided to postpone action until after election day. When we discovered that the Commissioner of Public Safety, Eugene "Bull" Connor, had piled up enough votes to be in the run-off, we decided again to postpone action until the day after the run-off so that the demonstrations could not be used to cloud the issues. Like many others, we waited to see Mr. Connor defeated, and to this end we endured postponement after postponement. Having aided in this community need, we felt that our direct-action program could be delayed no longer. 9

You may well ask, "Why direct action? Why sit-ins, marches, and so forth? Isn't negotiation a better path?" You are quite right in calling for negotiation. Indeed, this is the very purpose of direct action. Nonviolent direct action seeks to create such a crisis and foster such a tension that a community which has constantly refused to negotiate is forced to confront the issue. It seeks so to dramatize the issue that it can no longer be ignored. My citing the creation of tension as part of the work of the nonviolent-resister may sound rather shocking. But I must confess that I am not afraid of the word "tension." I have earnestly opposed violent tension, but there is a type of constructive, nonviolent tension which is necessary for growth. Just as Socrates felt that it was necessary to create a tension in the mind so that individuals could rise from the bondage of myths and half-truths to the unfettered realm of creative analysis 10 and objective appraisal, so must we see the need for nonviolent gadflies to create the kind of tension in society that will help men rise from the dark depths of prejudice and racism to the majestic heights of understanding and brotherhood.

The purpose of our direct-action program is to create a situation   11 so crisis-packed that it will inevitably open the door to negotiation. I therefore concur with you in your call for negotiation. Too long has our beloved Southland been bogged down in a tragic effort to live in monologue rather than dialogue.

One of the basic points in your statement is that the action that   12 I and my associates have taken in Birmingham is untimely. Some have asked: "Why didn't you give the new city administration time to act?" The only answer that I can give to this query is that the new Birmingham administration must be prodded about as much as the outgoing one, before it will act. We are sadly mistaken if we feel that the election of Albert Boutwell as mayor will bring the millennium to Birmingham. While Mr. Boutwell is a much more gentle person than Mr. Connor, they are both segregationists, dedicated to maintenance of the status quo. I have hoped that Mr. Boutwell will be reasonable enough to see the futility of massive resistance to desegregation. But he will not see this without pressure from devotees of civil rights. My friends, I must say to you that we have not made a single gain in civil rights without determined legal and nonviolent pressure. Lamentably, it is an historical fact that privileged groups seldom give up their privileges voluntarily. Individuals may see the moral light and voluntarily give up their unjust posture; but, as Reinhold Niebuhr has reminded us, groups tends to be more immoral than individuals.

We know through painful experience that freedom is never   13 voluntarily given by the oppressor; it must be demanded by the oppressed. Frankly, I have yet to engage in a direct-action campaign that was "well timed" in the view of those who have not suffered unduly from the disease of segregation. For years now I have heard the word "Wait!" It rings in the ear of every Negro with piercing familiarity. This "Wait" has almost always meant "Never." We must come to see, with one of our distinguished jurists, that "justice too long delayed is justice denied."

We have waited for more than 340 years for our constitutional   14 and God-given rights. The nations of Asia and Africa are moving with jetlike speed toward gaining political independence, but we still creep at horse-and-buggy pace toward gaining a cup of coffee at a lunch counter. Perhaps it is easy for those who have never felt the stinging darts of segregation to say, "Wait." But when you have seen vicious mobs lynch your mothers and fathers at will and drown your sisters and brothers at whim; when you have seen hate-filled policemen curse, kick, and even kill your black brothers and sisters; when you see the vast majority of your twenty million Negro brothers smothering in an airtight cage of poverty in the midst of an affluent society; when you suddenly find your tongue twisted and your speech stammering as you seek to explain to your six-year-old daughter why she can't go to the public amusement park that has just been advertised on television, and see tears welling up in her eyes when she is told that Funtown is closed to colored children, and see ominous clouds of inferiority beginning to form in her little mental sky, and see her beginning to distort her personality by developing an unconscious bitterness toward white people; when you have to concoct an answer for a five-year-old son who is asking, "Daddy, why do white people treat colored people so mean?"; when you take a cross-country drive and find it necessary to sleep night after night in the uncomfortable corners of your automobile because no motel will accept you; when you are humiliated day in and day out by nagging signs reading "white" and "colored"; when your first name becomes "nigger," your middle name becomes "boy" (however old you are) and your last name becomes "John," and your wife and mother are never given the respected title "Mrs."; when you are harried by day and haunted by night by the fact that you are a Negro, living constantly at tiptoe stance, never quite knowing what to expect next, and are plagued with inner fears and outer resentments; when you are forever fighting a degenerating sense of "nobodiness"—then you will understand why we find it difficult to wait. There comes a time when the cup of endurance runs over, and men are no longer willing to be plunged into the abyss of despair. I hope, sirs, you can understand our legitimate and unavoidable impatience.

You express a great deal of anxiety over our willingness to break   15
laws. This is certainly a legitimate concern. Since we so diligently urge people to obey the Supreme Court's decision of 1954 outlawing segregation in the public schools, at first glance it may seem rather paradoxical for us consciously to break laws. One may well ask: "How can you advocate breaking some laws and obeying others?" The answer lies in the fact that there are two types of laws: just and unjust. I would be the first to advocate obeying just laws. One has not only a legal but a moral responsibility to obey just laws. Conversely, one has a moral responsibility to disobey unjust laws. I would agree with St. Augustine that "an unjust law is no law at all."

Now, what is the difference between the two? How does one   16 determine whether a law is just or unjust? A just law is a man-made code that squares with the moral law or the law of God. An unjust law is a code that is out of harmony with the moral law. To put it in the terms of St. Thomas Aquinas: An unjust law is a human law that is not rooted in eternal law and natural law. Any law that uplifts human personality is just. Any law that degrades human personality is unjust. All segregation statutes are unjust because segregation distorts the soul and damages the personality. It gives the segregator a false sense of superiority and the segregated a false sense of inferiority. Segregation, to use the terminology of the Jewish philosopher Martin Buber, substitutes an "I-it" relationship for an "I-thou" relationship and ends up relegating persons to the status of things. Hence segregation is not only politically, economically, and sociologically unsound, it is morally wrong and sinful. Paul Tillich has said that sin is separation. Is not segregation an existential expression of man's tragic separation, his awful estrangement, his terrible sinfulness? Thus it is that I can urge men to obey the 1954 decision of the Supreme Court, for it is morally right; and I can urge them to disobey segregation ordinances, for they are morally wrong.

Let us consider a more concrete example of just and unjust laws.   17 An unjust law is a code that a numerical or power majority group compels a minority group to obey but does not make binding on itself. This is *difference* made legal. By the same token, a just law is a code that a majority compels a minority to follow and that it is willing to follow itself. This is *sameness* made legal.

Let me give another explanation. A law is unjust if it is inflicted   18 on a minority that, as a result of being denied the right to vote, had no part in enacting or devising the law. Who can say that the legislature of Alabama which set up that state's segregation laws was democratically elected? Throughout Alabama all sorts of devious methods are used to prevent Negroes from becoming registered voters, and there are some counties in which, even though Negroes constitute a majority of the population, not a single Negro is registered. Can any law enacted under such circumstances be considered democratically structured?

Sometimes a law is just on its face and unjust in its application.   19 For instance, I have been arrested on a charge of parading without a permit. Now, there is nothing wrong in having an ordinance which requires a permit for a parade. But such an ordinance becomes unjust when it is used to maintain segregation and to deny citizens the First-Amendment privilege of peaceful assembly and protest.

I hope you are able to see the distinction I am trying to point   20 out. In no sense do I advocate evading or defying the law, as would the rabid segregationist. That would lead to anarchy. One who breaks an unjust law must do so openly, lovingly, and with a willingness to accept the penalty. I submit that an individual who breaks a law that conscience tells him is unjust, and who willingly accepts the penalty of imprisonment in order to arouse the conscience of the community over its injustice, is in reality expressing the highest respect for law.

Of course, there is nothing new about this kind of civil disobe-   21
dience. It was evidenced sublimely in the refusal of Shadrach, Meshach, and Abednego to obey the laws of Nebuchadnezzar, on the ground that a higher moral law was at stake. It was practiced superbly by the early Christians, who were willing to face hungry lions and the excruciating pain of chopping blocks rather than submit to certain unjust laws of the Roman Empire. To a degree, academic freedom is a reality today because Socrates practiced civil disobedience. In our own nation, the Boston Tea Party represented a massive act of civil disobedience.

We should never forget that everything Adolf Hitler did in   22
Germany was "legal" and everything the Hungarian freedom fighters did in Hungary was "illegal." It was "illegal" to aid and comfort a Jew in Hitler's Germany. Even so, I am sure that, had I lived in Germany at the time, I would have aided and comforted my Jewish brothers. If today I lived in a Communist country where certain principles dear to the Christian faith are suppressed, I would openly advocate disobeying that country's anti-religious laws.

I must make two honest confessions to you, my Christian and   23
Jewish brothers. First, I must confess that over the past few years I have been gravely disappointed with the white moderate. I have almost reached the regrettable conclusion that the Negro's great stumbling block in his stride toward freedom is not the White Citizen's Counciler or the Ku Klux Klanner, but the white moderate, who is more devoted to "order" than to justice; who prefers a negative peace which is the absence of tension to a positive peace which is the presence of justice; who constantly says, "I agree with you in the goal you seek, but I cannot agree with your methods of direct action"; who paternalistically believes he can set the timetable for another man's freedom; who lives by a mythical concept of time and who constantly advises the Negro to wait for a "more convenient season." Shallow understanding from people of good will is more frustrating than absolute misunderstanding from people of ill will. Lukewarm acceptance is much more bewildering than outright rejection.

I had hoped that the white moderate would understand that law   24
and order exist for the purpose of establishing justice and that when
they fail in this purpose they become the dangerously structured
dams that block the flow of social progress. I had hoped that the
white moderate would understand that the present tension in the
South is a necessary phase of the transition from an obnoxious
negative peace, in which the Negro passively accepted his unjust
plight, to a substantive and positive peace, in which all men will
respect the dignity and worth of human personality. Actually, we
who engage in nonviolent direct action are not the creators of
tension. We merely bring to the surface the hidden tension that is
already alive. We bring it out in the open, where it can be seen and
dealt with. Like a boil that can never be cured so long as it is
covered up but must be opened with all its ugliness to the natural
medicines of air and light, injustice must be exposed, with all the
tension its exposure creates, to the light of human conscience and
the air of national opinion, before it can be cured.

In your statement you assert that our actions, even though   25
peaceful, must be condemned because they precipitate violence.
But is this a logical assertion? Isn't this like condemning a robbed
man because his possession of money precipitated the evil act of
robbery? Isn't this like condemning Socrates because his unswerv-
ing commitment to truth and his philosophical inquiries precipitated the act by the misguided populace in which they made him
drink hemlock? Isn't this like condemning Jesus because his unique
God-consciousness and never-ceasing devotion to God's will precipitated the evil act of crucifixion? We must come to see that, as
the federal courts have consistently affirmed, it is wrong to urge an
individual to cease his efforts to gain his basic constitutional rights
because the quest may precipitate violence. Society must protect
the robbed and punish the robber.

I had also hoped that the white moderate would reject the myth   26
concerning time in relation to the struggle for freedom. I have just
received a letter from a white brother in Texas. He writes: "All
Christians know that the colored people will receive equal rights
eventually, but it is possible that you are in too great a religious
hurry. It has taken Christianity almost two thousand years to
accomplish what it has. The teachings of Christ take time to come
to earth." Such an attitude stems from a tragic misconception of
time, from the strangely irrational notion that there is something in
the very flow of time that will inevitably cure all ills. Actually, time
itself is neutral; it can be used either destructively or constructively.
More and more I feel that the people of ill will have used time
much more effectively than have the people of good will. We will

have to repent in this generation not merely for the hateful words and actions of the bad people, but for the appalling silence of the good people. Human progress never rolls in on wheels of inevitability; it comes through the tireless efforts of men willing to be co-workers with God, and without this hard work, time itself becomes an ally of the forces of social stagnation. We must use time creatively, in the knowledge that the time is always ripe to do right. Now is the time to make real the promise of democracy and transform our pending national elegy into a creative psalm of brotherhood. Now is the time to lift our national policy from the quicksand of racial injustice to the solid rock of human dignity.

You speak of our activity in Birmingham as extreme. At first I 27 was rather disappointed that fellow clergymen would see my nonviolent efforts as those of an extremist. I began thinking about the fact that I stand in the middle of two opposing forces in the Negro community. One is a force of complacency, made up in part of Negroes who, as a result of long years of oppression, are so drained of self-respect and a sense of "somebodiness" that they have adjusted to segregation; and in part of a few middle-class Negroes who, because of a degree of academic and economic security and because in some ways they profit by segregation, have become insensitive to the problems of the masses. The other force is one of bitterness and hatred, and it comes perilously close to advocating violence. It is expressed in the various black nationalist groups that are springing up across the nation, the largest and best-known being Elijah Muhammad's Muslim movement. Nourished by the Negro's frustration over the continued existence of racial discrimination, this movement is made up of people who have lost faith in America, who have absolutely repudiated Christianity, and who have concluded that the white man is an incorrigible "devil."

I have tried to stand between these two forces, saying that we 28 need emulate neither the "do-nothingism" of the complacent nor the hatred and despair of the black nationalist. For there is the more excellent way of love and nonviolent protest. I am grateful to God that, through the influence of the Negro church, the way of nonviolence became an integral part of our struggle.

If this philosophy had not emerged, by now many streets of the 29 South would, I am convinced, be flowing with blood. And I am further convinced that if our white brothers dismiss as "rabble-rousers" and "outside agitators" those of us who employ nonviolent direct action, and if they refuse to support our nonviolent efforts, millions of Negroes will, out of frustration and despair, seek solace and security in black-nationalist ideologies—a development that would inevitably lead to a frightening racial nightmare.

Oppressed people cannot remain oppressed forever. The yearn-   30
ing for freedom eventually manifests itself, and that is what has
happened to the American Negro. Something within has reminded
him of his birthright of freedom, and something without has
reminded him that it can be gained. Consciously or unconsciously,
he has been caught up by the *Zeitgeist*, and with his black brothers
of Africa and his brown and yellow brothers of Asia, South America,
and the Caribbean, the United States Negro is moving with a sense
of great urgency toward the promised land of racial justice. If one
recognizes this vital urge that has engulfed the Negro community,
one should readily understand why public demonstrations are
taking place. The Negro has many pent-up resentments and latent
frustrations, and he must release them. So let him march; let him
make prayer pilgrimages to the city hall; let him go on freedom
rides—and try to understand why he must do so. If his repressed
emotions are not released in nonviolent ways, they will seek
expression through violence; this is not a threat but a fact of history.
So I have not said to my people, "Get rid of your discontent."
Rather, I have tried to say that this normal and healthy discontent
can be channeled into the creative outlet of nonviolent direct
action. And now this approach is being termed extremist.

But though I was initially disappointed at being categorized as   31
an extremist, as I continued to think about the matter I gradually
gained a measure of satisfaction from the label. Was not Jesus an
extremist for love: "Love your enemies, bless them that curse you,
do good to them that hate you, and pray for them which despitefully
use you, and persecute you." Was not Amos an extremist for justice:
"Let justice roll down like waters and righteousness like an ever-
flowing stream." Was not Paul an extremist for the Christian gospel:
"I bear in my body the marks of the Lord Jesus." Was not Martin
Luther an extremist: "Here I stand; I cannot do otherwise, so help
me God." And John Bunyan: "I will stay in jail to the end of my
days before I make a butchery of my conscience." And Abraham
Lincoln: "This nation cannot survive half slave and half free." And
Thomas Jefferson: "We hold these truths to be self-evident, that all
men are created equal. . . ." So the question is not whether we will
be extremists, but what kind of extremists we will be. Will we be
extremists for hate or for love? Will we be extremists for the
preservation of injustice or for the extension of justice? In that
dramatic scene on Calvary's hill three men were crucified. We must
never forget that all three were crucified for the same crime—the
crime of extremism. Two were extremists for immorality, and thus
fell below their environment. The other, Jesus Christ, was an
extremist for love, truth, and goodness, and thereby rose above his

environment. Perhaps the South, the nation, and the world are in dire need of creative extremists.

I had hoped that the white moderate would see this need. Perhaps I was too optimistic; perhaps I expected too much. I suppose I should have realized that few members of the oppressor race can understand the deep groans and passionate yearnings of the oppressed race, and still fewer have the vision to see that injustice must be rooted out by strong, persistent, and determined action. I am thankful, however, that some of our white brothers in the South have grasped the meaning of this social revolution and committed themselves to it. They are still all too few in quantity, but they are big in quality. Some—such as Ralph McGill, Lillian Smith, Harry Golden, James McBride Dabbs, Ann Braden, and Sarah Patton Boyle—have written about our struggle in eloquent and prophetic terms. Others have marched with us down nameless streets of the South. They have languished in filthy, roach-infested jails, suffering the abuse and brutality of policemen who view them as "dirty nigger-lovers." Unlike so many of their moderate brothers and sisters, they have recognized the urgency of the moment and sensed the need for powerful "action" antidotes to combat the disease of segregation. 32

Let me take note of my other major disappointment. I have been so greatly disappointed with the white church and its leadership. Of course, there are some notable exceptions. I am not unmindful of the fact that each of you has taken some significant stands on this issue. I commend you, Reverend Stallings, for your Christian stand on this past Sunday, in welcoming Negroes to your worship service on a nonsegregated basis. I commend the Catholic leaders of this state for integrating Spring Hill College several years ago. 33

But despite these notable exceptions, I must honestly reiterate that I have been disappointed with the church. I do not say this as one of those negative critics who can always find something wrong with the church. I say this as a minister of the gospel, who loves the church; who was nurtured in its bosom; who has been sustained by its spiritual blessings and who will remain true to it as long as the cord of life shall lengthen. 34

When I was suddenly catapulted into the leadership of the bus protest in Montgomery, Alabama, a few years ago, I felt we would be supported by the white church. I felt that the white ministers, priests, and rabbis of the South would be among our strongest allies. Instead, some have been outright opponents, refusing to understand the freedom movement and misrepresenting its leaders; all too many others have been more cautious than courageous and 35 have remained silent behind the anesthetizing security of stained-glass windows.

In spite of my shattered dreams, I came to Birmingham with the hope that the white religious leadership of this community would see the justice of our cause and, with deep moral concern, would serve as the channel through which our just grievances could reach the power structure. I had hoped that each of you would understand. But again I have been disappointed. 36

There was a time when the church was very powerful—in the time when the early Christians rejoiced at being deemed worthy to suffer for what they believed. In those days the church was not merely a thermometer that recorded the ideas and principles of popular opinion; it was a thermostat that transformed the mores of society. Whenever the early Christians entered a town, the people in power became disturbed and immediately sought to convict the Christians for being "disturbers of the peace" and "outside agitators." But the Christians pressed on, in the conviction that they were "a colony of heaven," called to obey God rather than man. Small in number, they were big in commitment. They were too God-intoxicated to be "astronomically intimidated." By their effort and example they brought an end to such ancient evils as infanticide and gladiatorial contests. 37

Things are different now. So often the contemporary church is a weak, ineffectual voice with an uncertain sound. So often it is an archdefender of the status quo. Far from being disturbed by the presence of the church, the power structure of the average community is consoled by the church's silent—and often even vocal—sanction of things as they are. 38

But the judgment of God is upon the church as never before. If today's church does not recapture the sacrificial spirit of the early church, it will lose its authenticity, forfeit the loyalty of millions, and be dismissed as an irrelevant social club with no meaning for the twentieth century. Every day I meet young people whose disappointment with the church has turned into outright disgust. 39

Perhaps I have once again been too optimistic. Is organized religion too inextricably bound to the status quo to save our nation and the world? Perhaps I must turn my faith to the inner spiritual church, the church within the church, as the true *ekklesia* and the hope of the world. But again I am thankful to God that some noble souls from the ranks of organized religion have broken loose from the paralyzing chains of conformity and joined us as active partners in the struggle for freedom. They have left their secure congrega- 40 tions and walked the streets of Albany, Georgia, with us. They have gone down the highways of the South on torturous rides for freedom. Yes, they have gone to jail with us. Some have been dismissed from their churches, have lost the support of their bishops and fellow ministers. But they have acted in the faith that right defeated is stronger than evil triumphant. Their witness has been the spiritual salt that has preserved the true meaning of the gospel in these troubled times. They have carved a tunnel of hope through the dark mountain of disappointment.

I hope the church as a whole will meet the challenge of this 41 decisive hour. But even if the church does not come to the aid of justice, I have no despair about the future. I have no fear about the outcome of our struggle in Birmingham, even if our motives are at present misunderstood. We will reach the goal of freedom in Birmingham and all over the nation, because the goal of America is freedom. Abused and scorned though we may be, our destiny is tied up with America's destiny. Before the pilgrims landed at Plymouth, we were here. Before the pen of Jefferson etched the majestic words of the Declaration of Independence across the pages of history, we were here. For more than two centuries our forebears labored in this country without wages; they made cotton king; they built the homes of their masters while suffering gross injustice and shameful humiliation—and yet out of a bottomless vitality they continued to thrive and develop. If the inexpressible cruelties of slavery could not stop us, the opposition we now face will surely fail. We will win our freedom because the sacred heritage of our nation and the eternal will of God are embodied in our echoing demands.

Before closing I feel impelled to mention one other point in 42 your statement that has troubled me profoundly. You warmly commended the Birmingham police force for keeping "order" and "preventing violence." I doubt that you would have so warmly commended the police force if you had seen its dogs sinking their teeth into unarmed, nonviolent Negroes. I doubt that you would so quickly commend the policemen if you were to observe their ugly and inhumane treatment of Negroes here in the city jail; if you were to watch them push and curse old Negro women and young Negro girls; if you were to see them slap and kick old Negro men and young boys; if you were to observe them, as they did on two occasions, refuse to give us food because we wanted to sing our grace together. I cannot join you in your praise of the Birmingham police department.

It is true that the police have exercised a degree of discipline in 43 handling the demonstrators. In this sense they have conducted themselves rather "nonviolently" in public. But for what purpose? To preserve the evil system of segregation. Over the past few years I have consistently preached that nonviolence demands that the means we use must be as pure as the ends we seek. I have tried to make clear that it is wrong to use immoral means to attain moral ends. But now I must affirm that it is just as wrong, or perhaps even more so, to use moral means to preserve immoral ends. Perhaps Mr. Connor and his policemen have been rather nonviolent in public, as was Chief Pritchett in Albany, Georgia, but they have used the moral means of nonviolence to maintain the immoral end of racial injustice. As T. S. Eliot has said, "The last temptation is the greatest treason: To do the right deed for the wrong reason."

I wish you had commended the Negro sit-inners and demon- 44 strators of Birmingham for their sublime courage, their willingness to suffer, and their amazing discipline in the midst of great provocation. One day the South will recognize its real heroes. They will be the James Merediths, with the noble sense of purpose that enables them to face jeering and hostile mobs, and with the agonizing loneliness that characterizes the life of the pioneer. They will be old, oppressed, battered Negro women, symbolized in a seventy-two-year-old woman in Montgomery, Alabama, who rose up with a sense of dignity and with her people decided not to ride segregated buses, and who responded with ungrammatical profundity to one who inquired about her weariness: "My feets is tired, but my soul is at rest." They will be the young high school and college students, the young ministers of the gospel and a host of their elders, courageously and nonviolently sitting in at lunch counters and willingly going to jail for conscience' sake. One day the South will know that when these disinherited children of God sat down at lunch counters, they were in reality standing up for what is best in the American dream and for the most sacred values in our Judaeo-Christian heritage, thereby bringing our nation back to those great wells of democracy which were dug deep by the founding fathers in their formulation of the Constitution and the Declaration of Independence.

Never before have I written so long a letter. I'm afraid it is much 45 too long to take your precious time. I can assure you that it would have been much shorter if I had been writing from a comfortable desk, but what else can one do when he is alone in a narrow jail cell, other than write long letters, think long thoughts, and pray long prayers?

If I have said anything in this letter that overstates the truth and 46 indicates an unreasonable impatience, I beg you to forgive me. If I have said anything that understates the truth and indicates my having a patience that allows me to settle for anything less than brotherhood, I beg God to forgive me.

I hope this letter finds you strong in the faith. I also hope that circumstances will soon make it possible for me to meet each of you, not as an integrationist or a civil-rights leader but as a fellow clergyman and a Christian brother. Let us all hope that the dark clouds of racial prejudice will soon pass away and the deep fog of misunderstanding will be lifted from our fear-drenched communities, and in some not too distant tomorrow the radiant stars of love and brotherhood will shine over our great nation with all their scintillating beauty.

> Yours for the cause of Peace and Brotherhood,
>
> Martin Luther King, Jr.

COMPREHENSION

1. Martin Luther King, Jr., says that he seldom answers criticism. Why does he decide to do so in this instance?

2. Why do the other clergymen consider King's activities to be "unwise and untimely"?

3. What reasons does King give for the demonstrations? Why does he feel it is too late for negotiations?

4. What does King say *wait* means to blacks?

5. What are the two types of laws King defines? What is the difference between the two?

6. Why is King disappointed in the white moderates?

7. What does King find illogical about the claim that the actions of his followers precipitate violence?

8. What two forces does King say he stands between?

9. Why is King disappointed in the white church?

PURPOSE AND AUDIENCE

1. What is King's purpose in writing his letter? Why, in the first paragraph, does he establish his setting (the Birmingham city jail) and define his intended audience?

2. In the beginning of his letter, King refers to his audience as men of good will. What passages in the letter indicate that he does not really believe this?

3. What indication is there that King is writing his letter to an audience other than his fellow clergymen?

4. What is the thesis of this letter? Is it stated or implied?

5. Why does King so carefully outline for his audience the reasons why he is in Birmingham?

STYLE AND STRUCTURE

1. Where does King seek to establish that he is a reasonable person? Why does he open with "My Dear Fellow Clergymen"?

2. Where does King address the objections of his audience?

3. At what point does King introduce the problem his letter is going to deal with?

4. What facts or examples does King use to support his thesis?

5. As in the Declaration of Independence, transitions are important in King's letter. Identify the transitional words and phrases that connect the different parts of his argument.

6. Why does King use Jewish, Catholic, and Protestant philosophers to support his position?

7. King uses both induction and deduction in his letter. Find an example of each, and explain how they function in the argument.

8. Throughout the body of his letter, King criticizes his audience of white moderates. In his conclusion, he seeks to reestablish a harmonious relationship with them. How does he do this?

WRITING WORKSHOP

1. Write an argumentative essay in which you support a deeply held belief of your own. Assume that your audience, like King's, is not openly hostile to your position.

2. Assume that you are a black militant writing a letter to Martin Luther King, Jr. Argue that King's methods do not go far enough. Be sure to address potential objections to your position. You might want to go to the library and read some newspapers and magazines from the 1960s.

3. Read the newspaper for several days, and collect articles about a controversial subject in which you are interested. Using the information from the articles, take a position on the issue, and write an essay in your own words supporting it.

How to Fix the Premedical Curriculum
LEWIS THOMAS

Lewis Thomas, a physician, held posts at various medical schools and hospitals before assuming his present position as president of the Memorial Sloan-Kettering Cancer Center in New York. In 1974 he won the National Book Award for his collection of essays, The Lives of a Cell. *"How to Fix the Premedical Curriculum" is from Dr. Thomas's second book,* The Medusa and the Snail. *In this essay, he argues that the present premedical curriculum should be overhauled. Although not as tightly organized as the other essays in this section, "How to Fix the Premedical Curriculum" nonetheless exhibits conventional strategies of argument as well as an awareness of audience.*

The influence of the modern medical school on liberal-arts education in this country over the last decade has been baleful and malign, nothing less. The admission policies of the medical schools are at the root of the trouble. If something is not done quickly to change these, all the joy of going to college will have been destroyed, not just for that growing majority of undergraduate students who draw breath only to become doctors, but for everyone else, all the students, and all the faculty as well. 1

The medical schools used to say they wanted applicants as broadly educated as possible, and they used to mean it. The first two years of medical school were given over entirely to the basic biomedical sciences, and almost all entering students got their first close glimpse of science in those years. Three chemistry courses, physics, and some sort of biology were all that were required from the colleges. Students were encouraged by the rhetoric of medical-school catalogues to major in such nonscience disciplines as history, English, philosophy. Not many did so; almost all premedical students in recent generations have had their majors in chemistry or biology. But anyway, they were authorized to spread around in other fields if they wished. 2

There is still some talk in medical deans' offices about the need for general culture, but nobody really means it, and certainly the premedical students don't believe it. They concentrate on science. 3

They concentrate on science with a fury, and they live for grades. If there are courses in the humanities that can be taken without 4 risk to class standing they will line up for these, but they will not get into anything tough except science. The so-called social sciences have become extremely popular as stand-ins for traditional learning.

The atmosphere of the liberal-arts college is being poisoned by premedical students. It is not the fault of the students, who do not start out as a necessarily bad lot. They behave as they do in the firm belief that if they behave any otherwise they won't get into medical school.

I have a suggestion, requiring for its implementation the following announcement from the deans of all the medical schools: henceforth, any applicant who is self-labeled as a "premed," distinguishable by his course selection from his classmates, will have his dossier placed in the third stack of three. Membership in a "premedical society" will, by itself, be grounds for rejection. Any college possessing something called a "premedical curriculum," or maintaining offices for people called "premedical advisers," will be excluded from recognition by the medical schools.

Now as to grades and class standing. There is obviously no way of ignoring these as criteria for acceptance, but it is the grades *in general* that should be weighed. And, since so much of the medical-school curriculum is, or ought to be, narrowly concerned with biomedical science, more attention should be paid to the success of students in other, nonscience disciplines before they are admitted, in order to assure the scope of intellect needed for a physician's work.

Hence, if there are to be MCAT tests, the science part ought to be made the briefest, and weigh the least. A knowledge of literature and languages ought to be the major test and the scariest. History should be tested, with rigor.

The best thing would be to get rid of the MCATs, once and for all, and rely instead, wholly, on the judgment of the college faculties.

You could do this if there were some central, core discipline, universal within the curricula of all the colleges, which could be used for evaluating the free range of a student's mind, his tenacity and resolve, his innate capacity for the understanding of human beings, and his affection for the human condition. For this purpose, I propose that classical Greek be restored as the centerpiece of undergraduate education. The loss of Homeric and Attic Greek from American college life was one of this century's disasters. Putting it back where it once was would quickly make up for the dispiriting impact which generations of spotty Greek in translation have inflicted on modern thought. The capacity to read Homer's language closely enough to sense the terrifying poetry in some of the lines could serve as a shrewd test for the qualities of mind and character needed in a physician.

If everyone had to master Greek, the college students aspiring   11 to medical school would be placed on the same footing as everyone else, and their identifiability as a separate group would be blurred, to everyone's advantage. Moreover, the currently depressing drift on some campuses toward special courses for prelaw students, and even prebusiness students, might be inhibited before more damage is done.

Latin should be put back as well, but not if it is handled, as it   12 ought to be, by the secondary schools. If Horace has been absorbed prior to college, so much for Latin. But Greek is a proper discipline for the college mind.

English, history, the literature of at least two foreign languages,   13 and philosophy should come near the top of the list, just below Classics, as basic requirements, and applicants for medical school should be told that their grades in these courses will count more than anything else.

Students should know that if they take summer work as volunteers   14 in the local community hospital, as ward aides or laboratory assistants, this will not necessarily be held against them, but neither will it help.

Finally, the colleges should have much more of a say about who   15 goes on to medical school. If they know, as they should, the students who are generally bright and also respected, this judgment should carry the heaviest weight for admission. If they elect to use criteria other than numerical class standing for recommending applicants, this evaluation should hold.

The first and most obvious beneficiaries of this new policy would   16 be the college students themselves. There would no longer be, anywhere where they could be recognized as a coherent group, the "premeds," that most detestable of all cliques eating away at the heart of the college. Next to benefit would be the college faculties, once again in possession of the destiny of their own curriculum, for better or worse. And next in line, but perhaps benefiting the most of all, are the basic-science faculties of the medical schools, who would once again be facing classrooms of students who are ready to be startled and excited by a totally new and unfamiliar body of knowledge, eager to learn, unpreoccupied by the notions of relevance that are paralyzing the minds of today's first-year medical students already so surfeited by science that they want to start practicing psychiatry in the first trimester of the first year.

Society would be the ultimate beneficiary. We could look forward 17
to a generation of doctors who have learned as much as anyone can
learn, in our colleges and universities, about how human beings
have always lived out their lives. Over the bedrock of knowledge
about our civilization, the medical schools could then construct as
solid a structure of medical science as can be built, but the bedrock
would always be there, holding everything else upright.

COMPREHENSION

1. What is the influence of the premedical curriculum on the liberal arts curriculum?

2. What does Thomas mean when he says, "The so-called social sciences have become extremely popular as stand-ins for traditional learning"?

3. How does Thomas propose to remedy the situation he describes? List the steps he suggests.

4. What qualities should medical schools require of their applicants?

5. How would students, medical schools, and society benefit from the changes Thomas suggests?

PURPOSE AND AUDIENCE

1. What is the thesis of this essay?

2. Thomas does not consider possible objections to his position. What clues does this give you about how he regards his audience? Who do you think would be more sympathetic to Thomas's position—a group of liberal arts professors or a group of physicians? Why?

3. Do you think Thomas expects his audience to accept his argument literally? Why do you think he overstates his case the way he does?

4. Will the facts that Lewis Thomas is himself a physician and president of the well-known Sloan-Kettering Cancer Center have any effect on his audience? Explain.

STYLE AND STRUCTURE

1. What premise does Thomas present in his first paragraph? How does he inject a note of urgency into it?

2. What two things does Thomas compare and contrast in paragraph 2? Why does he use this strategy at this point in his essay?

3. In what order of importance does Thomas list his points?

4. What elements does Thomas reinforce in his conclusion? What does he gain by ending this way?

WRITING WORKSHOP

1. Assume you are a premed major. Write a letter to Thomas refuting his argument. Be sure to address each of the points Thomas has presented in his essay.

2. How should your education to date have been different? Write an argumentative essay proposing changes that would improve the quality of education for someone now in the situation you have been in.

ACKNOWLEDGMENTS (continued from page iv)

DESCRIPTION

Lorus J. Milne and Margery J. Milne, "Water Striders." Reprinted by permission of Dodd, Mead & Company, Inc. from *A Multitude of Living Things* by Lorus J. Milne and Margery J. Milne. Copyright 1947, 1975 by Lorus J. Milne and Margery J. Milne.

Thomas Marc Parrott, "Shakespeare's Theatre." Used by permission of Charles Scribner's Sons from *William Shakespeare: A Handbook* by Thomas Marc Parrott. Copyright 1934, 1955 by Charles Scribner's Sons; renewal copyright © 1962 Frances M. Parrott Walters.

Mark Twain, "Reading the River." From *Life on the Mississippi* by Mark Twain. Harper & Row, Publishers, Inc. By permission Harper & Row, Publishers, Inc.

Nathan Irvin Huggins, "Uptown in Harlem." From *Harlem Renaissance* by Nathan Irvin Huggins. Copyright © 1971 by Oxford University Press, Inc. Reprinted by permission.

Studs Terkel, "Brett Hauser: Supermarket Box Boy." From *Working: People Talk about What They Do All Day and How They Feel about What They Do*, by Studs Terkel. Copyright © 1972, 1974 by Studs Terkel. Reprinted by permission of Pantheon Books, a Division of Random House, Inc.

EXEMPLIFICATION

Richard Wright, "The Ethics of Living Jim Crow." From pp. 3–5 of "The Ethics of Living Jim Crow" from *Uncle Tom's Children* by Richard Wright. Copyright 1937 by Richard Wright; renewed, 1965 by Ellen Wright. By permission of Harper & Row, Publishers, Inc.

Lawrence J. Peter and Raymond Hull, "The Peter Principle." From *The Peter Principle* by Lawrence J. Peter and Raymond Hull. Copyright © 1969 by William Morrow and Company, Inc. By permission of the publishers.

Nora Ephron, "Truth and Consequences." Copyright © 1973 by Nora Ephron. Reprinted from *Crazy Salad: Some Things about Women*, by Nora Ephron, by permission of Alfred A. Knopf, Inc.

J. B. S. Haldane, "On Being the Right Size." Originally published in 1928 in *Possible Worlds*.

PROCESS

Bernard Gladstone, "Applying an Antique Finish." Reprinted by permission of Times Books, a division of Quadrangle/The New York Times Book Co., Inc. from *The New York Times Complete Manual of Home Repair*. Copyright © 1978 by The New York Times Co.

S. I. Hayakawa, "How Dictionaries Are Made." From *Language in Thought and Action*, Third Edition by S. I. Hayakawa. © by Harcourt Brace Jovanovich, Inc., and reprinted with their permission.

Malcolm X, "My First Conk." From *The Autobiography of Malcolm X*, by Malcolm X with the assistance of Alex Haley. Copyright © 1964 by Alex Haley and Malcolm X. Copyright © 1965 by Alex Haley and Betty Shabazz. Reprinted by permission of Random House, Inc.

John Hostetler, "An Amish Wedding." From *Amish Society* by John Hostetler. Copyright © 1968. Reprinted by permission of the publisher, The Johns Hopkins University Press.

September 1977 *Reader's Digest.* Copyright © 1977 by the Reader's Digest Assn., Inc.

Patrick M. Kelley and Roger E. Masse, "A Definition of Technical Writing." Reprinted from the Spring 1977 *The Technical Writing Teacher* by permission of the journal and Patrick M. Kelley and Roger E. Masse of New Mexico State University.

Margaret Mead, "New Superstitions for Old." From *A Way of Seeing* by Margaret Mead and Rhoda Metraux. Copyright © 1966 by Margaret Mead and Rhoda Metraux. By permission of William Morrow & Company.

Edward Kasner and James R. Newman, "The Googol." From *World of Math.* Copyright © 1940, by Edward Kasner and James Newman. Renewed © 1967 by Ruth G. Newman and Edward Kasner. Reprinted by permission of Simon & Schuster, a Division of Gulf & Western Corporation.

Charles F. Berlitz, "The Etymology of the International Insult." Copyright 1970 by Penthouse International, Ltd. and reprinted with the permission of the copyright holder.

ARGUMENTATION

Steven Muller, "Our Youth Should Serve." Copyright 1978, by Newsweek, Inc. All Rights Reserved. Reprinted by Permission.

Isaac Asimov, "The Case Against Man." Copyright © 1975 Field Enterprises, Inc. Courtesy of Field Newspaper Syndicate.

Martin Luther King, Jr., "Letter from Birmingham Jail." "Letter from Birmingham Jail"—April 16, 1963—in *Why We Can't Wait* by Martin Luther King, Jr. Copyright © 1963 by Martin Luther King, Jr.

Lewis Thomas, "How to Fix the Premedical Curriculum." From *The Medusa and the Snail* by Lewis Thomas. Copyright © 1978 by Lewis Thomas. Reprinted by permission of Viking Penguin Inc. Originally appeared in *The New England Journal of Medicine.*

Index of Terms, Authors, and Titles